KENT PORTER

STRETCHING
QUICK C

BRADY
New York

BRADY

Simon & Schuster Inc.
Gulf + Western Building
One Gulf + Western Plaza
New York, NY 10023

DISTRIBUTED BY PRENTICE HALL TRADE

Manufactured in the United States of America

1 2 3 4 5 6 7 8 9 10

Library of Congress Cataloging-in-Publication Data
Porter, Kent.
    Stretching Quick C / Kent Porter.
        p.   cm.
    Bibliography: p.
    Includes index.
    ISBN: 0-13-662446-4
    1. C (Computer program language)   2. Microsoft Quick C (Computer
program)   I. Title.   II. Title: Stretching QuickC.
QA76.73.C15P674   1989
005.26—dc20   89-9801
                                                                  CIP

CONTENTS

PREFACE

This is a book for programmers who already write in C and who want to know more about how to use DOS in general and Quick C 2.0 in particular. If you're new to C, you need an introductory book right now and this one later.

This book proceeds from the assumption that you're fairly fluent in C, and that you haven't worked with Quick C before; and that you're intelligent enough to read the manuals and figure out how to work the product. Therefore, we scarcely mention the Quick C programming environment, and we spend very little ink and paper explaining basic concepts of the language. Nor do we restate what's in the Quick C 2.0 manuals; you can read them at no additional cost, since they come with the product.

Software manuals tell how to use the product—which buttons to push, how to compile, what features and built-in capabilities are available—but not what to do with it. They assume that you know intuitively how to apply the product and all its goodies to your software projects. But you probably don't. That's where guys like me make a living with books like this one. A software product manual is like the owner's guide for a radial-arm saw; it tells you how to use the saw, but not how to build a house. If you want to build a house, you have to buy another book that tells how to apply the saw. This book tells how to apply the software in building applications. In its turn, it assumes that you have the basic language skills analogous to carpentry skills such as driving nails, dropping a plumb line, and reading blueprints.

Someone once asked me what I was writing, and I said, "I'm writing a book that takes people competent in basic C to a truly advanced level." I stand by that as the objective for this book, and I hope it does that for you. It was never my intention to discuss every detail and pimple of Quick C, every function, option, bug, data structure, #include file, and possible usage. Instead, the thrust throughout has been to give you insights into the application of this remarkably supple C language implementation to the problems that confront programmers as they develop advanced software, especially for DOS-based machines.

That being the case, I have deliberately skirted around some of the obscure corners of C as implemented in the Microsoft product. Nowhere in this book (except here) will you find a mention of ssignal()/gsignal(), ioctl(), setjmp()/longjmp(), and other such oddities. That's not to say they're unimportant; perhaps they are for your application. If so, maybe you need yet another book to show you how to use them; or maybe the in-depth treatment of the subjects covered here will give you the broadened insights to apply topics not specifically discussed to your needs.

The benefit of a book like this is that it not only provides specific techniques and tools, but that it increases your understanding of the language as a whole and stimulates your imagination. A book that purports to cover every application of every feature of Quick C or any other language is either a superficial restatement of the documentation, or else so ambitious as to be unaffordable, and probably unwritable as well. The emphasis has instead been on providing workable solutions to common programming issues.

So what does the book cover? Here's a sampling:

- Part I furnishes programming techniques for working with disks, files, directories and subdirectories, and random-access files up to the level of indexing and cross-referencing records.
- Part II deals with the user interface, working from the lowest level of the **ROM BIOS** through windowing and display management to the keyboard. Much of this part is devoted to developing menus and pop-up/pull-down windows, and software tools and skeleton programs that you can adapt to your needs.
- Part III delves into computer graphics: natural coordinate systems, business charts, 2D objects, and complex curves.
- Part IV looks inward at methods for managing data dynamically with linked lists, queues, stacks, binary trees, and irregular data structures.
- Part V is a grabbag of sophisticated systems programming techniques: analyzing .EXE files, using DOS environment variables, managing parent and child processes such as exiting to and returning from DOS within a Quick C program, interrupt-handling, and using EMS.

So that's what this book covers. Before we get on with it, there is an additional, and perhaps sticky point that deserves clarification.

It's no secret; I'm the Senior Technical Editor of *Dr. Dobb's Journal*, the oldest and perhaps most technical of the commercial computer magazines. *DDJ* played a major role in making C the pre-eminent programming language that it is today, and while the magazine covers other languages (I used to write the Pascal/Modula-2 column, for example), *DDJ* remains chiefly a publication for C programmers.

As a professional computer journalist and a visible figure within the relatively small town of the personal computer industry, I unquestionably got more help from Microsoft and their support personnel than most users get. I was also a beta tester for Quick C 2.0, with which this book deals specifically.

Microsoft knows me personally, they were aware of what I was doing, and they treated me well. To pretend otherwise would be a charade.

But as a professional journalist, I am in no way beholden to Microsoft beyond acknowledging their support, for which I'm grateful. My job is to be fair and objective, and that's all. Microsoft understands that, I understand that, and you should as well. This book was written by an author and published by a company neither of whom has any financial affiliation whatsoever with Microsoft. In no way does the book represent an endorsement or promotion of Quick C, either by the Brady Books division of Simon and Schuster, or by me, or by *Dr. Dobb's Journal*. Instead, it is an aid to understanding how to use Quick C.

I should also point out that some of the material in this book was adapted from an earlier book I wrote entitled *Stretching Turbo C*, also published by Brady. The two products are similar in many ways and thus merit similar treatment. Additionally, these books are aimed at programmers of equivalent skill level using the competing compilers for the same kinds of programming projects. However, each of these books contain much information not found in the other as well, chiefly to accommodate differences between Borland's Turbo C and Microsoft's Quick C. Thus, while there is some overlap, the books are not the same things repackaged with different titles.

I can only hope that you learn as much from reading and using this book as I learned from writing it.

Happy programming.

K.P.

ACKNOWLEDGMENTS

In particular I want to thank Jeff Duntemann, Ron Copeland, and Al Stevens for being my tireless cheering section. Others who contributed to this project (whether they know it or not) are Joe Esposito, Julie Fallowfield, Herb Gellis, Kent Dahlgren, Neil Rubenking, Michael Abrash, Tyler Sperry, Ray Duncan, Laura McKenna, and Eloise Engle Paananen. There are lots of others besides.

Thanks to you all.

Trademarked products cited in text:

Name	Owner
Quick C	Microsoft
Microsoft C 5.n	Microsoft
Turbo Pascal	Borland International
IBM	International Business Machines
MS-DOS	Microsoft
PC-DOS	IBM
Lotus 1-2-3	Lotus Development Corp.
dBASE	Ashton-Tate
PS/2	IBM
UNIX	AT&T
OS/MVS	IBM
XTREE	Executive Systems, Inc.
CP/M	Digital Research
Norton Utilities	Peter Norton Computing
Norton Guides	Peter Norton Computing
Microsoft Windows	Microsoft
Framework	Ashton-Tate
Paradox	Ansa, a division of Borland International
Reflex	Borland International
pfs	Software Publishing

Limits of Liability and Discliamer of Warranty

STRETCHING
QUICK C

PART I

Finding Out About Disks in Quick C

When you were a neophyte programmer, you no doubt learned to read and write sequential files. Maybe you also learned to work with random files (or "direct" files as they're sometimes called), which let you jump around without regard to sequence. Many programmers, having mastered these two basic methods of file access, mistakenly assume that they have learned everything they'll ever need to know about disks and files.

After all, it's easy to take the disk system for granted. Quietly and reliably, it stores your data and coughs it back up on demand, which is exactly what one expects of a a storage medium. So what else is there to say?

Plenty, and the next few chapters will explore disks and files in some depth. Why? Because a thorough knowledge of the subject will make you a much more savvy programmer capable of writing highly sophisticated software. That's why you bought this book.

The chapters of Part One show how to get "secrets" kept in disk areas normally out of the sight of programs and how to produce directory listings, among other useful tricks. They also cover the various options Quick C offers for file I/O, and develop strategies for indexing random files so that you can go directly to the record you want in an instant.

Caveat: Some of the operations discussed here are armed and dangerous, capable of doing grievous injury to a disk until you've perfected them. **Never** use a hard disk or a floppy that you care about for testing. Instead, draw from your used-floppy pool, so that if something goes wrong you haven't lost anything of value.

CHAPTER 1

Exploring the Disk

The meat of this chapter has to do with getting the disk to reveal basic information about itself. For the sake of completeness, and in case it's something you don't know, we'll begin by discussing how a disk works and how DOS organizes it. If you're comfortable with your understanding of disks, you can skip a few pages to the discussion of inquiring about disk space.

Diskology 101: How a Disk Works

There are two basic kinds of disk technology at work in personal computers: *floppy* and *hard* (or fixed) disks. A third technology, *microfloppies*, is beginning to take hold with the advent of IBM's PS/2 machines. While the physical media differ, the principles of operation and organization are the same for all three, and also for variants such as Bernoulli Boxes and other removable disk cartridge products.

A disk rotates at some fixed rate of speed ranging from around 300 rpm for a floppy up to several thousand rpm for high-capacity hard drives. A movable device called the *head* writes data on the disk in the form of tiny magnetic spots. This occurs as the surface passes under the head. The spots are of reversed polarity, so that a spot with a negative charge might represent a 0 bit, and one with a positive charge represents a 1 bit. Later, the head retrieves data by sensing the charges as they pass, constructing bytes from them, and sending the information to the computer.

Naturally, the head doesn't write data wherever it feels like it. It follows rigid rules regarding the placement of data. The DOS FORMAT utility establishes the rules when it prepares the disk for use, subdividing the entire writable surface into manageable units.

The first unit in importance is the *track*. Tracks are concentric circles of data, and each has a number. The lowest-numbered track (0) is closest to the outside of the disk. Each track is further subdivided into several units called **sectors**, which are numbered starting from 1 (not 0). A sector holds a fixed number of bytes, usually 512. A normal 5¼" diskette has nine sectors per track,

3

or 4,608 bytes in each complete circuit of the disk. Since the diskette holds 360K (368,640 bytes) of data, simple math reveals that there are 80 tracks. Higher-capacity media have both more tracks and more sectors per track.

The FORMAT utility creates sectors by writing a uniquely identifiable control block at the start of each one. These control blocks are not accessible to programs, but instead are for the use of the disk controller in locating a specific address. The control block indicates the sector number and other information. For example, it tells whether the sector is usable, and, if in use, it includes linkage pointers to the adjacent sectors belonging to its occupant. Because files do not necessarily occupy contiguous sectors, the pointers give DOS a means for chaining through the file in logical sequence. Thus, the *sector control blocks* effect a linked list on the disk.

The sectors are set up in an interleaved fashion; that is, the logical sector structure is different from the physical sequence. If the interleave factor is 2, for example, the following might be the correspondence of physical to logical sectors:

Physical	Logical
1	1
2	21
3	2
4	22
5	3
etc.	etc.

The effect is that there is one physical sector between each pair of logical sectors. The purpose of this arrangement is to give the disk controller time to perform any necessary calculations and operations (e.g., sending the most recently read sector to the computer) between actual disk I/Os. The controller does these things while a sector of no interest is passing under the head, and completes them in time to watch for the next logical sector.

A diskette has two sides, of course, and DOS uses both of them. When it writes a large file, it fills the track on surface 0, then continues in the same track on surface 1 until it's full, then moves to the next track and resumes writing on surface 0. This goes on for as long as there are data. A new file always begins at the 0th byte of its first sector. If the file is not an even multiple of 512 bytes—few are—the unused remainder of the last sector is filled with hex character 1A (ASCII 26, or ∧Z from the keyboard), which DOS recognizes as an end-of-file marker.

From this, you can see that DOS has an addressing scheme for finding data on the disk. The address consists of three elements: track number, surface (or head) number, and sector number. Given those three elements, DOS can locate any 512-byte chunk of data on the disk, regardless of the disk's capacity, and direct the head to it. Random file access, which we discuss in Chapter 5, further narrows the selection down to the specific starting byte of a data record within that 512-byte sector.

This addressing information must, of course, be stored somewhere, so that DOS can later recall where it put a file and go there to fetch it. That's the purpose of the directory, which DOS places on a reserved part of the disk. For each file, DOS creates a 32-byte structure containing the file name, its date and time stamps, its attribute (normal, hidden, read-only, etc.), and its disk address, among other things. When you open a file, you tell DOS to find the directory entry for that file and prepare to read or write at its first sector address or some offset thereof, which it can calculate based on the addressing information in the directory entry.

Another level of control is also required in managing the disk. This level concerns itself with keeping track of disk space that is occupied and that which is available for assignment to new data. DOS maintains a structure on the disk called the *File Allocation Table*, or *FAT*, for this purpose. Each time DOS needs a place to put more data, it refers to the FAT to determine where to put it.

To avoid becoming unwieldy in size, the FAT doesn't keep track of individual sectors. Instead, it deals in units of storage space called *clusters*. A cluster is some power of two sectors. The following table shows common cluster sizes for IBM-class machines:

Disk	Power of 2	Sectors/cluster	Cluster size
Floppy	1	2	1,024
AT hard disk	2	4	2,048
XT hard disk	3	8	4,096

There are some inefficiencies inherent in this scheme. For example, if you write a file of 2,047 bytes to an AT hard disk, you'll take one cluster, or 2,048 bytes. However, if the file is 2,049 bytes—one more than the cluster size—DOS allocates two clusters, or 4,096 bytes, to it. That's a lot of wasted space for one additional byte. Because files are of random lengths, on average you waste one-half of a cluster for every file no matter what the cluster size. This is a particularly acute problem with the XT, which on average wastes 2K on every file it puts into a hard disk (since the XT cluster size is 4K). No doubt that's why the cluster size dropped with the later AT machines.

DOS reserves track 0 on every disk for its own use; user data are never written in this track. Track 0, head 0, sector 0 contains a record called the *boot sector*, which the operating system uses when the computer is started from the disk and which it reads when a disk is changed. This is followed by the FAT, which is in turn followed by the root directory of the disk. If the disk is bootable—i.e., you can start the computer by inserting it into drive A: or it's a hard disk containing the operating system—DOS also owns track 1, where it stores the programs necessary to get the machine up and running.

The directory of a bootable disk must have the two hidden system entries for IBMBIO.COM and IBMDOS.COM (or a clone manufacturer's equivalents) as its first two entries. These files contain the essence of the operating system. You cannot boot the computer from a disk that doesn't have these mandatory directory entries in the requisite place. And that explains why you can't install DOS with the SYS utility on a diskette that already contains other files. SYS responds that there isn't enough space; in fact, the first two directory entries are already committed, so the error message lies.

The DOS routines that control disk allocation always assign the lowest available cluster to new data. After extended use, this can lead to disk fragmentation, in which hunks of files get splattered all over the place in a crazy-quilt pattern that causes degradation of disk performance because the head spends so much time jumping from track to track. Hard disks are especially prone to this problem. Here's an example of how fragmentation occurs:

1. You write FILE.A, which occupies clusters 1 and 2.
2. You write FILE.B, which DOS places in cluster 3.
3. You erase FILE.A, freeing its clusters.
4. You append data to the end of FILE.B. When it goes beyond the end of cluster 3, DOS assigns the now-free cluster 1 to it.
5. You create FILE.C. The first part goes into cluster 2, which is free; but since FILE.A occupies the third cluster, the rest of FILE.C goes into cluster 4.

The problem is caused by erasing FILE.A and opening a hole in the Swiss cheese. Later, FILE.B's sequence is cluster 3, then cluster 1, while FILE.C's is cluster 2 followed by cluster 4. There are only two files on the disk, but both are fragmented and the head has to jump around to chain through them.

This is a situation that is inevitable in DOS, and there's not much you can do about it except to buy a disk optimization program that reshuffles files so that they occupy consecutive clusters. We raise the point here only because it's a fact of life, and so that you'll realize that your perception of slowing disk performance is factual and not subjective.

Now that we've laid out the basic organization of disks, let's see how your Quick C programs can put it to use.

Inquiring about the Disk's Characteristics

Software operates in the blind. That is, it can't look at the computer or read the manual to find out what sort of machine it's dealing with, but instead must grope around to learn about its environment. The software then adjusts its behavior accordingly.

An operating system, be it DOS, UNIX, OS/MVS, or whatever, is primarily a manipulator of control blocks. In C parlance, a control block is analogous to a structure: a predefined sequence of data elements describing something. Therefore, in interfacing with DOS, much of our concern is to define structures reflecting the operating system control blocks, fill them in, and work on them.

The rest of this chapter deals with disk inquiry functions and their applications.

Identifying the Disk

Perhaps the simplest inquiry we can make of a disk is to ask it to identify itself. Quick C has the library function _dos_getdrive(&drive), which passes the question along and returns the answer to the drive argument as a digit in which 1 = A, 2 = B, and so on. This number indicates the default disk, i.e., the one whose letter name appears as a prompt on the screen, and to which all disk I/Os are directed unless otherwise specified.

Note that Quick C inherits from DOS a degree of inconsistency in numeric drive indicators. Sometimes 0 means the A drive, and other times it means the default drive while A is indicated by 1. When a numeric drive indicator is required, always look up the function specifications to see which scheme to use.

If a disk operation takes the 0 = default mode and you want to perform the operation on the default disk, just pass it 0 for the drive. However, if it needs a specific drive indicator and you don't know which is the default, you can use _dos_getdrive() to find out the default disk unit, then pass the result instead of a literal digit as the drive parameter. This solves the problem neatly, and that's what _dos_getdrive() is for.

Getting Disk Information

Software can't blithely assume anything, especially considering the wide variety of disk hardware now on the market. Quick C uses the library function _dos_getdiskfree() to fill in the predefined structure (from DOS.H) with the most important information about a disk. The structure's format is:

```
struct  diskfree_t {
    unsigned  total_clusters;
    unsigned  avail_clusters;
    unsigned  sectors_per_cluster;
    unsigned  bytes_per_sector;
};
```

A call to _dos_getdiskfree (drive, &structure_variable) fills it in so that you can later look at the fields. The drive argument for this function has the following possible values:

Drive	Argument
Default	0
A:	1
B:	2
C:	3, etc.

The second argument is a pointer to a variable of type struct diskfree_t, defined in DOS.H. You might declare this variable as

    struct diskfree_t diskinfo;

and call the function with

    _dos_getdiskfree (driveno, &diskinfo);

So what do you do with this information when you have it? There are a couple of possibilities.

Computing the Disk Size

You can calculate the amount of total storage space on the disk. The expression is

    diskspace = diskinfo.sectors_per_cluster *
                  diskinfo.total_clusters *
                  diskinfo.bytes_per_sector;

which you can obtain from the structure after the call to _dos_getdiskfree(). Since the result of this calculation is inevitably a number greater than the capacity of an integer (32,767), the result must be assigned to a long.

Listing 1.1 is a simple program that demonstrates this discussion and also provides a useful utility for inquiring about a floppy disk. (NOTE: This program doesn't work with hard disks. We'll discuss them later.)

Listing 1.1 **Computing the capacity of a disk.**

```
/* DISKSIZE.C: Determines size of a specified diskette */

#include <stdio.h>
#include <dos.h>
#include <ctype.h>

main ()
{
struct diskfree_t diskinfo;          /* defined in DOS.H */
unsigned char     drive;             /* drive to inspect */
long              disksize,          /* disk size in bytes */
```

```
                    freespace;          /* free space in bytes */
    printf ("Which drive? ");
    drive = getche();
    drive = toupper (drive);         /* convert to upper case */
    printf ("\n\nInformation about drive %c:", drive);

    /* Convert letter to DOS indicator (1 = A, etc.) */
    drive -= "A" - 1;

    /* Get and report disk information */
    if (_dos_getdiskfree (drive, &diskinfo) == 0) {
      printf ("\n  Sectors per cluster  %8u",
        diskinfo.sectors_per_cluster);
      printf ("\n  Number of clusters   %8u",
        diskinfo.total_clusters);
      printf ("\n  Bytes per sector     %8u",
        diskinfo.bytes_per_sector);
      disksize = (long) diskinfo.sectors_per_cluster *
        diskinfo.total_clusters *
        diskinfo.bytes_per_sector;

      /* Show disk capacity and usage */
      printf ("\n  Disk capacity        %8lu", disksize);
      printf ("\n  Free clusters        %8u",
        diskinfo.avail_clusters);
      freespace = (long) diskinfo.sectors_per_cluster *
        diskinfo.bytes_per_sector *
        diskinfo.avail_clusters;
      printf ("\n  Bytes available      %8lu", freespace);
      printf ("\n  Occupied space       %8lu",
        disksize - freespace);
    } else puts ("\nNot a valid drive");
} /* ----------------------- */
```

Which Compiler Options to Use?

Since Listing 1.1 is the first program of the book, this an appropriate place to set up the Quick C 2.0 environment. In general, this book concerns itself with the utilization of the Quick C language, and not with the toolset itself. You can consult the documentation if you have questions about which button to push or how to answer a question from the compiler. However, the programs given here might or might not compile and run successfully depending on how your environment is set up. Consequently, I'll tell you how my environment is set (and why, in some cases). I recommend that you set yours the same way, so that we'll achieve the same results.

The default memory model for Quick C is small, and all the programs given in this book run in the small model. I've also run them all in large model, just to be sure. In later chapters we develop some libraries of functions that stretch Quick C 2.0 by providing tools you can use for your own projects. The libraries are written to be linked with programs compiled in *any* memory model; Quick C extensions to ANSI C make this possible by defining all library functions as *far*, and by passing far pointers to\from functions.

The Quick C Options menu is the gateway to setting up the environment. The menu contains two selections of concern here. The first governs the environment's menuing system. Set it to full. The default partial menuing system hides many of the Quick C 2.0 tools, and is intended chiefly for beginners. The other is the Make selection, which leads to a set of three dialog boxes.

In the top-level dialog box, set the build flags to *Debug*. The *Release* flag should only be set when a program is fully debugged and ready to go into production; set it and rebuild to make a smaller, faster .EXE program. During development, always have the Debug flag on. This dialog box leads to two others: *compiler* and *linker*.

The compiler flags box contains a number of selections. Leave the memory model at the default, which is small, unless you have a reason for preferring a different model. The warning levels range from none (0) to very persnickety (4). The default level 1 is usually sufficient to sniff out any questionable statements.

The C Language switch IS important. Set it to MS Extensions. This setting supports a superset of the ANSI C standard. Pure ANSI C doesn't recognize far pointers, which are used throughout this book, nor does it recognize other useful traits of the Quick C implementation. If ANSI compatibility is on, the compiler generates syntax error messages on encountering far pointers, and doesn't explain the problem further. Therefore you *must* set this switch to MS Extensions.

Set the Debug Info flag to Codeview, thus allowing you to use Quick C's integrated debugger as well as the standalone Codeview debugger. Turn Pointer Check off (no X); Quick C otherwise prevents you from using pointers to places outside the program's memory space. Such an inhibition is fine when learning C, but not for the advanced material covered here. Turn Incremental Compile on (X in box). This causes Rebuild to recompile only code that has changed since the last compile.

I recommend that you turn Optimization off completely while developing programs. Optimization sometimes causes bizarre errors at run time, and it usually rearranges the executable version almost beyond recognition. Debugging is hard enough without this added potential for troubles. Leave stack checking on. That way, if a program runs out of stack space, it quits with a run time error message rather than simply crashing (or worse yet, running amok and doing real damage to the machine).

The other dialog box controls the Linker flags. The global flags should be set to Ignore case off, Pause off, and Extended dictionary on. Change the latter only if you modify one of the Quick C libraries (a generally poor idea). The default stack size is 2,048 bytes, which is adequate for any program in this book unless noted otherwise.

As for Debug Flags, set Codeview and Incremental link on and Map file off. The latter is only useful if you're in deep trouble with a program and need to find out the addresses of routines. Otherwise it just clutters your directory with unneeded .MAP files.

Click the OK buttons to save this setup. These options become your default configuration for all programs. Now you're ready to go to work.

Building Appropriate Buffer Sizes

Your software can optimize disk performance by reading and writing buffers that exactly correspond to the disk cluster size. Calculate the cluster size as

Sectors per cluster * Bytes per sector

or, using the diskinfo structure, as

```
buffsize  =  diskinfo.sectors_per_cluster  *
             diskinfo.bytes_per_sector;
```

Since no existing version of DOS uses a cluster size greater than 32,767 bytes, the buffsize variable can safely be declared as an integer in C.

It might not be easy to use this information to your advantage, but it can be done. For example, if your program writes a byte at a time to a disk file, you could declare an array of buffsize bytes and continually add bytes to it, checking each time for buffer overflow. When the buffer is full, write it to disk, overlay it with 0x1A (end-of-file characters), and start again at the beginning. Although this entails some buffer-management overhead, it will usually result in improved disk performance.

Determining Free Space Left on the Disk

Often it's not enough simply to know the total capacity of a disk; you need to find out how much of that capacity is available. The Quick C diskfree_t structure contains the field avail_clusters, filled in by a call to _dos_getdiskfree(). You can use an expression similar to the one above to calculate the amount of free space:

```
freespace  =  diskinfo.sectors_per_cluster  *
              diskinfo.avail_clusters  *
              diskinfo.bytes_per_sector;
```

The DISKSIZE.C program in Listing 1.1 uses this expression to report the number of bytes available on the target disk.

One excellent application of this function is in giving your software the smarts to recognize in advance that it's going to run out of disk space during a file save. If you have data in lists, trees, or arrays, and you want to write them to disk, it's easy to calculate the number of bytes: Just multiply node size by number of items. Compare the result with the free space. If it is less than, it's safe to write; and if it's greater than, ask the user to mount a new floppy or whatever is appropriate. This simple precaution prevents the program from terminating abnormally via DOS's critical error handler, thus losing all the data.

If you want to make your program really smart, you can carry this idea a step farther, recognizing when it's a hard disk that's about to run out of space and diverting the data to a floppy. The next section covers how to get the disk to bare its soul.

Reading the Boot Sector

When FORMAT prepares a disk, it writes a special record called the *boot sector*. Located at track 0, head 0, sector 1, this record—i.e., structure in C terms—contains fundamental information about the disk that is not available anywhere else, and also a short bootstrap program that loads the operating system.

The boot sector is not a file, and consequently we have to go to some lengths to read it. Here we'll develop a couple of methods for inspecting absolute locations on disks.

Before we get into that, though, let's see what's in the boot sector. The structure defined in Listing 1.2 shows the contents, which yield a great deal of information about the physical disk.

Listing 1.2 **Contents of the disk boot sector.**

```
/* BOOTSEC.H: Header file describing DOS boot sector    */
/*     (track 0, head 0, sector 1) on any formatted disk */
/* ----------------------------------------------------- */
#pragma pack(1)

typedef struct {
  unsigned char signature;      /* E9h or EBh if formatted */
  unsigned      skip;                       /* no value */
  char          oem [8];                 /* OEM identifier */
  unsigned      byPerSec;   /* start of BPB: bytes/sector */
  char          secPerClus;      /* sectors per cluster */
  unsigned      resSecs;            /* reserved sectors */
  char          nFats;      /* # of FATs retained on disk */
  unsigned      nRootEnts;      /* # of root dir entries */
  unsigned      totSec;      /* # of sectors in volume */
  unsigned char mediaDescr;      /* media descriptor byte */
```

```
    unsigned        secPerFat;              /* sectors per FAT */
    unsigned        secPerTrack;            /* sectors per track */
    unsigned        nHeads;             /* # of heads (surfaces) */
    unsigned        nHidden;            /* # of hidden sectors */
    char            loader [482];       /* bootstrap loader area */
} BOOTSEC;

#pragma pack()
```

You should place this file as BOOTSEC.H in the directory where you'll be accumulating the programs from this book. Later we'll develop a couple of programs that use it.

Note the **#pragma** directives surrounding the structure definition. The Microsoft C compilers have an unfortunate tendency to take liberties with the alignment of data in structures. They like to start each field on a word boundary, expanding eight-bit objects to full 16-bit words, adding an extra character to odd-sized strings, and the like. This slightly improves performance, and in most situations it doesn't cause problems. However, when a structure is used as a disk buffer or a template overlaying a fixed area of memory, it can drive a programmer wild. The misalignments introduced by the compiler cause the program to report nonsensical values for fields. The pack pragma overrides this questionable "feature" by stipulating alignments.

The directive used here—**#pragma pack(1)**—tells the compiler to pack the structure on one-byte boundaries, or in other words to align the structure's fields as specified. An argument of 2 means to use two-byte (word) boundaries, and 4 specifies fullword 32-bit boundaries. The Quick C default is 2, so **#pragma pack(1)** is necessary when the structure must align as specified. The pragma without an argument at the end of the structure restores the default alignment.

One final note concerning structure packing. If you recompile your Quick C programs with Microsoft C or with QCL, you can force the compiler to pack all structures on byte boundaries with the /Zp command-line option.

Now let's consider the fields of the BOOTSEC structure. The signature byte tells whether or not the disk is formatted. This byte, which must be either 0E9h or 0EBh, is actually a jump instruction to the bootstrap loader further down in the boot sector. Anything else means the disk is either unformatted or else it's formatted for an operating system other than DOS; in both cases, the contents of the rest of the boot sector are probably useless.

The OEM identifier shows the computer manufacturer and DOS version used to format the disk. This is a normal null-terminated string.

Some of the following information is accessible through _dos_getdisk-free() discussed above; this is where the information comes from. Other information, such as the number of reserved sectors, FATs, and heads, is used by the disk device driver to calculate addresses.

The media descriptor byte tells what kind of disk this is. Its values map to media types as follows:

Value	Medium
0F7h	Microfloppy
0F8h	Hard disk
0F9h	5¼″ floppy, DS, 15 sectors
0FCh	5¼″ floppy, SS, 9 sectors
0FDh	5¼″ floppy, DS, 9 sectors
0FEh	5¼″ floppy, SS, 8 sectors
0FFh	5¼″ floppy, DS, 8 sectors

There's nothing you can learn about the disk from the loader[] field. It's merely a machine-language program for starting the computer, followed by some error messages. This program is always present in the boot sector, even if the disk is not bootable (i.e., if IBMBIO.COM and IBMDOS.COM are not the first two files in the root directory). Its only function on an unbootable disk is to display the nonsystem disk message if you attempt to start the system from it.

The Quick C library lacks a function for performing an absolute disk read, but we can write one of our own. Many of the library functions furnished with Quick C and other languages are "sugar-coated" calls to DOS or the ROM BIOS. When the built-in libraries don't include a function we need, it's often simple to write one, thus extending the language to suit our own requirements. We do a lot of that in this book, which is why it's called *Stretching Quick C 2.0.*

Absolute Disk Read for Floppies

The first absolute disk read function developed here is called bootsec(). It's syntactic sugar for interrupt 13h, function 2, which performs an absolute read via the ROM BIOS floppy disk services. That is, it bypasses all of DOS's normal disk-and file-management routines, positions the read/write head at a specific sector, and reads the boot sector of a specified drive into a structure of type BOOTSEC defined in Listing 1.2.

The bootsec() function requires an argument specifying the target diskette drive, where 0 = A:, 1 = B:, etc. After allocating space for one sector (512 bytes), it points the registers to head 0, track 0, sector 1, which is the first physical sector of the target disk. The ROM BIOS routine reads the sector into the allocated space. Bootsec() then returns a far pointer to this object. If unsuccessful, the returned pointer is NULL.

Listing 1.3 lists the program FDPARM.C, which includes the bootsec() function. This program asks you to type the drive letter for a floppy disk, and then it lists the disk parameters in the boot sector. Note how it computes the disk drive number. The function getche() gets a keystroke from the keyboard without echoing it. The toupper() macro converts it to uppercase, and the expression subtracts the ASCII value of "A" from the result to get the disk number. Thus, if you type either lowercase b or uppercase B, the disk variable is assigned the numeric value 1, which corresponds to the B drive indicator.

Listing 1.3 **Utility to list a diskette's boot sector.**

```
/* FDPARM.C: Shows contents of floppy disk's boot sector */

#include <stdio.h>
#include <string.h>
#include <dos.h>
#include <ctype.h>
#include <conio.h>
#include <malloc.h>
#include "bootsec.h"

main ()
{
char    disk, letter;
BOOTSEC *boot, *bootsec (int);

    printf ("\nWhich disk do you want to see? ");
    letter = getche();
    disk = toupper (letter) - "A";
    if ((boot = bootsec (disk)) != NULL) {
        printf ("\n\nBoot sector for drive %c:\n",
                    toupper (letter));
        printf ("\n  Signature                     %02X",
                    (unsigned char) boot->signature);
        printf ("\n  Bytes per sector              %d"
                    boot->byPerSec);
        printf ("\n  Sectors per cluster           %d"
                    boot->secPerClus);
        printf ("\n  Number of reserved sectors    %d"
                    boot->resSecs);
        printf ("\n  Number of FATs                %d"
                    boot->nFats);
        printf ("\n  Number of root entries        %d"
                    boot->nRootEnts);
        printf ("\n  Total number of sectors       %u"
                    boot->totSec);
        printf ("\n  Media descriptor              %02X",
                    (unsigned char) boot->mediaDescr);
        printf ("\n  Sectors per FAT               %d",
                    boot->secPerFat);
        printf ("\n  Sectors per track             %d",
                    boot->secPerTrack);
        printf ("\n  Number of drive heads         %d",
                    boot->nHeads);
        printf ("\n  Number of hidden sectors      %u",
                    boot->nHidden);
    } else
        printf ("\nError reading drive %c", disk + "A");
```

Listing 1.3 *(continued)*

```
    if (boot)
       free (boot);
} /* ------------------------ */


BOOTSEC *bootsec (int drive)
/* Use BIOS Int 13h, fcn 02h to read boot sector */
{
union REGS    reg;
struct SREGS sreg;
BOOTSEC       *buf;

    if ((buf = malloc (sizeof *buf)) != NULL) {
        reg.h.ah = 2;                        /* Int 13h, fcn 2 */
        reg.h.al = 1;                          /* one sector */
        reg.h.ch = 0;                            /* track 0 */
        reg.h.cl = 1;                    /* physical sector 1 */
        reg.h.dh = 0;                              /* head 0 */
        reg.h.dl = drive;                           /* drive */
        reg.x.bx = FP_OFF (buf);         /* buffer offset */
        sreg.es  = FP_SEG (buf);          /* and segment */
        int86x (0x13, &reg, &reg, &sreg);
        if (reg.x.cflag != 0) {               /* if failed */
            free (buf);
            buf = NULL;
        }
    }
    return buf;
}
```

Because they use the ROM BIOS diskette services, the FDPARM and DISK-SIZE programs are limited to reading the boot sectors of floppy disks. The reason is that a hard disk controller has its own ROM BIOS, of which the machine's low-level routines such as Int 13h are unaware. If we want to give our programs the ability to operate on hard disks, too, it's necessary to use a DOS function that knows which ROM BIOS to call upon.

Absolute Disk Read for Any Disk

DOS exists at a higher level than any BIOS and is thus able to communicate with both the machine and hard disk controller routines. Via Int 25h, DOS furnishes a routine capable of reading absolute sectors from any disk, floppy or hard (a hard disk is called a *fixed disk* in IBM parlance).

Unfortunately, a call to this interrupt cannot be written in "pure" C. This is because Int 25h pushes the flags register onto the stack, and a calling routine has to pop the old flags before attempting to return or else the program will return to the wrong address. The C language in general lacks an intrinsic pop instruction. Consequently, if we want to read absolute sectors from any disk including a hard drive, we have to include Assembly Language in the routine. Quick C 2.0 introduced an inline assembler that we can use to embed the requisite pop into our routine for Int 25h.

Quick C's inline assembly directive is _asm followed by a line of Assembly Language mnemonics and operands. You can also insert more than one line of inline code: To see how, consult the Microsoft document *C For Yourself*. The subprogram developed here (Listing 1.4) requires only one inline mnemonic, which we can code as

```
_asm  pop  ax
```

This clears the old flags from the stack, placing them into register AX. Because the function's return value is loaded into AX immediately following the pop instruction, no register corruption results.

This enables us to develop a general-purpose routine that uses DOS Int 25h to read any number of sectors from anyplace on any disk. We'll call it absread().

The prototype for this function is

```
int  absread (int drive, int startsec, int nsecs,
              char far *buf);
```

where:

- drive is a value 0 = A, 1 = B, etc.
- startsec is the logical sector number to start reading (with logical sector numbering, sector 0 is the boot sector and so on in numeric sequence up through total sectors on the disk − 1)
- nsecs is the number of sectors to read
- buf is a far pointer to any receiving buffer, such as a BOOTSEC structure. The buffer must be large enough to accommodate nsecs * 512 bytes.

The routine returns 0 if successful and − 1 if not.

Listing 1.4 is a listing of this routine, which is called ABSREAD.C.

Listing 1.4 **Function to read any disk sector.**

```
/* ABSREAD.C: Uses DOS fcn 25h to read absolute sector */
/*    on any disk drive                                 */

#include <dos.h>
#if !defined TRUE
#define FALSE 0
#define TRUE  !FALSE
#endif

int absread (int drive, int startsec, int nsecs,
```

Listing 1.4 *(continued)*

```
                char far *buf)
{
union REGS r;
struct SREGS seg;

  r.x.ax = drive;                          /* Set up arguments */
  r.x.bx = FP_OFF (buf);
  seg.ds = FP_SEG (buf);
  r.x.cx = nsecs;
  r.x.dx = startsec;
  int86x (0x25, &r, &r, &seg);             /* call DOS fcn 25h */

  /* Clear old flags from stack (inline assembler) */
  _asm pop ax

  /* Check for valid operation */
  return (r.x.cflag != 0) ? FALSE : TRUE;
}
```

Now we can revise **FDPARM.C** into a program that reads and displays the boot sector of any disk. This program is called **DISKPARM.C** and appears in Listing 1.5. It's essentially the same as **FDPARM**, except that it calls **absread()** and modifies its behavior to accommodate the return value, which is different from that of **bootsec()**.

This program must link with **ABSREAD**. If you're working at the DOS command line, compile and link with the command

    QCL DISKPARM.C ABSREAD.C

If you are in the Quick C environment, set a program list that includes **DISKPARM.C** and **ABSREAD.C**.

Listing 1.5 **Utility to list the boot sector of any disk.**

```
/* DISKPARM.C: Shows contents of disk boot sector */

#include <stdio.h>
#include <string.h>
#include <dos.h>
#include <conio.h>
#include <malloc.h>
#include "bootsec.h"

extern absread (int drive, int startsec,
                int nsecs, char far *buf);

void main ()
{
char    disk;
BOOTSEC far *boot;
```

```
    boot = malloc (sizeof *boot);            /* get buffer space */
    printf ("\nWhich disk do you want to see? ");
    disk = getche();
    disk = toupper (disk) - 'A';        /* compute disk indicator */
    if (absread (disk, 0, 1, (char far*) boot)) {
      printf ("\n\nBoot sector for drive %c:\n", disk + 'A');
      printf ("\n  Signature                    %02X",
                (unsigned char) boot->signature);
      printf ("\n  OEM                          %s",
                boot->oem);
      printf ("\n  Bytes per sector             %d",
                boot->byPerSec);
      printf ("\n  Sectors per cluster          %d",
                boot->secPerClus);
      printf ("\n  Number of reserved sectors   %d",
                boot->resSecs);
      printf ("\n  Number of FATs               %d",
                boot->nFats);
      printf ("\n  Number of root entries       %d",
                boot->nRootEnts);
      printf ("\n  Total number of sectors      %u",
                boot->totSec);
      printf ("\n  Media descriptor             %02X",
                (unsigned char) boot->mediaDescr);
      printf ("\n  Sectors per FAT              %d",
                boot->secPerFat);
      printf ("\n  Sectors per track            %d",
                boot->secPerTrack);
      printf ("\n  Number of drive heads        %d",
                boot->nHeads);
      printf ("\n  Number of hidden sectors     %u",
                boot->nHidden);
    } else
      printf ("\nError reading drive %c", disk + 'A');
    if (boot) _ffree (boot);
} /* ------------------------ */
```

It might be interesting and give you some small sense of power to unlock secrets about the disk not normally accessible to PC users. But one might reasonably ask what practical use this information has. Let's develop one.

A Disk-Checking Utility

Once in a while a disk—floppy or hard—develops a bad spot. Or you suspect that it might have because the system occasionally reports a disk error. The CHKDSK utility that comes with DOS reports file allocation discrepancies, but it doesn't tell you if there's a bad sector somewhere. Various "power user" packages, such as the Norton Utilities, furnish disk surface analysis programs. If you don't have such a utility, though, it's fairly easy to write one of your own, and that's what we'll do here.

By determining from the boot sector the number of heads, sectors, and so forth that a disk has, you can control loops that scan the disk a sector at a time looking for problems. The **absread()** function developed earlier will return an error whenever it can't read a sector, and the program can use the error return value to report the offending spot.

That's the main thrust of the DISKCHK.C program in Listing 1.6, and where it does most of its work. The three nested loops advance the head, the sector, and the track in order of frequency, stepping one logical sector at a time through the disk. The innermost loop calculates the current logical sector, reports where it is, and attempts to read that sector. If the read fails, the program lists the location on the lower portion of the display.

Like **DISKPARM** given above, this program must link with **ABSREAD**. The command line is

    QCL DISKCHK.C ABSREAD.C

or, alternatively, the environment program list should include both **DISKCHK.C** and **ABSREAD.C**.

Listing 1.6 **Disk check utility using absolute reads.**

```
/* DISKCHK: Checks a disk for bad sectors */

#include <stdio.h>
#include <]stdlib.h>
#include <malloc.h>
#include <graph.h>
#include <bios.h>
#include "bootsec.h"

extern int absread (int, int, int, char far*);

main ()
{
char     diskname, far *bfr;
int      drive, t, s, h, errline = 10;
unsigned logsec, ntracks, badsecs = 0;
BOOTSEC  far *boot;
void     tellwhere (int, int, int, unsigned),
         reporterror (int, int, int, unsigned,
                        int*, unsigned);

  _clearscreen (0);
  puts ("DISK CHECKING UTILITY\n");
  printf ("Which disk? ");
  diskname = toupper (getch());
  printf ("%c\n", diskname);

  /* Get workspace */
  if ((boot = _fmalloc (sizeof *boot)) == NULL) {
    puts ("\nOut of memory");
```

```
        exit (-1);
     }

   if ((bfr  = _fmalloc (512)) == NULL) {
     puts ("\nOut of memory");
     exit (-1);
   }

   /* Get disk boot sector */
   drive = diskname - "A";
   if (!absread (drive, 0, 1, (char far*) boot)) {
     printf ("\nError reading drive %c", diskname);
     exit (-1);
   }

   /* Compute number of tracks on disk */
   ntracks = (boot->totSec / boot->secPerTrack) /
             boot->nHeads;

   /* Report disk statistics */
   printf ("\n%u tracks, %d sectors/track, %d heads",
           ntracks, boot->secPerTrack, boot->nHeads);
   printf (" (%u logical sectors)", boot->totSec);
   puts ("\nStrike any key to stop disk scan");

   /* Check disk by reading each sector */
   for (t = 0; t < ntracks; t++)                    /* by track */
     for (s = 0; s < boot->secPerTrack; s++)   /* by sector */
       for (h = 0; h < boot->nHeads; h++) {       /* by head */
         logsec = (t * boot->secPerTrack * boot->nHeads) +
                  (s * boot->nHeads) + h;   /* logical sec */
         tellwhere (t, s, h, logsec);
   if (!absread (drive, logsec, 1, bfr)) {
           reporterror (t, s, h, logsec, &errline, badsecs);
           ++badsecs;
         }
         if (_bios_keybrd (_KEYBRD_READY) != 0) {
           puts ("\nProgram aborted at user request");
           getch();
           exit (0);                    /* quit if key pressed */
         }
       }

   /* End of run */
   puts ("\nDisk check completed");
   printf ("%u bad sectors found", badsecs);
   _ffree (bfr);                             /* free space */
   _ffree (boot);
 } /* ------------------------- */

void tellwhere (int track, int sector, int head,
                unsigned lsec)
{                    /* Show where the program is on the disk */
static char status [60];
```

Listing 1.6 *(continued)*

```
  sprintf (status,
    "Track %d, sector %2d, head %d (logical sector %u)",
    track, sector, head, lsec);
  _settextposition (7, 1);
  _outtext (status);
} /* ----------------------- */


void reporterror (int track, int sector, int head,
                  unsigned lsec, int *line, unsigned nerrs)
{                                        /* Report bad sector */
int   c;
static char errline [60];

  if (*line > 25) {      /* clear error area if screen full */
    while (c > 59) errline [c++] = ' ';
    errline [c] = '\0';
    for (c = 10; c < 26; c++) {
      _settextposition (c, 1);
      _outtext (errline);
    }
    _settextposition (10, 1);
    sprintf (errline,
             "(%u previous errors reported)", nerrs);
    _outtext (errline);
    *line = 11;
  }

  /* Report this bad sector */
  sprintf (errline,
    "%s track %d, sector %d, head %d (logical sector %u)",
    "Bad sector:", track, sector, head, lsec);
  _settextposition (*line, 1);
  _outtext (errline);
  ++(*line);
} /* ----------------------- */
```

This program runs for quite a long time, and it's likely that you'll want to bail out early. An example is when you've ascertained that there is indeed a defect on the disk; no point in continuing with the analysis. You can stop the program at any time during the scan phase by simply pressing a key. The code that detects the keypress is at the end of the innermost loop in DISKCHK. It uses the ROM BIOS keyboard status check available through Quick C's _bios_keybrd() function. This function normally returns 0, but when a key has been pressed it returns the keystroke. Thus a nonzero return means the user wants to quit, so the program does so. The keyboard status routine doesn't take the keystroke out of the buffer, so to avoid confusing the next program that looks for input, the program does a getch() to clear the keystroke.

This program uses some of Quick C's screen control functions to make the display "pretty." The tellwhere() function always places the status line in the same place on the screen. The reporterror() function is a little fancier. It constructs a sequential list of bad sectors starting in row 10 and working toward the bottom of the screen. When it tries to write past the bottom, it clears the list, posts a message stating how many errors have been found so far, and starts a new list in row 11.

If all this display formatting stuff is a little intimidating, don't worry. We'll have plenty to say about it in later chapters dealing with the user interface.

DISKCHK is a highly practical application of the material covered so far, and a good thing to keep handy.

We've seen how to find and use the internal information stored on disks, so now let's move on to means for exploring and managing disk space in Quick C.

CHAPTER 2

Directory Assistance

It's essential for software operating on MS-DOS machines to navigate among directories, which are an essential feature of the DOS landscape. Quick C provides a comprehensive set of tools for writing programs that do so easily and efficiently; the purpose of this chapter to familiarize you with them.

There are a number of things you can do with directories in Quick C, among them creating, changing, and deleting subdirectories, moving files between directories, searching all directories for a specific filename or pattern, and renaming files. We'll examine these operations with examples, combining them in various practical applications.

Before we begin, let's clear up one potentially confusing bit of terminology: the term path. A subdirectory is a child of a higher-level directory, which might in turn be the child of another yet higher. The highest-level directory on the disk is the root, designated in DOS notation by a singleton backslash; e.g., "C:\" indicates the root directory of the C drive. The entire sequence of directories that must be traversed to reach the current subdirectory is the *path* (or *pathname*). In the recommended Microsoft C setup, **SAMPLE** is a subdirectory under \BIN, whose parent is the root. Thus, on drive C the path to **SAMPLE** is

       C:\BIN\SAMPLE

Thus, a subdirectory is an entity such as **SAMPLE**, while the path is a description of the route to it.

Determining the Current Directory

Chapter 1 covered the _dos_getdrive() function that tells the calling program which disk drive is the current default. Quick C furnishes the analogous function getcwd() for determining the current directory. The "cwd" in getcwd() stands for "current working directory." The calling convention for this function (prototyped in **DIRECT.H**) is

```
char *getcwd (char *path, int n);
```

where path is a pointer to a buffer that will receive the pathname and n is the maximum allowable length including the null terminator. The function loads *buf with the pathname including the drive designator (letter plus colon). Since DOS allows pathnames up to 65 characters long and the drive information and null terminator are another three characters, the highest sensible value for the n parameter is 68.

The getcwd() function returns the address of the character string. Normally this is the same as the path argument and you can treat the call as if to a void function, i.e., disregard the returned value, as in

```
getcwd (&dir, 68);
```

However, you can pass NULL as the buf argument, and in that case getcwd() allocates an object of n characters on the heap, loads the pathname into it, and returns a pointer to the object, e.g.,

```
cwd = getcwd (NULL, 68);
```

This is useful if you only need to retain the pathname briefly or you're short on data space, since it doesn't use any memory in the program's working area (except for the two to four bytes for the cwd pointer). Thus, you can free the space later with

```
free (cwd);
```

The CURDIR.C program in Listing 2.1 illustrates the getcwd() function in action. It is analogous to typing ChDir at the DOS prompt without arguments. To build this program, your program list must include the entries

```
curdir.c
\lib\mlibce.lib
```

Listing 2.1 **Listing the current working directory.**

```
/* CURDIR.C: Shows the current working directory */

#include <direct.h>
#include <stdio.h>

main ()
{
char *path;

  path = getcwd (NULL, 68);
  printf ("Current working directory is %s\n", path);
}
```

One useful application of this function is in noting where you are before you change directories and/or drives. Later, you can use the path fetched by getcwd() to restore the system to its original state using the chdir() function; it would be rude to quit and leave the user off in some strange corner of the disk known only to your program.

Manipulating Directories

As a DOS user, you're no doubt well-acquainted with the DOS commands CHDIR, MKDIR, and RMDIR (alias CD, MD, and RD), which change, make, and remove directories, respectively. Quick C has exactly equivalent functions going by the unsurprising names chdir(), mkdir(), and rmdir().

Since these are such familiar DOS operations, they don't require much explanation. The same rules and effects apply. For example, chdir() switches from the current directory to a different one on the same or another drive, and all subsequent operations occur in the new directory. If you specify a different drive in the path given to chdir(), the directory becomes active on that drive, but the drive itself does not become the default. (The same thing occurs under similar circumstances with the command-level CHDIR in DOS, in case you didn't realize that; try it.) The rmdir() function cannot remove the current working directory, nor can it remove a subdirectory that still contains files, nor can it delete the root, just as in DOS's RMDIR. All three functions signal success by returning 0 and failure with a − 1 returned value.

As mentioned earlier, it's inconsiderate to change directories unless you provide a means for restoring the current one. Use getcwd() to note the current directory before rampaging off to a far corner of the disk system. The programs later in this chapter give examples.

Listing a Directory

Did you ever wonder how systems such as Lotus 1-2-3, dBASE III, and Quick C itself produce directory listings from within the software? You're about to find out, using the Quick C functions _dos_findfirst() and _dos_findnext().

The _dos_findfirst() and _dos_findnext() functions are C translations of DOS interrupt 21h, functions 4Eh and 4Fh. They search a directory for entries matching a specification. Each time a match is found, the search stops and the function fills in a structure from which you can fetch the file information.

_dos_findfirst() locates the first directory block satisfying the specification. Thereafter, call the _dos_findnext() function repeatedly to locate additional matches. _dos_findnext() always resumes the search immediately after the point where it (or _dos_findfirst()left off in a previous call, so that you don't get duplicate file entries. Both functions return 0 on success and −1 when either there's an error in the search specification or no further matching entries exist in the directory.

The Quick C #include file DOS.H defines struct find_t, which represents the structure of the DOS file entry block. This structure is defined as

```
struct  find_t  {
    char  reserved  [21];       /*  used  by  DOS  */
    char  attrib;               /*  file  attribute  */
    unsigned  wr_time;          /*  time  of  last  write  */
    unsigned  wr_date;          /*  date  of  last  write  */
    long  size;                 /*  file  length  in  bytes  */
    char  name  [13];           /*  filename.ext  */
};
```

All of the fields are useful to programs, and we'll discuss them at length in Chapter 3. For now, we'll only concern ourselves with the name and attribute fields.

Let's say you declare a pointer to the structured variable as

```
struct  find_t  *file;
```

and allocate heap space for the structure with

```
file  =  malloc  (sizeof  (*file));
```

Thereafter, upon successful return from _dos_findfirst() and _dos_findnext(), you can refer to the filename as

```
file->name;
```

The directory search process must always begin with a call to _dos_findfirst(). In addition to performing the first search operation, this function sets up the specifications in the find_t structure for subsequent use by _dos_findnext().

There are two elements in the specification: a *name pattern* and an *attribute pattern*. We say "pattern" because these elements typically include wildcards leading to the discovery of several matching file entries. The wildcards in the name field are as you might expect: an asterisk (*) to mean any number and combination of characters, and a question mark to indicate any single character. Thus the wildcard to find all files having the extension .BAT is *.BAT, while the wildcard to find all files having the form PAYROLL plus one character plus any extension is PAYROLL?.*.

The attribute describes characteristics of a file: hidden, read-only, normal, etc. The next chapter discusses file attributes at length. In searching a directory, we can set up a wildcard attribute that will find all matching file entries regardless of their characteristics. This is the hex byte 0FFh (all bits turned on). Specific attributes have predefined constants in DOS.H: for example, a subdirectory entry has the attribute _A_SUBDIR, and the attribute of a normal read/write file is _A_NORMAL.

The prototype for _dos_findfirst() is

```
int  _dos_findfirst (char *pattern,
                     struct  find_t  *found,
                     unsigned  attr);
```

To find the first entry in the current directory having the extension .C, you can issue the call

```
result  =  _dos_findfirst  ('*.C', file, 0xFF);
```

where result is an integer variable and file is a pointer to the allocated space as described earlier.

If _dos_findfirst() returns 0 to signal success, you can list file − >name, then begin a loop that repeatedly calls _dos_findnext() and lists subsequent filenames until the function returns − 1. The call to _dos_findnext() is

```
result  =  _dos_findnext  (file);
```

in accordance with the prototype

```
int  _dos_findnext (struct  find_t  *found);
```

Now let's write a program that lists all the .COM files in the root directory of the default disk. The equivalent DIR command at the DOS prompt level ("DIR *.COM") is less powerful than this program will be, because DIR doesn't list the hidden system files IBMBIO.COM and IBMDOS.COM or their equivalents in other MS-DOS implementations. Since we will search with the wildcard attribute 0FFh, our program will list all .COM files regardless of their attributes.

The program (ROOTCOM.C in Listing 2.2) uses several of the directory operations discussed in this chapter: chdir(), getcwd(), and _dos_findfirst() /_dos_findnext(). Note that the chdir() call to switch to the root directory needs a double blackslash. This is because backslash is a special lead-in character in C, normally indicating a nonprinting control sequence. To output a literal backslash, you have to code two of them in sequence.

The program uses getcwd() to jot down the current directory on entry. It then switches to the root to do its job. Just before quitting, it calls chdir(oldpath) to restore the old directory, so that the user isn't left stranded in the root. You must have a .MAK file to link the program with MLIBCE.LIB.

Listing 2.2 **Searching and listing a directory.**

```
/* ROOTCOM.C: List .COM files in root dir of default drive. */
/*    If disk is bootable, shows the hidden system files,    */
/*    which normally don't appear from the DIR command.      */
/* --------------------------------------------------------- */


#include <direct.h>
#include <dos.h>
#include <stdio.h>
#include <malloc.h>


#define  ANYFILE 0xFF


void main ()
{
struct find_t *file;                      /* file block pointer */
char          *oldpath;        /* directory where we are now */
int           result;          /* success code from searches */


/* Note where we are on entry */
  oldpath = getcwd (NULL, 80);                    /* get old path */
/* Begin search */
  chdir ("\\");                              /* switch to root */
  file = malloc (sizeof (*file));
  puts ("\nListing of .COM files in root directory:");
  result = _dos_findfirst ("*.COM", ANYFILE, file);


/* Continue search until all .COM files found */
  while (result == 0) {
    puts (file->name);                           /* list entry */
    result = _dos_findnext (file);            /* get next match */
  }
  puts ("\n-- End of list\n");


/* Restore status and quit */
  chdir (oldpath);                               /* old path */
  free (oldpath);
}
```

To become more comfortable with these directory operations, experiment with the program. You might modify it so that it goes to the \INCLUDE directory and lists all .H files, or to your Lotus directory to show all .WK? files, or whatever else strikes your fancy. Chapter 3 develops a generalized subdirectory listing utility that builds on this program.

Searching Directories _____

Now let's carry the ideas of this chapter one step further by creating a program that you'll want to keep in your library. This utility is called WHERE. If you type a command such as

WHERE .LIB

it will list every instance of a file with the .LIB suffix on your hard disk, showing the full path to the file. If you keep lots of directories for different projects, this utility can save you bundles of time by pinpointing exactly where a file is. You can search for specific files, such as

WHERE ROOTCOM.C

or for patterns. For example,

WHERE DATE*.?

tells you the exact location of every file that has DATE as the first four characters in its name and a one-character suffix. The program also reports how many matches it found.

WHERE.C (Listing 2.3) uses the directory manipulation functions discussed here. It also takes advantage of a programming concept known as *recursion*, in which a subroutine calls itself. The recursive function here is searchdir(). It first searches a directory for filenames matching the pattern and lists each one. Next it searches the directory for subdirectories; each time it finds one, it passes the name of the subdirectory to another invocation of itself. That invocation searches the named subdirectory and all of *its* subdirectories in the same fashion.

In this way, the function visits every directory on the disk. When its line of inquiry to successively lower levels is exhausted, recursion backs up to the next-higher level and finds the next downward chain of directories, and so on until it has no more directories to search. Because WHERE starts at the root, it examines every directory on the disk.

The WHERE program has two other features that merit an examination of the source code. The first is that the program expects to find a search pattern on the command line. When it doesn't find one (argc == 1), it asks the user to type the pattern. The other is the addition of explicit wildcards where one is implied.

This is done to ensure compatibility with the DOS DIR command. For example, you can type the command

DIR .C

and DOS interprets this to mean "DIR *.C." Similarly, you can type

DIR WHERE

and DOS takes that to mean "DIR WHERE.*." The statements labeled "Add wildcard prefix/suffix" accomplish the same thing by patching the asterisk wildcard as necessary.

This program needs a .MAK file to link with MLIBCE.LIB.

Listing 2.3 **Utility to search all directories for a pattern.**

```
/* WHERE.C: Searches directory structure from root and   */
/*    lists all occurrences of a filename matching the   */
/*    search argument from the command line              */
#include <stdio.h>
#include <dos.h>
#include <direct.h>
#include <conio.h>
#include <string.h>
#include <malloc.h>
/* Global to count matches found */
int   count = 0;
/* ------------------------------------------------- */
main (int argc, char *argv[])
{
char  *curdir,                    /* current directory on entry */
       sought [80],                   /* pattern to search for */
       *temp;                         /* temporary work string */
int   curdrive, newdrive,         /* current and new drives */
       p, n = 4;                       /* misc counters */
void  searchdir (char *dir, char *ptrn);       /* search fcn */

  /* Find out where we are */
  curdir = getcwd (NULL, 80);
  _dos_getdrive (&curdrive);

  /* Find out what we're looking for */
  if (argc > 1)
    strcpy (sought, argv[1]);          /* pattern from cmd line */
  else {
    printf ("Pattern to search for? ");          /* else ask */
    gets (sought);
  }
              /* Get designator for another drive if specified */
  if (sought [1] == ':') {
    newdrive = (toupper (sought [0])) - 64;          /* convert */
    _dos_setdrive (newdrive, &n);                /* set new drive */
    p = (sought [2] == '\\') ? 3 : 2;          /* start of pattern */
    strcpy (sought, &(sought [p]));            /* take out drive */
  }

                    /* Add wildcard prefix/suffix if necessary */
  if (sought [0] == '.') {
    temp = strcat ("*", sought);                 /* set prefix */
    strcpy (sought, temp);
  }
  if (!strchr (sought, '.' )
```

Listing 2.3 *(continued)*

```
    strcat (sought, "*.*");                         /* set suffix */
                        /* Perform search for pattern starting in root */
    searchdir ("\\", sought);
    printf ("\nNumber of matches = %d", count);
                            /* Restore original drive and directory */
    _dos_setdrive (curdrive, &n);
    chdir (curdir);
} /* ------------------------ */
void searchdir (char *path, char *ptrn)
                            /* recursive directory search routine */

#define ANYFILE 0xFF            /* wildcard attribute for any file */

{
struct find_t *f;
char           *wholepath;
unsigned       rtn;
    chdir (path);                              /* change to new dir */
    wholepath = getcwd (NULL, 80);             /* get full pathname */
    f = malloc (sizeof (*f));

                /* Search for filename matches in this directory */
    rtn = _dos_findfirst (ptrn, ANYFILE, f);
    while (rtn == 0) {                            /* list path */
      if (f->attrib != _A_SUBDIR)
        printf ("%s\\%s\n", wholepath, f->name);
      else
        printf ("%s\\%s <DIR>\n", wholepath, f->name);
      ++count;
      rtn = _dos_findnext (f);                /* find next match */
    }

            /* Now search any subdirectories under this directory */
    rtn = _dos_findfirst ("*.*", _A_SUBDIR, f);
    while (rtn == 0) {
      if ((f->attrib == _A_SUBDIR) && (f->name[0] != ".")) {
        searchdir (f->name, ptrn);              /* recursive call */
        chdir (wholepath);                      /* back to this dir */
      }
      rtn = _dos_findnext (f);                  /* search next dir */
    }

                                        /* Free allocated space */
    free (wholepath);
    free (f);
} /* ------------------------ */
```

Now that you're familiar with directory operations, let's see how to find out and interpret information specific to individual files.

CHAPTER 3

Finding Out More About Files

DOS stores a number of items of information about files in their directory entries, which are accessible to Quick C programs in a couple of ways. This chapter talks about how to obtain and interpret file information. During the discussion, we'll develop a library of miscellaneous file functions that stretch Quick C by providing services to your programs.

Before getting into details, let's discuss how DOS classifies disk files.

About File Attributes

DOS 2.0 and higher has six different classifications for disk files. These classifications—or "attributes" as they're more properly called—affect permissible operations on files. Additionally, DOS uses the attribute descriptor to flag files that have been modified since the last backup with a characteristic officially called *archive* but more commonly referred to as the *dirty bit*.

The file directory entry carries an eight-bit attribute byte whose bit meanings are shown in Table 3.1. Attributes are sometimes ORed together in various combinations. For example, _A_RDONLY I _A_HIDDEN (03h) indicates a read-only hidden file, while _A_SYSTEM I _A_ARCH (24h) means a system file that has been modified since its last backup.

Table 3.1 **File attributes.**

Bit	Meaning	Quick C constant(2)
00h	Normal read/write file(1)	_A_NORMAL
01h	Read-only	_A_RDONLY
02h	Hidden file (not listed by DIR)	_A_HIDDEN
04h	System file (ditto, owned by DOS)	_A_SYSTEM
08h	Volume label	_A_VOLID
10h	Subdirectory	_A_SUBDIR
20h	Archive ("dirty")(1)	_A_ARCH

1. The attribute constants are defined in DOS.H.
2. An attribute of 20h means a normal file eligible for backup
   due to modification since last backup.

The volume label (08h) is a special directory entry that carries the disk's "name" as shown on listings produced by the DOS **DIR** command. A label looks like a file entry, but it isn't one and can't be treated as such. Similarly, normal file operations cannot be carried out on subdirectories.

DOS uses the file attribute to control permissible operations on files. For example, you can delete only normal files (attribute 00h or 20h) with the **ERASE** alias **DEL** command. Similarly, **DIR** is blind to hidden and system files, and treats the volume label and subdirectory entries in special ways.

The read-only attribute places a file in a middling position between hidden and normal. A read-only file entry shows up when you type **DIR** and you can open it from a program for input, but not for output. You cannot erase a read-only file; it must first be changed to normal. Thus, read-only status is an effective way to prevent accidental erasure of important data. If you must write to such a file, have your application change its status, write the data, then change its attribute back to read-only.

In effect, DOS uses the attribute to support a somewhat defensive stance concerning file access. This is justified inasmuch as files that are other than "normal" are entitled to special protection. Otherwise, why flag them as such?

Consequently DOS surrenders information about the attribute somewhat reluctantly, and in ordinary file I/O doesn't even admit to the existence of non-normal files.

Let's say, for example, that you want to ascertain if the diskette in drive A is bootable. The presence of **IBMBIO.COM**, a hidden system file, indicates that it is, and its absence means it's not. You can find out if any normal file is present by attempting to open it with **fopen()** or **open()**, but that doesn't work with a hidden/system file; DOS returns an error code as if the special file didn't exist, even though it does. You can, however, use **_dos_findfirst()** to check for the existence of IBMBIO.COM; pass it the filename and the wildcard attribute 0FFh. If the operation is successful (0 returned), the diskette is bootable.

You can use the same method to check for the existence of other files that might not be visible to DIR. On a successful return, check the attrib field of the **find_t** structure if you need to find out the file's attributes.

The **access()** function defined in IO.H provides somewhat similar capabilities, except that it checks for specific permissions. The arguments are the pathname and one of the following mode values:

Value	Check for:
00	Existence only
01	Write permission
02	Read permission
03	Read/write permission

The **access()** function returns 0 if the test succeeded (i.e., if the file exists with mode 00, or it has the requested permission with the other modes). A return value of − 1 indicates that the test failed; in that case, the global value **errno** indicates why, giving either **ENOENT** (file doesn't exist) or **EACCES** (requested permission is invalid).

And finally there's **_dos_getfileattr()**, which is probably the easiest method that Quick C provides for checking the attributes of a file. Pass it the file path and a pointer to an unsigned integer, and the function drops the attributes into the pointed-to value. This function and **_dos_findfirst/next()** are the only ways to check the attributes of hidden and otherwise unusual files. It returns 0 normally and − 1 if it couldn't find the requested file.

Changing a File's Attributes

When you identify a non-normal file and you want to open it for ordinary I/O, you must first change its attributes to normal read/write. Note: You can open a read-only file for input using normal calls, but you can't write to it.

Although Quick C furnishes several ways to determine a file's attributes, it provides only one library function for changing them. The **chmod()** function, defined in IO.H, is limited to flipping a file between read-only and read/write access. Its constants are defined in **SYS\STAT.H** and consist of **S_IWRITE** and **S_IREAD**. Pass **S_IREAD** to set the file to read-only, and **S_IWRITE** to give the file normal read/write access.

If you need to do more with the attributes—say, change a file to or from hidden—you have to write a more flexible version of **chmod()** that calls DOS function 43h directly. Even better is to have a prewritten routine to do it, and that's what the first function in Listing 3.3 provides. Because this routine is a stretched replacement for the standard library's **chmod()** function, we'll call it **_chmod()**. The call works just like standard **chmod()** except that you can pass any attribute constant or ORed combination thereof from Table 3.1. For example, to hide a file, write

```
result  =  _chmod ("\\APATH\\SOMEFILE.EXT",  _A_HIDDEN);
```

The corresponding call to make the same file visible later is

```
result  =  _chmod ("\\APATH\\SOMEFILE.EXT",  _A_NORMAL);
```

Like the normal **chmod()**, **_chmod()** returns 0 if successful and − 1 if not, and it sets the global **errno** in the latter case. Listing 3.3 shows the possible **errno** values (more than for **chmod()**) and their meanings.

Your programs can use **_chmod()** to place a newly written file under DOS' protection if you don't want other users to tamper with it. After closing, change the attribute to **_A_RDONLY** or **_A_HIDDEN** to make it non-writable/nonerasable, or totally invisible to DIR and other programs, respectively. Authorized programs can then call _chmod() to change the attribute to _A_NORMAL prior to modifying the file, and then reset it later to the protected status.

Stretching Quick C File Handling

Listing 3.1 and 3.2 comprise a library of stretched file-handling functions for Quick C 2.0 programs, under the collective name FILEMISC. We'll discuss its routines as we progress through this chapter, developing some sample programs that show how to use them.

Listing 3.1 **Header for the FILEMISC library.**

```
/* Library FILEMISC.H: Miscellaneous file service func-    */
/*    tions that extend Quick C                            */
/* ------------------------------------------------------- */
/* _chmod(): Stretched version of Quick C chmod function   */
/* Changes a named file to any attribute except label      */
/*    and directory.                                       */
/* Returns 0 if successful, -1 if not, and sets global     */
/*    variable errno when unsuccessful.                    */


int _chmod (char far *path, int new_attrib);


/* ------------------------------------------------------- */
/* timestamp(): Converts the DOS file time stamp into:     */
/*      1. A formatted string of 12 chars (hh:mm:ss ?m)    */
/*      2. Its hour, min, and sec numeric components       */
/* For any component not to be converted, pass NULL arg    */


void timestamp (unsigned field,
        char *string, unsigned *hour,
        unsigned *min, unsigned *sec);


/* ------------------------------------------------------- */
/* datestamp(): Converts the DOS file date stamp into:     */
/*      1. A formatted string of 11 chars (mm/dd/yyyy)     */
/*      2. Its month, day, and year numeric components     */
/* For any component not to be converted, pass NULL arg    */


void datestamp (unsigned field,
        char *string, unsigned *year,
        unsigned *month, unsigned *day);
```

Listing 3.2 **Source for the FILEMISC library.**

```c
/* Library FILEMISC.C: Miscellaneous file service func-   */
/*    tions that extend Quick C                           */

#include <errno.h>
#include <dos.h>
#include <errno.h>
#include <stdlib.h>


/* ------------------------------------------------------ */
/* _chmod(): Stretched version of Quick C chmod function  */
/* Changes a named file to any attribute except label     */
/*    and directory.                                      */
/* Returns 0 if successful, -1 if not, and sets global    */
/*    variable errno when unsuccessful.                   */

int _chmod (char far *path, int new_attrib)
{
union REGS    inreg, outreg;
struct SREGS sreg;
int           retval = 0;

  inreg.h.ah = 0x43;                      /* Int 21h, fcn 43h */
  inreg.h.al = 0x01;                      /* set file attrib */
  inreg.x.cx = new_attrib;                 /* attrib to set */
  inreg.x.dx = FP_OFF (path);      /* point to file path */
  sreg.ds    = FP_SEG (path);
  int86x (0x21, &inreg, &outreg, &sreg);       /* call dos */

  switch (outreg.x.ax) {
    case 1:  errno = EINVAL;      /* invalid function call */
          retval = -1;
          break;
    case 2:                                  /* file not found */
    case 3:  errno = ENOENT;      /* bad path or filename */
          retval = -1;
          break;
    case 5:  errno = EACCES;       /* cannot change attrib */
          retval = -1;
          break;
    default: errno = 0;                      /* else no error */
  }
  return (retval);
}
/* ------------------------------------------------------ */


/* timestamp(): Converts the DOS file time stamp into:    */
/*     1. A formatted string of 12 chars (hh:mm:ss ?m)    */
/*     2. Its hour, min, and sec numeric components       */
/* For any component not to be converted, pass NULL arg   */

void timestamp (unsigned field,
```

Listing 3.2 *(continued)*

```
              char *string, unsigned *hour,
              unsigned *min, unsigned *sec)
{
struct TSTAMP {                           /* time stamp bitfield */
  unsigned sec  : 5,
         min  : 6,
         hour : 5;
};
union {
  struct TSTAMP stamp;
  unsigned        ftime;
} time;
char  ap[3];
int   h, m, s;

  strcpy (ap, "am");
  time.ftime = field;
  if (time.stamp.hour > 23)                    /* get hour */
    h = 0;
  else
    if (time.stamp.hour > 11) {
      h = time.stamp.hour - 12;
      ap[0] = "p";
    } else
      h = time.stamp.hour;
  m = time.stamp.min;                         /* get minute */
  s = time.stamp.sec * 2;                     /* get seconds */
  if (string)              /* convert time to text string */
    sprintf (string, "%02d:%02d:%02d %s", h, m, s, ap);
  if (hour) *hour = h;
  if (min)  *min  = m;
  if (sec)  *sec  = s;
}
/* ------------------------------------------------------ */

/* datestamp(): Converts the DOS file date stamp into:   */
/*      1. A formatted string of 11 chars (mm/dd/yyyy)   */
/*      2. Its month, day, and year numeric components   */
/* For any component not to be converted, pass NULL arg  */

void datestamp (unsigned field,
        char *string, unsigned *year,
        unsigned *month, unsigned *day)
{
struct DSTAMP {                     /* date stamp bitfield format */
  unsigned day   : 5,
         month : 4,
         year  : 7;
};
union {
  struct DSTAMP stamp;
```

```
    unsigned        fdate;
} date;
unsigned d, m, y;

    date.fdate = field;
    y = date.stamp.year + 1980;
    m = date.stamp.month;
    d = date.stamp.day;
    if (string)
      sprintf (string, "%02d/%02d/%02d", m, d, y);
    if (year)  *year  = y;
    if (month) *month = m;
    if (day)   *day   = d;
}
```

File Date and Time

DOS writes a time stamp into the directory entry each time a program modifies the file. A modification is any operation except read-only, and includes creating, rewriting, appending, and replacing records. The time stamp has two parts: date and time of day. At the same time that it updates the time stamp, DOS sets the dirty bit (20h) in the attribute byte.

The time stamp is accessible from Quick C in a couple of ways. If the file is not open, use _dos_findfirst() to load the fields wr_time and wr_date in the find_t strucuture. For an open file, call _dos_getftime(), which returns the date and time for the specified handle via arguments. The time and date values yielded by both the find and get functions are identical C bitfields.

Interpreting Time Stamps

The time stamp exactly parallels the format of timestamps maintained by DOS in the directory entry. It is a 16-bit word zoned into the bit fields shown in Figure 3.1.

The time-of-day stamp reflects the approximate time the file was last closed after a change (or created if new). The time is approximate in that its seconds field is actually the time-of-day seconds divided by two; e.g., 14 in this field means that the file was closed 28 or 29 seconds after the minute. Because one seldom cares about such hair-splitting as the exact second of file closure, this is "good enough."

Extracting the fields from this 16-bit word involves some shifting and ANDing to mask out unwanted bits and isolate those that we want. C has the necessary operators to do this, but it's easier to use the bitfield operations built into Quick C. In this case we can define the bitfield structure as

Figure 3.1 **File time stamp format.**

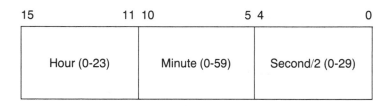

```
struct  {
    unsigned  sec  :  5,  min  :  6,  hour  :  5;
}  timefield;
```

A C bitfield is constructed from right to left, so the sec field occupies the low five bits, min the middle six, and hour the high five. This, then, is a description of Listing 3.2.

We can now refer to a field with notation such as timestamp.hour, and use the fields as though they were normal unsigned integers. However, the times- tamp() function in Listing 3.2 takes a slightly different approach than this discussion in an effort to enhance readability.

The timestamp() function explodes the time value obtained from the wr _time field in the find_t structure, or the value returned by _dos_getftime. Pass it the time value and four pointers corresponding to a text string, the hour, minute, and second, and timestamp() returns the extracted data. You can pass NULL for any pointer argument if you don't want the corresponding value returned. For example, to get only a text string and the month, call the function with

```
timestamp  (found.wr_time,  timestr,  NULL,  mo,  NULL);
```

The timestamp() function returns its results via indirection. We'll use it in an upcoming utility program.

Interpreting Date Stamps

The file date stamp is similar to the time stamp, but it has a different format shown in Figure 3.2. In this case, the seven high-order bits contain a number in the range 0-119, which must be added to 1980 to obtain the calendar year. The month and date fields correspond exactly to real-world calendars. Just as we did with time stamps, we can describe this 16-bit structure with the C bitfield

Figure 3.2 **File date stamp format.**

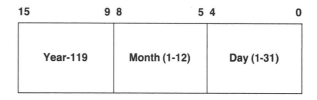

```
struct  {
        unsigned  day  :  5,  month  :  4,  year  :  7;
} datefield;
```

Listing 3.2 also lists the **datestamp()** function, which serves the same purpose for file date information as **timestamp()** does for the file time. The only real difference is that you pass the function a file date value and it explodes it into its various components plus a formatted string. As before, you can pass a NULL pointer for any component you don't want.

Note that the numeric parameters for both functions are passed in decreasing order of importance: hour, minute, second in the one case, year, month, day in the other. This makes it easy to remember the order of numeric pointer arguments.

Listing a Directory

Programs that produce listings of files give the impression of complexity and sophistication, as though the programmer knows some great technological secret. In fact, it can easily be done with a simple loop using the find functions. Here's how it works:

```
result  =  _dos_findfirst  (pattern,  attrib,  &fileinfo);
while  (result  = =  0)  {
        /*  do  any  output  preparation  here  */
        printf  ("%s...",  fileinfo.name,  ...);
        result  =  _dos_findnext  (&fileinfo);
}
```

Listing 3.3 illustrates this loop with a working example. Called LS.C after the UNIX command equivalent to DOS's DIR, it lists all the files in the default directory. Subdirectory names appear in uppercase, all other filenames in lowercase, and each entry includes its date and time stamps.

Listing 3.3 **A simple directory listing program.**

```
/* LS.C: lists files in current directory */

#include <stdio.h>
#include <io.h>
#include <dos.h>
#include <conio.h>
#include <direct.h>
#include <string.h>
#include "filemisc.h"

main ()
{
struct find_t file;
unsigned        result;
char            date [11], time [12];

  result = _dos_findfirst ("*.*", 0xFF, &file);
  while (result == 0) {
    if (!(file.attrib & _A_SUBDIR))
      strlwr (file.name);      /* non-directories in locase */
    datestamp (file.wr_date, date, NULL, NULL, NULL);
    timestamp (file.wr_time, time, NULL, NULL, NULL);
    printf ("\n%-20s %-14s %-14s", file.name, date, time);
    result = _dos_findnext (&file);
  }
}
```

LS isn't a very useful program, but it demonstrates how easy it is to list a directory with a Quick C program. At the end of this chapter, we'll flesh out LS into a highly flexible, powerful replacement for the DIR command.

Getting the Time and Date Stamps for an Open File

The find functions locate information about files that are not open. If a file is open, you can obtain its date and time stamps using the Quick C function _dos_getftime. To use this function, pass the file handle, plus pointers to the two unsigned integers that will receive the date and time values. The function returns 0 when successful and −1 when you've passed an invalid file handle (i.e., an unopened handle or one of the standard device handles discussed in Chapter 5).

_dos_getftime places the date and time values into the variables pointed to by the argument pointers. You can then pass these values to the datestamp() and timestamp() functions for interpretation, since their formats are the same as returned by the find functions.

For the record, Quick C has the offsetting function _dos_setftime, which you can use to deliberately falsify the time and date of an open file. It's unlikely that you'll have much application for this function, but if you need it, it's available.

File Size

Chapter 1 covered the way DOS allocates file space in clusters comprised of some multiple of the sector size. Since DOS assigns file space in these increments, it stands to reason that any given file's actual length is less than—or, at most, equal to—the space allocated to it. A file's size cannot be greater than its allocated space, but it might be as much as 4095 bytes less, depending on the cluster size.

As with time stamps, the method for determining file size depends on whether the file block was fetched from the directory with _dos _findfirst/next(), or the file is already open and associated with a handle. In both cases, the size is expressed in bytes; since files can potentially be very large, this quantity is of necessity a long integer.

The find_t structure filled in by _dos_findfirst/next() contains a field called *size*. Thus you can print it directly using a statement such as

```
printf ("\nFilesize  =  %lu", file.size);
```

For a file that is already open, you can obtain the size using the Quick C function filelength(), the prototype of which is specified in IO.H as

```
long    filelength (int  handle);
```

In other words, filelength() returns a long integer giving the length in bytes of the file associated with the handle.

Demonstration

Listing 3.4 lists FILETIME.C, which illustrates the discussion up to this point. The program uses _dos_findfirst() to locate the first version of itself in the default directory, which might be a .C, an .OBJ, a .BAK, a .MAK, or an .EXE file. When it finds such a file, the program lists the time and date stamps and file size from the find_t structure. Next it opens the same file and calls _dos_ getftime() and filelength() to obtain the same information using the handle. This shows how you can get the same information by two different means, depending on whether you're searching the directory or dealing with an open file.

Listing 3.4 **Getting file information by different means.**

```c
/* FILETIME.C: Demonstrates two methods for getting the   */
/*    time, date, and size of a file, depending on status */
/* ------------------------------------------------------- */

/* INCLUDES FOR PROTOTYPES AND STRUCTURES */
#include <dos.h>
#include <fcntl.h>
#include <io.h>
#include <stdio.h>
#include "filemisc.h"

/* LOCAL FUNCTION PROTOTYPES */
void dir_report (struct find_t *file);
void han_report (int han);
/* -------------------------- */

void main ()
{
struct find_t file;
int           handle;

/* Report file information from findfirst() */
  if (_dos_findfirst ("filetime.*", 0xFF, &file) == 0) {
    dir_report (&file);

/* Report same information from getftime() */
    handle = open (file.name, O_RDONLY);      /* open file */
    han_report (handle);                      /* report info */
    close (handle);                           /* close the file */
  } else
    puts ("Cannot find any instance of the file");
} /* ----------------------- */

void dir_report (struct find_t *file)
{                      /* print file info from directory block */
char time[12], date[11];
  /* Get the time and date strings */
  timestamp (file->wr_time, time, NULL, NULL, NULL);
  datestamp (file->wr_date, date, NULL, NULL, NULL);

  /* Report */
  puts ("File info obtained from findfirst:");
  printf ("\nFilename: %s", file->name);
  printf ("\n    Date: %s", date);
  printf ("\n    Time: %s", time);
  printf ("\n    Size: %lu", file->size);
} /* ----------------------- */

void han_report (int handle)
{                              /* print file info for open file */
unsigned  timefield, datefield;
```

```
char        time [12], date [11];

    /* Get time and date info */
    _dos_getftime (handle, &datefield, &timefield);
    timestamp (timefield, time, NULL, NULL, NULL);
    datestamp (datefield, date, NULL, NULL, NULL);

    /* Report */
    puts ("\n\n\nInfo for same file from handle functions:");
    printf ("\n    Date: %s", date);
    printf ("\n    Time: %s", time);
    printf ("\n    Size: %lu", filelength (handle));
}  /* ----------------------- */
```

An Alternative to the DOS DIR Command

Probably the most-used command in DOS's repertoire is DIR, which lists the files in a directory. As venerable and useful as it is, there are a couple of shortcomings in this command.

First, it doesn't let you know if there are hidden and system files in the directory. This is a problem when you're attempting to remove a directory from the disk. You issue the command

DEL *.*

which ostensibly deletes all the files, but in fact it doesn't touch those that are out of sight. Later you issue the RMDIR command and DOS mysteriously refuses to cooperate. The only way to find out why (that there are still files in the directory) is to use a DOS shell such as XTREE to inspect the directory for invisible contents. DOS itself won't tell you, and it contains no command for changing the survivors' attributes.

The second problem with DIR is that it doesn't tell you how much space the directory's contents occupy. This becomes an issue when you plan to back up the directory; how many diskettes do you need to have ready? The only way to figure it out is manually: Round each file's byte count to the next-higher cluster size and add them up. This is the kind of job we invented computers to do for us, yet DOS itself doesn't.

It was to overcome these disappointments that I decided to write the SUB.C program in Listing 3.5. It's an improved version of DOS's DIR command in that it shows:

- All files and their attributes, plus time stamps.
- The number of bytes in each file and the space in K allocated to it as a function of cluster size.

- Number of files in the directory, total bytes, and total space taken by all files in K.
- Free space remaining on the disk.

This program ties together many of the elements covered from Chapter 1 onward. Its general flow is:

- Get and remember the current directory.
- Find out what directory to search.
- List the specified contents of the target directory.
- Show summary information.
- Restore the original directory.
- Quit.

The details of these operations are broken down into a number of functions, as is usual in writing large C programs.

If you type the unadorned command

SUB

the program lists the entire contents of the current directory. You can also include command-line arguments. For example, to list all the .WKS files in your Lotus subdirectory, type

SUB \LOTUS*.WKS

The program is "considerate" in that it always returns to the original directory before ending. You can also use it to list the contents of directories on other drives.

The complexity of **SUB** is due partly to uncertainty about the format of the search pattern. There are many possible patterns that a user can type, each meaning something different. For example:

Pattern	Means
\DOS\UTILS*.com	Follow a path from the root and list all .COM files.
\DOS\UTILS	Follow a path from the root and list all files in the last directory.
\DOS\util*.*	List all files starting with "util" in the DOS directory.
DOS\UTILS	UTILS is a child of DOS, which is a child of the current directory. List all files in **UTILS**.
*.ext	All files in this directory with the suffix .**EXT**.
.ext	Same as above.

and so on.

SUB deals with this uncertainty by attempting to act on four possible interpretations of the search pattern:

1. No pattern entered, so assume the wildcards *.* for the current directory.
2. SUB DIR (DIR is a child of the current directory) or SUB \DIR (where DIR is a child of the root). The filename pattern is assumed to be wildcards *.*.
3. SUB DIR*.*, where *.* might be any pattern and DIR might be a path through several directory levels. A backslash preceding the first directory name indicates a path proceeding from the root, and its absence indicates a path starting in the current directory.
4. SUB *.*, where the pattern can be anything but no path is indicated. In other words, search the current directory.

If any of these attempts succeeds, the variable thru is set to TRUE and the program bypasses subsequent attempts. If none succeed, the program breaks the bad news with the message "PATH NOT FOUND."

Listing 3.5 A subdirectory listing utility.

```
/* SUB.C: Enhancement of DOS DIR command */

#include <stdio.h>
#include <dos.h>
#include <io.h>
#include <conio.h>
#include <stdlib.h>
#include <direct.h>
#include <string.h>
#include <malloc.h>
#include <graph.h>
#include "filemisc.h"
#ifndef  TRUE
#define  FALSE 0
#define  TRUE  !FALSE
#endif


/* Globals */
char             *olddir, searchpath [80],
                 filemask [13] = "*.mak";
unsigned         bps, nfiles, olddrive, drive;
long             totalbytes, totalK;
int              thru;
struct diskfree_t diskinfo;
/* ------------------------------------------------- */

main (int argc, char *argv[])
{
unsigned ndrives;
void listfiles (char*, char*), check (char*),
     separate (char*, char*, char*);
```

Listing 3.5 *(continued)*

```c
/* Initialize */
olddir = getcwd (NULL, 80);      /* get current directory */
_dos_getdrive (&olddrive);                        /* and drive */
totalbytes = totalK = 0L;
nfiles = 0;
drive = 0;
thru = FALSE;
strcpy (searchpath, olddir);      /* default search path */

/* Get desired search path, change drives if necessary */
if (argc > 1)
  strcpy (searchpath, argv [1]);
if (searchpath [1] == ':') {
  drive = (toupper (searchpath [0])) - 64;
  _dos_setdrive (drive, &ndrives);
}

/* Get info about selected drive */
_dos_getdiskfree (drive, &diskinfo);       /* drive info */
bps = diskinfo.sectors_per_cluster *     /* blocksize */
diskinfo.bytes_per_sector;

/* Show all files in current dir if no command-line arg */
if (argc == 1) {
  listfiles (searchpath, filemask);
  thru = TRUE;
}
/* Is command SUB <dir> or SUB <\DIR>? */
if (!thru) {
  strcpy (searchpath, argv [1]);
  if (chdir (searchpath) == 0) {
    listfiles (searchpath, filemask);
    thru = TRUE;
  }
}
/* Is command SUB <dir\*.*>? */
if (!thru) {
  separate (argv [1], searchpath, filemask);
  if (chdir (searchpath) == 0)
    if (strlen (filemask) > 0) {
      check (filemask);
      listfiles (searchpath, filemask);
      thru = TRUE;
    }
}
/* Is command SUB *.*? */
if (!thru) {
  strcpy (filemask, argv [1]);
  check (filemask);
  listfiles (olddir, filemask);
```

```
      thru = TRUE;
    }
    /* Have we exhausted all possibilities? */
    if (!thru)
      puts ("PATH NOT FOUND");

    /* Clean up and quit */
    _dos_setdrive (olddrive, &ndrives);      /* restore drive */
    chdir (olddir);                          /* and directory */
    free (olddir);
  } /* ----------------------------------------------- */

void check (char *mask)
/* Check file mask, complete with wildcards if necessary  */
{
char  temp [13];

  if (mask [0] == '.') {                    /* make .* into *.* */
    sprintf (temp, "*%s", mask);
    strcpy (mask, temp);
  }
  if (strchr (mask, '.') == NULL)           /* if no period */
    strcat (mask, "*.*");                   /* add wildcard */
} /* ----------------------- */

void separate (char *arg, char *path, char *mask)
   /* Break out path and mask from command-line arg */
{
char *brk;

  strcpy (path, arg);
  brk = strrchr (path, '\\');     /* find last '\' in path */
  if (brk) {                              /* if found */
    strcpy (mask, &(brk [1])); /* copy from right to mask */
    *brk = '\0';                /* chop off mask leaving path */
  }
} /* ----------------------- */

void listfiles (char *path, char *mask)
 /* List files in currently selected directory using mask */
{
struct find_t *file;
char          *heading;
unsigned      linecount, rc;
unsigned      startpage (char*);
void          writeinfo (struct find_t*);
void          showtotals (void);
unsigned      countlines (char*, unsigned);

  /* Get space for working objects */
  file = malloc (sizeof *file);
  heading = malloc (160);
```

Listing 3.5 *(continued)*

```
  /* Begin report */
  sprintf (heading, "Directory for %s in %s:", mask, path);
  linecount = startpage (heading);            /* first page */

  /* Write report */
  rc = _dos_findfirst (mask, 0xFF, file);
  while (rc == 0) {
    writeinfo (file);
    linecount = countlines (heading, linecount);
    rc = _dos_findnext (file);
  }
  showtotals ();
} /* ----------------------- */

unsigned startpage (char *header)     /* Begin output page */
{
  _clearscreen (_GCLEARSCREEN);
  puts (header);
  printf ("%-17s %-13s %-12s %-10s %-6s   KB",
    "Name", "Date", "Time", "Attrib", "Bytes");
  return 3L;
} /* ----------------------- */

unsigned countlines (char *head, unsigned count)
        /* Count line, start new page if full */
{
  ++count;
  if (count == 24) {
    printf ("\n-- MORE --");
    getch ();
    count = startpage (head);
  }
  return count;
} /* ----------------------- */

void showtotals (void)            /* End report with totals */
{
long   free, size;
  /* Compute totals */
  free = (long) diskinfo.avail_clusters * bps;
  size = (long) diskinfo.total_clusters * bps;

  /* Report results */
  printf ("\n%u files, %lu bytes, %luK space",
     nfiles, totalbytes, totalK);
  printf ("\n%lu bytes free out of %lu", free, size);
} /* ----------------------- */

void writeinfo (struct find_t *f)      /* list file entry */
{
```

```
char    tstring [12], dstring [11], *attribs (char);
unsigned kbytes (long), kb;

   /* Get file info */
   datestamp (f->wr_date, dstring, NULL, NULL, NULL);
   timestamp (f->wr_time, tstring, NULL, NULL, NULL);
   kb = kbytes (f->size);

   /* Non-directories shown in lower case */
    if (!(f->attrib & _A_SUBDIR)) strlwr (f->name);

   /* Write directory info */
   printf ("\n%-18s", f->name);                      /* name */
   printf ("%-14s", dstring);                         /* date */
   printf ("%-13s", tstring);                         /* time */
   printf ("%-10s", attribs (f->attrib));    /* attributes */
   printf ("%6lu", f->size);              /* size in bytes */
   printf ("%6u", kb);                        /* size in K */

   /* Update sums for this entry */
   totalK += kb;
   totalbytes += f->size;
   ++nfiles;
} /* ------------------------ */

char *attribs (char attrib)
         /* convert attribute byte to string */
{
static char attr [7];

   strcpy (attr, "......");
   if (attrib & _A_RDONLY) attr [5] = 'R';
   if (attrib & _A_HIDDEN) attr [4] = 'H';
   if (attrib & _A_SYSTEM) attr [3] = 'S';
   if (attrib & _A_VOLID)  attr [2] = 'V';
   if (attrib & _A_SUBDIR) attr [1] = 'D';
   if (attrib & _A_ARCH)   attr [0] = 'A';
   return attr;
} /* ------------------------ */

unsigned kbytes (long bytes)
     /* convert size to K, rounding up for cluster */
{
unsigned k = 0;
long     clust;

   if (bytes > 0L) {                       /* if file not empty */
     clust = bytes / bps;                 /* number of clusters */
     if ((clust % bps) != 0L) ++clust;            /* round up */
     if (clust == 0L) clust = 1;          /* minimum of one */
```

Listing 3.5 *(continued)*

```
    k = (clust * bps) / 1024L;                    /* space in K */
  }
  return k;
} /* ------------------------ */
```

Now that we've covered the directory manipulations of normal and protected files, let's consider the many ways of working with disk files in Quick C.

CHAPTER 4

101 Things to Do with a File

I f ever a subject begged for clarification, it's file handling in Quick C. The language provides dozens of functions—plus several variants thereon—for manipulating files. Some are general functions, others rely on a file handle, and still others deal with streams, requiring a special file descriptor structure. While so much flexibility provides for tremendous power in file operations, it's bewildering. This chapter and the next attempt to sort the mess of functions into something comprehensible.

This chapter illustrates practical uses for many of the Quick C file control functions, but not all; its thrust is to give an overview of the possibilities.

Handles and Streams

A fundamental matter needing clarification is the distinction between the two file-related terms *handle* and *stream*.

A *handle* is an identifier (an integer) that DOS assigns to input/output entities to keep track of them. It is, in effect, a reference number. If DOS assigns the handle 6 to file **XYZ.DAT** when it's opened, you specify handle 6 in subsequent file operations and DOS knows which open file you want to work on. Some two dozen file functions in Quick C use handles; the documentation often refers to these functions as "low-level I/O."

DOS predefines five handles, assigning them (whether actually used in a program or not) to logical devices that function as virtual files. Table 4.1 lists them.

Table 4.1 **Predefined handles and streams in Quick C.**

Handle	Purpose	DOS Device	C stream*
0	Standard input	CON	stdin
1	Standard output	CON	stdout
2	Standard error	CON	stderr

| 3 | Auxiliary | AUX | stdaux |
| 4 | List | PRN | stdprn |

The **CON** device is a catch-all name for the keyboard and display, **AUX** generally means a serial port, and **PRN** stands for the printer. DOS automatically opens these five I/O files for any program in execution.

Because DOS predefines the five handles 0–4, the first numeric handle it assigns to a program's file is 5, and so on upward. You'll probably never need to know the actual value of a given handle; the file-opening handle functions return it to a variable, and you pass that variable as an argument to other handle functions.

A *stream* is any source or destination for data that moves serially: i.e., byte by byte. For example, when you read data from a disk file, the data arrive in a stream of bytes and get stored in memory or processed sequentially in some other fashion. Similarly, if you write a string of characters to a file, you are sending a stream of data. The source and destination for these operations are thus stream files.

By this definition, the keyboard, printer, and display screen can also be stream files, and so can an auxiliary device such as a serial port. The concept of a stream file is therefore not limited to data on disk; any device that sends and/or receives data sequentially can be a "stream."

Consequently, for each predefined handle, there is a corresponding standard C stream that is generally more useful. That's what the "C stream" identifiers represent in Table 4.1. You can use the stream names as file variables, and it's not necessary to issue a **fopen()** before referring to them. For example, to write to the printer, simply code a statement such as

```
fprintf (stdprn, "\n%s", "This is printed output");
```

While a handle can, and often does, represent a stream, Quick C differentiates between handle functions and stream functions. A handle function is one that returns or requires the DOS-assigned handle. On the other hand, a stream function is one that utilizes a data structure known as the **FILE** object, and returns or requires a pointer to that structure in lieu of a handle.

The **FILE** object is defined in **STDIO.H**. A program using any of the numerous stream functions—i.e., virtually any program that does file operations—must thus #include <stdio.h> at the top to make the **FILE** structure available.

Stream files themselves are represented as pointers to **FILE** structures. For example, if you want to read from one disk file and write to another, you can declare the requisite pointers as

```
FILE    *inFile, *outFile;
```

The fopen() function and its variants fdopen() and freopen() return pointers to FILE structures when successful. Thus the call

```
inFile  =  fopen ("INPUT.FIL", "r");
```

assigns to inFile a pointer to the structure associated with INPUT.FIL. All subsequent stream operations on this file require the pointer. For example, to close the file later:

```
fclose (inFile);
```

Some of the handle and stream functions are parallel. Examples are read()/fread(), write()/fwrite(), eof()/feof(), close()/fclose(), and tell()/ftell(). In these cases and others, the *f* prefix indicates a stream function. However, an *f* prefix is not a dead giveaway: fstat() is a handle function. Many of the functions are unique to one or the other file-identification methods. For example, the file time and date can only be accessed via a handle function, while formatted text output to a file can only be accomplished via the stream function fprintf().

You can open a file with either a handle or a stream function: open() and fopen(), respectively. This would seem to pose a dilemma; if some operations are only possible with handles and others only with stream functions, which way should you open the file if you want to do some of both?

Fortunately, Quick C furnishes a bridge function to solve this problem. This is fileno(), which returns the handle associated with a stream. Use it as follows:

```
FILE   *infil;     /* declare stream pointer */
int     strhan;     /* handle for stream file */
{
       infil =  fopen ("SOME.FIL", "r");
       strhan =  fileno (infil);
       . . .

}
```

Now you can pass the strhan variable to functions requiring a handle; both infil and strhan identify the same file.

The fdopen() function provides a bridge in the opposite direction: associating a stream with an open handle. However, it's more complicated to use. Unless you know in advance that all operations you'll want to perform on a file are through handle functions, here's a general rule:

• Open files as streams with fopen().
• Before calling the first handle function (if any), use fileno() to get the handle for the stream.

Now let's classify some groups of file operations and see how to use this wealth of functions.

Operations on Unopened Files

Although most file operations occur on files that are opened—i.e., made accessible to the program via an internal communications link—there are a few that we can perform on unopened files. We discussed some in earlier chapters: for example, the _dos_findfirst/next() functions. Some others discussed here determine the accessibility of a file, change its read/write permission, rename, and erase.

A common technique in C is to open a file within an if() statement and check the value returned by open() or fopen() to find out if the operation was successful. Example:

```
if ((fp  =  fopen ("SOME.FIL", "r")) !=  NULL)
    /* process  the  file */
else
       /* file  was  not  opened  */
```

This method, though widely used, has a couple of drawbacks. First, the fopen() statement itself is intuitive only because it so often appears in programs. Try translating it into a concise statement in plain English sometime. The second drawback is that it often leads to difficult program logic; the "else" condition might appear a page or more after the open, where it's hard to find.

An easier way is to check first for the existence of a file and its access permission. If the file doesn't exist or perhaps is read-only when you intend to write to it, you can deal with the problem up front and not as the "otherwise" case in a failed open.

The QuickC access() function lets you check the accessibility of an unopened file. As a fringe benefit, you can also use it to see if a specified directory exists. The call is made as follows:

```
retval  =  access (filepath, accmode);
```

where:

- filepath is a pointer to the character string containing the path to the file or directory.
- accmode is a bit pattern described below.
- retval is an integer that receives 0 or −1 from the function to indicate success or failure, respectively.

The **accmode** bit patterns correspond to the access permission you're inquiring about. Those valid in DOS are:

Pattern	Meaning
06	Read and write permission
04	Read permission
02	Write permission
00	Existence

Suppose you want to see if the existing DATA.FIL can be written to. The call

```
retval  =  access  ("DATA.FIL", 2);
```

returns 0 to **retval**, indicating that it's a normal read/write file. You can proceed with the open and write operations.

But let's say that the file has a read-only attribute, meaning that DOS won't let you write to it. In that case, **access()** returns −1 to indicate that the requested permission is invalid for the file. You might handle this situation as follows:

```
if (access  ("DATA.FIL", 2)  = =  -1) {
    puts  ("File  is  read-only");
    exit  (1);
}
```

The program quits when DATA.FIL cannot be written to, and otherwise it falls through the condition to normal file operations following the closing curly brace.

A more elegant way to deal with this might be to change the mode of the file to read/write. To do this, #include <sys\stat.h> and issue the statement

```
chmod  ("DATA.FIL",  S_IWRITE);
```

Under DOS, write permission implies read permission, so a file set to **S_IWRITE** becomes read/write. If your program might be ported to UNIX, however, code the second argument as **S_IREAD—S_IWRITE**, since UNIX supports write-only files.

To check for the existence of a file or directory, pass permission pattern 0 as an argument to **access()**. The function returns 0 when the file exists and −1 when it does not.

The **unlink()** and **remove()** functions delete a file. They are equivalent to each other and to the DOS commands **DEL** and **ERASE**, and take the form

```
retval  =  unlink  (filename);
```

and

```
retval  =  remove (filename);
```

Their returned values are the same as for **access()**. Usually it's no big deal if **unlink/remove()** fails—the worst that can happen is that the file continues to exist—so you can safely ignore the returned value in most cases.

The last operation on unopened files that we'll discuss is renaming. It takes the form

```
retval  =  rename (oldname,  newname);
```

Assignment of 0 to retval indicates success, and -1 means failure. On -1, the global variable errno (defined in **ERRNO.H**) can have any of three possible values, which are:

ENOENT   No such file.

EACCES   Permission denied.

EXDEV   Not on same disk.

The last error might raise your eyebrows. That's because **rename()** is more powerful than it seems on the surface. Not only can it rename a file, but it can also move that file from one directory to another. For example, say that you want to remove **SOME.FIL** from the \APPLIC directory and place it in \BACKUP, retaining the same filename. The statement to do this is

```
retval  =  rename ("\\APPLIC\\SOME.DAT",
                            "\\BACKUP\\SOME.DAT");
```

Afterwards, **SOME.DAT** no longer appears in the \APPLIC directory. Note that the physical file doesn't move; instead, its directory entry is relocated into \BACKUP. This is a much more efficient way to shuffle files among directories than doing copies and deletes.

Opening Files

Quick C furnishes several functions for opening files, each with numerous options. Most of the time you'll use only one or two of them—**fopen()** and **open()**—but you should be aware of the alternatives. In general, the other open functions are specialized, and the options provide for a high degree of control over the subsequent status of the file.

The handle function **creat()** makes a new file, or erases an existing file's contents and prepares it to receive entirely new data. It fails when attempting to open existing files marked read-only.

The **creat()** function opens or creates a normal read/write file in text mode (unless the global variable _fmode is set to O_BINARY). In Quick C, a text mode file undergoes translation of new-line information: In memory, a new line, represented by the character '\n,' is a single line feed (LF), but when written to disk or a device, the newline character is translated into a carriage return/line feed (CRLF) sequence. The opposite translation occurs when reading from disk. The call to **creat()** is

```
newhandle = creat ("DATA.FIL", access);
```

where 'access' is one of the following constants defined in **SYS\STAT.H**:

Access constant	Meaning
S_IWRITE	Write access
S_IREAD	Read-only access
S_IWRITE—S_IREAD	Normal read/write access

Note that write access only (**S_IWRITE**) is equivalent to read/write access (**S_IWRITE—S_IREAD**), since in DOS permission to write implies permission to read. Thus the first and third entries achieve the same file access status.

The **creat()** function does nothing with this access information until the file is closed. At that time, it sets the attribute byte according to the access argument.

Another way to create a file is with the **O_CREAT** option of **open()**, which is discussed a little later.

The **fopen()** and **open()** functions have much in common. The chief difference is that **fopen()** is a stream function, and **open()** returns a file handle. But while they are otherwise parallel functions, the details of their options differ.

The usual way to open a file is to declare a pointer to a **FILE** structure as

```
FILE    *fp;
```

and then open it with

```
fp = fopen (filename, access);
```

where filename is the path and name of the file, and access is one of the following strings surrounded by double quotes:

Access type	Meaning
"r"	Read from file sequentially.
"w"	Begin sequential writing at start of file (see note 1).
"a"	Begin sequential writing at end of file (append).
"r+"	Read and write file (see note 2).
"w+"	Same as "r+".
"a+"	Same as "r+" except file pointer is positioned at end of file.

Note 1: The "w" access mode erases an existing file's contents upon opening it, so that new data start at the beginning. If the file does not exist when opened for writing, **fopen()** creates it.

Note 2: The plus-sign modifiers indicate update (read/write) modes, while their absence indicates one-way file operations.

The **fopen()** function returns a NULL pointer if the open attempt was unsuccessful. An example of an unsuccessful attempt occurs when you try to open a nonexistent file in access mode "r" (read). As mentioned earlier, you can open a file and test for success in the single (counterintuitive) statement

if ((fp = fopen (filepath, "r")) != NULL) { . . .

An alternative way to open a file is with the **open()** function. It returns a handle when successful, or −1 when it's not. You can specify a number of access options, which are defined in **FCNTL.H**. The most common are equivalent to those for **fopen()**:

Option	Equivalent to	Meaning
O_RDONLY	"r"	Read only
O_WRONLY	"w"	Write only
O_RDWR	"r+"	Read/write

Some less common access options are:

Option	Meaning
O_APPEND	Equivalent to **fopen()** "a"
O_CREAT	Create new file and set attribute byte per the optional permissions byte.
O_EXCL	Modifies O_CREAT, returns the EEXIST error if an attempt is made to create a file that already exists.
O_TRUNC	Erase file contents
O_BINARY	Explicitly open in binary mode (no newline translation)
O_TEXT	Explicitly open in text mode

As mentioned earlier in this chapter, it's generally advisable to open files as streams using **fopen()**. If you need to get the file handle, you can do so with the **fileno()** function, passing the stream pointer as an argument.

The **freopen()** function is useful for replacing one stream with another. It saves the step of closing a stream before associating its pointer with the next file. When you issue **freopen()**, the buffer for the currently open stream is flushed, the file is closed, and the replacement file is opened. This function is most often used to redirect I/O between a standard device and a disk file.

The program **REDIRECT.C** in Listing 4.1 illustrates I/O redirection using **freopen()**. The loop writes two lines to the display using normal **printf()** calls, then redirects stdout to DATA.FIL on disk. The target for **printf()** is now the disk, so the second iteration of the loop writes the same two lines to the file.

In order to reassociate stdout with its original device, it's necessary to reopen the stream using the standard device name "CON." That's the purpose of the freopen() call following the loop.

Next the program redirects the stdin device so that it receives input from the file instead of the keyboard. The output device stdout is unaffected, so the program loops to read lines from the file and display them on the screen, thus reading back the file contents as though they were being typed at the keyboard. This continues until the end of the file is reached, and then the program prepares to quit by resetting stdin back to its normal device.

Listing 4.1 Reopening a file and switching between stream and handle operations.

```
/* REDIRECT.C: Demos freopen(), redirecting stream I/O */

#include <stdio.h>
#include <io.h>

char     buf[] = "Now is the time for all good men",
         fil[] = "DATA.FIL";

main ()
{
FILE     *stream;
int      loop;
char     line [80];

  for (loop = 0; loop < 2; loop++) {
    printf ("These two lines go to screen and %s\n", fil);
    printf ("Text = %s\n", buf);

    /* Now redirect stdout to a file */
    if (loop == 0) {
      stream = freopen (fil, "w", stdout);
      if (stream == NULL) {
        printf ("Redirection failed\n");
        break;
      }
    }
  }

  /* Reopen stdout to console (closes old stream) */
  if (stream != NULL) {
    stream = freopen ("CON", "w", stream);
    printf ("\n\'stdout\' is back to the display\n");
    printf ("Here's what was written to %s:\n", fil);

    /* Read from disk file as though it were the keyboard */
    stream = freopen (fil, "r", stdin);
    gets (line);
    while (!feof (stream)) {
      printf ("    %s\n", line);
```

Listing 4.1 *(continued)*

```
    gets (line);
  }

  /* Reconnect stdin to keyboard */
  stream = freopen ("CON", "r", stream);
 }
}
```

Working with Temporary Files

Complex programs, especially those that work with large amounts of data, occasionally need a place to stash results as they work. Compilers are a good example, and so are sort utilities, editors that work on files larger than available memory, and other challenging applications. They write interim results for temporary safekeeping, and later return to reclaim them for further processing. That's what temporary files are about.

Because a temporary file exists only for the duration of the program run, there's no reason for the programmer or user even to know its name. The program itself can assign a unique name, create the file, use it, and later erase it with unlink/remove() during clean-up at the end of the job.

The Quick C mktemp() function exists for this purpose. Each time you use mktemp(), you pass an argument that is a character variable filled in with a template containing six 'X' characters, preceded by one or two optional literal characters that become part of the filename. The function scans the current directory and formulates a unique name that does not conflict with any existing file. It replaces the 'X' template with this new name.

Note that although mktemp() scans the directory to prevent conflict, it doesn't actually create a file with the new name. Thus, if you want to reserve the name before generating another, you must create a file by that name before calling mktemp() again. If you don't, mktemp() will repeatedly return the same name.

The program TEMP.C in Listing 4.2 illustrates mktemp() in action. It creates six temporary files and reports their names, then erases those files.

Listing 4.2 **Creating temporary files.**

```
/* TEMP.C: Makes temporary files with mktemp() */

#include <stdio.h>
#include <sys\types.h>
#include <sys\stat.h>
#include <io.h>
#include <string.h>
```

```
char *template = "tfXXXXXX";

main ()
{
char    name [6][13], *tempfile;
int     handle [6], f;

    for (f = 0 ; f < 6; f++) {
        strcpy (name [f], template);
        tempfile = mktemp (name [f]);       /* get tempfile name */
        handle [f] = creat (tempfile, S_IWRITE);    /* create */
        printf ("\nTempname %s, handle %d",          /* report */
            tempfile, handle [f]);
    }

  puts ("\n\nNow erasing tempfiles");
    for (f = 0; f < 6; f++)
        if (name [f] != NULL) {
            close (handle [f]);
            remove (name [f]);
        }
}
```

Sequential Operations on Files

There are two ways to perform I/O on open files: *sequential* and *random*. The latter is also called direct file *I/O* and, occasionally in C literature, *update mode*. The next chapter discusses random file operations, while here we concentrate on sequential mode.

Sequential I/O proceeds exactly as its name suggests: in chronological order. As a program processes data, it writes results to the file. Thus the file grows as new information is appended, until finally the program closes it. Later other programs read the file in precisely the same order as it was written.

Sequential processing has been with us for as long as computers have had external storage media. It's useful, time-honored, and proven, but not very flexible. If you want the 325th record in a sequential file, you have to read through 324 unwanted records to get to it. Sequential processing is thus inefficient for retrieving specific records. (If you want to do that, see the next chapter.) However, it's still the best method for automatically processing batches of related information, usually with a loop smart enough to handle all possible conditions in the data.

Computer applications abound with batch processing requirements: business sytems (payroll, billing), utilities such as compilers and text-printers, even some seemingly interactive programs such as editors. The latter read text from a file into the heap, let the user modify it, and then write the changed text back out, always maintaining the logical sequence of the characters. The standard devices—keyboard, display, printer, etc.—are purely sequential "files" in that operations involving them cannot be otherwise.

Unlike BASIC, Pascal, and most other languages, C makes little distinction between sequential and random I/O. The same functions are used for both, the primary difference being that in random I/O, additional instructions move the file pointer to the place where the next I/O will occur. In the absence of such functions (fseek()/lseek() et al., discussed in the next chapter), the file pointer automatically advances to the next position as data are written or read. Thus, sequential I/O occurs by default.

Quick C's libraries are rich with file I/O functions, which we can categorize as follows:

<u>Character input:</u>	fgetc(), fgets(), getc(), getw(), ungetc()
<u>Character output:</u>	fputc(), fputs(), putc(), putw()
<u>Record input:</u>	fread(), read()
<u>Record output:</u>	fwrite(), write()
<u>Formatted input:</u>	fscanf(), vfscanf()
<u>Formatted output:</u>	fprintf(), vfprintf()

An important aspect of sequential operations is detecting the end-of-file (EOF) condition during reads. Quick C furnishes two functions for this purpose: eof() and feof(). The first is for files being operated on with handles, the second for streams. Both work the same way, returning FALSE (zero) each time the file is read until the end of the file is reached, at which time they return TRUE (nonzero). In DOS text mode, EOF is signaled by the Ctrl-Z character (ASCII 26) embedded in text; in binary mode, by having exhausted the byte count indicated by the file size. The following code fragment opens and prints a stream text file until EOF:

```
if ((fp  =  fopen  (file,  "r"))  !=  NULL)
    while  (!feof  (fp))
    printf  ("%c",  fgetc  (fp));
```

Now suppose we're reading and processing a binary-image file in sequential mode, involving a buffer called image:

```
if ((handle  =  open  (file,  O_BINARY))  !=  −1)
    while  (!eof  (handle))
       if  (read  (handle,  image,  sizeof  (image)))
        process  (image);
```

In both cases, the EOF test can be read as "while not end-of-file do the following...." The while loop terminates when EOF is reached, and never executes if the file cannot be opened.

When you reach EOF (or even if you don't), you can go back to the start of a sequential disk file by issuing a rewind(). This stream function repositions the file pointer to the very first element. It gets its name and its spirit from operations on magnetic tape reels in the mainframe world. A call to rewind() automatically clears the EOF indicator returned by feof().

Detecting and Handling File Errors

Most file-handling functions in C return a value indicating success (a positive nonzero) or failure (zero or −1). For example, fread()/fwrite() return the number of items processed, read()/write() return the number of bytes handled, fopen() returns a pointer, open() a handle, and so on. In general, stream functions return an effective zero (including NULL) on failure, and handle functions return −1 since 0 is a valid handle.

This gives you a convenient method to test whether or not an operation was successful. Since 0 is a logical FALSE, you can perform a direct Boolean test on stream operations, as in

```
if (fread (buffer, 32, 2, stream))
 /* process the buffer contents */
```

No comparison is necessary; the test fails if fread() returns zero, and otherwise the operation was successful. A comparison *is* necessary with handle functions because −1 indicates failure. The handle equivalent of the test above is

```
if (read (handle, buffer, 64) != -1)
 /* process the buffer contents */
```

With streams, there's another way to detect an error: with the ferror() function. This function is TRUE (nonzero) when an error has occurred and FALSE when not. Maybe this seems backwards, but it makes sense in the context of its usage:

```
if (ferror (stream))
 /* an error has occurred */
else
 /* no error */
```

An error on input is most commonly EOF; on output, out of disk space. There are, of course, other errors that can occur as well, but they're much less common.

When an error on a stream has been detected, the error indicator stays on until you explicitly clear it. There are two ways of doing so. The rewind() function discussed above clears the EOF condition so that feof() again returns FALSE. The clearerr() function clears both the EOF condition and the stream's general error flag. Until you have cleared the error flag(s), further I/O to the stream will not work. Of course, if you issue clearerr() and retry the same failed operation, chances are good that you'll again encounter the error.

In that case, you might want to use a retry counter to keep the program from locking up in a loop; abort the job after a preset number of retries, or do something heroic like instructing the user to insert a fresh floppy in drive A so that data aren't lost due to a full disk. The circumstances of your application will dictate what sort of recovery is appropriate.

Closing Files

Some programmers tend to be lazy about closing files. After all, they reason, the compiler automatically inserts code to close any files that are still open when the program terminates. That's true, but it's sloppy programming. It's like failing to pick up your own mess on the theory that if you don't, somebody else will. Good programming practice dictates that if you open a file, you have the responsibility to close it.

There are two file closure functions, one for handles and one for streams. The handle function is close (handle). The way to detach a stream from the program is with fclose (stream).

This chapter has toured many of the Quick C functions associated with file handling and briefly reviewed sequential I/O, with which you are no doubt familiar. Now let's move on to a more complex and flexible way of managing data: random files.

Data Management with Random-Access Files

This chapter continues the discussion of Quick C file management begun in the last chapter, but it's a great deal more specific. Here we turn to random-access files and the construction of sophisticated, flexible databases that can deliver real power to your applications.

There is nothing special about a random-access file. Random files can be processed sequentially, and vice versa. The only hard-and-fast rule concerning files that will be processed randomly is that like records must have a fixed length and be grouped together. That's not necessarily true of pure sequential files, although it often is.

Random-access files often consist entirely of one fixed-length record type, but not always. An example of random-access files that don't is the .DBF file format used by dBASE. Here a single instance of a small data structure at the start of the file gives information about the number of data records, last update time, etc. It's followed by several structures, each describing one data field: type, size, and field name. Taken together, this information is called the *header record*. After the header begin the fixed-length data records, which occupy the rest of the file. Other programs create different, but analogous, kinds of random-access files; but all adhere to the rule that like records must be grouped together.

Because of this fixed-length requirement, it's convenient to think of a random file as consisting of many instances of a given data structure. Each instance is a record. You define the structure, then read and write it as often as necessary, always on a boundary that is an integral multiple of the structure size. If the file is all of one data record type, the point of reference is the start of the file; if of a header-and-data structure, the point of reference for finding random records is the start of the data record region.

Note that we said "read *and* write." Random access is bidirectional, allowing you to jump around in the file, reading a record here, writing another there. To update a record, you go to it, read it into memory, make the necessary changes, and then write it back into the same location.

Thus, random access lets you go directly to the record you need, jumping forward or backward over intervening records without having to read them as you must in sequential access. This makes any record in a random-access file instantly available to the program.

The problem with random access is in determining the location of a specific record. If the file contains records on 500 people, how do we know which one has information about Susan Brown? Fortunately, there are solutions to this problem, and later in the chapter we'll develop methods for indexing random files.

Text Versus Binary Mode

Quick C supports two basic ways of treating file contents. In the default text mode a newline character (written "\n" in C notation) is represented in program memory by the line-feed character 0Ah, but externally by two characters: carriage return and line feed (0Dh 0Ah). When a stream or handle I/O function operates in text mode, it performs the newline translation. Writing to a file, it expands newlines into the two-character sequence, and when reading from a file, the opposite.

Binary mode doesn't perform this translation. If it reads CR/LF, both characters appear internally; when it outputs a newline, the receiving device gets only the one character.

The newline translation mode is often important in random access, where record length and adherence to field boundaries within the structure are critical. If a random record containing a newline is written in text mode, one byte is automatically added and everything to the right of it in the record shifts one byte, disrupting the field alignment, causing numerics to become disastrously wrong, and potentially clobbering the first byte of the next record. Thus, random files should always be opened in binary mode.

The default mode—text or binary—is specified by the global variable _fmode, which is defined in STDLIB.H. The header file initializes _fmode as O _TEXT. You can override this default by making the assignment

        _fmode = O_BINARY;

and any subsequent opens (fopen(), open(), creat(), etc.) will be in binary mode.

However, it might not always be desirable to make files globally binary. If a program uses a couple of random files and several ordinary text files, including output to the printer, you don't want to lose newline translation for them all. In that event, you can override the default text mode, forcing only the random files to be binary.

The way to do this with a stream is to append the character "b" to the file mode argument for fopen(). For example, to open DATA.SET for random access in binary mode, write

stream = fopen ("DATA.SET", "r+b");

The equivalent handle open is even more explicit:

handle = open ("DATA.SET", O_BINARY);

Similarly, you can coerce a file into text mode with the "t" suffix in fopen() and O_TEXT with the handle open. If you set _fmode to O_BINARY, the text file opens must use the "t" suffix or else newline translation will not be in effect.

File Pointers

Just as variables in memory have pointers to indicate their locations, so do records in files. A file pointer is a long (32-bit) integer giving the offset of the element as a byte count relative to the start of the file. That is, if a file contains 32-byte records, the first is at 0, the second at 32, the third at 64, etc., and the file pointer must be set to the proper value—an integral multiple of 32 bytes in this case—for the I/O to occur correctly. Because a file is not segmented like memory in DOS machines, but instead one continuous address space of indeterminate size, the file pointer must be a long. Otherwise no file could ever contain more than 64K bytes.

When a file I/O occurs, the file pointer automatically advances by as many bytes as were read or written. That is, if the file pointer is set at 64 and a 32-byte I/O occurs, the file pointer afterwards has advanced to 96.

Ugly things happen if the file pointer gets out of sync with the record size. Say the record size is 100 bytes and you're stepping through the file a record at a time. The pointer should always be either 0 or some multiple of 100. But for some reason, perhaps you read only six bytes from one of the records. The pointer will then advance to 506, let's say, instead of a multiple of 100. Thereafter, if you keep adding 100 to the pointer for each record processed, it will always be off by six bytes. This means that on a read, you'll miss the first six bytes of the current record but get six from the next. In other words, the pointer will have lost its ability to locate records, and what you'll see in the structure fields is garbage. (NOTE: A similar problem can occur when a Quick C structure is the file buffer and you have not specified the #pragma pack(1) directive; *always* use the pragma when a structure describes a file record image.)

For this reason, random-access programs manage the file pointer carefully, ensuring that it always maintains integrity with respect to record boundaries.

The best rule when dealing with fixed-length record files is always to read and write entire records, and never portions.

Controlling the File Pointer

Two fundamental routines allow software to read and set the file pointer. As you might expect, there are variants for stream and handle files:

Stream	Handle	Effect
ftell()	tell()	Read file pointer
fseek()	lseek()	Set file pointer

These functions are only meaningful for disk files. If a file is actually a device—e.g., the keyboard—the concept of a pointer to a location within it is irrelevant, just as random access itself is.

If there's any doubt, you can determine if the file is a physical device with the function isatty(). Pass the file handle as an argument, and isatty() returns TRUE if the file is a device and FALSE if not. Supposing that the file was opened as a stream, you can instead pass fileno() as an argument, as in

```
if (isatty (fileno (stream))
   /* stream is a device */
else
   /* it's a disk file */
```

Of course, there's seldom much doubt; it's hard to think of a situation in which a particular file might be a sequential stream associated with a device under some circumstances and a random disk file under others.

In discussing pointers, we often refer to "moving" them. Of course, a software pointer doesn't physically move since it's a static variable located at some fixed memory address. Rather, to "move" a pointer is to change its value, so that it indicates a new position in the object pointed to (a file in this case).

The "tell" routines are the means for getting the current file pointer setting. The pointer automatically advances during read and write operations, so the "seek" routines don't have an exclusive right to control the pointer. Their purpose is to jump elsewhere in the file, as when you want to go directly from the 84th record to the 11th.

Most programming languages use a numbering system to indicate the relative positions of records within a file, so that the first record is #0, the second is #1, etc. C does not. Instead, it uses the actual byte offset from the start of the file, expressed as a long. The tell functions return a long, and the seek functions take a long argument.

At first glance this might seem a drawback, having to deal with byte offsets rather than relative record numbers, but in fact it's an advantage. It avoids the overly strict "typing" of random-access files that sometimes hinders Pascal programmers, while at the same time losing none of the advantages of random access. With C, you can write a header record that describes the file—its field names, data types, number of records, etc.—and begin the random-access data above the header. That's exactly how systems such as dBASE and Reflex treat files, and why they're written in C rather than the similar but more restrictive Pascal.

If you're more comfortable with relative record numbers, it's easy to translate between them and byte offsets. For a file containing only random records (no header record), derive the byte offset from the record number with

```
offset = (long) recno * sizeof (record);
```

and the record number from the byte offset with

```
recno = (int) offset / sizeof (record);
```

In this case, the lowest record number must be zero.

If you have a header record, you have to factor its size into the translation.

```
offset = (long) (recno * sizeof (record)) + sizeof (header);
```

Going the other way,

```
recno = (int) (offset − sizeof (header)) / sizeof (record);
```

The "tell" functions are very simple. Pass the stream or handle variable as the argument, assigning the result to a long variable:

```
longOffset = ftell (stream);
```

or

```
longOffset = tell (handle);
```

The "seek" functions are a little more complicated, because you have to provide, in addition to the file variable, a long offset and an origin indicator. The origin indicator answers the question "offset relative to what?" There are three origin indicators defined in **STDIO.H**, which are used in both **fseek()** and **lseek()**.

Indicator	Meaning
SEEK_SET	Byte offset from start of file
SEEK_CUR	Byte offset from current position
SEEK_END	Byte offset from end of file

Thus, to move the stream file pointer to absolute offset 1042 (relative to the start of the file), code

```
fseek (stream, 1042L, SEEK_SET);
```

The same thing in a handle file is

```
lseek (handle, 1042L, SEEK_SET);
```

Note that the "L" suffix is required after a literal offset to coerce the value to a long. You can also write the cast

```
(long) 1042
```

to accomplish the same thing, but the "L" suffix is more concise.

The "tell" functions return a positive long on success and −1L on failure. The only conceivable failure is passing an invalid file variable (bad value or file is a device), since in a true disk file the pointer must always be pointing somewhere.

The "seek" functions also return values that you can check for error. On success, a seek returns the byte offset of the new file position, and on failure, −1L. A seek failure occurs if you attempt to move the pointer to a location beyond the end of the file or to a negative offset (conceptually in front of the file's first byte).

Now let's put these ideas to work in a couple of scenarios that we can build upon.

Scenario #1: Deriving the Key from the Data

This scenario provides a simple working example of interactive random access. It also presents one possible solution to the problem of determining which record contains the information you want.

Here's the scenario. Suppose you work for a wholesaler who sells 1,000 different parts. Each item is identified by a part number, which ranges from 1,000 through 1,999. The company has a warehouse where it stores these items in any of 26 bays lettered A through Z. Your boss has given you the assignment of writing a program that, by part number, tells how many of the particular item are in stock and which bay they're in, and also allows clerks to adjust the inventory on hand as items are sold and restocked.

After studying the requirements, you decide that the system needs to keep three items of information for each part: the part number, the quantity on hand, and the bay where it's stored. Thus, the record structure is

```
#pragma pack(1)
struct {
    unsigned    partno,
                onhand;
    char        bay;
} PARTREC;
```

You need a file that reasonably approximates reality in order to test the application during development. This is easy to create; use the loop counter for the part number, a random number for the quantity on hand, and cycle through the alphabet for the bay. Listing 5.1 is a program MKINV.C that does this as it creates a test inventory file in sequential mode. Run it so that you'll have some data for the random-access program developed later.

Listing 5.1 **Program to create a test file for the inventory system.**

```c
/* MKINV.C: Creates test file for inventory system */

#include <stdio.h>
#include <stdlib.h>
#pragma   pack(1)

typedef struct {
  unsigned  partno, onhand;
  char      bay;
} PARTREC;

/* -------------------------- */

main ()
{
PARTREC    item;
FILE       *stream;
unsigned   n;
char       bay = 'A';

  if ((stream = fopen ("TEST.INV", "wb")) != 0) {
    for (n = 1000; n < 2000; n++) {
      item.partno = n;
      item.onhand = rand ();
      bay = (bay == 'Z') ? 'A' : ++bay;
      item.bay = bay;
      fwrite (&item, sizeof (item), 1, stream);
    }
    fclose (stream);
  } else
    puts ("Cannot create file");
}
```

The system for determining random-access record locations is quite simple. The part numbers run from 1,000 through 1,999, and the file is sorted in that order. Therefore record #0 is for part 1,000, record #1 for part 1,001, etc. You can compute a record's byte offset, then, as follows:

record number = part number − 1000

record offset = record number * sizeof (record)

For example, if the part number is 1,500, then it's at record 500, which is at byte offset 2,500 in the file (since the record length is five bytes).

This neatly solves the problem of locating a specific record based on a key value. Any time that some data element is serialized this way, you can use it as a locator key. Examples are customer, employee, and invoice numbers. If there are gaps in the sequence, write blank records as placeholders in the file. Those record slots will then be available when the keys are used, and the file positioning mechanism will remain intact.

The INVENTRY.C program in Listing 5.2 implements this scheme for locating records. Having opened the file successfully, the program enters an apparently endless loop (do while (1 = = 1)); the exit occurs when the user types a part number less than 1,000.

The main() function consists chiefly of this loop. It gets the part number from the user, fetches the record after computing its offset from the part number, and displays the record contents. If the user wants to do an update, a brief dialog ensues in function update() and the changed record is written back to the file. The message "No such part number" appears when the user has typed a number greater than 1,999; this is because the fseek() in gotrecord() fails, causing the function to return FALSE to main().

Note that file positioning with fseek() occurs immediately before the fread() in gotrecord() and the fwrite() in update(). That way you can be sure that the pointer is correctly positioned for the I/O. It's necessary to reposition the pointer back to the record's beginning before the fwrite() since the preceding fread() advanced it by five bytes.

The program never uses ftell() to determine where the pointer is. It doesn't need to. The controlling variable is the offset, which in turn is derived from the part number. The offset variable only changes in direct response to a keyboard command to fetch a specific record. Consequently you always know where you are in the file, making it unnecessary to query the file pointer to find out. This is an example of the "careful" pointer management mentioned earlier.

Run the program and play with it. Study it, too. Though simple, it's quite powerful and clearly illustrates the quantum leap in capability that random access brings to software.

Listing 5.2 **Random access in inventory management.**

```
/* INVENTRY.C: Parts inventory retrieval/update            */
/* This program processes TEST.INV in random-access mode,  */
/*     allowing user to pull the record for any item by    */
/*     part number and, if needed, update stock on hand    */
/* ------------------------------------------------------- */

/* INCLUDES */
#include <stdio.h>
#include <stdlib.h>
```

```c
#include <conio.h>
#include <process.h>

/* DEFINES */
#ifndef TRUE
#define FALSE 0
#define TRUE  !FALSE
#endif
#pragma pack(1)

typedef struct {
  unsigned  partno, onhand;
  char      bay;
} PARTREC;

/* LOCAL FUNCTION PROTOTYPES */
int  gotrecord (FILE*, long, PARTREC*);
void showrecord (PARTREC);
int  updating (void);
void update (FILE*, long, PARTREC*);

/* ------------- BEGIN HERE ------------- */
main ()
{
int     part;
char    input [6];
long    offset;
PARTREC item;
FILE    *f;

  if ((f = fopen ("TEST.INV", "r+b")) != NULL)
    do {
      printf ("\nPart number? (0-999 to quit) ");
      gets (input);                  /* get part # as string */
      part = (unsigned) atoi (input);   /* convert to nbr */
      offset = (long) (part - 1000) * sizeof (item);
      if (offset < 0L) {             /* if quitting then */
        fclose (f);                  /* close file and */
        exit (0);                         /* exit */
      }
      if (gotrecord (f, offset, &item)) {   /* if fetched */
        showrecord (item);                /* display record */
        if (updating ())              /* if update requested */
          update (f, offset, &item);        /* do it */
      } else
        puts ("\nNo such part number");
    } while (1 == 1);                /* loop until user quits */
  else
    puts ("Cannot open inventory file. Job ended.");
} /* ------------ LOCAL FUNCTIONS FOLLOW ---------------- */

int gotrecord (FILE *file, long position, PARTREC *record)
{             /* fetch record from indicated file position */
```

Listing 5.2 *(continued)*

```
int  success = FALSE;

  if (fseek (file, position, SEEK_SET) != -1L)
    if (fread (record, sizeof (*record), 1, file))
      success = TRUE;
  return (success);
} /* ----------------------- */

void showrecord (PARTREC record)          /* display record */
{
  puts ("\n------------------------------");
  printf ("       PART NUMBER %u", record.partno);
  printf ("\nQuantity on hand    %u", record.onhand);
  printf ("\nStored in bay       %c", record.bay);
} /* ----------------------- */

int updating (void)          /* see if user wants to update */
{
char    reply;

  printf ("\n\nDo you want to update stock? (Y/N) ");
  reply = toupper (getche ());
  return ((reply == "Y") ? TRUE : FALSE);
} /* ----------------------- */

void update (FILE *file, long position, PARTREC *record)
{                    /* update qty on hand if user wants to */
char    input [6];

  printf ("\nNew quantity on hand? ");
  gets (input);
  record->onhand = (unsigned) atoi (input);
  fseek (file, position, SEEK_SET);
  fwrite (record, sizeof (*record), 1, file);
} /* ----------------------- */
```

Scenario #2: Indexing Random Files

The first scenario showed how record locations can be derived from sequential data elements serving as the key. Now let's consider the case—occurring far more often—in which there is nothing about the data that lends itself to a relatively gap-free series of keys.

Examples of such data abound: people's names, Social Security numbers, manufacturers' part numbers, models of automobiles, equipment serial numbers, event time- and date-stamps, brand names, etc. In all cases, we can introduce order by alphabetizing or otherwise sorting, but the result can never be inherently serial in the same sense that integers follow a predictable sequence. For example, these Social Security numbers are in order:

132-91-7425

219-27-0778

223-01-6981

However, there's no way we can manipulate them mathematically to compute 0, 1, 2, the offsets of the records containing them. Thus, we need some other method for locating the relevant record in a random-access file.

This brings us to indexing. Like the index for this book, a random file's index provides a means for quickly looking up a key and finding out where it is.

An index entry is a simple structure consisting of two basic fields: the *key*, and the related record's *byte offset*. Given an argument (a *sought key*), you search the list until you find a match, then use the offset to reach into the file and grab the record. Shortly we'll implement an index.

First, though, let's set the scenario. The Personnel Department wants a company-wide locator system giving, for each employee, the first and last name, Social Security number, department, and extension. In order to locate someone, they want to type in the person's last name. The program will then locate the record and show the other information. If it's not the right person (there might be two or more with the same last name), the user can signal the computer to continue the search.

The record structure for the file is as follows:

```
#pragma  pack(1)
typedef  struct {
        char        last[12],
                    first[10],
                    ssn[12];
                    dept[6],
                    ext[5];
} LOCREC;
```

No such file exists, so it's first necessary to create it with a data entry program. MKLOCATR.C in Listing 5.3 accepts information about employees and saves it in LOCATOR.FIL, which has fixed record lengths based on the LOCREC structure. Note that, although written in sequential mode, we will later process this file with random access.

Run the program and type in a dozen or so entries. This will give you something to experiment with in the next program, and also we'll use this file later in the chapter.

Listing 5.3 **Sequential data entry for random access later.**

```
/* MKLOCATR.C: Data entry to build file for locator syst   */
/*     Data need not be in any particular order            */
/* ------------------------------------------------------- */


/* INCLUDES */
#include <stdio.h>
#include <string.h>

/* DEFINES */
typedef struct {
  char  last[12], first[10], ssn[12], dept[6], ext[5];
} LOCREC;
#define FILENAME "LOCATOR.FIL"

main ()
{
FILE   *loc;
LOCREC empl;
int    count = 0;

  if ((loc = fopen (FILENAME, "w+b")) != NULL) {
    putw (0, loc);        /* dummy rec count in file header */
    do {
      printf ("\nEmployee last name ");
      gets (empl.last);
      if (strlen (empl.last)) {
        printf ("  First name       ");
        gets (empl.first);
        printf ("  Social Sec #     ");
        gets (empl.ssn);
        printf ("  Department       ");
        gets (empl.dept);
        printf ("  Extension        ");
        gets (empl.ext);
        fwrite (&empl, sizeof (empl), 1, loc);
        ++count;                        /* count this record */
      }
    } while (strlen (empl.last));
    fseek (loc, 0L, SEEK_SET);          /* to start of file */
    putw (count, loc);    /* write record count in header */
    fclose (loc);
  } else
    puts ("Cannot open new locator file");
}
```

Because the resulting LOCATOR.FIL produced by this program will be indexed, it's not necessary to follow any particular order when keying the data. If the names are alphabetized that's fine, but it doesn't matter and yields no speed advantage in accessing records.

The data file now exists. The next step is to create an index. Sophisticated systems such as dBASE create and maintain the index automatically, adding, changing, and deleting index items as the contents of the indexed file change. For the sake of illustration, and to keep the sample programs from getting too long, we'll do it separately here. Once you're thoroughly familiar with the concepts, you can incorporate index management into your own applications.

Before we build the index, there's one thing you should note about LOCATOR.FIL. It has a header record consisting of a single integer giving the number of data records in the file. The count variable in Listing 5.3 keeps track of how many are entered. At the start of the program, a dummy value is written to LOCATOR.FIL to serve as a placeholder. Data records thus begin at offset 2. Just before closing the file, the MKLOCATR program seeks the header record and writes the count to it. Usually, header records are more complicated than this, but in this case it's all we need, and it does demonstrate how you can keep control of information in a file.

We can use the record count in constructing the index, and also in processing the indexed data file later. The index creation is quite simple. Open the data file and create a new file that will become the index: LOCATOR.NDX is an appropriate name, since its first part associates it with LOCATOR.FIL and the suffix suggests an index.

From the source file's header, you can fetch the record count and use that as a loop counter. Note that, since the first data record is numbered 0, the count will be 99 if there are 100 records. Therefore the file processing loop continues based on the condition

```
rec  <=  nrecs;
```

which is the second clause of a for() statement.

The loop itself first gets the offset for the current record using ftell(), then reads the record from the source file. This sequence is necessary since fread() advances the file pointer, so that after the read it points to the next record. The last name field is plucked from the data record, and then the program writes the name and offset to the index file. The loop repeats until all records have been read, and then the program closes the files and ends. The process is very quick, taking no more than a few seconds even for large files.

The MKLOCNDX.C program in Listing 5.4 implements these steps to create the index file. Run it, and then we'll use the two files to demonstrate indexed direct access.

Listing 5.4 **Creating the index for a random file.**

```
/* MKLOCNDX.C: Builds random-access index for LOCATOR.FIL */
/* INCLUDES */
#include <stdio.h>
#include <string.h>
```

Listing 5.4 *(continued)*

```
#pragma   pack(1)

/* DEFINES */
#define LOCATOR   "LOCATOR.FIL"
#define INDEX     "LOCATOR.NDX"
typedef struct {
  char  last[12], first[10], ssn[12], dept[6], ext[5];
} LOCREC;

typedef struct {
  char    name[12];
  long    offset;
} NDXREC;

main ()
{
int    nrecs, rec;
FILE   *loc, *ndx;
LOCREC empl;
NDXREC index;

  if ((loc = fopen (LOCATOR, "rb")) != NULL) {
    nrecs = getw (loc);                     /* read file header */
    ndx = fopen (INDEX, "wb");              /* create index file */
    for (rec = 0; rec <= nrecs; rec++) {
      index.offset = ftell (loc);           /* get file offset */
      fread (&empl, sizeof (empl), 1, loc);    /* get rec */
      strcpy (index.name, empl.last);       /* name to index */
      fwrite (&index, sizeof(index), 1, ndx); /* write it */
    }
    fcloseall ();                           /* close both files */
  } else
    puts ("Cannot open locator file");
}
```

The resulting index file has fixed-length records, each containing the last name and offset for a particular record in the data file. This is advantageous because we can place the entire index file on the heap as a table with a single entry point (the head) and search it rapidly.

The standard **calloc()** function is available specifically for this purpose. **calloc()** says, in effect, to allocate dynamic space for *n* elements of *m* bytes each. Here, *n* is the record count from the data file's header, plus one, and *m* is the size of an index record. The **NDXREC** structure is 16 bytes, so if there are 100 records, **calloc()** gets 1,600 bytes for the index table.

It's necessary, of course, to know the address of the first element in the table, which is assigned to a pointer of type **NDXREC**. Say we've declared the following pointers:

```
NDXREC    *list, *start;
```

Since calloc() returns a pointer to the allocated space, we can make the necessary assignment with

```
list  =  (NDXREC*) calloc (+ +nrecs, sizeof (NDXREC));
```

The list variable now points to the start of the table space. We can load the table by opening the index file and executing

```
fread (list, sizeof (NDXREC), nrecs, indexFile);
```

The index is now loaded and ready to do business.

The value of the list pointer is sacred and should never be changed, lest the program lose track of where the table begins. That's what the second pointer (start) is for: a working variable that we can use to indicate elements within the table.

Because the start pointer is bound to the NDXREC type, an interesting thing happens if we increment or otherwise perform arithmetic on it. Say we issue the statement

```
start  =  list;
```

The start pointer now points to the beginning of the table. But let's say we want to start searching the table at the second entry. We can advance the pointer with

```
+ +start;
```

The effect is to move the pointer to the next element. This is a logical increment; mathematically, the pointer's value increases by sizeof(objectPointedTo). The compiler does this automatically, relieving us of the burden of detailed pointer arithmetic.

To search the list, get the argument (a person's last name), and run through the index table comparing with the key. When a match is found, use the associated offset field to perform a seek in the data file, then read the data record.

You'll recall that duplicate last names are possible. Consequently, after displaying the fetched record, it's necessary to ask the user if it's the one he or she wants. If so, the search is completed. If not, however, advance the index pointer indicating the matching entry by one and resume the search.

The search concludes on one of two conditions: The desired data record is found, or the end of the list is encountered. The second case indicates that the desired record is not in the data file.

The LOCATE.C program in Listing 5.5 translates this discussion into action. The main() function performs all the necessary actions, farming out

details to other functions. The program repeats until the user enters a blank
line in response to the request for an employee's last name.

Listing 5.5 **Implementing an indexed file.**

```
/* LOCATE.C: Looks up employees in LOCATOR.FIL using        */
/*       random access index                                */
/* ----------------------------------------------------- */
/* INCLUDES */
#include <stdio.h>
#include <string.h>
#include <malloc.h>
#include <stdlib.h>
#include <conio.h>
#include <ctype.h>

/* DEFINES */
#ifndef TRUE
#define FALSE 0
#define TRUE !FALSE
#endif
#define FILENAME   "LOCATOR.FIL"
#define INDEX      "LOCATOR.NDX"

#pragma pack(1)
typedef struct {
  char  last[12], first[10], ssn[12], dept[6], ext[5];
} LOCREC;                                 /* file record format */

typedef struct {
  char  name[12];
  long  offset;
} NDXREC;                                 /* index record format */

/* LOCAL FUNCTION PROTOTYPES */
NDXREC *getIndex (int);
void get (char*);
NDXREC *search (NDXREC*, char*, NDXREC*);
void fetch (FILE*, NDXREC*, LOCREC*);
int  display (LOCREC*);
/* -------------- BEGIN HERE ------------ */

main ()
{
FILE       *loc;
char       key[12];
LOCREC     empl;
NDXREC     *head, *start, *matching, *tail;
int        located, nrecs;

  if ((loc = fopen (FILENAME, "r+b")) != NULL) {
    nrecs = getw (loc);                      /* read file header */
    head = getIndex (nrecs);    /* get index, set head ptr */
```

```
      tail = head + nrecs;                      /* set tail ptr */
      do {
        start = head;
        matching = NULL;
        get (key);
        if (strlen (key) > 0) {
          do {
            if ((matching = search (start, key,
                                    tail)) != NULL) {
              fetch (loc, matching, &empl);
              located = display (&empl);
              if (located)                      /* halt search */
                matching = NULL;
              else                              /* resume search */
                start = ++matching;  /* at next index entry */
            }
          } while (matching != NULL);
          if (!located)
            if (matching == NULL)
              puts ("\nNo match");
        }
      } while (strlen (key) > 1);
      fclose (loc);
    } else
      puts ("Cannot open locator file");
} /* ----------------------- */

NDXREC *getIndex (int recs)            /* load index on heap */
{
FILE    *index;
NDXREC *head;

  index = fopen (INDEX, "rb");
  head = (NDXREC*) calloc (recs, sizeof (NDXREC));
  fread (head, sizeof (NDXREC), recs, index);
  fclose (index);
  return (head);
} /* ----------------------- */

void get (char *key)              /* get search arg from user */
{
  printf ("\n\nLast name? ");
  gets (key);
} /* ----------------------- */

NDXREC *search (NDXREC *table, char *key, NDXREC *end)
{         /* search list for key, return pointer to match */
NDXREC   *next;

  next = table;
  while (next < end)
    if (strcmp (key, next->name) == 0)
      break;
```

Listing 5.5 *(continued)*

```
    else
      ++next;
  return ((next == end) ? NULL : next);
} /* ----------------------- */

void fetch (FILE *random, NDXREC *matched, LOCREC *buffer)
{                    /* fetch matched record from random file */
  fseek (random, matched->offset, SEEK_SET);
  fread (buffer, sizeof (*buffer), 1, random); /* get rec */
} /* ----------------------- */

int display (LOCREC *empl)    /* display employee data and */
{                             /* return TRUE if the one sought */
char reply;

  printf ("\nEmployee last name  %s", empl->last);
  printf ("\n   First name       %s", empl->first);
  printf ("\n   Soc Sec number   %s", empl->ssn);
  printf ("\n   Department       %s", empl->dept);
  printf ("\n   Extension        %s", empl->ext);
  printf ("\n\nIs this the one you want? (Y/N) ");
  reply = getche();
  return ((toupper (reply) == "Y") ? TRUE : FALSE);
} /* ----------------------- */
```

Relational Files

As user's information requirements have become more complex, it has become necessary to develop more sophisticated ways of accommodating them. One such technique is through the use of relational databases and their country cousin, discussed here, *relational files*. (A relational database has a specific and quite rigorous definition beyond the scope or interest of this book, but its chief component is the ability to cross-reference among records in different files, which is the meat of this discussion.)

A database is simply a collection of information, and as such it's fair to call any given file a data base. Usually, though, the term implies a collection of related items spread across several files. One file might contain employee names and Social Security numbers, another the addresses of those employees, still another their salary information, and so on. Taken as a whole, these files comprise a personnel database.

While it might seem, on first impression, that maintaining several separate files is more trouble than maintaining one that holds all the information, in fact there are a number of advantages that make splitting up the information worthwhile.

One of the most important advantages is in eliminating redundant data. Not only does this reduce disk space requirements, but it also does away with the need to make sure all instances of a given item are updated. For example, Jane Doe gets married and becomes Jane Smith. If all files are monolithic (containing everything needed for an application system), we have to update files containing Jane's employment records, salary information, pension plan, profit sharing, expense account, etc. Some clerk will spend half the day scrounging through files to get all these updates done, and will probably miss at least one. When separate files contain distinct, nonredundant information, only one file needs updating to rename Jane Doe as Jane Smith.

Another major advantage follows from the first. Since each file comprising a database contains only one or a few closely related items, we can combine files in a mix-and-match fashion to get exactly the information we want, without having to filter out masses of data we don't. Thus, the use of separate files allows many applications to share classes of information.

The only thing we need to link files together this way is some common element, a thread that ties Bill Johnson's name, which might be record #251 in **FILE.A**, to his salary, which is record #87 in **FILE.B**, to his address, record #194 in **FILE.C**, and so on.

There are a couple of ways to approach this problem. One is called a *hierarchical database*, which employs an elaborate system of pointers. The master file record for Bill Johnson might contain his name and Social Security number, plus pointers to all his other records in all the files of the database. Furthermore, in order to hold down the number of master file accesses, records in the lower-level files might also contain pointers to records in other files.

This approach is often used in mainframe databases, where it works well because there's a professional staff to look after it. The problem with hierarchical databases is complexity: The pointer structure is so bewildering that it requires vigilant maintenance and the judgment to recognize when it needs to be rebuilt.

An easier solution, and one that works best in small computers, is to crossrelate files. Here, every file is set up for random access and has an index. For two files to be relationally joined, they must contain one data element in common, which is the indexed item for the related-to file.

An example illustrates how it works. Say we want to expand the locator system to include the employee's current salary. The salary file contains, of course, the salary, plus it must have one unique identifier that also occurs in the locator file. The Social Security number is a good candidate, since no two people share the same number.

A quick one-time program can pull these two items from the payroll file and write them into a new file. (Later, in order to reap the benefits of crossrelating, you'll also have to modify the payroll system to refer to the new salary file, which then becomes the sole repository of salary information.)

When the salary file exists, use a program such as that in Listing 5.4 to make its index. All the information elements are now in place, and it remains only to modify the locator program for relational operation.

Here are the steps to perform a relational lookup for Bill Johnson:

1. Read the locator index onto the heap.
2. Read the salary index onto the heap.
3. Look up Bill Johnson's name and fetch his locator record as in Listing 5.5.
4. Using the Social Security number from his locator record as the search argument, find the matching entry in the salary index.
5. Use the associated file pointer to seek his related record in the salary file.
6. Fetch it and display the results.

Similar steps apply to the payroll system, or any other program that needs to find out Bill's salary. All any system requires is his Social Security number, and it can then locate any information about Bill in any file.

This concludes our discussion of disks and files in Quick C. It has been chiefly a look inward, from the program level toward the internal hardware and software aspects of data storage. The next part of the book looks outward toward the external world of the user interface.

PART II

The User Interface

Although shopworn, the term "user interface" owes its durability to sweeping breadth. The user interface encompasses all that the person using the system sees and touches: the keyboard, the display, the printer, and everything that happens to them. And that's the stuff of the next several chapters, including Part III. It's the longest part of the book because it's the most challenging and important part of programming, whether in Quick C or any other language.

A program might do wonderful things internally, but if it doesn't look good, doesn't produce readable output, isn't intuitive or at least reasonably simple to operate, the folks using it won't be impressed. In fact, they won't even like it. They might use it, but they'll grumble.

In a wonderful book entitled *The Network Revolution: Confessions of a Computer Scientist* (AC/DC, Berkeley, CA, 1984), author Jacques Vallee pokes a lot of good fun at us computer types and how we seemingly go out of our way to make life difficult for the less technologically endowed, but his point is clear. It is our responsibility to remove the barriers between the common sense of the thinking animal at the keyboard and the slavish, often idiotic tool at his or her fingertips. That's what a good user interface does.

It's not easy to write a program with a good user interface. Often such programs devote more lines of code to controlling the screen than to doing "real" work like calculations and data manipulation.

So our goal in this part of the book is to ease your task as a programmer. We'll examine the issues and the methods, and then, whenever practical, we'll develop libraries of routines that you can use in your programs, thus reducing the burdens of writing friendly software. After all, if your job is to make life easier for users, shouldn't that job be made easier for you, too?

CHAPTER 6

Basic Input/Output System

Paradoxically, our voyage to the most visible part of software begins at the deepest bowels of the machine: the ROM BIOS (pronounced like two words, "rom BY-oss").

If you're unfamiliar with hardware, perhaps we should explain that a ROM is a read-only memory device with software instructions electronically "burned" into it, so that the instructions don't disappear when power is removed. A ROM and the machine language it contains are sometimes collectively called "firmware" since they occupy a middle ground between pure hardware and software. When a program is burned into a ROM and the ROM is plugged into a socket, the program becomes a permanent part of the machine.

In this case, the program is the BIOS, or Basic Input/Output System. The term describes only part of what the ROM BIOS actually does, but it is descriptive of the portion accessible to programmers. The ROM BIOS actually has two broad missions to perform:

1. It takes control of the machine when power is first applied. It's the ROM BIOS that makes you wait while it checks memory, exercises the processor to make sure it's functioning properly, inventories the attachments, and performs other initialization. After that, it supervises the loading of DOS and hands control to the operating system. In addition, the ROM BIOS supervises the warm boot (or restart) that occurs when you "three-key" the machine by simultaneously pressing Ctrl, Alt, and Del.

2. The ROM BIOS furnishes a number of DOS-like system subroutines that programs can call to perform input/output, determine the status of various devices, alter the video mode, and do other fundamental tasks at the machine level.

The start-up routines in the ROM BIOS cannot be readily called by programs, nor should they be. No doubt that's why those who designed it chose to ignore this important task when they gave it a name.

The ROM BIOS services that you can call from Quick C programs break down into five categories as follows:

Interrupt	Purpose
10h	Video services: 20 functions for controlling the display.
13h	Floppy disk services: six functions.
14h	Serial port services: four functions.
16h	Keyboard services: three functions.
17h	Printer services: three functions.

Additionally, Quick C furnishes some built-in functions that call a subset of the ROM BIOS services. These are the _bios_..() functions. For example, _bios_disk() exercises some of the services of Int 13h, and _bios_keybrd() lets you make various inquiries of the keyboard via Int 16h. The DISKCHK program (Listing 1.6) illustrates a call to _bios_keybrd() when it checks to see if the user has pressed a key to tell the program to stop.

Our purpose here is to discuss the ROM BIOS in general and some of its particulars with respect to programming in Quick C. Thus, we'll talk about some specific calls in the appropriate places in later chapters, and some we won't cover at all. For a detailed description of the ROM BIOS, see Peter Norton's *Inside the IBM PC* (Brady Books, New York, 1986), and for exhaustive information about the ROM BIOS function calls, Ray Duncan's *Advanced MS-DOS* (Microsoft Press, Redmond, WA, 1986). Many other programmers' guides to the PC and clones also give the ROM BIOS extensive coverage.

Calling ROM BIOS Services from Quick C

During power-up, the ROM BIOS installs pointers to its service routines in the system interrupt vector table in lowest memory. The interrupts are those listed above.

Any program that calls a ROM BIOS service, then, must execute the appropriate software interrupt. Because each service routine performs more than one function, it's necessary to pass a function code in register AH to specify the action you want. Often the functions require further information in other registers, which are effectively parameters. Moreover, some ROM BIOS calls return information in one or more registers, while others return nothing.

As a result, it's not practical to have a single generalized routine for calling any ROM BIOS function from C. Instead, you have to set up a unique calling sequence for each function or use one of the _bios_..() functions if it performs the service you want. The _bios_..() calls are unique to Microsoft C and Quick C.

In order to attain compatibility with a number of other C packages (Lattice, Turbo, Aztec, UNIX, etc.), Quick C offers a number of alternatives for generating software interrupts. Because one isn't inherently "better" than another, we'll use the related calls int86() and int86x() in this book.

The int86() function has the prototype

```
int int86(int intNum, union REGS *inreg,
                       union REGS *outreg);
```

The REGS union is defined in DOS.H and covers all the byte registers AH through DL, all the word registers AX through DX, plus SI, DI, and the carry flag. For example, you might declare a variable as

```
union REGS reg;
```

and then assign a value to word register BX with

```
reg.x.bx = value;
```

and another value to byte register AH with

```
reg.h.ah = byteval;
```

The .x. infix represents a word register, and .h. a byte register, corresponding to the structures that comprise the REGS union.

As an example of a ROM BIOS call, let's use interrupt 10h (video services), function 3 to determine information about the cursor in video page 0. The call requires function code 3 in register AH and the page number in BH. It returns the following information:

Register	Information
CH	Scan line for top of cursor
CL	Scan line for bottom of cursor
DH	Row (Y) of current cursor position
DL	Column (X) of cursor position

Set up the call, make it, and extract the returned information like this:

```
reg.h.ah = 3;                          /* bios 10h function */
reg.h.bh = 0;                          /* video page 0 */
int86 (0x10, &reg, &reg);                       /* call */
curTop = reg.h.ch;                       /* cursor top */
curBott = reg.h.cl;                      /* and bottom */
y = reg.h.dh;                            /* current row */
x = reg.h.dl;                            /* and column */
```

The calls that return one or more values in registers are *inquiry functions*. Those that return nothing are *control functions*, such as positioning the cursor, writing to the display, or changing video mode. In the latter case, it's necessary only to set up the parameter registers and issue the interrupt; however, you must still pass two pointers to a REGS union. If they're the same, as in

```
int86 (0x10, &reg, &reg);
```

that's acceptable and no conflict occurs.

The int86x() function takes one more argument, which is a pointer to a structure of type SREGS, also defined in DOS.H. This structure represents the four CPU segment registers (CS, DS, ES, and SS), which you have to pass for some BIOS and DOS functions.

The ROM BIOS Data Area

Since the ROM BIOS responds to inquiries, it's natural to suppose that the ROM BIOS stores information about its status somewhere. And indeed it does. It owns a piece of memory called the ROM BIOS data area.

A ROM is a read-only memory, so the ROM BIOS cannot write temporary information into its own address space. Consequently, part of main memory is set aside in the IBM PC and compatibles to serve as a place where the ROM BIOS can keep its control and status information. This is a fixed block consisting of 132 bytes beginning at segment 40h. Because many commercial software packages refer directly to the ROM BIOS data area, IBM has publicly committed that it will keep this block intact for the foreseeable future.

Therefore it's safe to build programs that read the ROM BIOS data area. It is not safe to *write* to it, however, except in a very few cases that we'll discuss in due time. Be warned that indiscriminate tinkering with the contents is hazardous to the health of your computer and can potentially make real smoke.

Most of the BIOS data fields are unsigned bytes or integers, each of which has a unique meaning based on its position. Two of them are further broken down such that certain individual or grouped bits have a significance of their own. We can describe them in terms of Quick C bitfield structures.

A bitfield structure is simply a way of subdividing a 16-bit word and giving each subdivision an identifier, so that it can be referred to as a variable. The smallest field is one bit, the largest 16. Assignment of the fields, which are unsigned, proceeds to the left from bit 0. If the fields don't take the entire word, the leftover bits are unused and unnamed, but the object itself still occupies one word of storage. Similarly, if the total number of bits for all fields exceeds 16, the compiler packs as much as it can into one word and sticks the rest into a second word, but without splitting a given field between the two. Both bitfield structures in the BIOS data area occupy exactly 16 bits.

The first two typedefs in BIOSAREA.H (Listing 6.1) show how to define a bitfield structure. The only difference between this and a normal structure definition is the size specification following the field identifier; for example, nLPT consists of two bits, while nu13 is a one-bit field. Sum the sizes and you'll find they come to 16.

Incidentally, there's nothing "official" about the field names in Listing 6.1; they're of my choosing. Note that, in order to refer to members of the BIOS-

DATA structure, your program must initialize a pointer to its absolute address in memory (paragraph 40h). Example:

BIOSDATA far *bios = MK_FP (0x0040, 0);

using the macro defined in MK_FP.H (Listing 6.2).

Since we were just looking at the EQFLAGS structure, let's talk about what it contains.

Listing 6.1 Defining the ROM BIOS data area contents.

```
/* biosarea.h: ROM BIOS data area at 0x0040:0 in memory */

#ifndef  byte
#define  byte    unsigned char            /* define byte as a type */
#endif
#pragma  pack(1)

/* BIT FIELDS USED IN ROM BIOS DATA AREA */
typedef struct {
    unsigned  hasFloppies : 1,     /* 1 = system has floppy drives */
              nu1 : 1,                            /* not used */
              mbRAM : 2,          /* motherboard RAM size (obsolete) */
              initVideo : 2,                /* initial video mode */
              nDisks : 2,                  /* nbr of floppy drives */
              nu8 : 1,                            /* not used */
              nSerialPorts : 3,    /* nbr of serial ports attached */
              gamePort : 1,             /* 1 = game port attached */
              nu13 : 1,                           /* not used */
              nLPT : 2;                     /* number of printers */
} EQFLAGS;              /* this is the equipment flags structure */

typedef struct {
    unsigned  riteShiftDown : 1,       /* 1 = right shift key down */
              leftShiftDown : 1,        /* 1 = left shift key down */
              ctrlShiftDown : 1,      /* 1 = ctrl-shift combo down */
              altShiftDown : 1,        /* 1 = alt-shift combo down */
              scrollLockOn : 1,        /* 1 = scroll lock mode on */
              numLockOn : 1,             /* 1 = num lock mode on */
              capsLockOn : 1,           /* 1 = caps lock mode on */
              insOn : 1,                    /* 1 = ins mode on */
              unused : 3,                         /* spare bits */
              ctrlNumLockOn : 1,     /* 1 = ctrl-NumLock mode on */
              scrollLockDown : 1,     /* 1 = scroll lock key down */
              numLockDown : 1,          /* 1 = num lock key down */
              capsLockDown : 1,        /* 1 = caps lock key down */
              insDown : 1;                  /* 1 = ins key down */
} KBDFLAGS;             /* this is the keyboard flags structure */

typedef struct {
    unsigned  serialPortAddr[4];
    unsigned  parallelPortAddr[4];
```

```
        EQFLAGS     eqptFlags;
        byte        mfgrTestFlags;
        unsigned    mainMem;
        unsigned    expRAM;
        KBDFLAGS    kbdStat;
        byte        keypad;
        unsigned    kbdBuffHead;
        unsigned    kbdBuffTail;
        char        kbdBuff[32];
        byte        seekStat;
        byte        motorStat;
        byte        motorCnt;
        byte        diskErr;
        byte        NECStatus[7];
        byte        videoMode;
        unsigned    scrnWidth;
        unsigned    vidBuffSz;
        unsigned    vidBuffOfs;
        byte        cursPos[8][2];
        byte        cursBottom;
        byte        cursTop;
        byte        activeDispPage;
        unsigned    activeDispPort;
        byte        CRTModeReg;
        byte        palette;
        unsigned    dataEdgeTimeCount;
        unsigned    CRCReg;
        char        lastInputValue;
        unsigned    tick;
        int         hour;
        byte        timerOverflow;
        byte        brkStat;
        unsigned    resetFlag;
        long        hardDiskStat;
        byte        parallelTimeout[4];
        byte        serialTimeout[4];
        unsigned    kbdBuffOfs;
        unsigned    kbdBuffEnd;
} BIOSDATA;
```

The Equipment Flags

The third field in the BIOS data area is called the *equipment flags*, and it's brimming with information about the system configuration. Most of its bit fields are self-explanatory, either by their identifier names or from the comments, but a couple are not. You can fetch the flags either directly from the BIOSDATA structure or with Quick C's _bios_equiplist() function. In either case, the EQFLAGS bitfield structure helps you interpret the fields.

The initVideo field purports to describe the video mode that was in effect when the system first powered up, giving a clue as to which display adapter is present. The reliability of this field has eroded with the introduction of more advanced adapters such as Hercules, EGA, and VGA. Since it's a two-bit field, it can only convey four possible values, which are as follows:

Value	Meaning
0	Undefined
1	80 x 25 color
2	40 x 25 color
3	80 x 25 monochrome

Some CGA boards come up as undefined, as does the EGA. Except that when the EGA is working with a monochrome monitor, it comes up in mode 3. The Hercules card has an initial video mode of 1 and so does the MDS Genius full-page monitor, even though both are monochrome. The bottom line is: This bitfield is unreliable. You have to look elsewhere to identify the signature of the adapter, which we'll discuss presently.

The **mbRAM** field is another one that's obsolete, since it's based on early models of the PC. It used to indicate the motherboard RAM size, which went in 16K steps up to a maximum of 64K. Nowadays, with much more RAM on the motherboard, this field has become meaningless. If you need to find out the amount of RAM, look at the **mainMem** field elsewhere in the ROM BIOS data area or call **_bios_memsize()**, which returns the same value: the amount of memory present, expressed in K.

There are two related bitfields among the equipment flags that yield information about the attached floppy drives. The **hasFloppies** field is a Boolean; if 0, the machine is driveless, and otherwise you can look at **nDisks** to find out how many drives there are. The number of floppy drives is one more than the contents of the **nDisks** field. That is, if **nDisks** is zero, there's one drive, and if it's three, there are four.

Knowing how many diskette drives there are can make your programs smart. For example, if a drive malfunctions, you can instruct the user to mount a diskette in another drive if one exists.

The Keyboard Flags

The other bitfield structure in the BIOS data area is the one called **kbdStat**, described by the **KBDFLAGS** structure. This structure gives the status of various nonprinting, mode-setting keys such as Caps Lock and Insert. The "down" fields show if the related key is currently being pressed, while the "on" fields indicate if the specified mode is in effect. A yes is signified by a 1-bit.

This is one part of the ROM BIOS data area that you can safely modify. For instance, set Caps Lock on to make sure the user is entering case-sensitive data in uppercase. Or switch Num Lock on and tell the user to enter numerics via the keypad. Be sure to undo such sneaky mode settings later.

Video Information

A glance at the BIOSDATA structure in Listing 6.1 reveals that it contains more than anyone would ever want to know about the system. Such things as the manufacturer's test flags, the disk drive motor status and rotation count, and the data edge timer count have an extremely high yawn factor. At the other end of the who-cares spectrum are such things as cursor and video information, which are in the middle of the structure.

The videoMode field identifies which mode is currently in effect, using the following values:

Value	Mode
00h	40 x 25 B&W text, color adapter
01h	40 x 25 color text
02h	80 x 25 B&W text, color adapter
03h	80 x 25 color text
04h	320 x 200 4-color graphics (CGA)
05h	320 x 200 4-color graphics, color burst off (CGA)
06h	640 x 200 monochrome graphics (CGA)
07h	80 x 25 monochrome (MDA or EGA with mono display)
08h	160 x 200 16-color graphics (PCjr)
09h	320 x 200 16 color graphics (PCjr)
0Ah	640 x 200 4-color graphics (PCjr)
0Dh	320 x 200 16-color graphics (EGA)
0Eh	640 x 200 16-color graphics (EGA)
0Fh	640 x 350 monochrome graphics (EGA)
10h	640 x 350 4- or 16-color graphics (EGA)

You can infer the screen width from the video mode, but the scrnWidth field tells you directly. It's always 40 or 80 columns with standard monitor/adapter configurations.

The ROM BIOS keeps track of separate cursor positions on each of the (up to) eight video pages possible with color adapters. The activeDispPage field indicates which page is currently visible. It also furnishes an index into the cursPos array, which gives cursor position information. Ordinarily page 0 is active, and cursPos[0][0] and cursPos[0][1] contain the cursor column and row, respectively.

You can refer to these array fields to detect the cursor position in lieu of the Quick C function _gettextposition(). With some video adapters, you can also change them and thereby move the cursor. However, this isn't a safe method since it doesn't apply to all adapters. It's better to use Quick C's _settextposition() or to call ROM BIOS Int 10, function 2.

The cursTop and cursBottom fields identify the shape of the cursor, which applies to all pages. The cursor is a block shape that partially or completely fills a character cell, and it's composed of scan lines with 0 at the top. The bottom scan line is 12 in monochrome (video mode 7), 7 for CGA text modes, and varies in other modes. The default underscore cursor is the lowest two scan lines. As with cursor positioning, some adapters respond and others don't if you write directly to these fields. It's best to call ROM BIOS Int 10h, function 1 to set the cursor shape. The calling convention is as follows:

```
reg.h.ah  =  1;
reg.h.ch  =  newtop;
reg.h.cl  =  newbottom;
int86  (0x10,  &reg,  &reg);
```

You can also hide the cursor by setting bit 5 of cursTop (logical OR with 0x20), as in

```
reg.h.ah  =  1;
reg.h.ch  =  bios – ›cursTop  —  0x20;
reg.h.cl  =  bios – ›cursBottom;
int86  (0x10,  &reg,  &reg);
```

Afterward the cursor still has a position and behaves normally, but it isn't visible on the display. Make it visible again by ANDing cursTop with 0x1F in a similar call.

The palette field discloses which of the two four-color palette sets is selected for the CGA in a graphics mode. In any other mode, this field contains garbage. Also, writing to it has no effect. To change palettes, call ROM BIOS interrupt 10h, function 0Bh.

Keeping the Time

The two fields called hour and tick contain the values maintained by the ROM BIOS time-of-day clock. The hour field ranges from 0–23, keeping military time, while the tick field is an increment count. Each increment is 5/91 of a second; stated another way, 18.2 ticks occur per second. At first glance this ridiculous interval seems like one that only a committee would come up with, but it becomes sensible when you realize that, at that rate, 65,536 ticks work out to 3,600 seconds, or one hour. Since a 16-bit object can represent a maximum of 65,536 values, the interval has a sensible basis. When the count rolls over from its terminal value (FFFFh) to zero, a new hour begins and the hour field is incremented by the carry.

The dogged precision of computers produces a slight error in the interval, amounting to about 9.65 seconds in a 24-hour period. Consequently, as midnight draws nigh, the ROM BIOS clock appears to halt for that period in order to resynchronize itself with the real world.

Transcending the ROM BIOS

There are a couple of other interesting memory locations that are outside the ROM BIOS data area. Though not controlled by the ROM BIOS, they yield related hardware information.

The first of these is the EGA equipment byte, located three bytes beyond the end of the BIOS structure (at 0040h:0087h). The EGA board has its own ROM BIOS which, during power-up, notifies the world that it exists by writing data to this byte. If there's no EGA, the byte is zero, and otherwise it's nonzero to signify an active EGA. Thus, testing this byte is a quick way to determine if the computer is EGA-equipped. Note that 0 is FALSE and nonzero TRUE, so you can use the construct

```
if (ega)
    /* EGA is present */
else
    /* it's not */
```

If you want to know more about the EGA configuration, test bit 1 (AND with 02h). The bit is on when the EGA is connected to a monochrome monitor and off when it has a color display.

The other location of interest is at F000h:FFFEh, which contains the machine ID. This can be important if your program needs a specific hardware platform in order to run. For example, you might have some assembly code requiring an 80286. You can check the machine ID and gracefully decline to execute on anything smaller than an AT.

Here are the machine ID's for IBM PC's:

ID	Model
FFh	Standard PC
FEh	XT
FDh	PCjr
FCh	AT, XT286, PS/2-50, PS/2-60
FAh	PS/2-30
F9h	PC Convertible
F8h	PS/2-80

Some early Compaq portables have a machine ID of 00h, but in general, compatibles carry the same machine ID as the model they clone.

Creating Far Pointers

Microsoft gave us the FP_SEG and FP_OFF macros in DOS.H to extract the two portions of a far pointer. For some reason, they neglected to provide an offsetting macro for forming a far pointer, even though this is something that Quick C programs often need to do. A case in point is the initialization of a pointer to the ROM BIOS data area.

Let's create one to plug this gap. We'll call it MK_FP (for make far pointer) and place it in header file MK_FP.H, shown in Listing 6.2. Henceforth, any time we need to form a far pointer, we'll place the directive

```
#include "mk_fp.h"
```

at the top of the source file, then invoke the macro with a statement such as

```
farptr = MK_FP (segment, offset);
```

Listing 6.2 **Macro to make a far pointer.**

```
/* MK_FP.H: Macro to form a far pointer */

#define MK_FP(seg, off) ((void far *) \
        (((unsigned long)(seg) << 16) + (unsigned)(off)))
```

Putting It to Work

We've talked about the ROM BIOS data area. Now let's do something with it, both to demonstrate that in fact it works and to develop a handy utility.

The program is called HARDWARE.C, and it's shown in Listing 6.3. This program #includes BIOSAREA.H and uses many of the ROM BIOS fields to profile the system configuration. It reports on the following aspects of the hardware:

Machine type

Memory

Disk drives

Display

Ports

BIOSAREA.H doesn't define the two external locations we discussed earlier, so the program declares them itself. Both are far pointers to unsigned characters, initialized by the MK_FP macro. Why far pointers? Because the

EGA and machine ID bytes are outside the program's data segment, so it takes a far pointer to find them.

Note how the program sifts through several pieces of evidence to discern the signature of the video adapter. The method given here isn't 100 percent reliable, but it should be accurate most of the time. (Note: The Quick C graphics library discussed in Part III has an alternative method for identifying the video adapter.)

Listing 6.3 **Utility to list the hardware configuration.**

```
/* HARDWARE.C: Shows the system hardware configuration */

#include <stdio.h>
#include <dos.h>
#include <graph.h>
#include "biosarea.h"
#include "mk_fp.h"


main ()
{
unsigned n, far *ega = MK_FP (0x0040, 0x0087);
unsigned char far *machineID = MK_FP (0xF000, 0xFFFE);
BIOSDATA far *bios = MK_FP (0x0000, 0x0400);

        _clearscreen (0);
  puts ("SYSTEM HARDWARE CONFIGURATION");

  printf ("\nMachine type                             %02X ",
          *machineID);
  switch (*machineID) {
    case 0xFF: puts (" (PC)"); break;
    case 0xFE: puts (" (PC/XT)"); break;
    case 0xFD: puts (" (PCjr)"); break;
    case 0xFC: puts (" (PC/AT)"); break;
    case 0xF9: puts (" (PC Convertible)"); break;
    default:   puts (" (Unknown)");
  }

  printf ("\nMain memory size in K                    %u\n\n",
          bios->mainMem);

  puts ("Disk drives:");
  if (!bios->eqptFlags.hasFloppies)
    n = 0;
  else
    n = bios->eqptFlags.nDisks + 1;
  printf ("  Number of diskette drives              %u\n", n);
  printf ("  Hard disk installed                    %s\n\n",
          (bios->hardDiskStat == 0L) ? "No" : "Yes");
```

Listing 6.3 *(continued)*

```
puts ("Display:");
printf ("  Initial video mode                    %u",
       bios->eqptFlags.initVideo);
switch (bios->eqptFlags.initVideo) {
  case 0: puts (" (Undefined)"); break;
  case 1: puts (" (80 x 25 color)"); break;
  case 2: puts (" (40 x 25 color)"); break;
  case 3: puts (" (80 x 25 monochrome)"); break;
}
printf ("  Current video mode                    %u",
        bios->videoMode);
switch (bios->videoMode) {
  case 0: puts (" (40 x 25 B&W text, color adapter)"); break;
  case 1: puts (" (40 x 25 color text)"); break;
  case 2: puts (" (80 x 25 B&W text, color adapter)"); break;
  case 3: puts (" (80 x 25 color text)"); break;
  case 7: if (*ega != 0)
            puts (" (EGA 80 x 25 B&W text mode)");
          else
            puts (" (Monochrome 80 x 25 text)");
          break;
  default:puts (" (Graphics mode)");
}
printf ("  Video buffer size in bytes            %u\n'",
       bios->vidBuffSz);
printf ("  Active display page                   %u\n",
       bios->activeDispPage);
printf ("  Video adapter port address            %04Xh\n",
       bios->activeDispPort);
printf ("  Adapter type                          ");
if (*ega != 0)
  puts ("EGA");
else
  if ((bios->videoMode == 7) && (bios->vidBuffSz > 4096))
    puts ("Hercules");
  else
    if (bios->videoMode == 7)
      puts ("Monochrome");
    else
      if (bios->videoMode == 3)
        puts ("CGA");
      else
        if (bios->videoMode == 2)
          puts ("Compaq");
        else puts ("Unknown");

puts ("\nPorts:");
printf ("  Number of serial ports                %u\n",
       bios->eqptFlags.nSerialPorts);
printf ("  Number of parallel ports              %u\n",
       bios->eqptFlags.nLPT);
```

```
    printf ("  Game port attached                    %s\n",
            (bios->eqptFlags.gamePort) ? "Yes" : "No");
}
```

The ROM BIOS, though at the deepest accessible level of the machine, controls the highest level, which is the system's interaction with the outside world. Thus, in managing an effective user interface, our software lives at a middle level while manipulating the extremes. We'll see how in the chapters that follow.

CHAPTER 7

Managing the Text Screen

Most of the interaction between the computer and its user is accomplished by means of text. The computer asks questions and the user types answers, or vice versa. Even when graphics are the product of computer activity, they usually result from extended periods of text exchange.

Therefore, it can safely be said that text screens are the single most important aspect of the user interface. The user forms his or her impression of how "good" the program is from the appearance of text displays. Running time and even accuracy of results (within reason) are of lesser importance than understandable instructions, help panels, and the general accessibility of the program to human beings.

To a great extent, the "goodness" of the user interface is a matter of artistic judgement combined with the tools to make it happen. This is not a book about art, so we won't presume to tell you how to design your user interface. Instead, we'll concentrate on the tools. They are the bulk of this chapter.

Video Control Functions Built into Quick C

Quick C comes with a dozen built-in functions for manipulating text screens. The prototypes are in GRAPH.H and the functions themselves are located in GRAPHICS.LIB. They are as follows:

Function	Purpose
_displaycursor()	Turn cursor on and off.
_getbkcolor()	Get current background color.
_gettextcolor()	Get current text color.
_gettextposition()	Report cursor position.
_getvideoconfig()	Information about the display.
_outtext()	Write a string in color.
_setactivepage()	Select page for text activity.
_setbkcolor()	Set background color.
_settextcolor()	Set foreground color.

_settextposition()	Move cursor.
_settextwindow()	Create window on display.
_setvideomode()	Change display mode.
_setvisualpage()	View display page.

GRAPH.H defines not only the function prototypes, but also a host of constants and structures that you can use with them. For example, to clear the entire screen, you can issue the statement

```
_clearscreen (_GCLEARSCREEN);
```

and voila! it happens.

This is an unfortunately verbose statement. You can save some keystrokes by just typing

```
_clearscreen (0);
```

since the _GCLEARSCREEN constant maps to a zero value.

Many of these functions are so intuitive that they need little explanation. For example, _settextposition(7,1) places the text cursor at row 7, column 1. Note that the upper left corner of the display has the coordinate set {1, 1}.

Listing 7.1 is a program that illustrates text screen manipulation using several of these functions. This program is written for a color display, so on a monochrome device some of the colored text lines in the first screen might not show up at all, or might have strange attributes such as underlining.

Later we'll introduce a supplementary library of text display functions that could simplify this program somewhat. SCRNIO.C is a '"pure" Quick C program.

Listing 7.1 Manipulating text: a simple demonstration.

```
/* SCRNIO.C: demos screen management functions */

#include <graph.h>
#include <conio.h>

main ()

{
int    row, col, p;
int oldcolor = 1;
char str [80];
struct rccoord textpos;
struct videoconfig display;

  _clearscreen (0);
  _settextposition (1, 31);                  /* center following text */
  _outtext ("SCREEN MANAGEMENT");
  for (row = 2; row < 17; row++) {           /* write some text */
```

Listing 7.1 *(continued)*

```
     col = row;
     _settextcolor (oldcolor++);                      /* next color */
     _settextposition (row, col);
     sprintf (str, "This begins in column %2d, row %2d", col, row);
     _outtext (str);
   }

   textpos = _gettextposition();            /* get cursor location */
   _settextposition (19, 1);
   _settextcolor (7);
   sprintf (str, "At end of last row, cursor was at row %d, col
%d",
            textpos.row, textpos.col);
   _outtext (str);

   _outtext ("\nPress any key to erase row numbers...");
   getch ();                               /* wait for signal */
   for (row = 2; row < 17; row++) {
     col = row + 24;
     _settextposition (row, col);
     for (p = col; p < col+12; p++)
       putch (' ');                   /* erase col part of each line */
   }

   _settextposition (21, 1);
   _outtext ("Press any key to turn off cursor...");
   getch ();                                           /* wait */
   _displaycursor (_GCURSOROFF);              /* shut off cursor */

   _outtext ("\nPress any key to turn cursor back on...");
   getch ();                                           /* wait */
   _displaycursor (_GCURSORON);               /* cursor back on */

   _outtext ("\nPress any key to see your video configuration...");
   getch ();

   _getvideoconfig (&display);              /* get video config */
   _clearscreen (0);                          /* new screen */
   _outtext ("Text video configuration:");
   sprintf (str, "\n  Columns            %3d",
            display.numtextcols);
   _outtext (str);
   sprintf (str, "\n  Rows               %3d",
            display.numtextrows);
   _outtext (str);
   sprintf (str, "\n  Video pages available %3d",
            display.numvideopages);
   _outtext (str);
}
```

Of Video Pages

In 80 x 25 text mode, a display image consists of 2,000 character cells. Each character cell actually occupies two bytes of video memory. The first byte contains the character code, the second its attributes (discussed later). Thus, it takes 4,000 bytes of memory to represent one screen. This 4K region is called a page.

The memory that drives the monitor is separate from the computer's main memory (except on the PCjr). Display adapters typically come equipped with at least 16K of video memory starting at fixed address B800H:0000H, and most have much more. The only common exception is the monochrome display adapter (MDA), which has only 4K and can thus contain a single screen image; its memory originates at segment B000h. All others partition the display memory (in text modes) into several pages depending on how much memory there is. The maximum is usually eight pages (32K), even if the adapter is an EGA or VGA with several hundred K of video memory.

4,000 is a nice round number in decimal, but not in the computer's internal binary representation. Consequently, the partitioning occurs at intervals of 4,096, or 1000h, bytes. The 96 bytes at the end of each partition are unused in text modes.

Text pages are numbered starting at 0, which corresponds to the lowest 4K partition of video memory. You can find out how many text pages a machine supports by calling the Quick C function _getvideoconfig(). This function fills in a data structure of type **videoconfig** (defined in **GRAPH.H**), one of whose fields is called **numvideopages**. The highest available text page number is **numvideopages** − 1.

The existence of pages allows you to switch display images instantly. You do this by calling the Quick C function _setvisualpage(). This function changes the **vidBuffOfs** field in the ROM BIOS data area (see Listing 6.1), which causes the display adapter to change the place where it gets its information. The switch occurs in 1/60 second, the update frequency of the display. To the eye, this is instantaneous.

You can also switch around among preformatted screens, and create a display image "behind the scenes" in one video page while the user looks at another. The Quick C function _setactivepage() selects the video page where subsequent activity will occur. The visual page and the active page need not be the same, thus enabling you to construct a display out of the user's sight and only switch to the newly created image upon a signal of some sort.

The **SWAPSCRN** program in Listing 7.2 illustrates this. On successive keypresses, the program jumps back and forth between video pages 0 and 1. Most of the work is done in page 1 while you're looking at page 0. You'll note that the first peek at page 1 reveals garbage. Two keypresses later and you come back to a very different page 1, which has been given a green background and white lettering while you were reading the second set of instructions on page 0.

Listing 7.2 **Writing in one page while viewing another.**

```c
\* SWAPSCRN.C: Working with multiple display pages *\

#include <graph.h>
#include <conio.h>

main ()
{
struct videoconfig video;

  /* Check to see if we can run */
  _getvideoconfig (&video);
  if (video.numvideopages == 1)
    puts ("Only one video page available. Cannot run.");
  else {

    /* Start out in page 0 */
    puts ("Press a key to see page 1, again to come back here");
    getch();

    /* Show page 1 in uninitialized state */
    _setvisualpage (1);
    getch();

    /* Return to page 0 */
    _setvisualpage (0);
    puts ("Press a key to see page 1 after background activity");

    /* Construct an image behind the scenes in page 1 */
    _setactivepage (1);                        /* page 1 active */
    _setbkcolor (2L);                  /* set green background */
    _settextcolor (15);                /* and white foreground */
    _clearscreen (_GCLEARSCREEN);                     /* clear */
    _settextposition (11, 20);
    _outtext ("Page 1 changed while you weren't looking!");
    _settextposition (13, 27);
    _outtext ("Press any key to continue");

    /* Now wait for user keypress from page 0 */
    getch();
    _setvisualpage (1);

    /* Wait for another keypress to return to page 0 */
    getch();
    _setvisualpage (0);

    /* Clean up page 1, which is still active */
    _setbkcolor (0L);
    _settextcolor (7);
```

```
        _clearscreen (_GCLEARSCREEN);
        _setactivepage (0);                    /* restore default page */
    }
}
```

Text Attributes

As mentioned earlier, each character cell on the text display consists of two bytes. The first (on even addresses) is the ASCII code for the character to be displayed at that position. Its companion on the following odd address indicates the character's display attributes.

The attribute byte is a bit-zoned value conveying the foreground and background colors of the cell, the intensity of the character image, and two special effects: blinking and underlined. The format of this byte is:

7	6 5 4	3	2 1 0
Blink	Background	Intensity	Foreground

Quick C's _settextcolor() function controls the foreground field (bits 0–3). The _setbkcolor() function controls bits 4–6. There is no specific function for bit 7. However, you can easily set the blink bit by ORing 80h with the foreground color. For example, the statement

```
_settextcolor (15 | 0x80);
```

causes subsequent _outtext() calls to write blinking characters in bright white. The TEXTSCRN library introduced later in this chapter makes color and attribute setting more intuitive by defining some constants.

While the attribute bytes for monochrome and color adapters are identical, they have somewhat different effects depending on the video monitor's capabilities. A monochrome monitor can only display a limited subset of attributes:

Normal video (light on dark).

Intense normal video (bright on dark).

Reverse video (dark on light).

Underlined character.

Blinking character.

Light-on-light or vice versa.

You can turn on underlining on a monochrome monitor with

```
_settextcolor (1);
```

and turn it off with

```
_settextcolor (7);
```

Underlining is not available with a color monitor attached to a CGA, EGA, or VGA (you can't drive a color display with the MDA). Instead, the mono-chrome underline attribute produces a blue foreground, which is color 1. Otherwise, the zoning of the attribute byte is the same for both monochrome and color devices.

Bit 3 drives a basic color to its high-intensity counterpart. For example, when bit 3 is on, brown becomes yellow and gray becomes white. There are thus eight possible background colors and 16 for the foreground. Their values are:

Value	Basic	Value	Intense
0	Black	8	Dark gray
1	Blue	9	Light blue
2	Green	10	Light green
3	Cyan	11	Light cyan
4	Red	12	Light red
5	Magenta	13	Light magenta
6	Brown	14	Yellow
7	Light gray	15	White

The **TEXTSCRN** library discussed next furnishes constant names for the col-ors, and also enhances text operations in Quick C.

Stretching Text Manipulation _____

Programming in general, and graphics especially, tends to build hierarchies of functionality. One library serves as the foundation for another, which is further augmented by yet another, and so on. For example, DOS rests on the ROM BIOS, Quick C's graphics system builds on both, and application pro-grams using the graphics library perch atop them all like the capstone of a pyramid. What we're going to do here is add a level of functionality to Quick C's library. The objective is to make it easier to write programs that manage text screens.

Quick C offers a reasonably comprehensive set of tools for managing text screens, but it has a few holes and it could accomplish some things more eas-ily. The **TEXTSCRN** library stretches our Quick C repertoire by adding the following things:

- Color constants and blink
- Formatted output combining **_outtext()** with **printf()**

- Clear to end of line
- A single-character output function
- Text boxes with single and double borders
- Saving and restoring display pages
- Inquiry functions to determine:
  —Maximum column on the screen
  —Maximum row
  —Maximum page
  —Cursor column
  —Cursor row

The TEXTSCRN.H file in Listing 7.3 gives a more detailed picture of these enhancements.

Listing 7.3 **Header file for** TEXTSCRN **library.**

```
/* TEXTSCRN.H: Stretching text screen operations for QC 2.0 */

/* Text color constants */
#define BLACK      0
#define BLUE       1
#define GREEN      2
#define CYAN       3
#define RED        4
#define MAGENTA    5
#define BROWN      6
#define LTGRAY     7
#define DKGRAY     8
#define LTBLUE     9
#define LTGREEN    10
#define LTCYAN     11
#define LTRED      12
#define LTMAGENTA  13
#define YELLOW     14
#define WHITE      15
#define BLINK      0x80          /* OR with textcolor for blinking */

/* Added control functions */
void _cleareol (void);                      /* clear to end of line */
void _outtextf (char*, ...);                /* formatted _outtext */
void _outch (char);                         /* single-char output */
void _textbox (int top, int left, int bottom,  /* draw text box */
          int right, int style);
void _savescrn (int page);            /* save screen image in page */
void _restscrn (int page);          /* restore saved screen to page */
void _setbordwindow (int top, int left,      /* bordered window */
          int bottom, int right,
          int borderstyle, int fgcolor, int bgcolor);

/* Inquiry functions */
int maxcol (void);                          /* max column on display */
```

Listing 7.3 *(continued)*

```
int maxrow (void);                                /* max row on display */
int maxpage (void);                          /* highest avail video page */
int activepage (void);                        /* currently active page */
int visualpage (void);                       /* currently visible page */
int wherex (void);                         /* cursor col in active page */
int wherey (void);                         /* cursor row in active page */
```

The functions in the library source file **TEXTSCRN.C** (Listing 7.4) are all quite short, but several embody advanced programming techniques that make them worth studying. Consequently we'll discuss not only how to use these functions, but how they work.

The library includes one local function called initialize(). A number of the other functions rely on information about the video configuration. This information remains static, but there's no telling which function that needs it will be called first by an application program. This local function avoids the overhead of repeatedly calling _getvideoconfig(). The first function that needs configuration information calls it, and initialize() then obtains the configuration data and sets the Boolean switch init_done to indicate that it has already been called. All other using functions then check the switch and, finding it set, assume that the video configuration data are current.

If you add further functions to the library that might affect the video configuration—say, invoking EGA 43-line text mode—remember to call initialize() so that the configuration information is updated.

Listing 7.4 **Source for** TEXTSCRN **library.**

```
/* TEXTSCRN.C: Stretching text screen operations for QC 2.0     */
/* Library source                                               */

#include <graph.>
#include <dos.h>
#include <string.h>
#include <stdarg.h>
#include <malloc.h>
#include <stdio.h>
#include "biosarea.h"
#include "mk_fp.h"
#include "textscrn.h"

#if !defined TRUE
#define FALSE 0
#define TRUE  !FALSE
#endif

typedef struct scrnimage {
  unsigned char        dispmem [4000];
  struct scrnimage far *prev;
```

```
        struct rccoord        textpos;
        short                 fgcolor, bgcolor;
    } SCRNIMAGE;

    BIOSDATA far *bios = MK_FP (0x40, 0);       /* ROM BIOS data area */
    struct videoconfig video;                   /* video configuration */
    int init_done = FALSE;                          /* if initialized */
    SCRNIMAGE far *scrnstack = NULL;   /* screen image stack pointer */

    /* -------------------------------------------------        */
    /*                      LOCAL ROUTINE                       */
    /* -------------------------------------------------        */
    void near initialize (void)         /* initalize for these fcns */
    {
      _getvideoconfig (&video);                 /* get video info */
      init_done = TRUE;                         /* set switch */
    }
    /* -------------------------------------------------        */
    /*                    CONTROL FUNCTIONS                     */
    /* -------------------------------------------------        */

    void far _outtextf (char *ps, ...)          /* Formatted output */
    {                                   /* Pass args as for printf() */
    char    fline [80];
    va_list ap;

      va_start (ap, ps);
      vsprintf (fline, ps, ap);                    /* format string */
      va_end (ap);
      _outtext (fline);                     /* write to video memory */
    } /* ----------------------- */

    void far _outch (char ch)                   /* Single char output */
    {
    char  str [2];

      str [0] = ch;                          /* make a short string */
      str [1] = '\0';
      _outtext (str);                           /* and output it */
    } /* ----------------------- */

    void far _cleareol (void)           /* Clear to end of line from */
    {                                   /* current cursor position */
    register        c;
    char            blank [81];
    struct rccoord text;

      if (!init_done) initialize();          /* be sure we're set up */
      for (c = 0; c < 80; c++) blank [c] = ' ';       /* clear blank */
      text = _gettextposition();                   /* where are we? */
      c = video.numtextcols - text.col;  /* how far to right edge? */
      blank [c+1] = '\0';                      /* make blank that long */
      _outtext (blank);                           /* write spaces */
```

Listing 7.4 *(continued)*

```
  _settextposition (text.row, text.col);        /* restore cursor */
} /* ----------------------- */

void far _textbox (int top, int left,
                   int bott, int rite, int style)
                                       /* Draw box in text mode   */
                                       /* Style arguments:        */
                                       /*          0 = no box      */
                                       /*          1 = single-scored */
                                       /*          2 = double-scored */
{
register r, c;
char      horiz [81];
static    bord [][6] = {                        /* border characters */
          { 196, 179, 218, 191, 217, 192 },
          { 205, 186, 201, 187, 188, 200 }
        };

  if (style == 0) return;                /* no action, else... */

  /* Initialize */
  for (c = 0; c < 81; c++) horiz[c] = "\0";    /* horiz string */
  --style;                                     /* index to border set */

  /* Make sure coords are in proper order */
  if (left > rite) c = left, left = rite, rite = c;
  if (top > bott)  c = top, top = bott, bott = c;

  /* Draw top */
  for (c = 1; c < rite-left; c++)
    horiz[c] = bord [style][0];                  /* horiz char */
  horiz[c] = bord [style][3];                /* top right corner */
  horiz[0] = bord [style][2];                /* top left corner */
  _settextposition (top, left);
  _outtext (horiz);                                /* draw it */

  /* Draw bottom */
  horiz[c] = bord [style][4];                   /* bottom right */
  horiz[0] = bord [style][5];                   /* bottom left */
  _settextposition (bott, left);
  _outtext (horiz);                                /* draw it */

  /* Draw sides */
  for (r = top+1; r < bott; r++) {
    _settextposition (r, left);                  /* left side */
    _outch (bord [style][1]);                  /* vertical char */
    _settextposition (r, rite);                  /* right side */
    _outch (bord [style][1]);
  }
} /* ----------------------- */
```

```
      void far _savescrn (int page)                    /* save screen image */
                                                /* pushes image onto a stack */
      {
      SCRNIMAGE far *new;
      unsigned char far *vidmem;
      short oldpage;

        oldpage = _setactivepage (page);        /* remember where we are */
        new = _fmalloc (sizeof (SCRNIMAGE));            /* get space */
        new->prev = scrnstack;               /* point to previous image */
        scrnstack = new;                       /* update stack pointer */
        new->textpos = _gettextposition();   /* save cursor position */
        new->fgcolor = _gettextcolor();        /* save current colors */
        new->bgcolor = _getbkcolor();
        vidmem = (bios->videoMode == 7)            /* video memory addr */
                ? MK_FP (0xB000, (page * 0x1000))
                : MK_FP (0xB800, (page * 0x1000));
        movedata (FP_SEG (vidmem), FP_OFF (vidmem),      /* save image */
                FP_SEG (new), FP_OFF (new), 4000);
        _setactivepage (oldpage);             /* return to active page */
      } /* ------------------------ */


      void far _restscrn (int page)                /* restore screen image */
                                                /* pops image off a stack */
      {
      unsigned char far *vidmem;
      SCRNIMAGE far *top;
      short oldpage;

        if (scrnstack) {                    /* proceed if stack not empty */
          _settextwindow (1, 1, 25, 80);
          oldpage = _setactivepage (page);     /* remember where we are */
          top = scrnstack;                        /* top of stack */
          vidmem = (bios->videoMode == 7)          /* video memory addr */
                  ? MK_FP (0xB000, (page * 0x1000))
                  : MK_FP (0xB800, (page * 0x1000));
          movedata (FP_SEG (top), FP_OFF (top),            /* restore */
                  FP_SEG (vidmem), FP_OFF (vidmem), 4000);
          _settextcolor (top->fgcolor);              /* restore colors */
          _setbkcolor ((long)(top->bgcolor));
          _settextposition                 /* restore cursor position */
              (top->textpos.row, top->textpos.col);
          if (oldpage != page)
            _setactivepage (oldpage);            /* return to active page */
          scrnstack = top->prev;                /* update stack pointer */
          _ffree (top);                            /* free space */
        }
      } /* ------------------------ */


      void far _setbordwindow (int top, int left,  /* bordered window */
                      int bott, int rite,
                      int style, int fgcolor, int bgcolor)
      {
```

Listing 7.4 *(continued)*

```
int c;

   /* Make sure coords are in proper order */
   if (left > rite) c = left, left = rite, rite = c;
   if (top > bott)  c = top, top = bott, bott = c;

   /* Construct bordered window */
   _settextwindow (1, 1, 25, 80);                   /* use full screen */
   _settextcolor (fgcolor);                            /* set colors */
   _setbkcolor ((long)(bgcolor));
   _textbox (top-1, left-1, bott+1, rite+1, style);     /* border */
   _settextwindow (top, left, bott, rite);          /* open window */
   _clearscreen (_GWINDOW);                           /* clear it */
}
/* --------------------------------------------------------     */
/*                   INQUIRY FUNCTIONS                          */
/* --------------------------------------------------------     */

int far maxcol (void)                    /* max column on display */
{
   if (!init_done) initialize();
   return video.numtextcols;
} /* ----------------------- */

int far maxrow (void)                       /* max row on display */
{
   if (!init_done) initialize();
   return video.numtextrows;
} /* ----------------------- */

int far maxpage (void)                  /* highest avail video page */
{
   if (!init_done) initialize();
   return video.numvideopages - 1;
} /* ----------------------- */

int far wherex (void)                /* cursor col in active page */
{
struct rccoord text;

   text = _gettextposition();
   return text.col;
} /* ----------------------- */

int far wherey (void)                /* cursor row in active page */
{
struct rccoord text;

   text = _gettextposition();
   return text.row;
} /* ----------------------- */
```

Formatted Output

The Quick C display management subsystem doesn't recognize standard output functions such as printf() and cprintf(). These functions work, but they don't utilize the text color, nor do they update the cursor position maintained by the graphics library. The only text output function that interacts correctly with the other text management functions is _outtext().

Unfortunately, _outtext() is like puts(): It accepts only complete strings, and lacks the ability to format output from a variable number of arguments in the manner of printf(). That's why the SCRNIO.C program (Listing 7.1) had to call sprintf() prior to doing a screen write.

The first user-callable function in TEXTSCRN plugs this gap with _outtextf(). It works just like printf() in that you can pass it any number of arguments consisting of format specifiers, literals, and variable references. The function then constructs a string that can be up to 80 characters long and passes this string to _outtext() for output starting at the current cursor position.

The argument passed to _outtextf() is a pointer to a parameter string, with the ellipsis ("...") indicating a variable number of arguments. Formatting is accomplished by the va_start and va_end macros, with an intervening call to the vsprintf() function. Together, they form a loop. The va_start macro sets the next argument pointer from the parameter string, vsprintf() adds it to the string (fline in this case), and va_end takes the processed item off the start of the list. When all items have been formatted, va_end sets the argument pointer to NULL and the loop ends. At that point, control moves to _outtext(), which puts the formatted string fline onto the display.

The _outtextf() function thus replaces at least two lines of pure Quick C code with one. Here is an example derived from SCRNIO.C, Listing 7.1:

```
sprintf (str, "Column %d, row %d", col, row);
_outtext (str);
```

is replaced with

```
_outtextf ("Column %d, row %d", col, row);
```

It might also be unnecessary to declare the character array str, further saving coding effort and size.

Single-Character Output

The _outtext() function, in addition to providing no formatting capabilities, also expects a string as its argument. Therefore it cannot handle a single character. The only way to get a lone character onto the display under the control of the text management subsystem is to place it into a two-byte null-termi-

nated string, then call _outtext(). That's what the **TEXTSCRN** function _
outch() does.

To the programmer, _outch() is like putch() except that it can be expected to
behave properly on the display. For example, say that you want to echo a
user's keystroke using the current text attributes. The following sequence
accomplishes this:

```
response  =  getch();
_outch  (response);
```

Clearing to End of Line

In the **SCRNIO** program, we saw one way to trim away text to the right of the
current cursor location. It involved a brute-force loop that placed the cursor,
then wrote spaces to overlay the row numbers. Because clearing partial or
complete lines is a common operation on text displays, it calls for a more elegant solution. That's what the **TEXTSCRN** function _cleareol() provides.

This function fills a string with spaces. Then it measures the distance from
the cursor location to the right edge of the display and places a null terminator at the requisite position. The string is then passed to _outtext(). The
spaces erase everything to the right starting at the cursor position and ending
at the last column on the screen.

Thus, in **SCRNIO**, we could replace the nested loops that remove the row
numbers with the following:

```
for  (row  =  2;  row  ‹  17;  row + +)  {
        _settextposition  (row,  row + 24);
        cleareol();
}
```

Because the cursor position at the beginning of the cleared area is presumably important to the caller, _cleareol() puts the cursor back there after it finishes.

Drawing Text Boxes

Boxes around distinct areas of the screen add a professional touch to text displays. They visually fence off the things that you want the user to view separately: menus, popups, dialog boxes, error messages, and the like.

Machines in the IBM PC class furnish graphics characters for drawing
boxes. All such characters are in the extended ASCII set, with values in the
range 128–255. There are three kinds of box-drawing characters: single-score,
double-score, and conjunctions of the other two types (e.g., a single line join-

Figure 7.1 **Arrangement of values for a double box.**

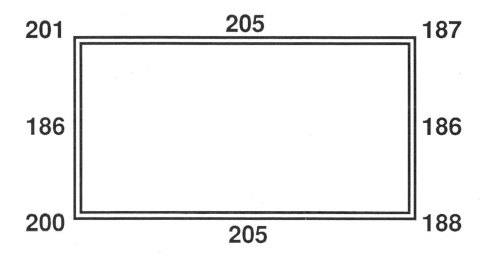

ing a double at right angles, two doubles crossing, etc.). Here we'll concentrate on simple boxes that use all of one type and form rectangles without interior lines. You might wish to expand this basic box-drawing capability into more sophisticated realms.

It takes six kinds of text characters to construct a simple box: horizontal, vertical, and corners. All of these text graphics characters pass through the center of the cells they occupy, and are thus equidistant from their neighbors both vertically and horizontally. Their ASCII values are as follows:

	Single	Double
Horizontal	196	205
Vertical	179	186
Upper left	218	201
Upper right	191	187
Lower right	217	188
Lower left	192	200

Figure 7.1 depicts the arrangement of ASCII values to construct a double-score box.

You can express the characteristics of a text box using five parameters: the coordinates of two opposite corners and its border style. As an example, say you want to surround the following string with a single-scored text box:

Hello, world!

This string contains 13 characters. If the string originates at row 13, column 10, its last character occurs in column 22. Therefore you can specify the surrounding box as

```
_textbox (12, 9, 14, 23, 1);
```

Note that _textbox() accepts the coordinates of any two opposite corners. It sorts them to derive the top left and bottom right corners. This means that you could specify the box above as

```
_textbox (12, 23, 14, 9, 1);
```

(upper right and lower left) and still get the same result.

One further assumption behind a box-drawing routine is that it might be called upon to draw any of three *kinds* of borders: none, single, or double. If none is specified, the routine should simply return, and otherwise it should draw the box as defined. The _textbox() function implements this.

The two-dimensional static array **bord** specifies the border characters for single- and double-scored boxes. The style argument selects which dimension to use; if it's 0 the function returns with no action, and otherwise style-1 selects the appropriate array dimension.

For the horizontal edges, the function constructs a string representing the top and draws it by calling _outtext(). It then replaces the corner characters and draws the bottom. The vertical edges are then drawn between corner characters, both sides at the same time, using _outch() discussed earlier.

Saving and Restoring a Screen Image

User interfaces often need to overlay a portion of the screen, then restore it later to its previous appearance. A good example is when creating a temporary object on the screen, such as a pull-down menu. The object obscures a portion of the screen; when it goes away, the information under the object reappears. How?

While it seems almost magical to make an object vanish, restoring the screen content it previously covered, in fact the operation is quite simple. You copy the video page into program memory, then alter the screen. Later, you restore the display by copying the saved information back into the video buffer. That's the purpose of the complementary functions _savescrn() and _restscrn() in the TEXTSCRN library.

These functions work together to manage a stack, which is a *last-in, first-out* (LIFO) dynamic data structure. Each call to savescrn() pushes an image on the top of the stack, and each call to restscrn() pops the image most recently saved. Why this order? Because, as you'll see in the next chapter, it prevents corruption of the display; you must remove a 1-2-3 sequence of pop-ups by backtracking in 3-2-1 order. That's how LIFO works.

The screen stack grows and shrinks on the heap, so it doesn't steal any memory from the program's data segment. It's implemented as a singly linked list, a form of dynamic data management that we'll discuss in more detail in Chapter 17. Each saved screen image goes into a node containing the 4,000-byte page, plus the cursor location at the time it was saved and a pointer to the preceding node. A variable called **scrnstack** functions as a stack pointer, always pointing to the most recent node. When you restore an image, **_restscrn()** copies its 4,000 bytes into the specified page of video memory, puts the cursor where it belongs in that page, and decrements the stack pointer to the next-lower node (or NULL if you've just popped the last image). The space occupied by the node is then released.

Unlike the other functions in the **TEXTSCRN** library, **_savescrn()** and **_restscrn()** don't automatically work on the currently active page. You must specify which page is affected. This enables your applications to do things like copying an image from one page to another without juggling the active page. For example, to copy the image from page 0 into page 5, the calls are:

```
_savescrn (0);
_restscrn (5);
```

It's as simple as that.

Now let's look at a program that demonstrates LIFO screen management. SAVEREST.C in Listing 7.5 creates three distinctive screens—black, green, and magenta—saving each one on successive keypresses. After the magenta screen is saved, the program writes the additional instruction "Saved: Press again" to begin the backtrack phase. This message disappears when you press a key. That's because the changed image has been overlaid by its previously saved copy. Successive keypresses return you to green, black, and finally to the DOS prompt. Because this program operates in video page 0, it works on both color and monochrome adapters, but the background color remains black on the MDA.

You can compile and link this program from the DOS command line with

```
QCL  saverest.c  textscrn.c
```

Listing 7.5 Saving and restoring images in LIFO order.

```
/* SAVEREST.C: Save and restore screens */

#include <conio.h>
#include <graph.h>
#include "textscrn.h"

main ()
```

Listing 7.5 *(continued)*

```
{
  _clearscreen (_GCLEARSCREEN);
  _outtext ("This is screen 1");
  _outtext ("\nPress any key");
  getch();
  _savescrn (0);


  /* Make and save screen 2 */
  _setbkcolor (GREEN);
  _settextcolor (WHITE);
  _clearscreen (_GCLEARSCREEN);
  _settextposition (11, 32); _outtext ("This is screen 2");
  _settextposition (13, 33); _outtext ("Press any key");
  getch();
  _savescrn (0);


  /* Make and save screen 3 */
  _setbkcolor (MAGENTA);
  _settextcolor (CYAN);
  _clearscreen (_GCLEARSCREEN);
  _settextposition (11, 32); _outtext ("This is screen 3");
  _settextposition (13, 33); _outtext ("Press any key");
  getch();
  _savescrn (0);


  /* Restore screen 3 */
  _settextposition (15, 31); _outtext ("Saved: Press again");
  getch();
  _restscrn (0);


  /* Restore screen 2 */
  getch();
  _restscrn (0);


  /* Restore screen 1 */
  getch();
  _restscrn (0);


  /* Restore screen defaults and quit */
  getch();
  _setbkcolor (BLACK);
  _settextcolor (LTGRAY);
  _clearscreen (_GCLEARSCREEN);
}
```

Inquiry Functions

The inquiry functions included in the **TEXTSCRN** library are conveniences to applications. They return specific items derived from the two Quick C functions _getvideoconfig() and _gettextposition(), relieving you of the need to declare structure variables, call those functions explicitly, and fetch values from the structures.

For example, if you want to move the cursor back to the start of the current row and clear the line, write

```
_settextposition (wherey(), 1);
_cleareol();
```

Similarly, you can clear all display pages with the loop

```
for (page = 0; page >= maxpage(); page++) {
    _setactivepage (page);
    _clearscreen (_GCLEARSCREEN);
}
```

Next let's examine using subsets of the display area.

Windowing

A window is a portion of the text display that functions as though it were a complete screen. That is, the upper left corner has text coordinates {1, 1}, text wraps to the next line when it reaches the right border, and the contents scroll upward as new lines are added at the bottom. Operationally, about the only difference (aside from size) is that, to clear a window, you issue the statement

```
_clearscreen (_GWINDOW);
```

Quick C's default window is the whole display, typically 80 columns by 25 rows. But let's say you want to set aside the lower right quadrant of the screen as an individual window. To do this, you issue the statement

```
_settextwindow (13, 41, 25, 80);
```

Now all text I/O occurs only in the lower right quadrant. The statement

```
_settextposition (1, 1);
```

places the cursor in row 13, column 41 of the overall screen, and all areas outside the window are unreachable. In effect, the window becomes a self-contained virtual display.

The window remains in effect until the program either ends or issues another _settextwindow() statement. For example, to restore full-screen operation, write

    _settextwindow (1, 1, 25, 80);

Similarly, to switch to another window occupying the space shown in Figure 7.2, the statement is

    _settextwindow (6, 20, 18, 50);

Note that the _settextwindow() statement works in the coordinate space of the screen as a whole and not of the current window.

Figure 7.2 **Selecting an area within the display.**

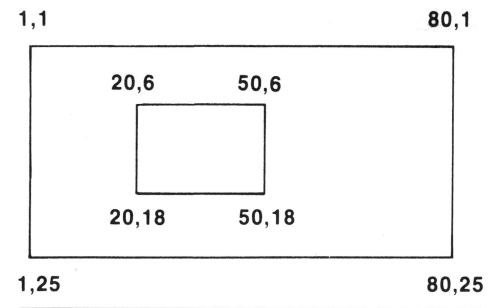

A Demonstration

Listing 7.6 is a program called WINDEMO.C. This program writes some background text, then prompts you to press any key. After each of the first three keypresses, the program creates a new window somewhere on the display and fills it with nonsense text in a different color. The program then requests three more keypresses, each time removing the most recent window and restoring the underlying screen.

As the program fills each window, the text wraps to the next line when it reaches the edge of the window, and the contents of the window scroll without affecting the rest of the display. The third window overlaps the second. When the third window is removed, the overlaid part of the second comes back into view; when the second goes away, the original text reappears. Thus a portion of the screen is actually buried under two layers, but it eventually gets uncovered as we strip away windows.

The DOS command to make this program is

        QCL windemo.c textscrn.c

Listing 7.6 **Windowing and screen save/restore.**

```
/* WINDEMO.C: Shows windowing, screen save/restore */

#include <conio.h>
#include <graph.h>
#include "textscrn.h"

/* DEFINE TYPES */
typedef struct {                          /* window descriptor */
   int     t, l, b, r;
   char    image [800];
} WINDESCR;

/* GLOBAL WINDOW DESCRIPTORS */
WINDESCR w [] = {
   { 10, 10, 20, 20 },
   {  5, 40, 15, 70 },
   { 12, 22, 17, 55 }
};

/* LOCAL FUNCTION PROTOTYPES */
void prompt (char*);
int  space (int, int, int, int);
void fillwin (int);
/* --------------------------- */

main ()
{
int  n;

  _clearscreen (_GCLEARSCREEN);          /* clear the screen */
  _settextcolor (BROWN);
  for (n = 1; n < 23; n++) {  /* write some backgrnd text */
    _settextposition (n, n);
    _outtextf ("This is at row %d, column %d", n, n);
  }

  for (n = 0; n < 3; n++) {       /* loop for three windows */
```

Listing 7.6 *(continued)*

```
      prompt ("Press any key for next window");
      _savescrn (0);                         /* save screen */
      _settextwindow (w[n].t, w[n].l,        /* set window */
            w[n].b, w[n].r);
      fillwin (n);                           /* fill window */
   }

   for (n = 2; n >= 0; n--){            /* step back, erasing */
      prompt ("Press any key to erase last window");
      _restscrn (0);                         /* LIFO restore */
   }

   prompt ("Press any key to quit");
   _settextcolor (LTGRAY);
   _clearscreen (_GCLEARSCREEN);
} /* --------------------- */


void prompt (char *mssg)

   /* Write prompt message at bottom of scrn and wait */

{
   _settextwindow (1, 1, 25, 80);       /* use whole screen */
   _settextposition (24, 1);            /* go to prompt line */
   _settextcolor (WHITE);
   _setbkcolor (0L);
   _cleareol ();                           /* clear line */
   _outtext (mssg);                        /* write message */
   getch ();                          /* hold until key pressed */
} /* --------------------- */


void fillwin (int number)

   /* Fill active window with scrolling text */

{
int  i, c;

   _clearscreen (_GWINDOW);             /* clear active window */
   _settextcolor (number + 1);          /* blue, green, cyan */
   for (i = 0; i < 30; i++)
      for (c = 33; c < 127; c++)           /* print all chars */
         _outch (c);
} /* --------------------- */
```

The array of window descriptors (w[] at the top of the listing) allows the program to handle the whole process with a pair of loops in main(). The first loop builds the windows. The second steps backward, removing windows in LIFO (last in, first out) order.

Outlining a Window with a Text Box

The final control function in the TEXTSCRN library is _setbordwindow(), which creates a window possessing a border and color attributes. Even if you want an unbordered window, you can save yourself some window setup steps by calling this function with a border style of 0.

Like _textbox(), _setbordwindow() accepts any two opposite corners and sorts them into northwest-southeast order. After making sure it's in full-screen mode, the function draws a box of the requested style immediately outside the new window. That is, if the window goes from {10, 5} to {20, 30}, the box is drawn from {9, 4} to {21, 31}. The process then completes by opening the window and clearing it, thus setting its foreground and background colors.

This function assumes that you want the border to have the same color characteristics as the window text. If not, draw the box separately, then call _setbordwindow() with a border style of 0.

Note too that _setbordwindow() doesn't save the display page. If you're going to remove the window later and restore whatever it overlays, call _savescrn() first.

The TBOX.C program in Listing 7.7 illustrates the use of bordered windows in connection with saving and restoring display pages. The program saves the screen it inherits on entry, then sets up a bordered window occupying most of the display surface. After writing some background text, it asks you to press any key to see the pop-up window, which appears in the center of the screen overlaying the text. The program prompts for another keypress to make the pop-up go away, thus restoring the overlaid text. A third keypress ends the program by redisplaying the entry screen.

All three border styles—single, double, and none—are used in this program. The prompt area at the bottom of the display is unbordered and operates like the command/status line found in many commercial software products.

Listing 7.7 **Implementing bordered windows.**

```
/* TBOX.C: Outlining windows with text boxes */

#include <conio.h>
#include <graph.h>
#include "textscrn.h"

/* Constants */
#define    MAINFORE YELLOW
#define    MAINBACK BROWN
#define    MSSGFORE BLACK
#define    BOXFORE  WHITE
#define    BOXBACK  RED
```

Listing 7.7 *(continued)*

```
main ()
{
int    n;
void prompt (char*);

  /* Set up main window, double border */
  _savescrn (0);                          /* save entry screen */
  _setbordwindow (2, 2, 22, 79, 2, MAINFORE, MAINBACK);

  for (n = 1; n < 22; n++) {              /* write some text */
    _settextposition (n, n + 5);
    _outtextf ("This is at row %d, column %d", n, n + 5);
  }
  prompt ("Press any key for pop-up...");

  /* Make a pop-up, single border */
  _savescrn(0);                              /* save display */
  _setbordwindow (10, 28, 10, 52, 1, BOXFORE, BOXBACK);
  _outtext ("This is a pop-up window");

  /* Hold pop-up until keypress */
  prompt ("Press any key to restore original screen...");
  _restscrn (0);                              /* restore */

  /* Shut down */
  prompt ("Press any key to quit...");
  _restscrn (0);                       /* restore entry screen */
} /* ----------------------- */

void prompt (char *mssg)
{                    /* write message to command line and wait */

  _setbordwindow (24, 1, 24, 80, 0, MSSGFORE, MAINBACK);
  _outtext (mssg);
  getch ();
} /* ----------------------- */
```

We've now developed the skills and some enhanced tools for managing text displays in Quick C. The next chapter builds on this one to create professional-quality displays with menu bars, pop-up windows, and pull-down menus.

CHAPTER 8

Creating the Visual Environment

This chapter builds on the tools and techniques covered in the last chapter to create the kinds of visual environments associated with high-powered software products. User interfaces typically use three kinds of visual objects: *free-form text screens, menu bars,* and *pop-ups.* The interactive environment of Quick C contains examples of all three and serves as a convenient point of reference.

A free-form screen is one in which the user or the data being presented have some control over the appearance of the display. The edit screen is an example; you as the user have the ability to move around within it, altering the way it looks by changing its contents.

A menu bar is a list of action items, usually running across the top or bottom of the display. There's one at the top of the Quick C screen. A menu bar might also appear in a pop-up; this commonly occurs in applications written to run under Microsoft Windows.

The third kind of object, a pop-up, is a window that appears and later vanishes. Pop-ups can take several forms. They share the characteristic that they temporarily overlay part or all of the screen and, when they disappear, the underlying display is restored. Three common examples are *pull-down menus, help panels,* and *dialog boxes.*

In the last case, the pop-up is a bordered window. A program uses a dialog box to request and receive information that it needs under special circumstances to do its job. An example from Quick C is the file pick list.

We'll examine these things in detail in this chapter and develop methods for creating them.

Structured Displays

A pop-up is, in effect, a subset of the screen ranging from a few rows by a few columns up to the entire visible display. As such, no matter where a pop-up is or what its size, we should be able to describe and manage it in a consistent fashion.

What are the elements essential for its management? Here's a list:

- Its position and size: coordinates of the left, top, right, and bottom of the pop-up.
- Its border style: 0–2 as defined in the _textbox() function from Chapter Eight.
- Its color attributes: foreground and background.
- A pointer to its text content: menu selections and other fixed text. If none, this pointer is NULL.

This suggests a pop-up data structure, and here it is:

```
typedef  struct  {
   int     top, left, bottom, right,
           style,
           normal, hilite,
           normback, hiback;
   char *text;
   int     lastrow, lastcol;
} POPUP;
```

We'll discuss the two additional fields (lastrow and lastcol) later in connection with returning to an open window.

Programs should initialize one such structure for each pop-up. Figure the coordinates of a pop-up in terms of fullscreen coordinates. The reference values are top and left. Bottom is the sum of top plus the number of text rows in the window. Right is the longest string's length, plus left. For example, say a window contains

```
This
is
a
popup
```

and its upper left corner is at {10, 10}. There are four lines, so the bottom is at row 14. The longest string contains five characters, so the right is at 15. This results in the smallest possible window to contain the text.

With pop-ups, which often pack text into a limited space, it's advisable to turn text wrap off with the Quick C statement

```
_wrapon (_GWRAPOFF);
```

You can get unexpected results if you leave text wrap on (it's the default in Quick C). In this case, for example, the final "p" is at the right edge of the pop-up. With text wrap on, the cursor will go to the next line, forcing all four lines to scroll and sending "This" off the top of the pop-up. Turning text wrap off prevents it from happening; the cursor simply stops when it can't move right and further output is truncated. The routine presented next automatically turns text wrap off.

Building the Pop-up Management Library

Now let's discuss a set of functions that provide simple calls for manipulating pop-up windows. These routines build on, and are thus extensions of, the Quick C library and the TEXTSCRN module presented in the last chapter.

Listing 8.1 is a header file for the new POPUP library. It defines a couple of data structures, one already discussed and the other to be covered later, plus prototypes for the library functions. Listing 8.2 is the library source itself.

You will need these files to use the programs in this and later chapters, and to make your own user interfaces. The rest of this chapter discusses how the functions work and how to use them.

Listing 8.1 **Header file for the** POPUP **library.**

```
/* POPUP.H: Prototype and typedef for POPUP.C library */

typedef struct {
  int  top, left, bottom, right,      /* border location */
       style,                            /* border style */
       normal, hilite,                 /* text attributes */
       normback, hiback;
  char *text;                       /* fixed text contents */
  int  lastrow, lastcol;            /* last cursor position */
} POPUP;

typedef struct {
  int  row,                        /* row where bar appears */
       interval,                   /* cols between first chars */
       fore, back;           /* foreground/background colors */
  char *choice;                    /* pointer to text contents */
} MENUBAR;

void popShow (POPUP *pop);             /* display popup window */

void popKeep (POPUP *win);              /* save window state */

void popUse (POPUP *win);               /* re-enable a window */

void popCenter (POPUP *win, int row, char *string);
                                      /* Center string in window */

void popRewrite (POPUP *win, int row,
              int fgcolor, int bgcolor);
```

Listing 8.1 *(continued)*

```
                              /* Rewrite pop-up row in new colors */
void popHilite (POPUP *win, int row);
                              /* Hilight text in popup row */

void popNormal (POPUP *win, int row);
                   /* Set text in popup row to normal attribs */

void menubar (MENUBAR *spec);
                   /* Write the menu bar described by spec */
```

Listing 8.2 **Source for the** POPUP **library.**

```
/* POPUP.C: Pop-up window library */

#include <stdio.h>
#include <dos.h>
#include <string.h>
#include <graph.h>
#include "textscrn.h"
#include "popup.h"

void popShow (POPUP *pop)            /* display popup window */
{
  _setbordwindow (pop->top, pop->left,     /* create popup */
                  pop->bottom, pop->right,
                  pop->style, pop->normal, pop->normback);
  _wrapon (_GWRAPOFF);                 /* disable text wrap */
  if (pop->text != NULL)
    _outtext (pop->text);              /* write fixed text */
} /* ----------------------- */

void popKeep (POPUP *win)    /* preserve state of a window */
{
  win->lastcol = wherex();
  win->lastrow = wherey();
} /* ----------------------- */

void popUse (POPUP *win)       /* re-enable existing window */
{
_settextwindow (win->top, win->left, win->bottom, win->right);
  _settextcolor (win->normal);
  _setbkcolor (win->normback);
  if (win->lastrow > 0)
    _settextposition (win->lastrow, win->lastcol);
} /* ----------------------- */

void popCenter (POPUP *win, int row, char *string)
                                     /* Center string in window */
{
int  i, tab;

  popUse (win);
```

```
      tab = 1 + (win->right - win->left - strlen (string) + 1) /
2;    _settextposition (row, tab);
     _outtext (string);
}  /* ------------------------- */

void popRewrite (POPUP *win, int row, int fgcolor, int bgcolor)
                        /* Rewrite pop-up row with new colors */
{
int          p, nchars, page, attrib;
union  REGS  reg;

   popUse (win);
   page = _setactivepage (0);                      /* which page? */
   _setactivepage (page);
   nchars = win->right - win->left + 1;       /* popup width */
   attrib = (bgcolor << 4) - fgcolor;     /* new text attrib */
   for (p = 1; p <= nchars; p++) {
     _settextposition (row, p);
     reg.h.ah = 8;                               /* get character */
     reg.h.bh = page;                            /* in active page */
     int86 (0x10, &reg, &reg);                     /* via ROM BIOS */
     reg.h.ah = 9;                         /* write back out with */
     reg.h.bl = attrib;                          /* hilite attribs */
     reg.h.bh = page;
     reg.x.cx = 1;                                   /* one char */
     int86 (0x10, &reg, &reg);
   }
}  /* ------------------------- */

void popHilite (POPUP *win, int row)
     /* Hilight text in popup row */
{
   popRewrite (win, row, win->hilite, win->hiback);
}  /* ------------------------- */

void popNormal (POPUP *win, int row)
     /* Set text in popup row to normal attribs */
{
   popRewrite (win, row, win->normal, win->normback);
}  /* ------------------------- */

void menubar (MENUBAR *spec)
     /* Write the menu bar described by spec */
{
int fore, back, p, s, row, col, c = 0;

   fore = _settextcolor (spec->fore);       /* get/set colors */
   back = _setbkcolor (spec->back);
   row = wherey();                       /* get cursor position */
   col = wherex();
   _settextposition (spec->row, 1);       /* start of menu bar */
   for (s = 1; s < maxcol(); s++)
     _outch (' ');                          /* set bar background */
```

Listing 8.2 *(continued)*

```
    _settextposition (wherey(), 1);      /* start of menu bar */
    for (p = 0; spec->choice [p]; p++)   /* copy text to bar */
      if (spec->choice [p] != '\n')
        _outch (spec->choice [p]);                   /* write char */
      else                      /* else move to next menu item */
        _settextposition (wherey(), spec->interval * ++c);

    /* Restore previous state */
    _settextcolor (fore);                        /* color scheme */
    _setbkcolor (back);
    _settextposition (row, col);          /* cursor position */
} /* ------------------------ */
```

Creating and Erasing Pop-ups

The **POPUP** data structure describes a pop-up window. The library furnishes routines that use the structure contents to do various things with these objects. The first and most obvious thing we need to do is convert the descriptor into something we can see on the display. That's what the **pop-Show()** function does.

Considering its importance, **popShow()** is actually quite simple. It passes the position and color information to _**setbordwindow()**, a **TEXTSCRN** function from Chapter 7, which does the work of drawing the border and opening the window. **popShow()** then turns text wrap off and, if its text pointer field is not **NULL**, writes the text into the window. Then it returns, leaving the newly created pop-up as the active window.

Consequently, it's very easy to create a pop-up window: Just initialize a structure of type **POPUP** and pass its pointer to **popShow()**.

The format of fixed text for a pop-up is a null-terminated string with newline characters embedded at the appropriate places. For example, if a pull-down menu has the entries

    Load
    New
    Save
    Quit

the string might be defined as

    pdtext = "Load\nNew\nSave\nQuit";

The **popShow()** routine doesn't save the screen. This is because, in some applications, you might want to place an object on the display permanently. Therefore, in creating a sequence of pop-ups that will be removed later in reverse order, it's your responsibility to call _savescrn() before each call to popShow().

Removing the pop-up(s) is therefore merely a matter of calling _restscrn(), once for each window created. The stack-like structure maintained by the TEXTSCRN library ensures removal in the proper order.

Sometimes you need to revisit a pop-up window after you've left it. Let's say the user is in a pull-down menu and does something to trigger a dialog box. Presently the dialog ends, the box is removed, and the user returns to the menu. In such cases, use the popKeep() and popUse() functions discussed next.

But first let's look at a program that illustrates the ease with which the library manages pop-ups. QUICKPOP.C in Listing 8.3 puts two small overlapping pop-up windows on the display and then removes them, advancing each step in response to a keypress. The action occurs against a grid filling the display. Note that QUICKPOP saves the entry screen as soon as it begins to run, and restores it just before ending.

Listing 8.3 **Popping up and removing windows.**

```
/* QUICKPOP.C: Creates and erases two pop-up windows on */
/*    successive keystrokes                              */

#include <graph.h>
#include <conio.h>
#include "textscrn.h"
#include "popup.h"

char   string1 [] = "This\nis\na\npopup",    /* literals */
       string2 [] = "So\nis\nthis";
POPUP  pop [] = {                            /* popup definitions */
  {5, 20,  8, 24, 2,   BLUE, MAGENTA, CYAN,  CYAN, string1},
  {8, 23, 10, 26, 1, YELLOW, WHITE,  BROWN, BROWN, string2}
};

main ()
{
int n;

  _savescrn (0);                       /* save entry screen */
  _clearscreen (_GCLEARSCREEN);

  for (n = 0; n < 1920; n++)           /* fill screen */
    _outch (197);

  for (n = 0; n < 2; n++) {            /* show the popups */
    getch ();
    _savescrn (0);
    popShow (&(pop [n]));
  }
  for (n = 1; n >=0; n--) {            /* then erase them */
```

Listing 8.3 *(continued)*

```
    getch ();
    _restscrn (0);
  }
  getch ();

  _restscrn (0);                          /* restore entry screen */
}
```

Returning to an Open Window

User interfaces occasionally need to shuttle between two or more pop-up windows. An example might be interacting with the user in a dialog box while a background process reports its status in another.

Cursor management is a problem in such instances. That's because Quick C regards a window as a singular item; the act of setting a text window automatically disables any other window currently active. The disabled window remains visible (unless overlaid by the new one), but inaccessible. Even after you've removed the new window, the cursor position for its predecessor is irrelevant since the point of reference has been lost. To see an example, rerun the **QUICKPOP** program and watch what happens to the cursor after the second pop-up is removed; it jumps to a location utterly unrelated to the remaining window. (Note: The cursor position is no longer corrupted when you eventually get back to a display page without a window.)

The **_savescrn()**/**_restscrn()** routines attempt to preserve and restore the cursor position for each page, but Quick C gets confused when windows are active. **_gettextposition()** returns the location of the cursor within the current window; it has no way of sensing if it's dealing with a window or the screen as a whole, nor does Quick C furnish a means for mapping text window coordinates to the full screen.

This is a problem only if you attempt to revisit windows after they've been abandoned. In that case, you need to prepare for the return visit by using the **POPUP** library's companion functions **popKeep()** and **popUse()**.

popKeep() should be called just before you abandon the pop-up window that you intend to reuse later. It stores the window-relative cursor position (the "window state") in the descriptor's **lastrow** and **lastcol** fields.

A new window certainly changes the cursor's position and point of reference; it might also change the color scheme. Therefore, to re-use a window after moving to another, call **popUse()** with the revisited window's descriptor as an argument. **popUse()** reinstates the window and its color scheme. It also restores the last cursor position within the window, using the state information saved by **popKeep()**. The routine assumes that the state is zero if **popKeep()** has never touched the descriptor; in that event it leaves the cursor at its default home position in the window.

   This is not an entirely perfect solution to the problems of one-at-a-time window management with Quick C. There is no way for the program to detect if the
revisited window is currently overlaid by another. Writes to a reopened window
could potentially clobber another window lying on top of it. Therefore you
should plan the placement of obscuring windows so that this can't happen.

   The TWOWINDS.C program in Listing 8.4 shows a simple application of
popKeep() and popUse(). On successive keypresses, the program shuttles
between two pop-up windows, writing alternatively in each. The first loop
opens the two windows in opposite quadrants of the screen. The second loop
writes to each window and, in the process, stores the text position by calling
popKeep(). The third loop then revisits the windows in turn, reinstating their
previous status by calling popUse() before doing another write.

   By extending this concept, you can easily track several windows and move
among them.

Listing 8.4 **Using more than one pop-up at a time.**

```
/* TWOWINDS.C: Shuttling between two popup windows */

#include <conio.h>
#include <stdio.h>
#include <graph.h>
#include "popup.h"
#include "textscrn.h"

POPUP w[] = {
    { 3, 10,  7, 26, 1, BLACK, 0,  CYAN, 0, NULL, 0, 0},
    {13, 50, 17, 66, 2, BLACK, 0, GREEN, 0, NULL, 0, 0}
};

main ()
{
int n;

  /* Save entry screen, open pop-ups */
  _savescrn (0);
  for (n = 0; n < 2; n++)
    popShow (&(w[n]));

  /* Write in one window, then other after keypress */
  for (n = 0; n < 2; n++) {
    popUse (&(w[n]));                       /* use window n */
    _outtextf ("Now in window %d", n);      /* write text */
    _outtext ("\nPress a key...");
    popKeep (&(w[n]));                      /* save state */
    getch ();                               /* wait */
  }

  /* Return to successive windows on further keypresses */
  for (n = 0; n < 2; n++) {
```

Listing 8.4 *(continued)*

```
    popUse (&(w[n]));                            /* use window n */
    _outtextf ("\n\nBack in window %d", n);
    _outtext ("\nPress a key...");
    getch();                                     /* wait */
  }

  /* Remove windows from screen and quit */
  _restscrn (0);
}
```

Writing to a Pop-up

We've already seen several cases in which text is written to a pop-up window using Quick C's _outtext(). You can also use the extended functions _outtextf() and _outch() from the TEXTSCRN library. Except for the smaller size of a window, it's the same as working on a full screen.

As Listing 8.4 shows, you can also use _settextposition() and _gettextposition() within a pop-up window. Keep in mind that these functions work in relation to the upper left corner of the active window, not of the screen as a whole. If you need to map window-relative coordinates to screen coordinates, add the row to the window's top and the column to the left edge position, as given by the descriptor.

Because text wrap is turned off by popShow(), any text element too wide to fit within the window's confines is truncated. In effect, the text seems to slide out of sight beneath the window's right edge. Text wrapping is normally enabled in Quick C programs, so you might find it necessary to turn it back on if you revert to a free-form text screen after handling some pop-ups. You can do this by issuing

    _wrapon (_GWRAPON);

Next we'll consider some special output requirements in pop-up windows.

Centered Text

A bordered pop-up with centered text has a pleasing appearance. It also attracts attention, which is of course the purpose in popping up a window. Examples of centered text are titles, error messages, and prompts such as "Press any key to continue . . .". Sometimes variable data looks better centered, too.

To center a character string, find the width of the window (from its descriptor structure), subtract the string length, divide by two, and add one. This gives the number of character offset positions to achieve centering.

The popCenter() function in Listing 8.2 uses the character offset (the variable tab) to set the horizontal position within the window row specified by the argument. If text already exists in the row, you should move the cursor to column 1 and issue a call to _cleareol() before calling popCenter(). Use sprintf() if you need to center a string containing variable information. After building the string, pass it as an argument.

Word of caution: Don't put a leading newline into a string that is to be centered. The routine will insert the leading spaces, but then advance to the start of the next line before writing the text. Consequently, the line will not be centered, and it will appear in the wrong row.

Listing 8.5 contains a short program illustrating a pop-up with centered text.

Listing 8.5 **Centering text in a pop-up window.**

```
/* CENTERED.C: Shows text centered in a pop-up window */

#include <conio.h>
#include "popup.h"
#include "textscrn.h"

POPUP pop = {8, 30, 14, 50, 2, YELLOW, 0, BROWN, 0};

main ()
{
  _savescrn (0);                           /* save entry screen */
  popShow (&pop);                                    /* pop up */
  popCenter (&pop, 2, "This text");                   /* write */
  popCenter (&pop, 4, "is centered.");
  popCenter (&pop, 6, "Press any key...");
  getch();                                 /* wait for keypress */
  _restscrn (0);                    /* restore entry screen */
}
```

Highlighted Text

Here's where we get to the meat of pull-down menus. Many applications using pop-ups employ highlighting for prompt lines, to show which menu choice is currently indicated for selection, for warning messages, and so forth. They do this by setting a different foreground/background attribute to create a distinctive bar. The pull-down menus in Quick C 2.0 are an example. The menu consists of dark letters on a light background, but the selection bar reverses the color scheme and moves in response to the cursor keys.

Highlighting is accomplished by changing the attributes for a row using the POPUP structure's hilite and hiback fields. The popRewrite() function scans across the width of the window, changing the attribute byte at each character position.

The Quick C library doesn't include a function for detecting what's on the screen at a given character position, but the ROM BIOS does. Interrupt 10h, function 8, returns the character at the current cursor position. Function 9 writes a character and attribute to the display. Thus, by advancing across the row one character at a time, popRewrite() reads the current character and rewrite sit with the highlighting attributes.

The same process applies to removing highlighting and restoring the normal color schemes. Simply substitute the POPUP structure's normal and normback values. That's the purpose of the popHilite() and popNormal() functions; they pass the appropriate character attributes to popRewrite(), a subroutine common to both.

The expression for building an attribute byte used by the ROM BIOS call is

attribute = (background << 4) | foreground;

That is, shift the background value left four bits and OR it with the foreground. The result is consistent with the attribute structure shown in Chapter 8.

Listing 8.6 shows the highlighting routines in action. It pops up a box. The second line of text in the box tells what's going to happen the next time you press a key. First the line is highlighted, then restored to normal colors, and finally the program ends.

Listing 8.6 **Highlighting and restoring text lines.**

```
/* HILITE.C: Highlighting a line within a pop-up */

#include <conio.h>
#include <graph.h>
#include "popup.h"
#include "textscrn.h"

POPUP pop = {8, 30, 12, 50, 2,
             GREEN, BLACK, BLACK, GREEN, 0};

main ()
{
  _savescrn (0);                        /* save entry screen */
  _displaycursor (_GCURSOROFF);
  popShow (&pop);                                /* pop up */

  /* Write original message */
  popCenter (&pop, 2, "Press any key");          /* write */
  popCenter (&pop, 4, "to highlight...");
  getch ();

  /* Change second line and hilite */
  _settextposition (4, 1); _cleareol ();
  popCenter (&pop, 4, "to restore...");
  popHilite (&pop, 4);
```

```
    getch();

    /* Change second line and restore normal colors */
    _settextposition (4, 1); _cleareol();
    popCenter (&pop, 4, "to quit...");
    popNormal (&pop, 4);
    getch();

    /* Erase popup and quit */
    _displaycursor (_GCURSORON);
    _restscrn (0);                          /* restore entry screen */
}
```

A common application for the **popHilite()** and **popNormal()** functions is highlighting selections on pull-down menus. When the highlight moves from one selection to another (often, but not always, in response to a cursor arrow key, as covered in the next chapter), three actions are necessary:

1. Set the currently-indicated row back to the normal attributes (**popNormal()**).
2. Increment or decrement the selection indicator as appropriate.
3. Highlight the newly indicated row (**popHilite()**).

The menuing subsystem given in Listing 8.7 at the end of this chapter illustrates this algorithm.

Menu Bars

Another familiar device of professional user interfaces is the menu bar, which usually runs across the top of the window but can run across the bottom, or even somewhere in between. Many software systems use it: Framework, Paradox, Reflex, dBASE, and the pfs family of products, to name but a few. Quick C's is at the top, and like most of its kind, it names several broad categories of action which, when selected, lead to a pull-down submenu from which the user picks the specific task to be performed.

A menu bar is a much simpler visual object than a pop-up. It's simply one line on the display possessing the following properties:

- The row where it appears.
- Interval in columns between choices' first characters.
- Foreground and background colors.
- Text contents.

This leads naturally to the second descriptor structure that appears in POPUP.H:

```
typedef  struct {
   int     row,            /* row  where  bar  appears  */
           interval,       /* cols  btwn  first  chars  */
           fore, back;              /* text  colors  */
   char *choice;           /* ptr  to  text  contents  */
} MENUBAR;
```

As in the case of pop-ups, the text component of the descriptor is a pointer to an initialized string. You can preserve memory space by packing this string with a byte indicating where it is to be broken and the next character written at the following interval. Any nonprinting character will do: A convenient one, used here, is the newline. Thus the string

   "File\nPrint\nData\nGraph\nOptions"

is expanded into five separate selections spread evenly across a menu bar.

The interval between selections is simple to figure. If there are n selections, the interval is 80/n on the full 80-column screen. The string above contains five selections, so their interval is 80/5 = 16 characters. If the menu bar is to appear inside a window 50 characters wide, then the interval is 50/5 = 10 characters.

A complete menu bar specification, then, consists of a string initialization followed by a structure initialization, as in:

```
char  menutxt[]  =
          "File\nPrint\nData\nGraph\nOptions";

MENUBAR bar  =  {0, 16, BLACK, GREEN, menutxt};
```

This specifies a menu bar containing the selections in menutxt[], with the bar located in row 0, interval between selections' first characters of 16 columns, and black-on-green. Convert the specification into a visual object by passing its pointer to the POPUP library's menubar() function.

The only tricky part of menubar() occurs in the loop that copies the text to the screen. The p index keeps track of the source location, while the c variable gives the current selection (0, 1, 2, etc.). Whenever a newline is encountered in the source string, c is incremented and multiplied by the interval to give the new column where output resumes. Thus the routine expands the source string to fill the bar with proper spacing between selections.

Menu Bars and Pull-down Menus: A Skeleton Program

We now have nearly all the software mechanisms in place to develop a sophisticated program driven by a menu bar and pull-down menus. The only things lacking are "pointing" refinements via the keyboard, which we'll cover in the next chapter.

PULLDOWN.C in Listing 8.7 is a skeleton containing a complete menu-driven program relying on the pop-up management routines developed here. The program displays a menu bar containing five selections. When you type the first letter of any selection, an associated pull-down appears with the first choice highlighted. You can step through the choices by pressing the space bar. To leave the pull-down, press the Esc key, and to select an item, press Enter.

PULLDOWN doesn't do any useful work beyond providing a working user interface. It's up to you to customize it and flesh it out, chiefly in the actOn() function, which we'll discuss later. One selection does work, however, and that's the Quit choice in the File menu. To stop the program, type F, then space down to Quit and press Enter.

The first major step in defining a system of menus is to initialize structures and their related strings. Doing so outside the scope of any function including main() makes these objects visible to all ensuing functions in the compile unit. A sensible way is to define, one by one at the top of the primary file, the text components followed by their related descriptors. That's what the OBJECTS DEFINITION portion of Listing 8.7 does.

The main() function has three phases. The first sets up the basic screen and, for purposes of demonstrating how the removal of a pull-down restores the underlying text, writes some text just below the menu bar. Notice that the screen preparation phase tailors the menu bar to the display adapter type. By checking the monitor field in the videoconfig structure loaded by a call the _ getvideoconfig(), the program determines if the display is monochrome. If so, the program changes the menu bar color scheme so that the bar will show up as a lighted band with dark characters.

The last phase of main() simply cleans up by restoring the screen to its default state. Most of the real work occurs in the middle phase.

This loop drives the menu bar selections. It waits for the user to press a key, then uses the keystroke value to set an index to the appropriate pulldown menu. If a valid selection, the loop calls a routine to displays the menu and process the user's request. This function, doMenu(), returns TRUE if the loop is to reiterate and FALSE if the user has decided to stop (File menu, Quit selection).

The doMenu function changes the status line at the bottom of the display to reflect appropriate instructions, then displays the pull-down. There are three possible actions (which will be expanded in the next two chapters to include others). These are:

- The space bar moves the highlight to the next choice in the pull-down.
- The Esc key abandons the pull-down and reverts to the initial (menu bar only) display.

- The Enter key executes the pull-down choice.

The switch() in doMenu() processes these keyboard entries, with the case clauses setting control variables as appropriate to continue the local and main() loops. Note that the CR case either halts all loops (user pressed Enter when Quit is chosen from the File menu) or passes control to another function called actOn().

The actOn() function is what you must flesh out if you adapt this user interface to your own application. As written here, it merely displays which choice the user has made. Normally this function would act as a dispatcher via nested switch() statements, as in:

```
switch (pick) {
  case 0:
    switch (indic) {
      case 0: getFile(); break;
      case 1: saveFile (); break;
      case 2: combFiles(); break;
      case 3: backup(); break;
    }
    break;
  case 1:
    switch (indic) {
      case 0: prtReport(); break;
      case 1: prtGraph(); break;
      case 2: prtNewPage(); break;
    }
    break;
  case. . . etc.
```

The libraries developed here make PULLDOWN surprisingly compact, considering that it's a complete user interface. The tools presented in these chapters enable us to confine it to less than 160 lines of code.

Listing 8.7 **A complete menuing skeleton.**

```
/* PULLDOWN.C: Skeleton of menu bar with pull-down menus */

/* INCLUDES */
#include <graph.h>
#include <stdio.h>
#include <dos.h>
#include <conio.h>
#include <ctype.h>
#include "textscrn.h"
#include "popup.h"

/* DEFINES */
#if !defined TRUE
```

```
#define   FALSE  0
#define   TRUE   !FALSE
#endif
#define   CR     13
#define   SPC    32
#define   ESC    27
#define   NONE   99


/* OBJECT DEFINITIONS */
POPUP full = {1, 1, 25, 80, 0, YELLOW, 0, BLACK};
POPUP action = {12, 25, 14, 55, 2, RED, 0, LTGRAY, 0};


/* Menu bar */
char  menutext [] = "File\nPrint\nData\nGraph\nOptions";
MENUBAR bar = {1, 16, WHITE, BLUE, menutext};


/* Text of pull-down menus */
char  p0text [] = "Retrieve\nSave\nCombine\nBackup\nQuit",
      p1text [] = "Report\nGraph\nNew page",
      p2text [] = "Edit\nDelete\nInsert\nBrowse",
      p3text [] = "Type\nView\nDelete\nSave",
      p4text [] = "Colors\nKeyboard\nRecalc";


POPUP pop [] = {
      {3,  2, 7,  9, 1, BLACK, BLACK, LTGRAY, GREEN, p0text},
      {3, 16, 5, 23, 1, BLACK, BLACK, LTGRAY, GREEN, p1text},
      {3, 32, 6, 37, 1, BLACK, BLACK, LTGRAY, GREEN, p2text},
      {3, 48, 6, 53, 1, BLACK, BLACK, LTGRAY, GREEN, p3text},
      {3, 64, 5, 71, 1, BLACK, BLACK, LTGRAY, GREEN, p4text}
};


/* LOCAL FUNCTIONS */
void prompt (char*, POPUP*);
int  doMenu (int, POPUP*);
void actOn (int, int);
/* ---------------------------------------------------------- */


void main ()
{
int    repeating, pick;
char   sel;
POPUP  *popup;
struct videoconfig video;


/* Prepare main screen */
  _settextcolor (YELLOW);
  _setbkcolor (BLACK);
  _clearscreen (_GCLEARSCREEN);
  _getvideoconfig (&video);
  if (video.monitor == _MONO) {      /* change colors for mono */
    bar.fore = BLACK;
    bar.back = LTGRAY;
  }
```

Listing 8.7 *(continued)*

```
      menubar (&bar);                                    /* display menu bar */
      _settextposition (4, 1);
      _outtext ("Three of the pull-down menus overlay this text");

/* Loop to drive menu bar selections */
      do {
        repeating = TRUE;                                   /* set switch */
        prompt ("Pick menu selection by letter", &full);
        sel = getch();                                     /* get selection */
        switch (toupper (sel)) {
          case 'F': pick = 0; break;
          case 'P': pick = 1; break;
          case 'D': pick = 2; break;
          case 'G': pick = 3; break;
          case 'O': pick = 4; break;
          default:  pick = NONE; break;
        }
        if (pick < NONE) {
          popup = &(pop [pick]);                        /* select pulldown */
          repeating = doMenu (pick, popup);              /* display it */
        }
      } while (repeating);

/* Clean up at end of job */
      _settextcolor (LTGRAY);
      _setbkcolor (BLACK);
      _clearscreen (_GCLEARSCREEN);
} /* ----------------------- */

void prompt (char *message, POPUP *current)

                   /* Display a prompt message at bottom of screen */
{
  popKeep (current);                            /* save current state */
  popUse (&full);                               /* use full screen */
  _settextposition (24, 1);                     /* go to prompt line */
  _cleareol();                                  /* and clear it */
  popCenter (&full, 24, message);               /* display prompt */
  popUse (current);                       /* return to calling popup */
} /* ----------------------- */

int doMenu (int pick, POPUP *menu)

                     /* Display pull-down menu, get selection */
{
int  indic = 1, keepOn = TRUE, looping = TRUE, last;

  _savescrn (0);                                   /* save the display */
  prompt ("Space to advance, Enter to select, ESC to quit", menu);
  popShow (menu);                           /* display the pulldown */
  popHilite (menu, indic);                  /* highlight first choice */
```

```
      last = menu->bottom - menu->top + 1;          /* last menu row */
      do {
        switch (getch ()) {
          case SPC:                                       /* advance */
            popNormal (menu, indic);            /* reset to normal */
            if (++indic > last)
              indic = 1;                             /* wrap to top */
            popHilite (menu, indic);              /* hilite next */
            break;
          case ESC:                                          /* quit */
            looping = FALSE;
            break;
          case CR:                                         /* select */
            if ((pick == 0) && (indic == 5))
              keepOn = FALSE;                  /* if picked "Quit" */
            else
              actOn (pick, indic);               /* act on choice */
            looping = FALSE;
            break;
        }
      } while (looping);
      if (!looping)
        _restscrn (0);                   /* erase menu when done with it */
      return (keepOn);
    } /* ------------------------ */

void actOn (int barchoice, int menuchoice)

                 /* stub of dispatcher for acting on menu choice */
{
char  report [30], key;

  _savescrn (0);                                    /* save screen */
  sprintf (report, "You selected menu %d, item %d",
           barchoice, menuchoice);
  popShow (&action);
  popCenter (&action, 2, report);
  prompt ("Press any key to continue...", &action);
  getch();
  _restscrn (0);                            /* restore after keypress */
} /* ------------------------ */
```

Of course there are other approaches to menus; this is just one. Expand the capabilities of the routines given here as your needs dictate. The next chapter will help you do that.

CHAPTER 9

Keyboard Virtuoso

Just as the display is the most important output device of a personal computer, so is the keyboard the most important input device. It's not merely a means for entering data, but also the primary device—indeed, the *only* device in most cases—by which a user controls the system. For that reason, mastery of the keyboard is essential to successful software.

The C language in general makes it easy to take the keyboard for granted, and Quick C is no different. It provides character-at-a-time input functions such as **getch()** (get a character without echo) and **getche()** (same but echo to the display), as well as string-input functions such as **gets()** and **scanf()**, which take advantage of DOS's input editing operations.

The problem with the standard C functions is that they don't accommodate the peculiarities of the PC-style keyboard: There are no standard functions, for example, to obtain a cursor-control key, a function key, or others such as PgUp, Home, End, and so on.

Consequently, this chapter concentrates chiefly on the things that *don't* come built into Quick C.

Of ASCII and Codes

Since you've been programming for a while, you probably don't need another description of what ASCII is all about. If you do, refer to any of the numerous works for beginning programmers. Here we'll discuss its extensions on PCs.

Formally, ASCII defines only 128 unique characters in the numeric range 0–127. Because an eight-bit byte can represent 256 possible values, the IBM PC and related machines furnish an extended character set that utilizes the upper range of 128 values by turning on the high-order bit. These "extended ASCII" values furnish the box-drawing characters discussed in Chapter 7, plus mathematical symbols, foreign-language characters, and other things unavailable in standard ASCII. This book gives some of them; the rest you can get from IBM Technical References, language manuals, and, often, word processing product documentation.

To display one of these extended ASCII characters from Quick C, all you need is the numeric code. For example, if you want to display the Greek letter omega, write

```
putchar (234);
```

You can also place it into a text string with sprintf():

```
sprintf (string, "The omega symbol is %c", 234);
```

Unfortunately, those who designed the PC forgot to make it so easy to capture these special symbols from the keyboard. There is no keystroke or key combination that produces the omega character, a double-scored northwest box corner, or the summation symbol. That doesn't mean it can't be done, but only that it's a little more difficult than displaying these characters. We'll cover this later in the chapter.

The PC also has a special set of keyboard codes that relate to the nonprinting control keys: notably the function keys F1–F10 (F1–F12 on newer keyboards), any Alt-key combination, and the cursor control keys. They all generate two-byte character sequences in which the first is a null (ASCII 0) followed by a value corresponding to the depressed key. For example, the two-byte sequence 00h, 4Dh (in decimal, 0 followed by 77) indicates that the cursor-right key has been pressed.

In the case of these keys, an ASCII zero indicates that the receiving software must fetch the next character to determine which nonprinting key has been operated, as discussed next.

The Keyboard Buffer

Chapter 6 defined the ROM BIOS data area, part of which contains the keyboard buffer. This is a 15-byte circular buffer that stores ASCII values coming from the keyboard. How it works isn't germane to our discussion here; if you want details, see Robert Jourdain's *Programmer's Problem Solver*, (Brady Books, New York, 1986) pages 92–93.

What you do need to know is that Quick C calls the DOS keyboard routines, which in turn call the ROM BIOS interrupt 16h functions to fetch successive values from the keyboard buffer. When the user presses one of the nonprinting control keys, *two* values go into the keyboard buffer: a null followed by the key's value.

Therefore, when your program fetches a null from the keyboard, it should get the next value with getch() and act on it not as a normal ASCII code, but as a special case. The next section shows how.

Handling the Nonprinting Control Keys

There's a startling number of nonprinting keys. For example, any Alt-letter combination generates a valid two-byte sequence that you can associate with a unique software function. Jourdain covers them all on page 136 of his book. Here we'll concentrate on the major ones, for which Table 9.1 lists the second-byte values.

Table 9.1 **Values of the major nonprinting keys.**

Value	Keystroke
Lead-in byte is 0, followed by:	
16–25	Alt-Q through Alt-P (top row of letters)
30–38	Alt-A through Alt-L (middle row)
44–50	Alt-Z through Alt-M (bottom row)
59–68	F1 through F10
71	Home (keypad 7)
72	Cursor up (keypad 8)
73	PgUp (keypad 9)
75	Cursor left (keypad 4)
77	Cursor right (keypad 6)
79	End (keypad 1)
80	Cursor down (keypad 2)
81	PgDn (keypad 3)
84–93	Shift + F1–F10
94–103	Ctrl + F1–F10
104–113	Alt + F1–F10

Say you've declared ch as a character variable. You can handle the special keys with a test such as

```
if ((ch = getch()) != 0) {
    . . .                /* handle char normally */
} else
    specKey ();  /* process special key */
```

The specKey() routine can then fetch the next character and act on it as appropriate, as in

```
keyVal = getch();  /* get second byte */
switch (keyVal) {
    case 59: help(); break;     /* F1 key */
    case 60: edit(); break;     /* F2 key */
    . . .                        /*   etc.  */
}
```

Let's translate this discussion into a working program that reports which key has been operated.

Keyboard Sampler

Listing 9.1 is a program that processes both ordinary keystrokes and extended keys. The **setUpScreen()** function creates a "pretty" display with operating instructions in the upper box and a large text work area in the lower.

The main loop captures keystrokes. If the user presses a normal (one-byte) key, the program displays the generated character. It branches to a subprogram on detecting the ASCII null signifying an extended key. There it uses **getch()** to fetch the second byte from the keyboard buffer. A **switch()** statement identifies the main extended keys: F1–F10 and those of the keypad. An unspecified keystroke such as Ctrl-Fn generates the message "Other ext code." The program terminates on Alt-X.

Note that the program produces output in column format within the work area. The variables **row**, **col**, and **c** manage the output using **gotoxy()**. When the program runs out of screen space—i.e., the next item would be beyond the right side of the display—it quits automatically.

Note also the compound statement

```
if  (++row  >  17)
    row  =  TOP, c  += 16;
```

The second line is not an error, but a valid C construction. Multiple statements separated by commas count as a single statement. This construction allows you to resolve two or more independent expressions controlled by the if(), but without using curly braces to isolate the block.

Listing 9.1 **Keyboard sampler.**

```
/* KEYS.C: Captures and displays keypresses */

#include <stdio.h>
#include <conio.h>
#include <dos.h>
#include <graph.h>
#include "textscrn.h"

#ifndef TRUE
#define FALSE 0
#define TRUE  !FALSE
#endif

/* Local functions */
void setUpScreen (void);
int  extended (void);

main ()
{
char   key;
```

Listing 9.1 *(continued)*

```
int    row = 1, col, repeating, c = 2;

  setUpScreen ();                               /* create work screen */

/* Loop to process keypresses */
  do {
    col = c;
    _settextposition (row, col);                    /* place cursor */
    key = getch();                              /* get next keypress */
    if (key == 0)                                    /* if null char */
      repeating = extended ();              /* handle extended code */
    else
      if (key == ' ')
        _outtext ("Space");
      else
        if (key == 27)
          _outtext ("Esc");
        else
          _outch (key);                         /* else show char */
    if (++row > 17)
      row = 1, c += 16;
    if (c > 78) repeating = 0;               /* quit if screen full */
  } while (repeating);

/* End of run */
  _setbordwindow (1, 1, 25, 80, 0, LTGRAY, BLACK);
  _displaycursor (_GCURSORON);
} /* ----------------------- */

void setUpScreen (void)
      /* Build display */
{
  /* Set up instruction box */
  _displaycursor (_GCURSOROFF);                  /* turn off cursor */
  _setbordwindow (1, 1, 5, 80, 2, WHITE, BLUE);
  _settextposition (2, 32);                   /* print instructions */
  _outtext ("Keyboard Sampler");
  _settextposition (3, 16);
  _outtext ("Press any key and the program reports what it is");
  _settextposition (4, 32);
  __outtext ("Quit with Alt-X");

  /* Construct program workarea */
  _setbordwindow (7, 2, 23, 79, 1, WHITE, BLACK);
} /* ----------------------- */

int  extended (void)                       /* process extended codes */
{
char   ext;
int    keepOn = TRUE;                            /* TRUE is default */
```

```
      ext = getch();                              /* get second byte */
      switch (ext) {
        case 45: keepOn = 0; break;               /* Alt-X for quit */
        case 59: _outtext ("F1"); break;
        case 60: _outtext ("F2"); break;
        case 61: _outtext ("F3"); break;
        case 62: _outtext ("F4"); break;
        case 63: _outtext ("F5"); break;
        case 64: _outtext ("F6"); break;
        case 65: _outtext ("F7"); break;
        case 66: _outtext ("F8"); break;
        case 67: _outtext ("F9"); break;
        case 68: _outtext ("F10"); break;
        case 71: _outtext ("Home"); break;
        case 72: _outtext ("Cursor up"); break;
        case 73: _outtext ("PgUp"); break;
        case 75: _outtext ("Cursor left"); break;
        case 77: _outtext ("Cursor right"); break;
        case 79: _outtext ("End"); break;
        case 80: _outtext ("Cursor down"); break;
        case 81: _outtext ("PgDn"); break;
        case 82: _outtext ("Ins"); break;
        case 83: _outtext ("Del"); break;
        default: _outtext ("Other ext key");
      }
      return keepOn;
    }
```

Controlling Menu Selections with Cursor Keys

Now that we've seen how to capture and interpret the cursor control keys, we can improve on the menu-handling discussed in the last chapter. Instead of using the space key to advance the highlight bar, we can use the cursor keys to move it up and down and select a choice.

Suppose you have the following menu on the display:

Accounts payable
Receivables
Payroll & Personnel
General ledger
Quit

The usual ground rules for such menus are:

- Pick an entry by typing its unique first letter, or;
- Use the cursor keys to move the highlight to the desired item, then press Enter to select it.

Thus, if the highlight is over Receivables and you want to quit, you can either type **Q** or use any of the cursor keys to move to the **Quit** entry and press Enter. The up or left cursor keys move the highlight up, down or right move it down. The lighted bar wraps to the opposite end of the menu when it reaches an extreme. Furthermore, in accordance with usual practice, the F1 key summons help.

You can handle these conditions with a loop that waits for a keypress, then decides what to do with it using a **switch()** statement. The A, R, G, and P keys dispatch the appropriate task, while Q sets a TRUE/FALSE variable to FALSE, thus signalling the loop to terminate and end the program. Operation of the Enter key selects the currently indicated task for execution or, if the lighted bar is over **Quit**, has the same effect as pressing Q.

Any cursor control or function key generates a two-byte sequence in which the first is ASCII null, also handled by a case in the **switch()** statement. However, in this event, the program must fetch the second byte and then act on it with a nested **switch()**. In the case of F1, it dispatches the help task. The cursor keys are handled by multiple cases, in which up and left are identical and have the same entry point, and down and right have a different common case.

Both switches ignore extraneous keystrokes. For example, J has no effect, nor do Ins and F3. This is accomplished by omitting the default case from the **switch()** constructs.

The **process()** function in Listing 9.2 implements these ideas. If the indicator is not on menu row 6 (**Quit**), the **run()** function is called and otherwise the looping variable is set to FALSE, which signals the function to stop and return. The looping variable also changes to FALSE if the user actually presses Q, and the indicated job runs for any other valid letter entered.

At the start of the loop in **process()**, the current selection is highlighted only for as long as the program is waiting for a keystroke, and then it reverts to normal. Why? Because the user will likely press one of the initials (A, R, P, or G) to select a task, regardless of where the bar is. It wouldn't do to have the program run Payroll while **A/P** is still highlighted. Thus, **process()** turns off the highlight as soon as it receives a keystroke.

Because this is a skeleton program, the **run()** function only simulates the execution of a task by flashing up a pop-up showing the task (indicator) number and pausing to wait for a keystroke. In reality, you'd probably dispatch different tasks as appropriate from the outer **switch()** in the **process()** function. Each task under this scheme should be a function that performs the following steps:

1. Save the current display.
2. Run the task itself.

3. Restore the display.

4. Return.

Listing 9.2 is the program APPMENU.C, which simulates a hypothetical business application and furnishes a skeleton that you can flesh out to suit your needs.

Listing 9.2 **A full-featured menuing program.**

```
/* APPMENU.C: Menuing skeleton for a hypothetical appli-  */
/*    cation, showing cursor control in menu selection     */
/* ------------------------------------------------------- */

/* INCLUDES */
#include <stdio.h>
#include <dos.h>
#include <conio.h>
#include "textscrn.h"
#include "popup.h"

/* DEFINES */
#define   CR      13
#define   F1      59
#define   UP      72
#define   LEFT    75
#define   RITE    77
#define   DOWN    80
#ifndef   TRUE
#define   FALSE   0
#define   TRUE    !FALSE
#endif

/* LOCAL FUNCTIONS */
void    process (POPUP*);
void    run (int);
void    help (void);

/* MENU TEXT DEFINITION */
char menutext[]=
"  ** MAIN MENU **\n Accounts payable\n Receivables\n\
 Payroll & Personnel\n General ledger\n Quit";

/* POP-UP DEFINITIONS */
POPUP menu  = { 4, 31, 9, 50, 2, BLACK, RED,
                 CYAN, BLACK, menutext};
POPUP jobid = {17, 31, 21, 47, 1, RED, 0, GREEN, 0};
POPUP helps = { 7, 34, 13, 76, 1, LTGRAY, 0, MAGENTA, 0};
/* -------------------------- */

main ()
{
  /* Set up base screen */
```

Listing 9.2 *(continued)*

```
  _savescrn (0);
  _setbordwindow (1, 1, 25, 80, 0, YELLOW, BLACK);
  _settextposition (1, 27);
  _outtext ("The Empire Corporation, Inc.");

  /* Run the program */
  popShow (&menu);                              /* display menu */
  process (&menu);                              /* process choices */
  _restscrn (0);                               /* Clean up and quit */
} /* ----------------------- */

void process (POPUP *menu)    /* Process main menu choices */
{
int  indic = 2, looping = TRUE;
char key;

  do {
    popHilite (menu, indic);       /* hilite indic selection */
    key = getch ();                           /* get a keystroke */
    popNormal (menu, indic);             /* un-hilite selection */
    switch (toupper (key)) {              /* act on keystroke */

      /* If an alpha selection */
      case 'A': run (1); indic = 2; break;
      case 'R': run (2); indic = 3; break;
      case 'P': run (3); indic = 4; break;
      case 'G': run (4); indic = 5; break;
      case 'Q': looping = FALSE; break;

      /* If user hit Enter on current selection */
      case CR : if (indic != 6)
                    run (indic-1);          /* run indic task */
                else
                    looping = FALSE;              /* or quit */
                break;

      /* If user hit a function or cursor key */
      case 0  : key = getch ();          /* get second byte */
                switch (key) {                /* act on it */
                  case F1  : help (); break;
                  case UP:
                  case LEFT: if (--indic == 1)
                                 indic = 6;     /* wrap down */
                             popHilite (menu, indic);
                             break;
                  case DOWN:
                  case RITE: popNormal (menu, indic);
                             if (++indic == 7)
                                 indic = 2;     /* wrap up */
                             popHilite (menu, indic);
                             break;
```

```
                    }                              /* end of nested switch */
        }                                          /* end of outer switch */
    } while (looping);
}  /* ----------------------- */

void run (int job) /* Simulate running the menu selection */
{
char mssg [20], key;

    _savescrn (0);                                    /* save screen */
    popShow (&jobid);                       /* pop up job ident window */
    sprintf (mssg, "Running job %d", job);
    popCenter (&jobid, 2, mssg);           /* identify job number */
    popCenter (&jobid, 4, "Press any key...");
    key = getch();                            /* wait for keypress */
    if (key == 0) getch();                  /* ignore extended key */
    _restscrn (0);                             /* delete pop-up */
}  /* ----------------------- */

void help (void)       /* Pop up help panel if F1 is pressed */
{
char mssg [40], key;

    _savescrn (0);                                    /* save screen */
    popShow (&helps);
    popCenter (&helps, 1, "** H E L P **");
    popCenter (&helps, 3, "Select by typing first letter, or");
    sprintf (mssg, "Move up with %c or %c, down with %c or %c,",
             24, 27, 25, 26);
    popCenter (&helps, 4, mssg);
    sprintf (mssg, "then press %c%c", 17, 217);
    popCenter (&helps, 5, mssg);
    popCenter (&helps, 7, "Press any key to resume . . .");
    key = getch ();                           /* wait for keypress */
    if (key == 0) getch();                  /* ignore extended key */
    _restscrn (0);                             /* restore screen */
}  /* ----------------------- */
```

Reassigning Keys

One of the design shortcomings in PCs is the inaccessibility of the extended ASCII characters from the keyboard. The only way to display characters with values above 7Fh (127 decimal) is to generate them within software; there is no keystroke to generate, for example, the Greek letter pi, which is E3h (227 decimal), nor are there keystrokes for the foreign-language symbols (most of those are in 80h through ADh). Thus, it's necessary for software to trap key-strokes and reassign values to them.

A simple way is through direct replacement. Say, for example, that you want to give the user the ability to type the pi symbol. The backwards apos-trophe (French accent grave, written "`") is a character of very limited usefulness to most applications, yet it's available directly from the keyboard and thus a good candidate for reassignment.

Your keyboard handler can simply look for this ASCII value (60h) and replace it with the ASCII value for pi (E3h):

```
if ((ch = getch())  = = 0x60)
  putchar (0xE3);     /* replace with pi */
else
  putchar (ch);       /* treat normally */
```

A simple if() is fine for a single keystroke reassignment, but it won't do for multiple substitutions, especially when Alt-key combinations are a factor. Let's say you want to write software that accepts and faithfully replays the French language. Here are the key reassignments:

Keystroke	Produces
Alt-A (0 + 30)	a-grave (), 85h
Ctrl-E (5)	e-acute (), 82h
Alt-E (0 + 18)	e-grave (), 8Ah
Alt-C (0 + 46)	cedille (), 87h

Note that three of the keystrokes produce a null lead-in, while one does not. This complicates reassignment.

A way to overcome the problem is to process keystrokes with a switch() inside a function that returns the "final" value after substitutions. The returned value is displayed, emulating echo of keyboard entries. That's what the keystroke() function does in the FRENCH.C program shown in Listing 9.3.

Listing 9.3 **Keyboard reassignment.**

```
/* FRENCH.C: Illustrates keyboard reassignment to produce */
/*    text typed in French. Replacements are:              */
/*          Alt-A     a-grave                               */
/*          Ctrl-E    e-acute                               */
/*          Alt-E     e-grave                               */
/*          Alt-C     cedille                               */
/* ------------------------------------------------------- */

#include <stdio.h>
#include <conio.h>

#define    A_GRAVE    0x85
#define    E_ACUTE    0x82
#define    E_GRAVE    0x8A
#define    CEDILLE    0x87
#define    CR         0x0D

char  keystroke (void);                         /* prototype */

main ()
```

```
{
char    ch, input [80];
int     p = 0;

  puts ("\nEDITEUR FRANCAIS:\n");
  puts ("\nEcrivez une ligne");               /* ask for a line */

  do {                                   /* get a line of input */
    if (kbhit) {                            /* wait for keypress */
      ch = keystroke ();        /* get it after substutution */
      if (ch != NULL) {               /* ignore unknown key */
        putchar (ch);                       /* echo to display */
        input [p++] = ch != CR ? ch : NULL;     /* save it */
      }
    }
  } while (ch != CR);

  puts ("\n\nVOUS AVEZ ECRIT LA LIGNE SUIVANTE:");
  puts (input);                    /* repeat what was typed */
} /* ------------------------ */
char   keystroke (void)     /* substitute keystrokes as reqd */
{
char    key;

  key = getch();                     /* get ASCII for keypress */
  switch (key) {
    case 5: key = E_ACUTE; break;                    /* Ctrl-E */
    case 0: key = getch();          /* get second key on Alt */
            switch (key) {
              case 30: key = A_GRAVE; break;        /* Alt-A */
              case 18: key = E_GRAVE; break;        /* Alt-E */
              case 46: key = CEDILLE; break;        /* Alt-C */
              default: key = NULL;          /* unknown key */
            } /* end of nested switch */
  } /* end of outer switch */
  return (key);
}
```

The program first identifies itself as "EDITEUR FRANCAIS" (a French-language editor), and asks you to "Ecrivez une ligne" (type a line of text). To see it in action, type the line

   Je suis élève de la langue française

meaning "I'm a student of the French language." Type the appropriate key combinations to produce the special French characters. The program echoes your keystrokes, making the necessary substutitions. When you press Enter, the program reports that "VOUS AVEZ ECRIT" (you have written) followed by the line of input. This full-line echo shows that the substitutions—and not the keystrokes—were stored in the input[] string.

   A word about the kbhit() macro in the main() function's input loop: This macro, which is defined in CONIO.H, waits for a keypress. It does not actually fetch the keystroke from the keyboard buffer. Rather, it puts the program in a tight loop until you press a key, and then it allows execution to resume. That's why the first thing **keystroke()** does is to call **getch()**; the ASCII value is still in the buffer. The rest of the program's operation should be clear, based on the discussion earlier in this chapter.

This concludes our discussion of text-oriented user interfaces. These chapters have covered a number of useful techniques that stretch the capabilities already built into Quick C, incorporating them into the **TEXTSCRN** and **POPUP** libraries. Using these tools, you can quickly write your own professional, intuitive user interfaces.

A final recommendation before we move on is to combine the two .OBJ files into a linkable library. You might choose to call it **TEXT.LIB**, in which case the DOS command is

```
LIB  TEXT  + TEXTSCRN + POPUP;
```

Having done that, you can link any program that uses the routines with the TEXT library (plus any Quick C libraries you need).

Now let's investigate another aspect of user interfaces: computer graphics.

PART III

Computer Graphics in Quick C

Quick C 2.0 comes with an extensive set of tools for creating interesting and useful visual effects on computers equipped with more than the minimal Monochrome Display Adapter (MDA), which is suitable only for text displays. This graphics library, while not entirely device-independent, fits itself with a remarkable degree of flexibility to a variety of graphics subsystems ranging from the early IBM Color Graphics Adapter (CGA) up through the recent, and highly versatile, Virtual Graphics Adapter, or VGA. It also handles such non-IBM standards as the Hercules board.

The Quick C manuals describe the numerous graphics library functions in detail. You can obtain an excellent quick reference to these functions and constants by listing the GRAPH.H file that comes with Quick C. This is almost indispensible, in fact, when doing graphics programming.

With good documentation already in existence, it would be a waste of time and paper to describe the library again in this book. Instead, what is needed are concrete examples that show how to put the library to work in practical applications, as well as a discussion of computer graphics issues that digs deeper than the product documentation. That is what we will cover in the next several chapters.

We should point out, however, that like so many other programming topics, graphics is an entire arena of computer science, and there are numerous subjects that we won't cover here. Our aim is to lay a reasonably solid foundation for creating practical graphics.

CHAPTER 10

Graphics 101

It's necessary for a Quick C program to find out about its environment before it can intelligently produce graphics. In Chapter 6 we explored the ROM BIOS data area, which contains low-level information about the machine. Later we used the Quick C function _getvideoconfig() to determine things about the text display. Between the two, our programs can also learn a great deal about the graphics configuration.

The Quick C 2.0 data structure videoconfig, loaded by _getvideoconfig(), contains a number of useful fields. Some are relevant only to text modes, others only to graphics. If you're upgrading from Quick C 1.0, you should know that this structure is greatly expanded in the newer version. Here's its definition from GRAPH.H:

```
struct  videoconfig {
        short numxpixels;           /* number of pixels on X axis */
        short numypixels;           /* number of pixels on Y axis */
        short numtextcols;          /* number of text columns available */
        short numtextrows;          /* number of text rows available */
        short numcolors;            /* number of actual colors */
        short bitsperpixel;         /* number of bits per pixel */
        short numvideopages;        /* number of available video pages */
        short mode;                 /* current video mode */
        short adapter;              /* active display adapter */
        short monitor;              /* active display monitor */
        short memory;               /* adapter video memory in K bytes */
};
```

Information not available here can often be found in the ROM BIOS data area, or inferred from knowledge of the video system's characteristics.

An example of inferred information is the location of the video display buffer, which we discussed in Chapter 7. The buffer changes location depending on the display mode and adapter type. Table 10.1 lists the common adapters and the memory segment of the display buffer.

Table 10.1 **Locations of video display buffers.**

	Text	Graphics
Monochrome	B000h	N/A
Hercules (HGC)	B000h	B000h#
CGA	B800h	B800h
MCGA	B800h*	A000h#
EGA	B800h*	A000h#
VGA	B800h*	A000h#

* B000h when operating with monochrome monitor
\# B800h when in CGA emulation mode

It's nice to know the location of the video buffer, but unnecessary in order to use the Quick C graphics library. What you do need to know is the various graphics modes supported by different adapters. This information allows your program to select a mode suited to the hardware capabilities.

The monochrome adapter (MDA) doesn't support graphics modes at all. Consequently it's excluded from Table 10.2, which shows modes available on the common video adapters. GRAPH.H defines constant names for these and other modes.

Table 10.2 **Graphics modes supported by common adapters.**

	HGC	CGA	MCGA	EGA	VGA
320 x 200, 4 colors	X	X	X	X	X
320 x 200, 4 gray scales	X	X	X	X	X
640 x 200, B&W	X	X	X	X	X
720 x 348, B&W	X				
320 x 200, 16 colors			X	X	X
640 x 200, 16 colors			X	X	X
640 x 350, 16 colors				X	X
640 x 480, B&W					X
640 x 480, 16 colors					X
320 x 200, 256 colors			X		X

Note that the EGA and VGA support most of the modes furnished by earlier adapters such as the CGA. The color mode common to all is CGA 320 x 200 4-color. It's tempting to avoid the complexities of programming for multiple adapters and all their differences by opting to make all graphics programs operate in this mode. In many of the example programs given here, that's exactly what we'll do. But the purpose of example programs is to show how something works, with a minimum of clutter to obscure the point. If you opt in your programs for the lowest common denominator, you'll lose most of the advantages of better display technologies. The CGA modes aren't very good. Later in this chapter, we'll discuss virtual coordinates, which ease the burden of programming for multiple display adapters and thus allow you to more easily take advantage of higher resolution.

Meanwhile, Listing 10.1 lists the program VIDEO.C, which reports important information about the computer's video hardware. It's not only a useful
utility, but it also shows how to detect facts about the video configuration.

Listing 10.1 **Detecting and reporting video information.**

```
/* VIDEO.C: Displays information about video configuration      */
/*          Common IBM PC devices only                          */

#include <stdio.h>
#include <graph.h>
#include "mk_fp.h"
#include "biosarea.h"
#if !defined TRUE
#define FALSE 0
#define TRUE  !FALSE
#endif

main ()
{
BIOSDATA far *bios = MK_FP (0x40, 0);
struct videoconfig text, grafix;
short best;

  /* Get text and general video information */
  _getvideoconfig (&text);

  /* Get info about best graphics mode available */
  if (text.adapter != _MDPA) {
    switch (text.adapter & 0x2F) {
      case _CGA  : best = _MRES4COLOR;   break;
      case _EGA  : best = _ERESCOLOR;    break;
      case _VGA  : best = _VRES16COLOR;  break;
      case _MCGA : best = _MRES256COLOR; break;
      case _HGC  : best = _HERCMONO;     break;
    }
    _setvideomode (best);              /* go to best graphics mode */
    _getvideoconfig (&grafix);                        /* get info */
    _setvideomode (_DEFAULTMODE);           /* return to text mode */
  }

  /* Report video information */
  puts ("Video configuration information:");
  printf ("  General: Adapter type          %02X",
          text.adapter);
  switch (text.adapter & 0x2F) {
    case _MDPA : puts ("(_MDPA)"); break;
    case _CGA  : puts ("(_CGA)");  break;
    case _EGA  : puts ("(_EGA)");  break;
    case _VGA  : puts ("(_VGA)");  break;
    case _MCGA : puts ("(_MCGA)"); break;
    case _HGC  : puts ("(_HGC)");  break;
    default    : puts ("(Other)"); break;
  }
```

Listing 10.1 *(continued)*

```
   printf ("                    Monitor type              %02X ",
           text.monitor);
   switch (text.monitor) {
     case 0x0001: puts ("(_MONO)");           break;
     case 0x0002: puts ("(_COLOR)");          break;
     case 0x0004: puts ("(_ENHCOLOR)");       break;
     case 0x0008: puts ("(_ANALOGMONO)");     break;
     case 0x0010: puts ("(_ANALOGCOLOR)");    break;
     case 0x0018: puts ("(_ANALOG)");         break;
     default:     puts ("(Other)");           break;
   }
   printf ("             Video memory size     %3d Kbytes\n",
              text.memory);
   printf ("             Video hardware port   %04Xh\n\n",
           bios->activeDispPort);


   printf ("   Text:     Rows                 %3d\n",
           text.numtextrows);
   printf ("             Columns              %3d\n",
           text.numtextcols);
   printf ("             Video pages          %3d\n",
           text.numvideopages);
   printf ("             Normal video mode    %3d\n",
           text.mode);
   printf ("             Video buffer size    %4d bytes\n",
           bios->vidBuffSz);
   printf ("             Video memory segment  %4Xh\n\n");
           text.monitor == _MONO ? 0xB000 : 0xB800);


   if (text.adapter != _MDPA) {
     printf (" Graphics: Width in pixels      %3d\n",
             grafix.numxpixels);
     printf ("             Height in pixels   %3d\n",
             grafix.numypixels);
     printf ("             Bits per pixel     %3d\n",
             grafix.bitsperpixel);
     printf ("             Number of colors   %3d\n",
             grafix.numcolors);
     printf ("             Video pages        %3d\n",
             grafix.numvideopages);
     printf ("             Video buffer segment  ");
     switch (text.adapter){
       case _HGC : printf ("%Xh\n", 0xB000); break;
       case _CGA : printf ("%Xh\n", 0xB800); break;
       default   : printf ("%Xh\n", 0xA000); break;
     }
   }
}
```

Figure 10.1 **A diagonal line in computer graphics.**

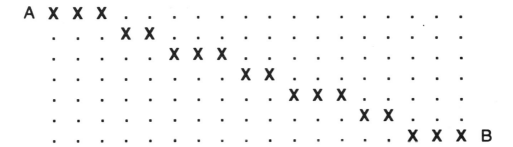

The Basis of Computer Graphics

The fundamental proposition of graphics is this: All visual objects on a computer screen are composed of small blips of light. To the machine, each one is an individual entity known in computer parlance as a *pixel*, short for *picture element*. The eye connects them together to form an image. It might be something as simple as the letter A or as complex as a multicolored topographical map of North America. No matter, the process is the same; the computer software throws little splashes of light and color on the display and leaves it to us to interpret them as "things."

The simplest "thing" is a line segment, which connects point A with point B. If the line is perfectly horizontal, the computer easily represents it with a sequence of pixels, all on the same scan row, between the two points. A perfectly vertical line is similar, except that the pixels are in the same horizontal position on successive scan rows. A diagonal line is a different matter and something of a challenge. Here the pixels occur on successive scan rows, but without the benefit of strict vertical alignment. Figure 10.1 illustrates a typical diagonal line, where an X indicates a lighted pixel and a period is one not lighted.

This pixel pattern approximates a diagonal line, but it's not smooth. That's because each pixel on the screen has a fixed position. If you squint at Figure 10.1, your eyes will perceive a reasonably smooth line, which is the best that a digital device can do. The irregularities from one row to the next are called "jaggies," and they're an unfortunate but inescapable feature of the graphics landscape.

Jaggies appear everywhere in computer graphics. Any object that is not exactly vertical or horizontal has them: circles, triangles, polygons, even the letters of text. Examine your screen closely. They're there.

Jaggies are minimized by increasing the resolution of the display, and that's the intent in advancing the technology of computer graphics. The now-obsolete CGA has jaggies in spades; everything seems to be made of stair-steps. Later adapters, such as the EGA and VGA, have more horizontal positions and more vertical scan rows within the same physical display space. More positions mean higher resolution and thus less apparent jaggies.

In its color graphics modes, the CGA has 320 pixels horizontally by 200 vertically, for a total of 64,000. The VGA presents, in the same display area, 640 x 480 pixels, or 307,200 pixels. Consequently the VGA has 4.8 times the resolution of the CGA or, stated another way, the jaggies are about 20 percent as apparent as on the CGA.

Look again at Figure 10.1. The line is composed of three pixels on one scan row, two on the next, three on the next, and so on. Figuring out how many pixels per row in order to connect point A with point B is a complex process. There are a number of algorithms for doing this. The most common is Bresenham's, which introduces minimal overhead and is used by the Quick C graphics library. Nevertheless, it's still a computationally intensive task, and for that reason graphics don't appear with the same lightning speed as text.

The Source of Graphics Images

The display screen of most computers is a cathode ray tube, or CRT, a roughly conical glass tube. The inside of the viewing surface is coated with a phosphorescent substance that glows momentarily when struck by electrons, which emanate from a group of "guns" located in a neck at the back of the tube. Under the control of some circuitry, the guns ceaselessly fire this beam in a fixed pattern that sweeps to and fro across the viewing surface.

The beam is carefully synchronized so that it sweeps across any given point on the viewing surface at regular intervals. As the beam crosses a point to be lighted—a pixel location—the guns fire; when a pixel is dark, they don't. The objective is to cross all points often enough that the phosphor remains illuminated without flickering.

The sweep speed affects screen resolution. In a CGA, for example, each cycle of the beam horizontally crosses the display 200 times. Thus, there are 200 scan rows, and hence a maximum of 200 pixels stacked vertically. Similarly, the number of times the guns can be fired during a single sweep governs the horizontal resolution.

Display technologies developed after the CGA have higher resolutions, since the controlling electronics have gotten faster, enabling the guns to sweep more times and fire more often. The electronics can also control more guns, leading to a greater number of colors on the screen at one time.

Display adapters get the information they need to control the electron guns from an on-board memory called the *video buffer*. Through either output commands or direct memory addressing, software writes to the video buffer. The adapter's circuitry then reads this memory and translates what it finds there into actions that control the firing of the guns. That, in brief, is how graphics get from your program to the display.

But how do you tell the display adapter which pixels to light, and in what colors?

Of Coordinates

For each type of display there exists an addressing scheme to identify individual pixels. Each pixel position has a row and column number, or X and Y coordinate. This is a concept borrowed from Cartesian geometry, in which the X axis expresses a horizontal position and the Y axis a vertical position. Taken together, the X and Y coordinates represent the location of any point on a plane with respect to a fixed point (the origin, where X and Y are both 0). No doubt you recall this system from high school algebra.

All graphics displays have a common origin, which is the upper left corner of the screen. X grows to the right, while Y grows downward (never mind for now that downward-increasing Y coordinates are backwards from what they taught you in school; we'll deal with this problem later). The resolution of a specific display device and the active graphics mode determine the maximum X and Y values, as Figure 10.2 shows.

In CGA four-color graphics, the maximum X is 319. Counting the origin itself, then, the width of the screen can hold 320 pixels. The maximum Y is 199, for a total of 200 pixels vertically. Any point can be represented within these two ranges: The center, for example, is at {160, 100}. On the other hand, most EGA graphics modes are 640 wide x 350 high, while the VGA can go up to 640 x 480, as shown earlier in Table 10.2.

Note that, by convention, the computer industry describes the resolution of a display in terms of "X by Y" and never "Y by X." Similarly, graphics coordinates themselves are expressed in X-then-Y order (which is opposite from Quick C's text coordinates, expressed in row-then-column [or Y-then-X] sequence).

Using Traditional Coordinates

The device coordinates of a computer screen are upside-down, since the Y value increases toward the bottom of the screen. For many drawing applica-

Figure 10.2 **Graphics coordinate systems.**

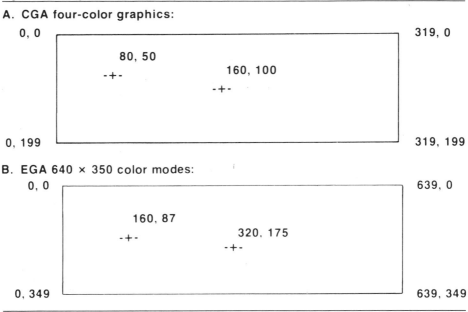

A. CGA four-color graphics:

B. EGA 640 × 350 color modes:

tions, that's not a problem. It complicates matters, though, when doing mathematical plots of the sort you learned in algebra. Fortunately, it's fairly simple to adjust coordinates.

Say you're working on a CGA, whose Y ranges from 0 at the top through 199 at the bottom (Figure 10.2A). Intuition says 0 should be at the bottom and Y should increase upward. In devising the program, you can pretend that the latter is the case, creating a conceptual screen in which the origin is at the lower left corner, as in Figure 10.3. The two inner points are now specified more naturally, so that the point physically higher has a higher Y value.

The computer, of course, doesn't know that you've flipped the Y scale, so if you start drawing without telling it, it will produce your plot upside down. All you have to do to is remap coordinates by subtracting your Y's from 199 (or whatever the maximum Y of the display mode is) as you output them.

Extending this idea a bit further, you can move the conceptual origin any place. In Figure 10.4, for example, it's in the center of the screen.

Here you can work in a coordinate system whose extremes are at the four corners of the display. To translate from your coordinates to device coordinates:

1. For X, add the physical location of the X origin. Here it's at 160. Thus the left side of the screen is at device coordinate $-160 + 160 = 0$, and

Figure 10.3 **Traditional coordinates on the CGA.**

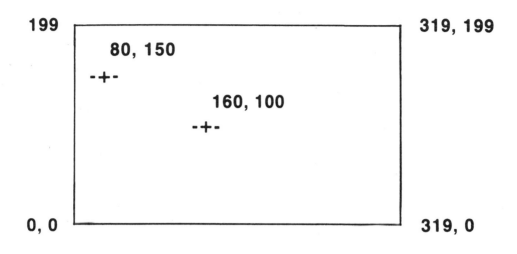

the right side is at 159 + 160 = 319. Figure 10.2A shows that this is correct.

2. For Y, add the physical location of the Y origin (100 in this case) and subtract from 199. Thus the top of the screen translates to 199 − (99 + 100) = 0, and the bottom to 199 − (−100 + 100) = 199.

Virtual Coordinates

The techniques we just covered work fine for the CGA, and you can easily adapt them to the EGA and VGA by substituting the maximum X and Y values. Often, however, you don't know which adapter your program will use, as in writing software for distribution. If you specify the lowest common denominator—320 x 200 CGA—your graphics will fill the screen, but they'll put the EGA and VGA into CGA emulation mode, which is grainy and hard on the eyes, and which doesn't take advantage of more up-to-date technology. On the other hand, graphics that use the adapter's capabilities but hardwire the coordinates to the CGA limits will look pretty silly squished into the upper left quarter or less of the screen. To make graphics that self-adjust to the display's dimensions, you can apply a technique called *virtual* (or "normalized") *coordinates*.

Virtual coordinates assume arbitrary X and Y scales independent of actual device coordinates. In establishing virtual coordinates, you say in effect, "All

Figure 10.4 **Relocating the origin on the CGA.**
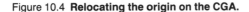

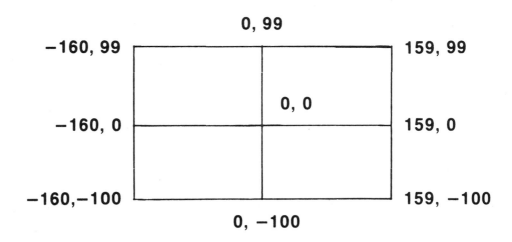

screens are n units wide by m units high." You then work within this assumed coordinate system, and translate to device coordinates at output time.

The normal screen for PCs has a height that is 75 percent of its width. Therefore, to get square squares and round circles and other correct proportions, the range of virtual Y coordinates should be 75 percent of the X range. The only common graphics standard that currently provides this ratio in physical device coordinates is the VGA's 640 x 480 mode. Even if you don't have one of these high-end adapters, you can fake "square pixels" on any display using virtual coordinates.

Set the scale to anything you want, observing the 75 percent Y rule: 400 x 300, 640 x 480, 600 x 450, etc. Your conceptual screen might be as shown in Figure 10.5. Note that Y coordinates increase upwards.

Because the object in using virtual coordinates is to overcome the differences among devices, you can't make any hard assumptions when translating to device coordinates. Instead, use the numxpixels and numypixels fields from the videoconfig structure to determine the device's physical characteristics, where:

```
maxx  =  numxpixels  -  1;
maxy  =  numypixels  -  1;
```

Figure 10.5 **A screen using virtual coordinates.**

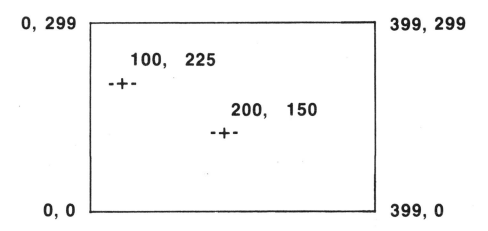

Then remap your coordinates to the display using the following algorithms (where vw and vh are thc maximum virtual X and Y, and vx and vy are the virtual coordinates to be translated).

```
1. For X:
   xf  =  (double)(maxx)/vw;  /*  x  translation  factor  */
   dx  =  (int)  (xf  *  vx);              /*  device  x  */
2. For Y:
   yf  =  (double)(maxy)/vh;    /*  y  translation  factor  */
   dy  =  (int)  (maxy-(yf  *  vy));             /*  device  y  */
```

The most sensible way to handle these calculations, which occur every time you output to the screen, is with functions. The variables **maxx**, **maxy**, xf and yf should be statics initialized outside the translation functions in order to reduce overhead.

Because many of the graphics programs in succeeding chapters (and ones you write yourself) will use virtual coordinates, let's create a **VCOORDS** library. Its two major components, header and source, are shown in Listings 10.2 and 10.3. The library furnishes an 800 x 600 virtual display area for Quick C graphics. A program later in the chapter shows how to use the library.

Listing 10.2 **Header file for virtual coordinate library.**

```
/* VCOORDS.H: Header for implementing 800 x 600 virtual
                display area in Quick C graphics */

#define VH 600                                      /* height */
#define VW 800                                      /* width  */

/* GLOBALS DEFINED IN LIBRARY, EXTERNALLY VISIBLE */
extern int    maxx, maxy;            /* max x and y coords */
extern double xf, yf;        /* x and y translation factors */

void setFactors (void);      /* compute translation factors */
int dx (int vx);             /* translate virt X to device X */
int dy (int vy);             /* translate virt Y to device Y */
```

Listing 10.3 **Library source for virtual coordinates.**

```
/* VCOORDS.C: Library for implementing virtual */
/*     coordinates in Quick C graphics          */
/* Virtual coordinate range defined by VW, VH  */
/*     in VCOORDS.H                             */

#include <graph.h>
#include "vcoords.h"

/* GLOBALS */
int    maxx, maxy;                     /* max x and y values */
double xf, yf;               /* x and y translation factors */

void setFactors (void)       /* compute translation factors */
{                            /* call after entering graphics mode */
struct videoconfig video;

  _getvideoconfig (&video);
  maxx = video.numxpixels - 1;
  maxy = video.numypixels - 1;
  xf = (double) (maxx) / VW;
  yf = (double) (maxy) / VH;
} /* ------------------------ */

int dx (int vx)                       /* map virt X to device X */
{
  return (int) (xf * vx);
} /* ------------------------ */

int dy (int vy)                       /* map virt Y to device Y */
{
  return (int) (maxy - (yf * vy));
} /* ------------------------ */
```

Listing 10.4 (GEOM.C) uses virtual coordinates to construct three simple
geometric objects. Because the program selects the appropriate video mode
for the adapter present in the system, it runs without modification on any of
the common graphics boards. And because it uses virtual coordinates, the
displayed objects are the same shapes and locations on any graphics-capable
machine; the only differences are colors and resolution. What you see is a
square standing on its corner in the left half of the screen, a rectangle in the
upper right corner, and a circle in the lower right corner, with the display
area outlined. If you have an EGA or VGA, run the program as is to see how it
looks, then change line 24 to

      _setvideomode(_MRES4COLOR);

This will force the adapter into CGA four-color mode. After recompiling,
you'll see that the output is almost identical to that of the original version.
This would be difficult to achieve without virtual coordinates.

Listing 10.4 **Using virtual coordinates.**

```
/* GEOM.C: Plots some geometric figures using            */
/*         virtual coordinates for device independence    */

/* INCLUDES */
#include <graph.h>
#include "vcoords.h"

main ()
{
short mode = -2;
struct videoconfig video;

  /* Select display mode for installed adapter */
  _getvideoconfig (&video);
  switch (video.adapter) {
    case _MCGA :
    case _CGA  : mode = _MRES4COLOR;  break;
    case _EGA  : mode = _ERESCOLOR;   break;
    case _VGA  : mode = _VRES16COLOR; break;
    case _HGC  : mode = _HERCMONO;    break;
  }

  /* Display graphics objects */
  if (_setvideomode (mode)) {
    setFactors();                     /* initialize variables */
    _setcolor (1);
    _moveto (dx   (0), dy   (0));                    /* home pen */
    _lineto (dx (799), dy   (0));           /* outline screen */
    _lineto (dx (799), dy (599));
    _lineto (dx   (0), dy (599));
    _lineto (dx   (0), dy   (0));
```

Listing 10.4 *(continued)*

```
    _setcolor (2);          /* rectangle, upper right corner */
    _rectangle (_GBORDER, dx (600), dy (550),
                          dx (760), dy (300));

    _setcolor (3);              /* tilted square, left half */
    _moveto (dx (100), dy (300));
    _lineto (dx (300), dy (500));
    _lineto (dx (500), dy (300));
    _lineto (dx (300), dy (100));
    _lineto (dx (100), dy (300));

    _setcolor (1);              /* circle, lower right screen */
    _ellipse (_GBORDER, dx (550), dy (250),
                        dx (750), dy ( 50));

    getch();                            /* wait for keypress */
    _setvideomode (_DEFAULTMODE);       /* leave graphics */
} else
    puts ("Graphics not available on this machine");
}
```

Now that we've covered some of the conceptual aspects of graphics, let's discuss particulars of working with the Quick C graphics library.

Working with the Graphics Library

The Quick C graphics library is an entire subsystem that isolates programs from the usual low-level tedium of pixel graphics: ROM BIOS calls and the like. It handles all the hardware interfaces for you, via high-level functions. The constants and calls are all spelled out in **GRAPH.H.** Don't try going around the graphics system and calling the ROM BIOS directly while in a graphics mode, as this is almost a guarantee of catastrophe.

The graphics library has a single door leading in and out: the function _ setvideomode(). Pass one of the constants defined in **GRAPH.H** to enter a graphics mode. For example, to place the machine in EGA 640 x 350 16-color mode, code

    _setvideomode (_ERESCOLOR);

The graphics library records the mode in effect when you call this function. Thus you can leave graphics and return to the original mode by passing _ DEFAULTMODE in another call to _setvideomode().

The _setvideomode() function returns a Boolean result to indicate its success, where 0 means failure and nonzero indicates that the display is now in the requested mode. Unless you know your program will always run on a system that supports the specified mode, it's best to perform graphics inside a conditional statement, as in:

```
if  (_setgraphmode (mode_val)) {
      /* do graphics */
} else
      /* mode not supported */
```

Listing 10.5 implements this program construct. CGAMODE attempts to place the video system into CGA four-color mode. If successful, it says so and awaits a keypress before reverting to the original text mode, and otherwise it informs the user that the CGA mode isn't available.

Listing 10.5 **Detecting a successful switch to graphics mode.**

```
/* CGAMODE.C: Sets CGA 4-color mode if available, */
/*        then restores original text mode           */

#include <graph.h>
#include <conio.h>

main ()
{
  if (_setvideomode (_MRES4COLOR)) {      /* if successful, */
    _outtext ("CGA four-color mode");     /* announce mode */
    _outtext ("\nPress any key to quit");
    getch();                              /* wait for keypress */
    _setvideomode (_DEFAULTMODE);         /* leave graphics */
    puts ("Back in text mode");
  } else
    puts ("Your adapter doesn't support CGA 4-color mode");
}
```

Coordinate Spaces

The Quick C graphics routines operate in two conceptually separate coordinates spaces on the same screen. Text output relies on the row-and-column basis discussed in preceding chapters. That is, for routines such as _outtext(), the screen consists of 25 rows by some number of columns: usually 40 or 80, depending on the graphics mode. Drawing routines, on the other hand, consider the screen to consist of pixel positions expressed in XY order.

When graphics objects and text must appear adjacent to one another (labels, call-outs, and such), it's necessary to convert between coordinate spaces.

A character cell is always eight pixels wide. Therefore graphics modes with a width of 320 pixels contain 40-column text lines, and 640-wide graphics modes support 80 columns of text. To find the character position in which a graphics pixel occurs, divide by eight and add one. That is, a pixel at X coordinate 5 is in text column 1 (since (5/8) = 0 + 1 = 1 in integer arithmetic), and the pixel at X = 213 is in text column 27. The opposite calculation converts a text column to its leftmost X coordinate: that is, (column − 1) * 8 = X. Thus, text column 27 begins at X coordinate 208.

It's a little more complicated on the vertical axis. The number of Y pixels per character cell depends on the vertical density of the display mode. Divide vertical resolution by 25 to find the number of Y pixels per row. In 200-line modes, for example, a character is eight pixels in height, while in the EGA 350-line mode its height is 14 pixels. Once the cell height is known, conversion between text rows and graphics Y coordinates is the same as above. That is, to find the text row for a Y, divide by cell height and add one. Going the other way, subtract one from the text row and multiply by cell height to find the Y coordinate at the top of the row.

The Graphics Cursor

The Quick C line-drawing routines employ a conceptual device known as the graphics cursor. Unlike the text cursor, the graphics cursor is never visible. Instead, it represents the point of departure for the next line to be drawn.

When you enter a graphics mode, the graphics cursor is initialized to the center of the display. This is its default position. If you then issue the statement _lineto(0, 0), the first line goes from the center of the screen to the upper left corner. The line appears in the highest available color (also a default). The next _lineto() call draws a line from the upper left corner to the specified coordinates.

You can change the location of the graphics cursor at any time by issuing a _moveto() statement. This is the same as _lineto() except that the cursor leaves no line as it moves. If you want to know where the graphics cursor is, call _getcurrentposition(). This function fills in a structure of type xycoord (defined in GRAPH.H) via an assignment. For example:

```
struct  xycoord  gc;      /* declare  struct  variable */
gc  =  _getcurrentposition();
_moveto  (gc.xcoord + 10,  gc.ycoord + 10);
```

This code sequence declares a variable of type struct xycoord and moves the cursor ten pixels to the right and below its current position.

The _arc() function also changes the location of the graphics cursor. All other drawing routines work in absolute coordinates and do not affect the current graphics cursor location. Thus, for example, you can draw a line, then a rectangle elsewhere on the screen. The next line you draw proceeds from the end of the line previously drawn and NOT from a point somewhere on the rectangle. That's precisely what the LINE&BOX.C program in Listing 10.6 does.

Listing 10.6 Graphics cursor is unaffected by other objects.

```
/* LINE&BOX.C: Draws line, box, and line to show that
       graphics cursor is not affected by _rectangle */

#include <graph.h>
#include <conio.h>

main ()
{
  if (_setvideomode (_MRES4COLOR))  {
    _setcolor (1);                                /* line color */
    _moveto (0, 0);               /* start at top left corner */
    _lineto (160, 50);                            /* draw a line */

    /* now draw a box */
    _setcolor (2);                                /* box color */
    _rectangle (_GBORDER, 0, 100, 100, 199);        /* draw */
    /* and now another line */
    _setcolor (1);                            /* line color again */
    _lineto (319, 25);                            /* draw */

    /* quit after keypress */
    getch();                                      /* wait */
    _setvideomode (_DEFAULTMODE);         /* restore text */
  } else
    puts ("Your adapter doesn't support CGA mode");
}
```

Inheritance

The Quick C graphics system obeys rules of inheritance that observe the distinction between text and graphics. The _set...() functions such as _setlinestyle() and _setcolor() establish characteristics globally, and all eligible objects created thereafter inherit those characteristics.

For example, after you issue the statements

```
_setcolor (1);
_setlinestyle (0xCCCC);
```

all drawn objects will be of the color specified in palette register 1 (more on this below). Text is excluded, however, because its color is separately controlled by the _settextcolor() function. Furthermore, all drawn objects consisting of straight lines (_lineto() and _rectangle()) will be closely dotted rather than solid.

The Quick C documentation for individual _set...() functions tells which graphical elements are affected.

Color Palettes

Graphics video adapters support a concept known as the *color palette*. It's analogous to the painter's palette, on which a number of colors are arrayed from which the artist selects one for his next brush strokes. When a color adapter drives a monochrome monitor, colors show up as gradations of a gray scale. The size and number of available palettes depends on the graphics mode. Only one palette can be in use at a time.

The palettes' default colors increase in intensity from 0 up to some numeric limit. The 0 value is always the background color. Unless specified otherwise, the adapter selects the highest available palette color for text and drawing. Use _setcolor() and _settextcolor() to override the default output colors.

A palette is an array in which each element ("register") contains a value representing a color. The statement

    _setcolor (n);

tells the video system to index into the nth element of the array and write all succeeding pixels using the color found there. That being the case, we can change the value stored in the nth element so that all pixels of value n assume a new color. This change takes place on the screen instantly.

The means for changing a palette register is Quick C's _remappalette() function. Its arguments are the register number and a new color value. Thus, to change the background from default black to blue, write

    _remappalette (0, _BLUE);

Similarly, you can change the entire palette at once with _remapallpalette(). The argument here is a pointer to an array of n long integers (where n is the number of colors supported by the video mode). The array reloads the palette registers starting at 0 with the new values from your array.

The Quick C graphics package provides no means for inquiring about the current setting of a palette register. If your program must know, it has to remember any changes it makes to the palette.

The simplest palette belongs to CGA 640 x 200 mode (_HRESBW). There's only one palette, which contains two registers: background (0) and foreground (1). By default, the color scheme is white on black. You can change it to any other combination by remapping the palette. A favorite technique of desktop publishing programs and other software that copies the Macintosh appearance is to remap the palette to black on white.

Color palettes for the CGA four-color modes are at the opposite extreme in complexity. Some boards support two palettes, others four. By default you get the highest-numbered palette when you enter a 320 x 200 graphics mode. You can switch to a different palette with the Quick C _selectpalette() function. Each palette has a preset color scheme. Table 10.3 lists them.

Table 10.3 **CGA default palette colors.**

Palette	1	2	3
0	Green	Red	Brown
1	Cyan	Magenta	Light gray
2	Light green	Light red	Yellow
3	Light cyan	Light magenta	White

Note: Color 0 is black in all palettes

The CGA supports 16 simultaneous colors in text mode. All 16 are also available in graphics mode, but only four at a time. If you don't like a particular default color in one of the palettes, change the register to any of the other 15 colors using _remappalette(). Call _remapallpalette() to modify all colors at once. These functions only work on the active palette, so you can't remap an out-of-use palette behind the scenes. However, any palette change takes effect in 1/60 second, which is the refresh frequency of the display, so the change is virtually instantaneous.

Listing 10.7, CHPALET.C, demonstrates various palette changes on the CGA. Successive keypresses advance the program. First it draws three filled rectangles in colors ascending from 1. Then the program steps downward through four palettes; the results of the first two steps are unpredictable if your board supports only two palettes. The next step changes the highest color in palette 0 from brown to yellow. Note that the text color changes also. This is because the default text color is taken from the highest palette register, which is the one we're changing. With the following keypress, the background color changes from default black to blue, thus placing four true colors on the screen at once. Next we remap the entire palette to the color scheme given by the newcolors[] array. Finally, the box in color 2 seems to disappear. It's still in color 2, but palette register 2 has been changed to the same value as the background. One last keystroke ends the program.

Listing 10.7 **Manipulating CGA palettes.**

```
/* CHPALET.C: Changing CGA color palettes */

#include <graph.h>
#include <conio.h>
#include "textscrn.h"

long newcolors[] = {_MAGENTA, _LIGHTMAGENTA,
                    _LIGHTYELLOW, _BRIGHTWHITE};
```

Listing 10.7 *(continued)*

```
main ()
{
int n, x;

  if (_setvideomode (_MRES4COLOR)) {
    for (n = 1; n < 4; n++) {              /* draw 3 colored boxes */
      _setcolor (n);
      x = n * 60;
      _rectangle (_GFILLINTERIOR, x, 40, x+59, 190);
    }

    /* Step down through color palettes */
    for (n = 3; n >= 0; n--) {
      _selectpalette (n);
      _settextposition (1, 1); _cleareol();
      _outtextf ("Color palette %d", n);
      getch();
    }

    /* Change brown to yellow in palette 0 */
    _remappalette (3, _LIGHTYELLOW);
    _settextposition (1, 1); _cleareol();
    _outtext ("Remapped palette 0, color 3");
    getch();

    /* Change background */
    _remappalette (0, _BLUE);
    _settextposition (1, 1); _cleareol();
    _outtext ("Remapped background color");
    getch();

    /* Change entire palette */
    _remapallpalette (newcolors);
    _settextposition (1, 1); _cleareol();
    _outtext ("Remapped entire palette");
    getch();

   /* Make color 2 disappear by changing to background color */
    _remappalette (2, newcolors[0]);
    _settextposition (1, 1); _cleareol();
    _outtext ("Remapped color 2 to background color");
    getch();

    _setvideomode (_DEFAULTMODE);          /* restore text mode */
  } else
    puts ("Your adapter doesn't support CGA graphics modes");
}
```

The EGA provides considerably more flexibility than the CGA in color
selection. Although it has only one palette, it is capable of displaying up to 16

colors at a time selected from a possible 64. A color results from the combination of blue, green, and red. Each of these color components can have one of four intensities, which are the same for all:

Intensity	Value
Black	00h
Dark	15h
Medium	2Ah
Bright	3Fh

(Black indicates the absence of that color component.)

The meaning of an intensity value depends on its position within a 32-bit integer (type long). Working right to left, the lowest eight bits affect red, the next eight bits green, and the next eight bits blue. The high-order byte is unused.

You create a color by ORing its components. Thus, for example, you can achieve fuchsia by mixing medium red and dark blue with the expression

```
fuchsia  =  0x150000L  |  0x00002AL;
```

or, more simply,

```
fuchsia  =  0x15002AL;
```

Note that green is not a component of fuchsia, and thus the middle byte is zero.

The EGA palette is automatically initialized to the same values as 16-color text mode, where 0 = black, 1 = blue, 2 = green, and so on up through 15 = white. If you want to replace the default yellow with fuchsia, mix the color as described, then change EGA palette register 14 to the new color value using _ remappalette(). Thereafter any pixel of value 14 will appear on the display as fuchsia. That's what the program in Listing 10.8 does.

Listing 10.8 Creating fuchsia on the EGA.

```
/* FUCHSIA.C: Remaps EGA palette reg 14 to fuchsia */

#include <graph.h>
#include <conio.h>

main ()
{
long fuchsia;

  if (_setvideomode (_ERESCOLOR)) {
    _setcolor (14);                        /* show original color */
    _rectangle (_GFILLINTERIOR,            /* draw filled box */
              160, 100, 480, 250);
    getch();                               /* wait for keypress */
```

Listing 10.8 *(continued)*

```
    fuchsia = 0x00002AL - 0x150000L; /* Med red - dark blue */
    _remappalette (14, fuscia);          /* change palette */
    getch();                                /* wait again */
    _setvideomode (_DEFAULTMODE);              /* quit */
  } else
    puts ("Not an EGA");
}
```

The VGA immensely extends this color-intensity concept. Here, colors are
blended from 64 possible shades each of blue, green, and red, giving a total of
262,144 potential colors, of which 256 can be visible at any time. Each base
shade is a byte containing a value from 0 through 63, with the upper two bits
always 00. As with the EGA, these bytes are concatenated to form a long integer.

The MIX.C program in Figure 10.9 allows you to experiment with different
colors on an EGA or VGA. The program displays swatches of the four intensities of each base color arranged in rows across the screen. The leftmost column is black, with intensity increasing to the right. At the bottom of the
display is a large box that shows the current color mix. A white rectangle in
each row outlines the intensity of that color present in the large box.

To operate the program, press r (lowercase) to decrease the intensity of red
and R (uppercase) to increase red. The same effects are true for green (g/G)
and blue (b/B). When you change an intensity, the outlining rectangle moves
appropriately and the color of the sample box changes.

Quit by pressing Esc. This restores the display to text mode, and the program reports the last color combination. MIX.C is therefore a tool for design-
ing custom colors on the EGA; use the results to build the colors for other
programs.

Listing 10.9 **Utility for mixing EGA colors.**

```
/* MIX.C: Utility for mixing EGA colors */

#include <conio.h>
#include <stdio.h>
#include <graph.h>

#define RED0      0x000000L   /* basic hues for mixing */
#define RED1      0x000015L
#define RED2      0x00002AL
#define RED3      0x00003FL
#define GRN0      0x000000L
#define GRN1      0x001500L
#define GRN2      0x002A00L
#define GRN3      0x003F00L
#define BLU0      0x000000L
#define BLU1      0x150000L
```

```
        #define BLU2        0x2A0000L
        #define BLU3        0x3F0000L

        #define ESC   27       /* Esc char */
        #define ERASE  0
        #define SHOW  15

        int ri = 1, gi = 5, bi = 9;              /* rgb indices in palette */
        int col[] = {30, 190, 350, 510};            /* box horiz locations */
        int row[] = {30, 110, 190};                 /* box vert locations  */
        long palreg[] = {_BLACK, RED0, RED1, RED2, RED3,
                        GRN0, GRN1, GRN2, GRN3,
                        BLU0, BLU1, BLU2, BLU3,
                        _BRIGHTWHITE, 0, _BRIGHTWHITE
        };


        main ()
        {
        int r, g, b;
        void setup_screen (void), mix_colors (int*, int*, int*);

          if (_setvideomode (_ERESCOLOR)) {
            _remapallpalette (palreg);           /* change entire palette */
            setup_screen();                         /* construct display */
            mix_colors (&r, &g, &b);                /* do the real work */
            _setvideomode (_DEFAULTMODE);           /* restore text mode */

            /* Report results */
            printf ("\nMixed color has value 0x%06X", palreg [13]);
            printf ("\nComponent breakdown:\n");
            printf ("    Blue: 0x%061X  ", palreg[b+bi]);
            switch (b) {
              case 0: puts ("(BLU0)"); break;
              case 1: puts ("(BLU1)"); break;
              case 2: puts ("(BLU2)"); break;
              case 3: puts ("(BLU3)"); break;
            }
            printf ("    Green: 0x%061X  ", palreg[g+gi]);
            switch (g) {
              case 0: puts ("(GRN0)"); break;
              case 1: puts ("(GRN1)"); break;
              case 2: puts ("(GRN2)"); break;
              case 3: puts ("(GRN3)"); break;
            }
            printf ("    Red:   0x%061X  ", palreg[r+ri]);
            switch (r) {
              case 0: puts ("(RED0)"); break;
              case 1: puts ("(RED1)"); break;
              case 2: puts ("(RED2)"); break;
              case 3: puts ("(RED3)"); break;
            }
          } else puts ("Your adapter doesn't support EGA mode");
        } /* --------------------------------------------------- */
```

Listing 10.9 *(continued)*

```
void draw_box (int reg, int c, int r)        /* box around color */
{
int xl, yl, x2, y2;

  xl = col[c] - 5; yl = row[r] - 5;                /* upper left */
  x2 = xl + 110;   y2 = yl + 70;                   /* lower right */
  _setcolor (reg);
  _rectangle (_GBORDER, xl, yl, x2, y2);
} /* ------------------------------------------------------- */

void setup_screen (void)                 /* construct work screen */
{
int r, c, reg = 1,
    xl, yl, x2, y2;

  for (r = 0; r < 3; r++)
    for (c = 0; c < 4; c++) {
      _setcolor (reg++);                       /* select color reg */
      xl = col[c]; yl = row[r];                /* rectangle coords */
      x2 = xl+100; y2 = yl+60;
        _rectangle (_GFILLINTERIOR, xl, yl, x2, y2); /* fill */
      }
  _setcolor (13);                        /* mixed color display area */
  _rectangle (_GFILLINTERIOR, 30, 280, 610, 340);

  for (r = 0; r < 3; r++)                    /* rubberband most intense */
    draw_box (SHOW, 3, r);
} /* ------------------------------------------------------- */

void mix_colors (int *red, int *green, int *blue)
                            /* interactive portion mixes colors */
{
#define RAISE(col) col = (col < 3) ? ++col : 3
#define LOWER(col) col = (col > 0) ? --col : 0

char reply;
int  r, rc = 3, gc = 3, bc = 3;
long mixture;

  do {
    reply = getch();
    switch (reply) {
      case ESC : break;                        /* quit program */
      case 'r' : r = 0;                         /* lower red */
                 draw_box (ERASE, rc, r);
                 LOWER (rc);
                 draw_box (SHOW, rc, r);
                 break;
      case 'R' : r = 0;                         /* raise red */
                 draw_box (ERASE, rc, r);
                 RAISE (rc);
```

```
                    draw_box (SHOW, rc, r);
                    break;
         case 'g' :  r = 1;                              /* lower green */
                    draw_box (ERASE, gc, r);
                    LOWER (gc);
                    draw_box (SHOW, gc, r);
                    break;
         case 'G' :  r = 1;                              /* raise green */
                    draw_box (ERASE, gc, r);
                    RAISE (gc);
                    draw_box (SHOW, gc, r);
                    break;
         case 'b' :  r = 2;                              /* lower blue */
                    draw_box (ERASE, bc, r);
                    LOWER (bc);
                    draw_box (SHOW, bc, r);
                    break;
         case 'B' :  r = 2;                              /* raise blue */
                    draw_box (ERASE, bc, r);
                    RAISE (bc);
                    draw_box (SHOW, bc, r);
                    break;
      }
      *red    = rc;                          /* update color components */
      *green  = gc;
      *blue   = bc;
      mixture = palreg[bc+bi] - palreg[gc+gi] - palreg[rc+ri];
      _remappalette (13, mixture);                       /* update display */
   } while (reply != ESC);
}
```

Study this program. It contains a number of useful programming techniques. One example is the use of the **RAISE** and **LOWER** macros in the mix_ colors() function. These macros determine if the color selection can move farther right or left, respectively. If not, the selection remains as is. Another is the use of the variable ri, gi, and bi, which furnish offset indices into the palreg array for red, green, and blue intensities. They're used during the reporting of results, and also to create the new color mixture near the bottom of the listing. The state variables rc, gc, and bc in mix_colors() keep track of the current intensity of each base color. Additionally, passed to draw_box() along with the row, these state variables serve as an index to the col array containing the X location of the affected color swatch. The Y coordinate is found by indexing into the row array using the r argument. In this way, draw_box() determines the position of the color swatch to be outlined. The command constants ERASE and SHOW issued by mix_colors() are regarded by draw_ box() as the registers for the box color; ERASE maps to black and SHOW to white. Consequently each case in mix_colors() first ERASEs the present box by telling draw_box() to redraw it in black, then moves the selection indicator (if possible) and SHOWs the box in its new location.

It's time now to move on to geometric objects and other interesting visual effects using Quick C graphics.

CHAPTER 11

Controlling the Graphics Display

This chapter covers some of the fun stuff of computer graphics. It's about drawing interesting and useful objects on the display, and about programming techniques that convert imagination into something you can see. Consistent with the title and spirit of the book, we'll stretch the Quick C graphics library a little, but mostly we're going to explore ways of using the toolkit to create visual effects.

The Quick C library furnishes routines for creating six basic kinds of visual objects:

pixels

lines

rectangles

arcs

ellipses

pie slices

This might not seem like a very large set of tools, yet from it we can create an astonishing variety of visual images. Supporting routines let us set the styles of lines and fill patterns, open viewports, and apply other artistic techniques that further expand the possibilities. Let's get started.

In Praise of the Lowly Pixel

Pixels might be mere specks of light on the display, but they are the grains of sand that make the seashore. Without the pixel (an abbreviation for "picture element"), we wouldn't have graphics.

The pixel is to graphics what the bit is to data: the smallest unit of information. Both a bit and a pixel have two characteristics in common: positional significance, and a binary (on/off) state. A pixel has one more dimension than a bit, though, and that is color. A group of adjacent pixels sharing a common color form an object. If we're successful in arranging the pixels, the viewer's eye will recognize their totality as a "thing" and assign meaning to them.

Many of the Quick C graphics routines arrange large numbers of pixels into patterns. For example, line-drawing routines place pixels as close as possible to the actual path of a line, and _rectangle() using the _GFILLINTERIOR control argument creates a solid block of pixels. These routines relieve you from worrying about individual pixels; they abstract the elements of the image to a higher level.

However, when you do need to operate at the pixel level, the Quick C graphics library furnishes a matched pair of routines called _getpixel() and _setpixel(). Both take an XY coordinate pair as their arguments. (Quick C 2.0 also has the variants _getpixel_xy() and _setpixel_xy(). They work the same, but accept a structure of type xycoord as their arguments.) The _getpixel() routine senses and returns the pixel value at the specified coordinate position. Its companion _setpixel() does the same thing, but also writes a new pixel at the same location in the current foreground color; you can disregard the returned value if you don't care what the new pixel overlaid.

This pair of functions lets you create smart drawing routines that avoid overlaying other objects already on the screen. Using _getpixel(), the routine can feel its way along and change direction when it encounters an obstacle. Listing 11.1 contains FEEL.C, which does just that. The program operates in CGA 4-color mode.

Listing 11.1 A smart pixel-drawing routine.

```
/* FEEL.C: A line "feels" its way along, changing direction
        when it encounters the edge of a rectangle */

#include <graph.h>
#include <conio.h>
#include <stdio.h>

main ()
{
short x = 200, y = 160,            /* line's starting point */
      xi = 1, yi = -1;             /* movement increments */

   if (_setvideomode (_MRES4COLOR)) {   /* use CGA 4-color */
      _rectangle (_GBORDER, 50, 30,     /* drawn in color 3 */
                  269, 170);
      _setcolor (2);
      while (!kbhit()) {              /* run until key pressed */
         if (_getpixel (x+xi, y) == 3)   /* edge at next x? */
```

```
              xi = -xi;                    /* reverse x direction if so */
         if (_getpixel (x, y+yi) == 3)         /* edge at next y? */
              yi = -yi;                    /* reverse y direction if so */
         x += xi, y += yi;              /* advance to next position */
         _setpixel (x, y);                        /* and draw pixel */
      }
      getch();                          /* clear keyboard buffer */
      _setvideomode (_DEFAULTMODE);       /* restore text mode */
   } else
      puts ("Your adapter doesn't support CGA mode");
}
```

After going into graphics mode, the program draws a rectangle in default color 3, then changes the foreground color to 2 in preparation for writing pixels. The main loop does most of the work. It runs until you press a key, as detected by kbhit(). This function senses a keypress, but it doesn't clear the keyboard buffer; that's what getch() does after the loop.

The direction of movement is controlled by xi and yi. The line begins in the lower right quadrant of the box and initially moves up and to the right. In each iteration, the loop checks the next pixel position to see if it contains a barrier color. If so, the appropriate movement increment (xi or yi) changes to the opposite sign. The position variables x and y are then updated, and the routine draws a new pixel at that location.

This program creates a lattice of gradually fattening diagonal lines that eventually fill the entire rectangle. It continues retracing the same path, but you can't see that because it's redrawing pixels in the same color.

Drawing Lines

We've already drawn a number of lines in previous programs and discussed the _lineto() routine in the last chapter, so the subject needs no introduction beyond a brief summary. _lineto() draws a line from the current graphics pen position to a new location, using the prevailing foreground color. The pixel at the end of the line becomes the new graphics cursor position.

A new function related to _lineto() is _lineto_xy(), which accepts a structure of type xycoord as its argument. We'll put it to work a little later when we discuss a multiple line-drawing routine.

In addition to the default solid line, both of these functions are capable of drawing stylized lines in a repeating pattern. To establish a new line pattern, call _setlinestyle() and pass a 16-bit mask of type unsigned short. Thereafter all lines drawn by the _lineto() routines, and also all rectangles, will assume the pattern.

The mask defines a sequence of 16 pixels in which a 1 bit turns the corresponding pixel on, and a 0 bit turns it off. The mask is implemented left to

right through the mask in the drawing direction. For example, a line consisting of long dashes with equally long spaces between them has the mask
F0F0h: Four pixels are on, then four are off, and so on. A dash-dot pattern
might be defined as FAFAh, with five pixels on, one off, one on, one off, and
then repeating for the next eight bits. Listing 11.2 lists LINES.C, a program
that draws a few line patterns and labels them. The command line to make
this program is

     QCL lines.c textscrn.c

Listing 11.2 **Drawing stylized lines.**

```
/* LINES.C: Standard and user-defined line patterns */

#include <graph.h>
#include <conio.h>
#include "textscrn.h"


typedef struct {
  char           name [15];
  unsigned short ptrn;
} LINETYPE;


LINETYPE line[] = {
    {"Solid",         0xFFFF},
    {"Dotted",        0xAAAA},
    {"Long dashes",   0xF0F0},
    {"Short dashes",  0xCCCC},
    {"Dash-dot",      0xFAFA}
};
void main ()
{
short n, y;

   if (_setvideomode (_MRES4COLOR)) {       /* Use CGA 4-color */
     for (n = 0; n < 5; n++ ) {                /* show patterns */
       _setlinestyle (line[n].ptrn);               /* set style */
       y = ((n + 1) * 32) + 4;            /* line and text row */
       _moveto (0, y);                            /* move pen */
       _lineto (175, y);               /* draw line in style */
       _settextposition ((y / 8) + 1, 24);
       _outtextf ("%s", line[n].name);         /* report name */
     }
     getch ();                           /* wait for keypress */
     _setvideomode (_DEFAULTMODE);
   }
}
```

Stretching the Quick C Graphics Library _____

Now let's do for graphics what we did earlier for text handling: Add a layer of functionality that eases the effort in writing graphics applications. This library is called EXGRAPH, short for extended graphics. First we'll list the library's header and source files in Listings 11.3 and 11.4, and then we'll discuss the things it does.

Listing 11.3 **Header file for stretched graphics.**

```
/* EXGRAPH.H: Extended graphics functions for Quick C 2.0 */

short far bestmode (void);   /* get best graphics mode for adapter */

void far wait (double seconds); /* stop execution for timed period */
                            /* also quits on detecting a keypress */

void far _polyline (int nsegs, struct xycoord vert[], int next[]);
          /* draw a polyline of nsegs line segments, where:       */
          /*     vert[] contains vertices for nsegs+1 vertices     */
          /*     and next[] contains nsegs+1 indexes for end points */
          /* NOTE: vert[] must contain device coords, not virtual  */

void far _saveimage (int x1, int y1, int x2, int y2);
   /* push defined graphics screen area onto a stack in the heap */
                            /* retrieve later with _restimage() */

void far _restimage (void);
                /* pop graphics screen area off top of image stack */
                    /* restore to screen at original location */
```

Listing 11.4 **Source for extended graphics library.**

```
/* EXGRAPH.C: Extended graphics functions for Quick C 2.0 */
/* Library source */

#include <graph.h>
#include <conio.h>
#include <malloc.h>
#include <stdio.h>
#include <dos.h>
#include "exgraph.h"
#include "mk_fp.h"
#pragma pack(1)                                     /* pack structs */

typedef struct imstacknode {                       /* image stack node */
  char far *image;                            /* pointer to save buffer */
  int x, y;                                     /* upper left corner */
  struct imstacknode far *prev;
} IMSTACKNODE;
```

Listing 11.4 *(continued)*

```
/* Global to this library */
IMSTACKNODE far *imstack = NULL;                          /* image stack pointer */
/*------------------------------------------------------------------- */

short far bestmode (void)              /* return best graphics mode for adapter */
{
short best;
struct videoconfig grconfig;

  _getvideoconfig (&grconfig);
  switch (grconfig.adapter) {
    case _MDPA: best = -1; break;                        /* error return for MDA */
    case _CGA : best = _MRES4COLOR;     break;
    case _EGA : best = _ERESCOLOR;      break;
    case _VGA : best = _MRES256COLOR; break;
    case _MCGA: best = _MRES4COLOR;     break;
    case _HGC : best = _HERCMONO;       break;
  }
  return best;
} /*------------------------------------------------------------------- */

void far wait (double seconds)                /* stop execution for timed period */
                                        /* also quits on detecting a keypress */
{
unsigned far *biostick = MK_FP (0x0040, 0x006C);
unsigned endtime;
double   et;

  et = (seconds * 18.2) + *biostick;                      /* proposed end time */
  if (et > 65535.0) {                          /* clock is about to roll over */
    endtime = (unsigned)(et-65535.0);          /* period after clock resets */
    while (*biostick < 0)                            /* wait for rollover */
      if (kbhit()) {                                       /* or keypress */
        getch();
        return;
      }
  } else
    endtime = (unsigned)(et);
  while (*biostick < endtime)                  /* wait until end of timed period */
    if (kbhit()) {                             /* or quit early on keypress */
      getch();
      return;
    }
} /*------------------------------------------------------------------- */

void far    _polyline (int nsegs, struct xycoord vert[], int next[])
          /* draw a polyline of nsegs line segments, where:          */
          /*    vert[] contains coordinates for the line vertices    */
          /*    and next[] contains nsegs+1 indexes for end points   */
          /* NOTE: vert[] must contain device coords, not virtual    */
{
```

```
int seg;


  _moveto_xy (vert [next[0]]);                          /* set starting point */
  for (seg = 1; seg <= nsegs; seg++)                        /* draw figure */
    _lineto_xy (vert [next[seg]]);
} /*------------------------------------ ------------------------------- */



void far _saveimage (int x1, int y1, int x2, int y2)
                    /* push defined screen area onto a stack in the heap */
                                    /* retrieve later with _restimage() */
{
IMSTACKNODE far *new;
char far *image;
long imsize;
  imsize = _imagesize (x1, y1, x2, y2);                    /* get image size */
  new = _fmalloc (sizeof *new);                               /* get node */
  if (imstack == NULL) {                                  /* set pointers */
    new->prev = NULL;                                    /* for first node */
    imstack = new;
  } else {
    new->prev = imstack;                              /* or additional node */
    imstack = new;
  }
  image = _fmalloc (imsize);                    /* allocate space for image */
  _getimage (x1, y1, x2, y2, image);                        /* save image */
  new->image = image;                               /* set node pointer */
  new->x = x1; new->y = y1;                         /* save origin of image */
} /*--------------------------------------------------------------------- */



void far _restimage (void)
                    /* pop graphics screen area off top of image stack */
                            /* restore to screen at original location */
{
IMSTACKNODE far *top;


  if (imstack != NULL) {                        /* work only if stack not empty */
    top = imstack;                                        /* get top node */
    imstack = top->prev;                              /* update stack pointer */
    _putimage (top->x, top->y, top->image, _GPSET);            /* restore */
    _ffree (top->image);                              /* free image space */
    _ffree (top);                                    /* and stack node */
  }
} /*--------------------------------------------------------------------- */
```

Selecting the Best Graphics Mode

The assortment of available graphics modes for various adapters is bewildering, and if every graphics program we write has to automatically select the most appropriate mode, it's a task best performed by a library routine.

That's why EXGRAPH includes the bestmode() function. It senses the adapter type and returns its best graphics mode. Thus you can automatically switch to graphics with a call such as

```
_setvideomode (bestmode());
```

and save yourself a lot of repetitive coding.

The "best" mode is of course a matter of judgement, as well as being application-dependent. Mathematical functions, for example, might best be plotted on the CGA in 640 x 200 monocolor (defined as _HRESBW in GRAPH.H). In that case, don't call bestmode(), but instead insert your own mode selection routine. The criterion I used in devising bestmode() was the most colors at the highest resolution. If the ones given here don't work for your needs, rewrite bestmode() or go around it.

Inserting Timed Delays

Some graphics applications require a "slide show" approach, in which the program advances from one display to the next on a timed basis, without human intervention. Examples are sales demos and business presentations. The EXGRAPH library function wait() provides the mechanism.

The argument to wait() is a floating-point number representing the number of seconds that you want to halt execution. The use of a double allows you to specify fractional seconds, such as 10.5.

The ROM BIOS maintains a time-of-day clock in its data area (see Chapter 6) that we can use to time the delay. The clock "ticks" 18.2 times per second, counting up from 0 at the start of the hour to 65,535 at the end, then rolling back to 0 to begin a new hour. Therefore the end of the delay period is the seconds to delay times 18.2, plus the current tick. A loop can simply repeat until the current tick value equals or exceeds the ending time.

However, we have to consider the possibility that the tick count is high and the ending time will occur in the next hour, after the clock has rolled over. In that case, we subtract 65,535 from the ending time, wait for the tick to reset to 0, and then proceed as above.

The user might want to override the timed interval, especially if it's long. For that reason, the delay loops check the keyboard during each iteration, using kbhit() to detect a keypress. If one occurs, the routine clears the keyboard buffer and returns early.

So that's how the **wait()** function inserts an interruptable delay into a program.

Drawing Multiple Lines

Most graphics packages include a routine for drawing multiple connected lines with a single call. It's surprising that the Quick C library doesn't, so let's plug the gap.

Such routines, of which there are a number of variants, commonly go by the name polyline. Hence the name of the function in **EXGRAPH**, which includes an underscore prefix to look like other graphics library functions. The _polyline() function itself is quite simple; explaining it and setting up for it are more complex.

_polyline() accepts three arguments. The first is the number of line segments to be drawn. To draw a triangle, for example, the **nsegs** argument is 3. The second argument is an array of type **struct xycoord**, defined in **GRAPH.H**. This structure type contains the X and Y coordinates of a point (or vertex). The array, therefore, defines the points at which line segments converge to form a figure. For a closed polygon, the vertices represent the corners; for an open figure such as the letter W, the vertices give the starting and ending points for each line segment.

The final argument is the most complex. It is an array of indices indicating the order in which vertices are selected. A single line segment requires two vertices—start and end—and, by extension, two lines are defined by three vertices, three lines by four vertices, etc. Therefore the **next[]** argument must be an array of **nsegs + 1** integers each indicating the position of a point's coordinates within the **vert[]** array. The order of values in the **next[]** array gives the sequence in which vertices are selected for consecutive line segments, with element 0 indicating the starting point of the first line and the element **nseg** indicating the end of the last line.

As an example, say we have five points evenly spaced around a circle. The vertices thus form a pentagon or, if we rearrange their order, a star. To draw a pentagon, the order specified in the **next[]** array is 0, 1, 2, 3, 4, 0. For a star, we join every second point in the order 0, 2, 4, 1, 3, 0. In both cases the figure is closed because the last point coincides with the first.

The program **PENTAGON.C** in Listing 11.5 illustrates this discussion of polylines and shows how the same set of vertices can be used to draw more than one figure depending on the specified order. The program also uses the other two extended graphics functions discussed so far. Make this program with

```
QCL pentagon.c vcoords.c exgraph.c
```

Listing 11.5 **Drawing two polygons from one set of vertices.**

```
/* PENTAGON.C: Draws an enclosed star in virtual space */
/* Illustration of _polyline() routine */

#include <graph.h>
#include <stdio.h>
#include "vcoords.h"
#include "exgraph.h"
#define SIDES 5

struct xycoord vert[] = { /* virtual vertices of pentagon */
   {400, 560}, {660, 360}, {560,   60},
   {240,   60}, {140, 360}
};
int order[] = {            /* order of points to form a star */
   0, 2, 4, 1, 3, 0
};

void main ()
{
int seq;

  if (_setvideomode (bestmode())) {
    setvcoords (800, 600);                   /* set virt coords */
    for (seq = 0; seq < SIDES; seq++){   /* convert coords */
      vert[seq].xcoord = dx (vert[seq].xcoord);
      vert[seq].ycoord = dy (vert[seq].ycoord);
    }
    _polyline (SIDES, vert, order);      /* draw star first */
    for (seq = 0; seq < SIDES; seq++)    /* reorder points */
      order [seq] = seq;                     /* for outline */
    _setcolor (_getcolor() - 1);
    _polyline (SIDES, vert, order);          /* draw outline */
    wait (5.0);                                /* wait 5 sec */
    _setvideomode (_DEFAULTMODE);
  } else
    puts ("Your adapter doesn't support CGA 4-color mode");
}
```

The vertices are defined in virtual coordinates to ensure a "square" display aspect, and their order is set to form a star. The program's body then takes over, placing the adapter into the best graphics mode and establishing a virtual coordinate space of 800 x 600. The _polyline() routine doesn't understand virtual coordinates, so the for() loop converts the vertices into device coordinates. The star is then drawn.

To differentiate the polygons visually, the program reduces the current color to the next-lower palette value. Next it reorders the points into numeric sequence 0, 1, 2, 3, 4, 0 with a loop, thus specifying a pentagon formed from consecutive points. The second call to _polyline() draws it as an outline around the star. After freezing the display for five seconds, the program ends.

Figure 11.1 **Output of the** PENTAGON Program.

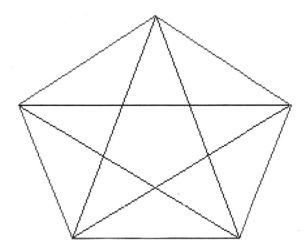

Figure 11.1 shows a black-and-white image of the display produced by the PENTAGON program. On the screen, the star and its enclosing polygon are of different colors.

EXGRAPH has the two additional functions _saveimage() and _restimage(). These are the graphics counterparts to _savescrn() and _restscrn() from the TEXTSCRN library we developed earlier. Before we discuss them, let's talk about Quick C's "native" functions for operating on portions of the graphics display.

Capturing and Restoring Graphics Images in Pure Quick C

The Quick C graphics library furnishes a set of routines for making and reproducing "snapshots" of the screen or a portion thereof: _imagesize(), _getimage(), and _putimage(). Like real-life snapshots, these images are rectangular. The _imagesize() function tells how many bytes of memory are needed to hold the image within an area delineated by the northwest and southeast corners. _getimage() copies a portion of the screen out to a memory buffer, and _putimage() goes the other way by placing a buffered image onto the display. Graphics literature often refers to the getimage() and putimage() operations as "bitblt" (pronounced "bit blit"), meaning a high-speed bit-image transfer.

Use _imagesize() to determine the amount of space needed to contain the portion of the screen that you want to capture. It takes into account the number of bits per pixel when calculating the space requirement, and returns that value. You can then use it to allocate storage. Here is an example:

```
nbytes  =  _imagesize (left, top, right, bottom);
buffer  =  malloc (nbytes);
```

Having allocated a heap buffer of the appropriate size, you can save the image with

```
_getimage (left, top, right, bottom, buffer);
```

To copy a saved image back to the screen, write

```
_putimage (left, top, buffer, action);
```

In a sense, _putimage() is the opposite of _getimage() in that it copies the bitblt stored in buffer back to the screen, at a location specified by the left and top coordinates. The original width and height are preserved. However, the action argument gives _putimage() considerable flexibility in controlling the way the image is restored. You can use this flexibility to create various visual effects.

GRAPH.H defines five action "verbs" for _putimage(). These verbs govern the way in which the new image's pixels affect those they overwrite. They are:

_GAND   Logical AND, retaining pixel bits common to both the new and existing images. CGA example: 0&2 = 0, 1&2 = 0, 2&2 = 2, 3&2 = 2.

_GOR   Logical OR, changing colors. CGA example: 0 | 2 = 2, 1 | 2 = 3, 2 | 2 = 2, 3 | 2 = 3.

_GPRESET   Inverts the new image's original colors, erasing the overlaid image. CGA example: 0: = = 3, 1: = = 2, 2: = = 1, 3: = = 0.

_GPSET   The image overwrites the background and has exactly the same colors as before. This is the usual way of restoring images.

_GXOR   Foreground (nonzero) pixels in the new image invert the existing pixels, while the new image's background pixels allow the overlaid image to "show through" without change. Thus the shape of the new image is seen, but not in its original colors. Successive writes to the same space cause the new image to flash.

One of the most overworked cliches in the English language says that a picture is worth a thousand words. Cliches may be tired, but they remain cliches because they contain wisdom. So let's turn the preceding description into working reality with the BITBLT.C program in Listing 11.6. Make the program with the command line

    QCL bitblt.c exgraph.c textscrn.c

Listing 11.6 **Illustrates effects of** _putimage() "verbs".

```
/* BITBLT.C: Demos effects of the _putimage() action verbs */

#include <stdio.h>
#include <graph.h>
#include <malloc.h>
#include "exgraph.h"
#include "textscrn.h"

void main()
{
char *buffer;
int c, left=30, top=30, rite=290, bottom=170;
long size;
void setbackground (char*);

  /* Set graphics mode */
  if (!(_setvideomode (_MRES4COLOR))) {
    puts ("CGA not supported");
    exit (-1);
  }

  /* Construct and save foreground object */
  _setcolor (2);
  _moveto (left, top); _lineto (rite, bottom);
  _moveto (left, bottom); _lineto (rite, top);
  for (c = 0; c < 5; c++)
    _rectangle (_GBORDER, left--, top--, rite++, bottom++);
  size = _imagesize (left, top, rite, bottom);
  buffer = malloc (size);
  _getimage (++left, ++top, --rite, --bottom, buffer);
  _outtext ("Basic image");
  wait (3.0);

  /* Put image with _GAND */
  setbackground ("_GAND");
  _putimage (left, top, buffer, _GAND);
  wait (3.0);

  /* With _GOR */
  setbackground ("_GOR");
  _putimage (left, top, buffer, _GOR);
```

Listing 11.6 *(continued)*

```
   wait (3.0);

   /* With _GPRESET */
   setbackground ("_GPRESET");
   _putimage (left, top, buffer, _GPRESET);
   wait (3.0);

   /* With _GPSET */
   setbackground ("_GPSET");
   _putimage (left, top, buffer, _GPSET);
   wait (3.0);

   /* With _GXOR */
   setbackground ("_GXOR");
   for (c = 0; c < 12; c++) {
     _putimage (left, top, buffer, _GXOR);
     wait (0.5);
   }

   /* End of run */
   free (buffer);
   _setvideomode (_DEFAULTMODE);
   printf ("Image size was %ld bytes", size);
} /* ----------------------- */

void setbackground (char action[])
{
int x1, x2, i;

   _clearscreen (_GCLEARSCREEN);
   _outtextf ("Put using %s", action);
   for (i = 1; i < 4; i++) {
     _setcolor (i);
     x1 = i * 80; x2 = x1 + 79;
     _rectangle (_GFILLINTERIOR, x1, 10, x2, 199);
   }
   wait (1.0);
} /* ----------------------- */
```

This program, operating in CGA four-color mode, creates and saves a criss-crossed rectangle, then puts it against a striped background, successively using each of the _putimage() action verbs. Each verb appears at the top of the screen during its reign. The program advances in a slide show manner by calling wait(). The effect is a vivid demonstration of how the various verbs differ in their effects. Especially note the _GXOR loop; repeatedly executing the same _putimage() call makes the image flash.

Because _putimage() allows you to specify a destination, you can restore the image to the screen at a different place than it originated. This capability provides for animation, and also for creating visual patterns based on repetitive images. An example of the latter is the TILES.C program in Listing 11.7.

Note that the tile variable is an array of 2 x 2356 bytes on the heap (where _getimage() places it). The heap exists in the stack segment, which is 2K by default in Quick C. Consequently, you have to override the default stack size in order to avoid a stack overflow. The array occupies about 4.6K, so 8K (8192 bytes) gives the program plenty of space. You can set this stack size at the command line by compiling with the statement

    QCL /F 8192 tiles.c vcoords.c exgraph.c

In the environment, set the stack size via Options/Make/Linker flags.

Listing 11.7 **Creating a complex pattern with _putimage().**

```
/* TILES.C: Creates a tiled pattern with repeated bitblts */

#include <graph.h>
#include <conio.h>
#include <stdio.h>
#include "vcoords.h"
#include "exgraph.h"

void main()
{
void tile0 (char*), tile1 (char*);
char tile[2][2356];
int  x, y, t=0;

  if (_setvideomode (_MRES4COLOR)) {
    setvcoords (320, 256);                /* set coord space */
    tile0 (tile[0]);            /* make/save original tiles */
    wait (1.0);
    tile1 (tile[1]);
    wait (1.0);

    /* copy alternating tiles to display */
    for (y = 63; y < 256; y+=64)
      for (x = 0; x < 319; x+=64) {
        _putimage (dx(x), dy(y), tile[t], _GPSET);
        t = (t == 0) ? 1 : 0;      /* toggle tile selector */
      }
    getch();                              /* wait for keypress */
    _setvideomode (_DEFAULTMODE);
  } else
    puts ("CGA mode not available");
} /* ------------------------ */

void tile0 (char *buf)          /* create image for tile 0 */
{                                       /* and store in buf */
  _setcolor (1);
```

Listing 11.7 *(continued)*

```
   _rectangle (_GBORDER, dx(0), dy(63), dx(63), dy(0));
   _setcolor (2);
   _moveto (dx(28), dy(63)); _lineto (dx(63), dy(28));
   _moveto (dx( 0), dy(36)); _lineto (dx(36), dy( 0));
   _setcolor (3);
   _moveto (dx( 0), dy(48)); _lineto (dx(16), dy(48));
   _lineto (dx(48), dy(16)); _lineto (dx(48), dy( 0));
   _moveto (dx(63), dy(16)); _lineto (dx(48), dy(16));
   _moveto (dx(16), dy(63)); _lineto (dx(16), dy(48));
   _getimage (dx(0), dy(63), dx(63), dy(0), buf);
} /* ---------------------- */


void tile1 (char *buf)              /* create image for tile 1 */
{                                           /* and store in buf */
   _setcolor (1);
   _rectangle (_GBORDER, dx(64), dy(63), dx(127), dy(0));
   _setcolor (2);
   _moveto (dx( 64), dy(28)); _lineto (dx(100), dy(63));
   _moveto (dx(127), dy(36)); _lineto (dx( 92), dy( 0));
   _setcolor (3);
   _moveto (dx(112), dy(63)); _lineto (dx(112), dy(48));
   _lineto (dx( 80), dy(16)); _lineto (dx( 80), dy( 0));
   _moveto (dx( 64), dy(16)); _lineto (dx( 80), dy(16));
   _moveto (dx(127), dy(48)); _lineto (dx(112), dy(48));
   _getimage (dx(64), dy(63), dx(127), dy(0), buf);
}
```

Working in a virtual coordinate space, this program creates two square patterns that are mirror images of each other and saves them in indexed buffers. You see one, then the other, at the lower left corner of the display; a one-second delay after creating each image lets you view them individually. Then the program fills the screen with these images, placing them into a gridwork of alternating tiles. The result is a complex pattern that remains on the display until you press a key.

The overall effect is achieved by placing similar images diagonally adjacent to each other. Since the tiles are numbered 0 and 1, the image arrangement is

$$
\begin{array}{ccc}
0\ 1 & & 1\ 0 \\
1\ 0 & \text{-or-} & 0\ 1
\end{array}
$$

The ternary operator in the main display loop toggles the selector variable t between 0 and 1, thus alternating the tile displayed during the current iteration. This simple solution works because there is an odd number of tiles in each row.

Stacking Graphics Images

As in text screens, you might want to create graphics pop-ups that later vanish by restoring the overlaid area. For that reason, the **EXGRAPH** library in Listing 11.4 includes the _saveimage() and _restimage() functions, graphics counterparts to _savescrn() and _restscrn().

Like their text cousins, these graphics functions automatically manage a stack in dynamic memory. Thus _restimage() always restores the most recently saved image area, effecting a last-in, first-out order.

Unlike the text functions, _saveimage() and _restimage() deal with a portion of the display area and not the entire screen. This is because it takes many more bytes to store even a relatively small graphics region for an entire text display. Consequently, for _saveimage() you specify opposite corners of the area to be saved. The origin of the area is stored along with the graphics image, so _restscrn() takes no arguments; it restores the image at its original location.

GRPOP.C, Listing 11.8, provides a working example of graphics pop-ups. In the interest of simplicity, the pop-ups are filled rectangles, each of a different color and at a different location. All overlap in the center of the screen. Using timed delays, the program stacks the pop-ups, pauses for three seconds, then removes them in LIFO order. Make the program at the command line with

    QCL grpop.c exgraph.c

Listing 11.8 **Stacking and removing graphics pop-ups.**

```
/* GRPOP.C: Graphics pop-ups */

#include <conio.h>
#include <graph.h>
#include <stdio.h>
#include "exgraph.h"

void main()
{
int pop;

  if (_setvideomode (_MRES4COLOR)) {

    /* First popup */
    _setcolor (1);
    _saveimage (70, 40, 210, 110);
    _rectangle (_GFILLINTERIOR, 70, 40, 210, 110);
    wait (1.5);

    /* Second popup */
    _setcolor (2);
    _saveimage (160, 70, 280, 140);
```

Listing 11.8 *(continued)*

```
    _rectangle (_GFILLINTERIOR, 160, 70, 280, 140);
    wait (1.5);

    /* and third */
    _setcolor (3);
    _saveimage (120, 90, 190, 170);
    _rectangle (_GFILLINTERIOR, 120, 90, 190, 170);
    wait (3.0);

    /* Now remove the pop-ups */
    for (pop = 3; pop > 0; pop--) {
      _restimage();
      wait (1.5);
    }
    _setvideomode (_DEFAULTMODE);
  } else
    puts ("CGA not supported");
}
```

Filling

Filling a closed figure with some pattern and color makes it distinct from its surroundings, as well as adding realism or otherwise enhancing the visual meaning of the object. It's an important aspect of graphics presentation. So important, in fact, that Quick C furnishes four functions for controlling filling, and offers filling as an option in its built-in _rectangle(), _pie(), and _ellipse() functions. There is also an explicit fill function called _floodfill(), which we'll discuss here.

The default fill style is solid, as we've already seen in several programs that call _rectangle() with the _GFILLINTERIOR option. The fill is always done in the current foreground color. The _pie() and _ellipse() functions similarly create visually solid filled objects when called with _GFILLINTERIOR, or outlines only with _GBORDER.

If you want to use a different fill pattern, you have to define it in terms of an eight-bit by eight-row array of type char (the elements are not really regarded as characters, but instead as bytes). The Quick C graphics library's filling routine repeats this 8x8 pattern throughout the designated area much as TILES.C (Listing 11.7) filled the screen with square images. Filling stops at the object's boundaries, so in most cases (where the width or height are not a multiple of eight) the pattern is truncated at an edge.

In the pattern specification, a 1-bit means the corresponding pixel is on, and a 0-bit means the pixel is off. This is similar to the line pattern discussed earlier, except each segment (scan line) of the fill pattern is eight pixels in length instead of 16. For example, if every other pixel in a scan line is on, the

Figure 11.2 **Defining a striped fill pattern.**

Pattern	Hex
X . . . X . . .	0x88
. X . . . X . .	0x44
. . X . . . X .	0x22
. . . X . . . X	0x11
X . . . X . . .	0x88
. X . . . X . .	0x44
. . X . . . X .	0x22
. . . X . . . X	0x11

binary pattern is 10101010, or AAh in hex. If you want a tightly cross-hatched pattern, the second line would have the opposite bit configuration, or 99h. Alternating these two values through eight array elements defines the fill pattern.

. Figure 11.2 illustrates this concept further by defining a diagonally striped pattern, where the X's represent lighted pixels. Note that the bit configurations make for continuous lines. That is, if a second copy of the pattern is placed adjacent in any direction to the one shown, each line of lighted pixels continues unbroken. Having worked out this pattern, you can define it in a C program as

```
char  striped[]  =  {0x88,  0x44,  0x22,  0x11,
                     0x88,  0x44,  0x22,  0x11};
```

The pattern becomes active with the call

```
_setfillmask  (striped);
```

and thereafter all filled objects assume the striped pattern.

The _setfillmask() function returns a pointer to the currently active (superseded) pattern. Consequently, if you're going to want later to reactivate the default solid mask, you can define a pointer as

```
char  far  *solid;
```

Then, when activating the striped mask, issue the call

solid = _setfillmask (striped);

Restore the original mask later with

_setfillmask (solid);

You can also obtain a pointer to the current mask at any time by calling _getfillmask(), as in

char far *currfill;
    ...
    _getfillmask(currfill);

FILLER.C, Listing 11.9, illustrates three different fill patterns within rectangles: tightly hatched, loosely hatched, and striped. Each is in a different color on the CGA display. Note that the two boxes within the full-screen fill must first be cleared by filling with color 0 (the background). If we don't do this, the new pattern will become mixed with the one it overlays.

Listing 11.9 **Using different fill patterns.**

```
/* FILLER.C: Draws objects and fills them using floodfill */
#include <graph.h>
#include <stdio.h>
#include "vcoords.h"

/* Fill pattern definitions */
unsigned char tight_hatch[] = {
    0xAA, 0x55, 0xAA, 0x55, 0xAA, 0x55, 0xAA, 0x55
};
unsigned char loose_hatch[] = {
    0x99, 0x66, 0x99, 0x66, 0x99, 0x66, 0x99, 0x66
};
unsigned char stripes[] = {
    0x88, 0x44, 0x22, 0x11, 0x88, 0x44, 0x22, 0x11
};

main ()
{
unsigned char far *solid_mask;

  if (_setvideomode (_MRES4COLOR)) {    /* use CGA 4-color */
    setvcoords(800, 600);              /* init virtual coords */
    _selectpalette (0);                        /* set palette */
    solid_mask = _getfillmask (NULL); /* get default mask */

    /* Border and fill whole screen */
    _setfillmask (tight_hatch);
    _rectangle (_GFILLINTERIOR,
```

```
                          dx (0), dy (599), dx (799), dy (0));

        /* Large box in center */
        _setcolor (0);                          /* clear area first */
        _setfillmask (solid_mask);
        _rectangle (_GFILLINTERIOR,
                    dx (200), dy (200), dx (600), dy (400));
        _setcolor (2);                          /* now draw filled box */
        _setfillmask (loose_hatch);
        _rectangle (_GFILLINTERIOR,
                    dx (200), dy (200), dx (600), dy (400));

        /* Small box, lower right */
        _setcolor (0);                          /* clear area first */
        _setfillmask (solid_mask);
        _rectangle (_GFILLINTERIOR,
                    dx (650), dy ( 50), dx (750), dy (150));
        _setcolor (1);                          /* now draw filled box */
        _setfillmask (stripes);
        _rectangle (_GFILLINTERIOR,
                    dx (650), dy ( 50), dx (750), dy (150));

        /* Wait for keypress and quit */
        getch();
        _setvideomode (_DEFAULTMODE);
    } else
        puts ("Your adapter doesn't support CGA 4-color mode");
}
```

You can achieve interesting effects by overlaying one fill pattern with
another. One example is called dithering, in which colors are mixed to form a
blend. The technique is to have one colored pattern fill in empty pixels in
another. Listing 11.10 (DITHER.C) illustrates this. Dithering is not very successful on the CGA, so this program operates in EGA 16-color mode. It
divides the EGA display into three color bars. The one on the left is brown,
the one on the right yellow. In between is a dithered pattern combining the
two. The display favors bright colors, so the result is a shade of dark yellow,
with the bit pattern discernible at close range.

Listing 11.10 **Dithering to blend two colors.**

```
/* DITHER.C: Blends brown and yellow on the EGA */
/*           by using offsetting fill patterns */

#include <graph.h>
#include <stdio.h>

char a[] = {0xCC, 0x33, 0xCC, 0x33, 0xCC, 0x33, 0xCC, 0x33};
char b[] = {0x33, 0xCC, 0x33, 0xCC, 0x33, 0xCC, 0x33, 0xCC};

void main()
```

Listing 11.10 *(continued)*

```
{
  if (_setvideomode (_ERESCOLOR)) {

    /* Draw brown color bar */
    _setcolor (6);
    _rectangle (_GFILLINTERIOR, 0, 0, 209, 349);

    /* Draw yellow color bar */
    _setcolor (14);
    _rectangle (_GFILLINTERIOR, 420, 0, 629, 349);

    /* Dither a color bar from yellow and brown */
    _setfillmask (a);
    _rectangle (_GFILLINTERIOR, 210, 0, 419, 349);
    _setcolor (6);
    _setfillmask (b);
    _rectangle (_GFILLINTERIOR, 210, 0, 419, 349);

    getch();                              /* wait for keypress */
    _setvideomode (_DEFAULTMODE);
  } else
    puts ("EGA color mode not supported");
}
```

Quick C's _floodfill() function fills an area bounded by a border color, including irregular polygons. If you're unfamiliar with the term, an irregular polygon is any closed shape. It can include vertices that intrude into the figure, forming a concavity. Most objects in the real world are irregular polygons: a house key, for example, or the petal of a flower, or a coffee cup.

_floodfill() requires three arguments: the origin of the fill (X and Y coordinates) and the boundary color. It then begins spreading the current fill style outward from the origin until it encounters a pixel of the border color. If it can go around the pixel it will do so, leaving the pixel intact but continuing to spread the pattern until progress is blocked in all directions by the border color. _floodfill() can thus fill an object, and it can also fill everything around another contained polygon but not invade it.

Listings 11.11 and 11.12 are two programs that illustrate _floodfill() in action. Listing 11.11 is BOOM!.C, which depicts a lightning bolt. This image shows that _floodfill() can work its way through a complex shape, backtracking to handle concavities. Listing 11.12, DIAMOND.C, draws a white diamond surrounded by a cyan frame. The background within the frame is magenta. It's actually four triangles, each of which is individually filled. The frame is also filled by _floodfill(), illustrating how this general filling routine can work around a contained object (the diamond and its background) without entering it.

Listing 11.11 **Filling an irregular polygon.**

```c
/* BOOM!.C: Lightning bolt is filled irregular polygon */

#include <graph.h>
#include <stdio.h>
#include <stdlib.h>
#include "exgraph.h"

struct xycoord bolt[] = {
   {160,    0}, {155,   45}, {165,   40}, {150, 100}, {160,   95},
   {130, 190}, {175,   90}, {165,   95}, {185,   35}, {175,   40},
   {185,    0}
};
int order[] = {0, 1, 2, 3, 4, 5, 6, 7, 8, 9, 10, 0};

void main()
{
  if (_setvideomode (_MRES4COLOR)) {
    _polyline (11, bolt, order);
    _floodfill (170, 10, 3);
    wait (5.0);
    _setvideomode (_DEFAULTMODE);
  } else
    puts ("CGA not supported");
}
```

Listing 11.12 **Filling several objects.**

```c
/* DIAMOND.C: Diamond in a frame */

#include <graph.h>
#include <stdio.h>
#include "exgraph.h"

struct xycoord diamond[] = {
   {160, 60}, {220, 100}, {160, 140}, {100, 100}
};
int order[] = {0, 1, 2, 3, 0};

void main()
{
  if (!(_setvideomode (_MRES4COLOR))) {
    puts ("CGA not supported");
    exit (-1);
  }

  /* Draw filled diamond */
  _selectpalette (1);                /* cyan, magenta, lt gray */
  _polyline (4, diamond, order);
  _floodfill (160, 100, 3);               /* fill from center */

  /* Draw surrounding frame, fill quadrants */
```

Listing 11.12 *(continued)*

```
_rectangle (_GBORDER, 100, 60, 220, 140);
_setcolor (2);                     /* fill with magenta */
_floodfill (110,  70, 3);              /* upper left */
_floodfill (110, 130, 3);              /* lower left */
_floodfill (210, 130, 3);              /* lower right */
_floodfill (210,  70, 3);              /* upper right */

/* Draw and fill outer frame */
_setcolor (3);                     /* outline in white */
_rectangle (_GBORDER, 80, 40, 240, 160);
_setcolor (1);                     /* fill with cyan */
_floodfill (90, 50, 3);

/* Freeze display and quit */
wait (5.0);
_setvideomode (_DEFAULTMODE);
}
```

Scaling the Coordinate Space

The virtual coordinates introduced in Chapter 10 were discussed only in the context of removing distortion by forcing pixels to be square. We can also use virtual coordinates to scale the virtual display area so that the data to be displayed make the maximum use of it. Also, by adding constants to the virtual coordinates, we can arithmetically shift the origin of the coordinate system. The application discussed here is plotting mathematical functions.

Many mathematical functions have a domain that is both positive and negative. Examples are the trigonometric functions sine and cosine, of which the result (Y) fluctuates smoothly between +1.0 and −1.0 depending on the angle (X) argument. If we want to view the result of one of these functions through one full circle, or 360 degrees, then the virtual plot area must be 360 units in width.

There are two problems with using virtual coordinates in this case. First, the coordinate space as defined in the **VCOORDS** library always has a positive Y, with the origin (X = 0, Y = 0) in the lower left corner. Therefore it seemingly cannot contain negative values.

The solution is to shift the Y origin upward. In the case of sine and cosine, values are evenly divided between negative and positive, so the sensible place to put the Y origin is in the vertical center of the display. We can do this by adding a constant to the virtual Y each time we resolve it using the library's dy() function. The constant represents the upward shift (in virtual Y units) of the Y origin. We'll see how in a moment.

The other problem is that virtual coordinates are integers. If we attempt to plot the range −1.0 <= Y <= 1.0, we'll get a line that fluctuates at most one pixel in either direction from the Y origin; hardly a useful graph. To solve this problem, multiply the virtual Y by a constant large enough to yield a value that allows fine gradations to become meaningful. For trig functions, 100.0 is sufficient because it increases the domain such that $-100.0 <= Y <= 100.0$.

Consequently, to plot a sine or cosine through one full rotation, the virtual space must be at least 360 x 200. To resolve a fractional value to its device coordinate, the expression is

```
dy ((int)(frac_val * 100.0)  +  100);
```

The constant 100.0 expands the fractional value into a meaningful integer, and the integral constant 100 places it in relation to a Y origin in the vertical center of the screen. If you want to shift the X origin someplace besides the left edge of the display and use fractional X's, you can apply a similar expression to the argument of dx().

Now let's see a working example. We're going to plot the equation

```
y  =  sin 2x  +  cos x
```

Because the two factors of the equation are out of sync with each other and additive, the deviation of Y can be as much as 2.0, suggesting a vertical dimension of 400 (where 100.0 is the Y multiplier). We want to leave room at the top and bottom for a label and a legend, so we'll set the virtual height to 440 units. Therefore the Y addition constant is 220. This value is called YO in the TRIGPLOT program (Listing 11.13). Furthermore, we'll plot the functions through two full cycles, so the domain of X is 720 degrees (constant MAXX). We now have our virtual coordinate space, defined as

```
setvcoords  (MAXX, YO*2);
```

Listing 11.13 Fitting the display space to the data.

```
/* TRIGPLOT.C: Plots equation y = cos x + sin 2x */
/* 0 <= x <= 720 degrees, y = +- 2.0 */

#include <graph.h>
#include <math.h>
#include <stdio.h>
#include <conio.h>
#include <string.h>
#include "vcoords.h"
#include "exgraph.h"
#define LABEL "y = sin 2x + cos x"                    /* graph label */
#define DEG2RAD 0.01745           /* conversion: degrees to radians */
#define MAXX 720                               /* max value of X */
#define YM 100                                  /* y multiplier */
#define YO 220                       /* y origin in virtual coords */

struct videoconfig video;                       /* global variable */
```

Listing 11.13 *(continued)*

```
main()
{
int x, y;
double theta, ys, yc;
void legend (int, char*);
void plot (int, double);

  if (!(_setvideomode (bestmode()))) {
    puts ("Graphics not available");
    exit (-1);
  }

  /* Label the graph */
  _getvideoconfig (&video);
  x = (video.numtextcols - strlen (LABEL)) / 2;
  _settextposition (1, x);
  _outtext (LABEL);

  /* Set coordinate space */
  setvcoords (MAXX, YO*2);              /* 720 x 240 virtual pixels */
  _setlinestyle (0x8888);                        /* dotted X axis */
  for (y = -2; y < 3; y++) {
    _moveto (dx(  0), dy((y*YM)+YO));
    _lineto (dx(719), dy((y*YM)+YO));   /* mark unity increments */
  }

  /* Plot sin 2x */
  _setcolor (1);
  legend (0, "sin 2x");
  for (x = 0; x < 720; x++) {
    theta = (double)(x) * DEG2RAD;              /* angle in radians */
    ys = sin (theta * 2.0);                        /* y for sin 2x */
    plot (x, ys);
  }

  /* Plot cos x */
  _setcolor (2);
  legend (1, "cos x");
  for (x = 0; x < 720; x++) {
    theta = (double)(x) * DEG2RAD;
    yc = cos (theta);
    plot (x, yc);
  }

  /* Plot sum */
  _setlinestyle (0xFFFF);
  _setcolor (video.numcolors-1);              /* use brightest color */
  legend (2, "sum");
  for (x = 0; x < 720; x++) {
    theta = (double)(x) * DEG2RAD;
    ys = sin (theta * 2.0);
```

```
    yc = cos (theta);
    plot (x, ys+yc);
  }

  /* Hold for keypress, then quit */
  getch();
  _setvideomode (_DEFAULTMODE);
} /* ----------------------- */

void legend (int item, char *legendtext)
                      /* insert legend for item at bottom of plot area */
{
int stx, gx, gy;
struct rccoord text;

  stx = (((video.numtextcols/3)+2) * item);          /* text col */
  _settextposition (video.numtextrows, stx);
  _outtext (legendtext);                             /* write legend */
  text = _gettextposition();                  /* where is text cursor? */
  gx = text.col * 8;                                /* graphics x */
  gy = (text.row-1) *
      (video.numypixels / video.numtextrows) + 4;      /* and y */
  _moveto (gx, gy);
  _lineto (gx+40, gy);                          /* draw legend line */
} /* ----------------------- */

void plot (int x, double y)            /* plot next curve segment */
{
  if (x > 0)
    _lineto (dx(x), dy((int)(y*YM)+Y0));
  else
    _moveto (dx(x), dy((int)(y*YM)+Y0));
}
```

The **TRIGPLOT** program tailors its appearance to the best graphics mode available. Between the CGA and the EGA/VGA, the only differences are colors and the size of text. The program centers the label at the top and marks the unity intervals $(-2, -1, 0, 1, 2)$ on the Y axis with dotted lines. In successive colors, it plots sin 2x, then cos x, and finally (in the brightest available color) their sum.

Make the **TRIGPLOT** program with the command line

    QCL trigplot.c vcoords.c exgraph.c

Figure 11.3 shows the result as it appears on the CGA. The black-and-white reproduction here doesn't do the plot justice; colors distinguish the three curves. The most sinuous and widely varying is the sum.

Further notes on this program: Quick C trig functions require radians, not degrees, as their argument (this is true of almost all programming languages). There are 0.01745 radians per degree, accounting for the constant **DEG2RAD**.

Figure 11.3 **Output from** TRIGPLOT.C on the CGA.

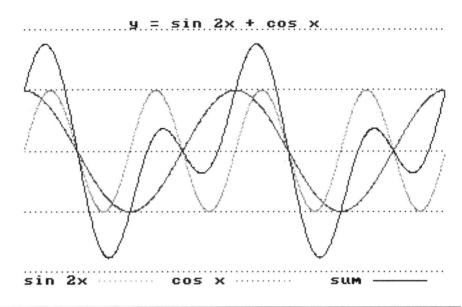

The legend() function places evenly spaced legends across the bottom of the graph by relating text and graphics coordinates. The plot() function positions the graphics pen when the angle is 0, and otherwise draws to the next vertex of the curve. Use of the _lineto() function (rather than _setpixel()) keeps the curves from becoming sparse on steep slopes.

The following section further expands on these concepts.

Computing Regular Polygons

The vertices of a regular closed polygon are simply points spaced at even intervals around an imaginary circle. The outline of the polygon is obtained by joining these points, as in a square or a hexagon. Similarly, we can join the points in other orders to form figures such as a star. And by relocating the virtual X and Y reference points for the center of the figure, we can locate it anywhere on the display surface.

All vertices of a polygon are equidistant from the center of the circle they lay on. In fact, if you create a polygon with a great many vertices, it will approximate a circle, and it's valid to describe a true circle as a polygon with infinitely many vertices. Consequently, the trigonometry of circles is useful for creating polygons.

The distance from the center to the circle is its radius. The angle to the point is customarily represented by the Greek letter theta. Thus, if the origin is at coordinates {0, 0}, the coordinates for a point r units away at angle theta are found as follows:

$$x = r \cos theta$$

$$y = r \sin theta$$

Suppose you want to define a hexagon. The number of sides is six, so the arc for each vertex is 360 / 6 = 60 degrees. The successive values of theta are thus 0, 60, 120, .., 360. However, computer graphics throws in a couple of small complications.

The first is that, as mentioned earlier, the sin() and cos() functions don't work with degrees, but instead with radians. Radians is a measure of angular motion based on pi (3.1415927). A full circle is 360 degrees or 2*pi radians. Therefore a half circle is pi radians, and the number of radians per degree is pi / 180.0 = 0.0174532. If we call this conversion value DEG2RAD, we can convert degrees into equivalent radians with

$$radians = degrees * RAD;$$

The virtual coordinates are then derived from

$$x = r \cos (radians)$$
$$y = r \sin (radians)$$

By placing these expressions into a loop that steps degrees by some even sub-multiple of 360, we can build a set of points that describe a regular polygon. For example, to construct the vertices of a nine-sided polygon, the stepping value for degrees is 360/9 = 40. The results are placed into an array of virtual coordinates.

The next trick has to do with getting these virtual coordinates onto the screen. The assumed center of the array of coordinates is {0, 0}. Consequently, some three-fourths of the coordinates are in the negative domain: Either left of the virtual origin, or below it, or both. Therefore applying dx() and dy() to the coordinates will display only the upper right quadrant. As in the case of the Y axis for the curves discussed earlier, it's necessary to offset the coordinates in order to relocate their point of reference.

Let's call this point of reference {CX, CY}, which can be any arbitrary place. If we want to place the polygon in the center of an 800 x 600 virtual display, the offsetting coordinates are CX = 400 and CY = 300. Consequently, the relocated virtual coordinates for any point become

$$x = CX + (r \cos [radians])$$
$$y = CY + (r \sin [radians])$$

Use dx() and dy() to resolve them to device coordinates.

The HEXMANIA.C program in Listing 11.14 builds on this idea. The program computes a large hexagon, storing the virtual coordinates of the vertices in the array big[]. The array is then displayed around a point at the center of the screen by constructing an outline. After a brief delay to let you see the outline, the program draws six smaller hexagons, each centered on a vertex of the larger figure.

The command line to make this program is

QCL hexmania.c vcoords.c exgraph.c

Listing 11.14 **Regular polygons with movable centers.**

```
/* HEXMANIA.C: Hexagons superimposed on a larger hexagon */
/* Illustrates moving the center of a polygon */

#include <graph.h>
#include <math.h>
#include "vcoords.h"
#include "exgraph.h"
#define DEG2RAD 0.0174532
#define RADIUS  200
#define CX 400
#define CY 300

void main()
{
struct xycoord big[6], small[6];
int x, xoff, yoff;
double theta;
void draw (struct xycoord*, int, int);

  /* Initialize the large hexagon */
  for (x = 0; x < 6; x++) {
    theta = (double)(x*60) * DEG2RAD;        /* angle x in radians */
    big[x].xcoord = (int)(cos (theta) * RADIUS);       /* x coord */
    big[x].ycoord = (int)(sin (theta) * RADIUS);       /* y coord */
  }

  /* Initialize the small hexagon */
  for (x = 0; x < 6; x++) {
    small[x].xcoord = big[x].xcoord / 3;
    small[x].ycoord = big[x].ycoord / 3;
  }

  /* Set graphics */
  if (!(_setvideomode (bestmode()))) {
    puts ("Graphics not available");
    exit (-1);
  }

  /* Draw the big hexagon in outline only, wait 3 seconds */
```

```
    setvcoords (CX*2, CY*2);
    _moveto (dx (big[0].xcoord+CX), dy (big[0].ycoord+CY));
    for (x = 1; x < 6; x++)
      _lineto (dx (big[x].xcoord+CX), dy (big[x].ycoord+CY));
    _lineto (dx (big[0].xcoord+CX), dy (big[0].ycoord+CY));
    wait (3.0);

    /* Draw the little hexagons at vertices of the big one */
    for (x = 0; x < 6; x++) {
      xoff = big[x].xcoord + CX;             /* offsets for center */
      yoff = big[x].ycoord + CY;
      draw (small, xoff, yoff);              /* draw the hexagon */
    }

    /* Wait 5 seconds, then quit */
    wait (5.0);
    _setvideomode (_DEFAULTMODE);
  } /* --------------------- */

void draw (struct xycoord *hex, int x, int y)
                 /* draw hex joining all vertices centered on x, y */
{
int p, v;

    for (p = 0; p < 6; p++)
      for (v = 0; v < 6; v++) {
        _moveto (dx (hex[p].xcoord+x), dy (hex[p].ycoord+y));
        _lineto (dx (hex[v].xcoord+x), dy (hex[v].ycoord+y));
      }
}
```

Each small hexagon is drawn from a common array, which was taken from the larger array through division of all points by three. The center offset of a small hexagon is the sum of the screen center {CX, CY} plus the vertex around which it is drawn. The loop that calls **draw**() and the local function itself show how this is done. The **draw**() function also illustrates a method for joining all vertices to all others, forming a jewel-like figure.

This chapter has illustrated a number of techniques for controlling the graphics display and for creating visual images constructed from straight lines. Now let's widen the graphics repertoire with curves.

CHAPTER **12**

Drawing Simple Curves

The last chapter concentrated on developing graphics images from straight lines. This one and the next introduce techniques and tools for drawing various kinds of curved objects using Quick C graphics.

It's possible to regard a curve as a series of many straight line segments, each joining its neighbors at a very slight angle of incidence. For example, a regular polygon with 200 sides would be indistinguishable from a circle on a computer screen. However, this is an inconvenient way to think of and work with curves, which are visual and mathematical entities in their own right. Hence this chapter.

First we'll deal with the curve-making tools built into the Quick C graphics library, and then we'll stretch your repertoire with additional ways of drawing them.

Quick C Library Functions

The Quick C library has three functions for creating curved objects of various classes: _ellipse() draws closed curves such as circles, _arc() draws open curves, and _pie() is a variant on _arc() for making pie slices.

The library functions all rely on a concept known as the bounding rectangle. This is an imaginary box that represents the outer limits of the curve it contains, specified in terms of its northwest and southeast corners. For example, an ellipse is drawn within its bounding rectangle such that it touches all four sides.

Figure 12.1 illustrates this principle by depicting both the bounding rectangle and its contained ellipse. Listing 12.1 is the program BOUNDCIR.C that produced this drawing.

Listing 12.1 **Program that produced Figure 12.1.**

```
/* BOUNDCIR.C: Illustrates bounding rectangle of an ellipse */

#include <graph.h>
#include <conio.h>

void main()
```

```
  {
    if (_setvideomode (_MRES4COLOR)) {
      _setcolor (1);
      _rectangle (_GBORDER, 0, 0, 199, 199);/* show rectangle */
      _setcolor (3);
      _ellipse (_GFILLINTERIOR, 0, 0, 199, 199);* and ellipse */
      getch();
      _setvideomode (_DEFAULTMODE);
    }
  }
```

It's important to note that the image in Figure 12.1 is mathematically a circle, since its bounding rectangle is a square of 200 x 200 pixels. The circle isn't perfectly round, however, because of the distortion introduced by non-square pixels. This occurs to one degree or another in all graphics modes except VGA 640 x 480. The elliptical appearance of the circle is another example of the problem first discussed in Chapter 10.

One solution is to manually calculate dimensions for the bounding rectangle that counteract the screen's inherent distortion. An easier one is to let the computer do it by applying virtual coordinates as discussed earlier. Either way, in order to draw a circle that looks round, you need to make an ellipse that is mathematically either shorter along the vertical axis, or longer along the horizontal. The degree of intentional distortion depends on the amount of inherent discrepancy you have to correct. That's a function of the graphics

Figure 12.1 **An ellipse and its bounding rectangle.**

mode. As I said, it's easier to use virtual coordinates to define the bounding rectangle.

Listing 12.2 shows how to perform this in CIRCLE.C, Figure 12.2 is a photo of the result. The images in Figures 12.1 and 12.2 are the same physical height: 200 pixels. In this case, we achieved roundness by stretching the ellipse horizontally, the result of shortening the virtual X axis to 267 units (200 vertical / .75 to get the proper square ratio). We could also have done it the other way, defining a virtual space of, say, 320 x 240. The result of a 200 x 200 bounding rectangle in that case would have been a circle the same physical width as the ellipse in Figure 12.1, instead shrunken along the vertical axis.

Listing 12.2 **Drawing a round circle with virtual coordinates.**

```
/* CIRCLE.C: Illustrates bounding rectangle of an ellipse */
/*     using virtual coordinates to achieve a circle */

#include <graph.h>
#include <conio.h>
#include "vcoords.h"

void main()
{
  if (_setvideomode (_MRES4COLOR)) {
    setvcoords (266, 200);          /* 266 x 200 virtual space */
    _setcolor (1);                              /* show rectangle */
    _rectangle (_GBORDER, dx(0), dy(0), dx(199), dy(199));
    _setcolor (3);                              /* and circle */
    _ellipse (_GFILLINTERIOR, dx(0), dy(0), dx(199), dy(199));
    getch();
    _setvideomode (_DEFAULTMODE);
  }
}
```

Of course there are times when you really do want to draw an ellipse. The same problems hold true as for circles, though; it's hard to get the right proportion of width to height unless you use virtual coordinates. An ellipse bounded by the virtual coordinates {0, 0} and {100, 50} will indeed be twice as long as it is high when it appears on the screen.

Note that the Quick C _ellipse() function only supports variability along the vertical and horizontal axes. Later we'll discuss a method for producing rotated ellipses using conic splines.

You can produce partial, open curves with the Quick C function _arc(). The _pie() function is closely related to _arc() and differs in only two respects:

- Straight lines are drawn from the ends of the arc to the point around which the arc rotates, forming a pie slice.
- You must specify one of the two options _GBORDER or _GFILLINTERIOR to produce an outline or a slice filled using the current fill mask.

Figure 12.2 **Output from the** CIRCLE program.

Therefore we'll discuss only _arc() here, and you can generalize the discussion to _pie() as well.

Like ellipse(), arc() relies on a bounding rectangle to define the extent of its sweep. The center of rotation is the midpoint between the opposite corners of the rectangle. Therefore a bounding rectangle squished along one axis produces an elliptical arc, and a physically square (on the display) rectangle yields a circular arc. The curve shown in Figure 12.3 shows an elliptical arc, the result of the bounding rectangle having greater width than height.

The arc is conceptually a portion of the complete ellipse filling the bounding rectangle defined by {X1, Y1} and {X2, Y2}. The visible portion begins where the ellipse intercepts an imaginary line running between its center and the point specified by {X3, Y3}. The arc then rotates counterclockwise until it intercepts another imaginary line extending from the center to {X4, Y4}. You can see this by examining Figure 12.3, a drawing produced by the ARC.C program in Figure 12.3.

Listing 12.3 **Program to illustrate the components of an arc.**

```
/* ARC.C: Illustrates how Quick C draws an arc */

#include <stdio.h>
#include <graph.h>
#define X1  80
#define Y1  50
```

Listing 12.3 *(continued)*

```
#define X2 240
#define Y2 150
#define X3   0
#define Y3  50
#define X4 240
#define Y4 150

main()
{
int cx, cy, tx, ty;

  if (_setvideomode (_MRES4COLOR)) {
    /* Draw bounding rectangle */
    _setcolor (2);
    _rectangle (_GBORDER, X1, Y1, X2, Y2); /* bounding rectangle */

    /* Draw vectors */
    cx = ((X2 - X1) / 2) + X1;
    cy = ((Y2 - Y1) / 2) + Y1;
    _moveto (X3, Y3);
    _lineto (cx, cy);
    _lineto (X4, Y4);

    /* Draw the arc */
    _setcolor (3);
    _arc (X1, Y1, X2, Y2, X3, Y3, X4, Y4);

    /* Label the points */
    _settextcolor (1);
    _settextposition ( 6,  9); _outtext ("X1,Y1");
    _settextposition (19, 32); _outtext ("X2,Y2");
    _settextposition ( 6,  1); _outtext ("X3,Y3");
    _settextposition (20, 32); _outtext ("X4,Y4");
    cx /= 8; cy /= 8;
    _settextposition (cy, cx); _outtext ("cx,cy");

    /* Wait for keypress and quit */
    while (!kbhit());
    _setvideomode (-1);
  } else
    puts ("Graphics mode not available");
}
```

There are many things to admire about the Quick C graphics library, but its way of making arcs is not among them. For one thing, it's nearly impossible to determine the coordinates where an arc began and ended; a necessity if the arc is part of a larger pattern such as a rounded box or a meandering line. For another, this business of intercepting with imaginary lines is counterintuitive.

There's a better way, so let's begin stretching our curve-making methods in Quick C.

Figure 12.3 **Anatomy of a Quick C arc.**

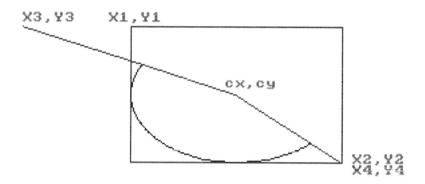

Conic Splines _____

A spline is to the graphics programmer as a French curve is to the draftsman: a tool for drawing endlessly variable curves. More specifically, a spline is a mathematical description of a curve, but don't let that turn you off. The nice thing about splines is that they're defined in terms of reference points that approximate the shape of the curve. Having visualized the curve you want, it's a simple and intuitive matter to plot its control points.

There are several kinds of splines. This book discusses two. Conic splines define a simple curve in terms of three control points. They provide not only a useful programming tool, but also serve as a conceptual basis for the more complex curves possible using a type of cubic spline known as the *Bezier curve*, discussed in the next chapter.

A conic spline gets its name from the layout of three control points that, if joined by straight lines, form a cone. The curve itself is a line moving between two end points (the "knots") and attracted toward the middle point at the apex of the cone. The curve never reaches this third point, but simply tends toward it, forming a smooth arc between the knots. When it reaches a knot, the curve's direction is exactly the same as the line moving from the control point through the knot. Thus, any conic spline forms a perfect quarter of an ellipse. Figure 12.4 illustrates several conic splines along

Figure 12.4 **Several conic splines.**

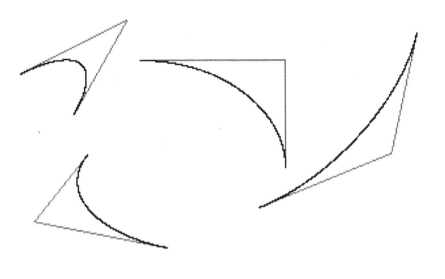

with their defining cones. Normally, of course, we wouldn't show the cones; they're here to illustrate the relationship between the curve and its control points.

Since a conic spline can be described in terms of two knots and a control point, it's easy to imagine a function that does it with the call

```
_curve (x1, y1, x2, y2, xc, yc);
```

Here {x1, y1} are the coordinates of one knot, {x2, y2} the coordinates of the other, and {xc, yc} those of the control point. The actual implementation of such a function is a lot more involved than simply imagining it, but not insurmountable.

Traditionally, the mathematics of curves involves trigonometry to find each point as a curve swings around its center. Trigonometric functions consume a lot of overhead on computers, however, making traditional methods unacceptably slow. For that reason, a lot of research has been done in recent years to find a better way. The method described here is an amalgamation of some of that research, taken primarily from Newman and Sproull *(Principles of Interactive Computer Graphics*, McGraw-Hill, New York, 1979) and several papers published by the scholar James Blinn.

Because the path of a curve changes by very small amounts as it progresses from one point to the next, it's necessary to employ fractional numbers in computing the variances. Fractional numbers are synonymous in most programmers' minds with floating point arithmetic. We'll develop an algorithm here using floating point, and later we'll present an alternative that yields much better performance.

The floating-point version of the conic _curve() function is shown in Listing 12.4. This routine begins by measuring the distance from the control point to each knot, and uses that information to locate the center of the ellipse of which the conic spline is a quadrant. The center coordinates are given by {x0, y0}.

This version of the _curve() function is illustrative only and—although it works—is not used in any programs in this book. Don't bother typing it into your computer.

Listing 12.4 **Conic spline algorithm using floating point.**

```
/* Draw a conic spline using floating point          */
/* Knots are at x1, y1 and x2, y2, control pt at xc, yc */

#include <graph.h>
#define HALFPI 3.1415927 / 2.0                        /* PI/2 */
#define DEN    1024.0             /* pixel density constant */

void _curve (int x1, int y1, int x2, int y2, int xc, int yc)
{
short i, x, y, prevx, prevy;
double vx, vy, ux, uy, x0, y0;

  vx = (double)(xc - x2);                   /* distance to P2 */
  vy = (double)(yc - y2);
  ux = (double)(xc - x1);                   /* distance to P1 */
  uy = (double)(yc - y1);
  x0 = (double)(x1) - vx + 0.5;             /* center of arc */
  y0 = (double)(y1) - vy + 0.5;
  for (i = (short)(HALFPI * DEN); i >= 0; --i) {
    x = (short)(x0 + vx);                 /* current position */
    y = (short)(y0 + vy);
    if (x != prevx || y != prevy)/* don't duplicate pixels */
      _setpixel (x, y);
    prevx = x;                          /* remember this position */
    prevy = y;
    ux -= vx / DEN;                           /* advance arc */
    uy -= vy / DEN;
    vx += ux / DEN;
    vy += uy / DEN;
  }
}
```

The terms of the for() statement might seem a little strange, so let's figure them out. A full circle (or ellipse) travels through PI*2 radians of arc. Therefore a quarter-turn is PI/2 radians, as represented by the HALFPI constant. Okay, so what's DEN? It's a pixel density constant; the higher the value, the more densely pixels are packed together to form a line. Experimentation reveals that a density constant of 1,024 is sufficient to make a solid-line curve from one corner of the display to the other in EGA 640 x 350 mode. A higher value slows down the line-drawing process without adding further resolution. Thus, 1,024 is the optimum. The expression HALFPI * DEN yields 1608, which is the maximum number of pixels to form any conic spline. Cast to type short, 1,608 becomes the loop counter's initial value.

The algorithm draws the curve by repeating the loop. The x and y variables are the computed current pixel position at each step. Note that this is calculated with reference to the center coordinates {x0, y0}. In other words, the curve is rotating around this point. The vx and vy variables are responsible for keeping track of the current offset from the center. They do this by interacting ingeniously with ux and uy; each updates the other with 1/DEN of its value. Because each changes with respect to the other, the continuous and smooth variance of the curve is obtained without using trig functions.

Nevertheless, the extensive use of floating point operations makes the algorithm slow. The if test in the loop improves performance slightly by avoiding duplicate pixel writes in small curves, but it's not enough to overcome the inherent slowness of floating-point arithmetic in machines lacking a math coprocessor.

The workaround is to use fixed-point arithmetic involving long integers. The resolution of computer graphics displays doesn't require the exacting precision of floating-point math. Thus we can get by with decimal approximation, which is much faster than floating point.

Fixed-point arithmetic works like this. All integers are promoted to longs and shifted left 16 bits, placing the integral portion of the value in the high-order word. The low-order word contains the fractional value. To get back to an integer, simply shift 16 bits right. This conversion truncates the fraction, but it doesn't matter since the only time we do it is to derive the X and Y coordinates of the pixel to be written; the fractional portion is present during all computations that yield the coordinates.

Shifting left by 16 bits is the same as multiplying by 65,536. Consequently, HALFPI becomes 102,942 (1.5708 * 65,536). Similarly, shifting left or right 10 bits is the same as mutiplying or dividing by 1,024, so DEN becomes a shift value of 10.

Listing 12.5 **Conic spline algorithm using fixed point.**

```
/* CURVE.C: Draws a conic spline using fixed point        */
/* Knots are at x1, y1 and x2, y2, control pt at xc, yc */


#include <graph.h>
#define HALFPI  102942L                /* fixed-point PI/2 */
#define HALF     32768L                 /* fixed point 0.5 */
#define DEN          10           /* pixel density constant */
```

```
void _curve (int x1, int y1, int x2, int y2, int xc, int yc)
{
short i, x, y, prevx, prevy;
long vx, vy, ux, uy, x0, y0;

  vx = (long)(xc - x2) << 16;                    /* distance to P2 */
  vy = (long)(yc - y2) << 16;
  ux = (long)(xc - x1) << 16;                    /* distance to P1 */
  uy = (long)(yc - y1) << 16;
  x0 = ((long)(x1) << 16) - vx + HALF;       /* center of arc */
  y0 = ((long)(y1) << 16) - vy + HALF;
  for (i = (short)((HALFPI << DEN) >> 16); i >= 0; --i) {
    x = (short)((x0 + vx) >> 16);           /* current position */
    y = (short)((y0 + vy) >> 16);
    if (x != prevx || y != prevy) /* don't duplicate pixels */
      _setpixel (x, y);
    prevx = x;                              /* remember this position */
    prevy = y;
    ux -= vx >> DEN;                              /* advance arc */
    uy -= vy >> DEN;
    vx += ux >> DEN;
    vy += uy >> DEN;
  }
}
```

The fixed-point algorithm in Listing 12.5 otherwise works the same as the floating point version, but several orders of magnitude faster. Consequently we'll use it in programs.

Create the file CURVE.H containing the following function prototype:

```
void far _curve (int x1, int y1, int x2, int y2,
                 int xc, int yc);
```

Now let's put the fixed-point conic splines algorithm to work. Listing 12.6, SPLINES.C, produces the drawings that you saw in Figure 12.4. Make this program from the command line with

```
QCL splines.c curve.c exgraph.c
```

Listing 12.6 **Program to draw assorted conic splines.**

```
/* SPLINES.C: Draws several conic splines */

#include <graph.h>
#include "exgraph.h"
#include "curve.h"

void main()
{
  if (_setvideomode (_MRES4COLOR)) {                    /* CGA 4-color */
    /* Right angle in center of display */
```

Listing 12.6 *(continued)*

```
    _setcolor (1);
    _moveto (100, 50); _lineto (210, 50); _lineto (210, 130);
    _setcolor (3);
    _curve (100, 50, 210, 130, 210, 50);

    /* Sharp angle, lower right */
    _setcolor (1);
    _moveto (60, 120); _lineto (20, 170); _lineto (120, 190);
    _setcolor (3);
    _curve (60, 120, 120, 190, 20, 170);

    /* Wide angle, lower left */
    _setcolor (1);
    _moveto (190, 160); _lineto (290, 120); _lineto (310, 30);
    _setcolor (3);
    _curve (190, 160, 310, 30, 290, 120);

    /* Small tight curve upper left */
    _setcolor (1);
    _moveto (10, 60); _lineto (90, 20); _lineto (50, 90);
    _setcolor (3);
    _curve (10, 60, 50, 90, 90, 20);

    getch();                                    /* wait for keypress */
    _setvideomode (_DEFAULTMODE);
  }
}
```

Forming Objects with Conic Splines

Because we know the locations of the control points forming a conic spline, it's simple to combine curves with lines to draw complex shapes. The spline's cone forms a V with the control point at the juncture and the knots at the tips. Each leg of the cone is composed of a line beginning at the apex and passing through the knot. Each line is tangent to the curve. Thus, when the curve arrives at a knot, it is moving away from the control point along this line.

The curve can thus flow smoothly into a straight line that continues the vector passing through its knot. The joint occurs at the knot. The other end of the straight line segment must be colinear with the knot and the control point. That is, if the knot and the control point both lie on Y coordinate 100, then the other end of the continuing line segment must be on Y coordinate 100 also. The same idea holds true when the line slants; in that case, you have to use geometry or graph paper to find the end point of the continuation line.

An example best illustrates this idea. Listing 12.7 contains ROUNDBOX.C, which draws a parallelogram with rounded corners. After taking a snapshot of this object with _getimage(), the program adds the corner cones and saves the image. It then alternates the two images in the same place on the display, in effect making the cones flash. This allows you to see how the straight sides of the parallelogram continue the cones, forming smooth joints with the curves.

You can make this program from the command line with

QCL roundbox.c curve.c exgraph.c

Listing 12.7 Joining conic splines with straight lines.

```
/* ROUNDBOX.C: Forming a rounded parallelogram */
/*    with lines and conic splines */
/* Box and its containing outline flash */

#include <graph.h>
#include <malloc.h>
#include "exgraph.h"
#include "curve.h"

void main()
{
char far *box, far *outline;
long size;
int  t;

  if (_setvideomode (_MRES4COLOR)) {

    /* Draw the rounded box */
    _moveto (170, 70); _lineto (210,   70);       /* top    */
    _curve (210,   70, 215,  85, 230,   70);      /* NE cor */
    _moveto (215, 85); _lineto (185, 115);        /* right  */
    _curve (185, 115, 150, 130, 170, 130);        /* SE cor */
    _moveto (150, 130); _lineto (110, 130);       /* bottom */
    _curve (110, 130, 105, 115,  90, 130);        /* SW cor */
    _moveto (105, 115); _lineto (135, 85);        /* left   */
    _curve (135,  85, 170, 70, 150,  70);         /* NW cor */

    /* Save the image */
    size = _imagesize (90, 70, 230, 130);
    box = _fmalloc (size);
    _getimage (90, 70, 230, 130, box);

    /* Draw the containing outline */
    _moveto (150,  70);
    _lineto (230,  70); _lineto (170, 130);
    _lineto ( 90, 130); _lineto (150,  70);

    /* Save outline */
    outline = _fmalloc (size);
    _getimage (90, 70, 230, 130, outline);

    /* Alternate the images 20 times */
    for (t = 0; t < 20; t++) {
      wait (0.5);
```

Listing 12.7 *(continued)*

```
    _putimage (90, 70, box, _GPSET);
    wait (0.5);
    _putimage (90, 70, outline, _GPSET);
  }

  /* Clean up and quit */
  _ffree (box);
  _ffree (outline);
  _setvideomode (_DEFAULTMODE);
  }
}
```

Let's use the northeast corner as an example to see how it works. The cone has knots at {210, 70} and {215, 85}, with the control point at {230, 70}. One side of the cone is easy; the first knot and the control point both lie on Y plane 70, so any smoothly adjoining line must be on the same plane. Indeed, the other end of the line forming the top of the parallelogram is at {170, 70}.

The other side of the cone slants. Between the control point and the knot, X changes by 15, and Y by the same amount (disregarding the signs). Consequently, there's a one-to-one ratio of change along the line. Extending the plane onward by 30 pixels, then, we come to an end point at {185, 115}.

The same general idea holds true when joining two conic splines in a continuing curve. The splines join at coincident knots, and the sides of their cones are colinear; that is, the two control points and the joining knot are all on the same plane.

The TILTOVAL.C program in Listing 12.8 illustrates this. The figure drawn by the program is similar to that of the previous program, except that it consists entirely of conic splines joined to form a continuum. It's not possible to draw this shape with Quick C's _ellipse() routine, which limits variations to the two orthogonal axes of an ellipse. This program also demonstrates using virtual coordinates with the conic _curve() function. The program draws the large tilted oval and freezes the display for five seconds, then adds the cones and freezes it again for the same period before ending.

The DOS command to make this program is

     QCL tiltoval.c vcoords.c exgraph.c curve.c

Listing 12.8 **Drawing an object consisting only of splines.**

```
/* TILTOVAL.C: Tilted oval uses conic splines and virt coords */

#include <graph.h>
#include "vcoords.h"
#include "exgraph.h"
#include "curve.h"

void main()
```

```
{
  if (_setvideomode (bestmode())) {
    setvcoords (640, 480);

    /* Draw the ellipse and freeze 5 seconds */
    _curve (dx(200), dy(240), dx(500), dy(420), dx(380), dy(420));
    _curve (dx(500), dy(420), dx(440), dy(240), dx(620), dy(420));
    _curve (dx(440), dy(240), dx(140), dy( 60), dx(260), dy( 60));
    _curve (dx(140), dy( 60), dx(200), dy(240), dx( 20), dy( 60));
    wait (5.0);

    /* Now add the cones and freeze again */
    _moveto (dx(380), dy(420));
    _lineto (dx(620), dy(420));      _lineto (dx(260), dy( 60));
    _lineto (dx( 20), dy( 60));      _lineto (dx(380), dy(420));
    wait (5.0);

    _setvideomode (_DEFAULTMODE);
  }
}
```

Now let's combine a number of lines and conic splines to draw a common household object: the clothes hanger. A hanger is an interesting shape because its ends are tightly bent acute-angle curves joining the triangular sides, and also because its hook is formed of several curves, one of which reverses the direction of the others. Listing 12.9 is the HANGER program. The layout of the shape was done on a piece of graph paper (indispensible for graphics programming), with the points translated into the coordinates given in the program. The direction of drawing is counterclockwise, starting at the point where the hook joins the top of the triangle. The hook itself is drawn last. The knots for the curves in the hanger's body are colinear with the sides, the overall triangle being defined by the apex (where the hook attaches) and the conic control points at the ends.

You can make this program from the command line with

QCL hanger.c exgraph.c curve.c

Listing 12.9 **Drawing a clothes hanger.**

```
/* HANGER.C: Draws a coat hanger with lines and conic splines */

#include <graph.h>
#include "exgraph.h"
#include "curve.h"

void main ()
{
  if (_setvideomode (_MRES4COLOR)) {

    /* draw body of hanger */
```

Listing 12.9 *(continued)*

```
_moveto (160, 90); _lineto (70, 120);
_curve (70, 120, 70, 130, 40, 130);
_moveto (70, 130); _lineto (250, 130);
_curve (250, 130, 250, 120, 280, 130);
_moveto (250, 120); _lineto (160, 90);

/* draw hook at top */
_curve (160, 90, 155, 80, 160, 84);
_curve (155, 80, 150, 70, 150, 77);
_curve (150, 70, 160, 60, 150, 60);
_curve (160, 60, 170, 70, 170, 60);

wait (10.0);
_setvideomode (_DEFAULTMODE);
}
}
```

The most complex part of the hanger is its hook, which consists of four conic splines smoothly joined. Three curves rotate clockwise, and the fourth (at the bottom) counterclockwise. What's more, as the close-up view in Figure 12.5 shows, the lower two hooks join on the slant. This kind of joint is tricky to program, which is why we've broken out the hook for separate discussion. (Listing 12.10 lists HOOK.C, which drew the close-up image.)

Figure 12.5 **Close-up view of the hanger hook.**

Listing 12.10 **Program to draw the magnified hook.**

```
/* HOOK.C: Anatomy of the hanger hook splines */

#include <graph.h>
#include "exgraph.h"
#include "curve.h"

void main()
{
  if (_setvideomode (_MRES4COLOR)) {

    /* Draw the cones */
    _setcolor (1);
    _moveto (160, 175);
    _lineto (160, 145); _lineto (110, 105);
    _lineto (110, 25); _lineto (210, 25);
    _lineto (210, 75);

    /* Then the splines */
    _setcolor (3);
    _curve (160, 175, 135, 125, 160, 145);
    _curve (135, 125, 110, 75, 110, 105);
    _curve (110, 75, 160, 25, 110, 25);
    _curve (160, 25, 210, 75, 210, 25);

    /* Freeze 5 seconds and quit */
    wait (5.0);
    _setvideomode (_DEFAULTMODE);
  }
}
```

The upper two splines are no problem to draw since they're simple quarter-circles whose cones are orthogonal (vertical and horizontal). The challenge is figuring out where the control points should be for the lower two.

We'll use the coordinates from HOOK.C; they map directly to the smaller hook drawn by HANGER.C. The bottom of the lower curve begins at {160, 175}, where it connects to the hanger. The top of the upper curve is at {110, 75}, the joint with the remainder of the hook. These are the two extremes for the curves in question.

The curves should join halfway between the extremes. By simple arithmetic, we find this point to be at {135, 125}. We now have the four knots for the splines, with the midpoint being common to both.

The lower spline curves counterclockwise moving upward, so its control point lies somewhere to the right of the common knot. Furthermore, it has the same X coordinate as the starting point: 160. The easiest way to find its Y coordinate is to locate the midpoint between the two knots, then draw a line through this point perpendicular to the knot-to-knot line. The point where this perpendicular line crosses X coordinate 160 is the control point for the lower spline; its Y is 145.

The control point for the upper curve must be on the same X as the extreme knot for that curve, or 110. We can find its Y by drawing a line from the lower spline's control point through the common knot. This line crosses X 110 at the control point for the upper spline (since the control points and common knot for smoothly joined splines are on the same plane). It happens at Y coordinate 105.

Geometry provides the mathematics for performing these calculations within programs. However, there's an easier way to draw complex curves of this kind. It's called a Bezier spline, and we discuss it in the next chapter.

Let's wrap up our coverage of conic splines with a program that's fun, in addition to furnishing models for a number of programming tricks with splines. Remember the old juke boxes with their bright, colorful neon lights? They were a legitimate form of folk art in their day, and have now become prized collector's items. The one drawn by JUKEBOX.C (Listing 12.11) won't fetch anyone a high price, but it makes for a stunning display showing the power conic splines bring to computer graphics. Because of its lavish use of colors and fine resolution, this program runs on EGA and VGA adapters.

The command line to make this program is

```
QCL jukebox.c textscrn.c vcoords.c exgraph.c curve.c
```

Listing 12.11 **Dazzling graphics with conic splines.**

```
/* JUKEBOX.C: Draws an old-fashioned juke box on EGA/VGA */
/* Uses conic splines and lines */

#include <graph.h>
#include <conio.h>
#include "textscrn.h"                         /* for std color names */
#include "vcoords.h"
#include "exgraph.h"
#include "curve.h"

struct xycoord star[] = {
  {225, 105}, {238, 95}, {233, 80}, {217, 80}, {212, 95}
};
int order[] = {0, 2, 4, 1, 3, 0};

void main()
{
int x, y;

  if (_setvideomode (_ERESCOLOR)) {
    setvcoords (450, 350);

    /* Yellow arches at top */
    _setcolor (YELLOW);
```

```
_curve (dx(145), dy(230), dx(225), dy(310), dx(140), dy(310));
_curve (dx(225), dy(310), dx(305), dy(230), dx(305), dy(310));
_curve (dx(165), dy(230), dx(225), dy(290), dx(165), dy(290));
_curve (dx(225), dy(290), dx(285), dy(230), dx(285), dy(290));

/* Red arch at top */
_setcolor (LTRED);
_curve (dx(155), dy(230), dx(225), dy(300), dx(155), dy(300));
_curve (dx(225), dy(300), dx(295), dy(230), dx(295), dy(300));

/* Red boxes at sides */
_setcolor (RED);
for (x = 140; x < 300; x+=140)
  for (y = 215; y < 235; y+=15)
    _rectangle (_GBORDER, dx(x), dy(y), dx(x+30), dy(y-10));

/* Neon lines between boxes and down sides */
_setcolor (YELLOW);
for (x = 145; x < 170; x+=20) {
  _moveto (dx(x), dy(219)); _lineto (dx(x), dy(216));
  _moveto (dx(x), dy(204)); _lineto (dx(x), dy( 91));
}
for (x = 285; x < 310; x+=20) {
  _moveto (dx(x), dy(219)); _lineto (dx(x), dy(216));
  _moveto (dx(x), dy(204)); _lineto (dx(x), dy( 91));
}
_setcolor (LTRED);
for (x = 155; x < 300; x+=140) {
  _moveto (dx(x), dy(219)); _lineto (dx(x), dy(216));
  _moveto (dx(x), dy(204)); _lineto (dx(x), dy( 91));
}


/* White boxes at bottom corners */
_setcolor (WHITE);
for (x = 140; x < 170; x+=10)
  _rectangle (_GBORDER, dx(x), dy(90), dx(x+10), dy(30));
for (x = 280; x < 310; x+=10)
  _rectangle (_GBORDER, dx(x), dy(90), dx(x+10), dy(30));

/* Lighted crown */
_moveto (dx(220), dy(285));
_lineto (dx(215), dy(315)); _lineto (dx(220), dy(315));
_lineto (dx(220), dy(320)); _lineto (dx(230), dy(320));
_lineto (dx(230), dy(315)); _lineto (dx(235), dy(315));
_lineto (dx(230), dy(285)); _lineto (dx(220), dy(285));
_setcolor (LTGRAY);
_floodfill (dx(225), dy(300), WHITE);
_setcolor (WHITE);
_moveto (dx(220), dy(285)); _lineto (dx(220), dy(320));
_moveto (dx(230), dy(285)); _lineto (dx(230), dy(320));

/* Bottom of box */
_setcolor (MAGENTA);
```

Listing 12.11 *(continued)*

```
_moveto (dx(171), dy(35)); _lineto (dx(279), dy(35));

/* Scallops in window at top */
_curve (dx(181), dy(259), dx(200), dy(277), dx(200), dy(259));
_curve (dx(200), dy(277), dx(225), dy(285), dx(217), dy(270));
_curve (dx(225), dy(285), dx(250), dy(277), dx(234), dy(270));
_curve (dx(250), dy(277), dx(269), dy(259), dx(250), dy(259));

/* Outline of scalloped window */
_setcolor (LTGREEN);
_curve (dx(177), dy(249), dx(225), dy(285), dx(188), dy(285));
_curve (dx(225), dy(285), dx(273), dy(249), dx(262), dy(285));
_curve (dx(273), dy(249), dx(260), dy(235), dx(275), dy(235));
_curve (dx(177), dy(249), dx(190), dy(235), dx(175), dy(235));
_moveto (dx(190), dy(235)); _lineto (dx(260), dy(235));

/* Stacks of records */
_setcolor (DKGRAY);
for (x = 190; x < 250; x+=25)
  for (y = 250; y > 235; y-=3) {
    _moveto (dx(x), dy(y)); _lineto (dx(x+20), dy(y));
  }

/* Music selection panel */
_setcolor (WHITE);
_rectangle (_GBORDER, dx(179), dy(225), dx(270), dy(195));
_setcolor (LTGRAY);
for (y = 222; y > 196; y-=4) {
  _moveto (dx(185), dy(y)); _lineto (dx(269), dy(y));
}
_setcolor (RED);                                    /* buttons */
for (x = 180; x < 250; x+=23)
_rectangle (_GFILLINTERIOR, dx(x), dy(224), dx(x+5), dy(196));

/* Inner border around lower part of box */
_setcolor (LTBLUE);
_moveto (dx(169), dy(204)); _lineto (dx(169), dy(95));
_curve (dx(170), dy(95), dx(175), dy(90), dx(175), dy(95));
_moveto (dx(175), dy(90)); _lineto (dx(175), dy(50));
_curve (dx(175), dy(50), dx(185), dy(40), dx(185), dy(50));
_moveto (dx(185), dy(40)); _lineto (dx(265), dy(40));
_curve (dx(265), dy(40), dx(275), dy(50), dx(265), dy(50));
_moveto (dx(275), dy(50)); _lineto (dx(275), dy(90));
_curve (dx(275), dy(90), dx(280), dy(95), dx(275), dy(95));
_moveto (dx(281), dy(95)); _lineto (dx(281), dy(204));

/* Belly bar below music selection box */
for (x = 195; x < 260; x+=5) {
  _moveto (dx(x), dy(182)); _lineto (dx(x), dy(173));
}
_rectangle (_GBORDER, dx(191), dy(185), dx(259), dy(171));
```

```
_setcolor (CYAN);
_curve (dx(190), dy(175), dx(185), dy(180), dx(185), dy(175));
_curve (dx(185), dy(180), dx(180), dy(185), dx(185), dy(185));
_curve (dx(180), dy(185), dx(175), dy(190), dx(175), dy(185));
_moveto (dx(175), dy(190)); _lineto (dx(275), dy(190));
_curve (dx(275), dy(190), dx(270), dy(185), dx(275), dy(185));
_curve (dx(270), dy(185), dx(265), dy(180), dx(265), dy(185));
_curve (dx(265), dy(180), dx(260), dy(175), dx(265), dy(175));

/* Speaker gridwork */
_setcolor (BROWN);
_moveto (dx(240), dy(170));
_lineto (dx(255), dy(155));   _lineto (dx(210), dy(110));
_lineto (dx(195), dy(125));   _lineto (dx(240), dy(170));
_moveto (dx(225), dy(170));
_lineto (dx(255), dy(140));   _lineto (dx(225), dy(110));
_lineto (dx(195), dy(140));   _lineto (dx(225), dy(170));
_moveto (dx(210), dy(170));
_lineto (dx(255), dy(125));   _lineto (dx(240), dy(110));
_lineto (dx(195), dy(155));   _lineto (dx(210), dy(170));
_moveto (dx(195), dy(170));   _lineto (dx(255), dy(110));
_moveto (dx(255), dy(170));   _lineto (dx(195), dy(110));
_setcolor (RED);
_rectangle (_GBORDER, dx(195), dy(170), dx(255), dy(110));

/* Cowling around speaker */
_setcolor (YELLOW);
for (x = 190; x < 265; x+=70) {                /* inner verticals */
  _moveto (dx(x), dy(170)); _lineto (dx(x), dy(105));
}
for (x = 180; x < 275; x+=90) {                /* outer verticals */
  _moveto (dx(x), dy(165)); _lineto (dx(x), dy(105));
}
_curve (dx(190), dy(174), dx(180), dy(164), dx(180), dy(174));
_curve (dx(190), dy(105), dx(225), dy( 70), dx(190), dy( 70));
_curve (dx(260), dy(174), dx(270), dy(164), dx(270), dy(174));
_curve (dx(260), dy(105), dx(225), dy( 70), dx(260), dy( 70));
_curve (dx(180), dy(105), dx(225), dy( 60), dx(180), dy( 60));
_curve (dx(270), dy(105), dx(225), dy( 60), dx(270), dy( 60));

/* Draw star below speaker */
for (x = 0; x < 5; x++) {          /* convert to device coords */
  star[x].xcoord = dx(star[x].xcoord);
  star[x].ycoord = dy(star[x].ycoord);
}
_setcolor (LTCYAN);
_polyline (5, star, order);

/* Crescents around star */
_setcolor (LTBLUE);
_moveto (dx(195), dy(105)); _lineto (dx(215), dy(105));
_curve (dx(215), dy(105), dx(205), dy( 85), dx(195), dy(105));
_curve (dx(205), dy( 85), dx(195), dy(105), dx(195), dy( 90));
```

Listing 12.11 *(continued)*

```
_moveto (dx(235), dy(105)); _lineto (dx(255), dy(105));
_curve (dx(235), dy(105), dx(245), dy( 85), dx(255), dy(105));
_curve (dx(245), dy( 85), dx(255), dy(105), dx(255), dy( 90));

/* Embellishments at bottom */
_setcolor (MAGENTA);
for (x = 185; x < 260; x+=70) {
  _rectangle (_GBORDER, dx(x),    dy(57), dx(x+10), dy(53));
  _rectangle (_GBORDER, dx(x+3), dy(60), dx(x+ 7), dy(50));
}
_setcolor (GREEN);
_rectangle (_GBORDER, dx(205), dy(55), dx(245), dy(45));
_moveto (dx(210), dy(50)); _lineto (dx(240), dy(50));

/* Quit after keypress */
getch();
_setvideomode (_DEFAULTMODE);
  }
}
```

Conic splines furnish an intuitive way to draw simple curves that arc through a quarter of an ellipse. As you've seen, it's easy to string them together. An even easier way to create complex curves is with the Bezier splines that are the subject of the next chapter.

CHAPTER 13

Drawing Complex Curves

The conic splines discussed in Chapter 12 are good for many graphics programming applications, but not all. Examples where conic splines fall short are curlicues, handwriting, and solid curved objects such as a vase. Of course you can use them to depict such things, but the effort of constructing and stringing together all those conic splines makes for tedium and discouragement. Enter the Bezier spline, a method for expressing elaborate curves in terms of a few control points.

The method takes its name from its inventor, P. E. Bezier (pronounced "bay-zee-AY"), a French mathematician who developed it in the early 1970s to assist in the computer-aided design of Renault automobiles. The Bezier algorithm belongs to a group of mathematical curios called *cubic splines*, all of which have the same general objective of describing complex curves. Bezier's proposition is that a polygon can approximate a curve, which wends its way among the vertices like the Voyager spacecraft navigating among the outer planets. If the polygon closes back to its origin, the curve is also closed. An open polygon, on the other hand, describes a curve with two end points. The curve only touches the end points, with the other vertices exerting an influence over its path. Figure 13.1 shows a Bezier curve.

How a Bezier Curve Works _____

A science fiction analogy helps explain how a Bezier curve works. Suppose a spacecraft is moving from one galaxy to another. As it travels, it encounters other celestial bodies whose gravity pulls it away from a straight line. All the objects in the universe influence its path to some extent, but the nearest ones have the most effect. When it finally arrives at its destination, the space ship's track will have described a complex, constantly varying curve.

Figure 13.1 **A Bezier curve.**

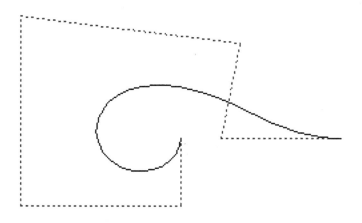

In the course of the journey, the craft's position at any instant is represented by two kinds of information. One is its coordinates, which are x, y, and z (for horizontal, vertical, and depth, respectively) and give its absolute location with respect to some point. The other is a value called u in the calculations in Listing 13.1. This is a relative indicator ranging from 0 to 1, representing the percentage of the total distance that the craft has to travel from start to finish. When u = 0.0, the craft hasn't left yet; when u = 1.0, it's arrived; and when u = 0.5, it's halfway there. Thus, if you were the navigator, you could determine your position at any time by deriving the coordinates from u, which is, in effect, the controlling variable of the voyage. Bezier furnishes a formula for doing this.

Calculus 101

Unfortunately, no one has yet come up with a way to do more than the most primitive graphics without resorting to heavy math, and Bezier curves are no exception. The Bezier equation for a curve is

$$P(u) = \sum_{i=0}^{n} p_i B_{i,n}(u)$$

In other words, for any point u, the location is the sum of n + 1 control-point factors proceeding from point 0. This factor is a blending function

$$B_{i,n}(u) = C(n,i)\, u^i\, (1 \cdot u)^{n \cdot i}$$

which in turn is derived from the binomial coefficient

$$C(n,i) = nl/(il(n \cdot i)!)$$

So much for the equations. Now let's talk about what they do.

The blending function is where the real work of the Bezier method gets done. It calculates a "gravity factor" for each control point relative to the current u. The closer a control point, the more "gravity" it has and thus the more it influences the outcome, which is the coordinates. When u = 0, the metaphorical spacecraft is still at the point of origin, or p[0], and no other points have any say-so about its position. As it leaves the origin, p[1] begins to pull it. Halfway between p[0] and p[1], both points have the same influence. However, p[2] also attracts the craft enough to pull it away from a straight line between p[0] and p[1], and other points beyond p[2] also draw it in diminishing proportion to their distance. As it approaches the end point, there is nothing beyond to draw it away, and so it arrives.

The blending function is a mathematical statement of this effect. For each control point, it returns a fractional value by which the coordinates of that control point are multiplied. The sums of these x, y, and z products are the coordinates of the position at u.

By drawing lines between successive u's, we make a map of the route, which is the Bezier curve based on the control point layout.

Of Hulls and Such _____

The power of Bezier curves lies in their ability to represent a complex curve with a few points expressed in coordinates. The simplest curve is described by three points: the origin, the destination, and one intermediate vertex. The outcome in this case is a smooth arc from origin to destination, tending toward the intermediate point. This is exactly the same as a conic spline. So why not throw out conic splines and use Bezier as a general curve-drawing algorithm? Because the Bezier algorithm is considerably more complex, and therefore introduces more overhead.

The Bezier method has to be more involved because it takes numerous points into account. The curves it draws result from several points laid out in an order that roughly approximates the desired trajectory, as in Figure 13.1. That curve derives from seven control points. The straight lines join the

Figure 13.2 **A closed Bezier curve.**

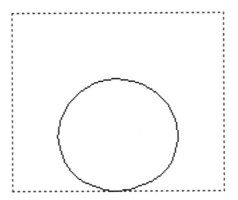

points in order, forming an open polygon, or "hull." Normally, of course, you wouldn't draw the hull itself, since the object of the game is the curve. However, we show the hull here so that you can see how it provides an intuitive notion of the curve's shape.

Bezier curves are insensitive to orientation. It happens that in Figure 13.1 the origin is at the center of the curl and the destination at the far right. However, if we had specified the control points in the opposite order, exactly the same curve would have resulted.

As mentioned earlier, a hull can be closed, producing a circle or something like it. Figure 13.2 illustrates a closed Bezier curve. The hull has six control points. The four corners are obvious. Less so are the origin and destination, which are coincident at bottom center where the circle and hull meet. If you pulled one of the corners of the hull out or pushed it in, the Bezier curve would form a misshapen circle.

Implementing the Bezier Algorithm

Listings 13.1 and 13.2 are the header and source files for a library of routines that partially implement the Bezier algorithm: "partially" because, although the Bezier algorithm can create three-dimensional curves, the method given here only works in two dimensions. The reason is that 3D graphics is a subject for a thick book beyond the scope of this one. If you want to learn more, see *Principles of Interactive Computer Graphics* by W. Newman and R. Sproull (McGraw-Hill, New York, 1979). The Bezier algorithm in Listing 13.2 is based in part on Newman and Sproull, (pp. 315–319), who provide lucid explanations and Pascal listings for some of the more opaque concepts of this dense topic.

Listing 13.1 **Bezier library header file.**

```
/* BEZIER.H: Prototypes for drawing Bezier curves in 2D */


/* Return q factorial */
double fact (int q);

/* Return coordinates for current 'u' */
void far bezierFcn (double *x, double *y, double u,
            double  coeff[], int n, struct xycoord p[];

/* Draw a Bezier curve */
void far drawBezier (struct xycoord p[], int npts, int
segments);
```

Listing 13.2 **Bezier library source listing.**

```
/* BEZIER.C: Functions for drawing Bezier curves in 2D    */
/*    Assumes display is in graphics mode                 */
/* ------------------------------------------------------ */
#include <graph.h>

double fact (int q)

     /* Return q factorial */
{
int   f = 1, c;

  for (c = q; c > 1; c--)
    f *= c;
  return (f);
} /* ----------------------- */

double c (int n, int i)

   /* Binomial coefficient used in blending function */
{
  return (fact (n) / (fact (i) * fact (n - i)));
} /* ----------------------- */

double blend (int i, int n, double u, double binomial)

   /* Bernstein blending function */
{
double partial;
```

Listing 13.2 *(continued)*

```c
int     j;

  partial = binomial;
  for (j = 1; j <= i; j++)
    partial = partial * u;
  for (j = 1; j <= (n - i); j++)
    partial = partial * (1.0 - u);
  return (partial);
} /* ----------------------- */


void far bezierFcn (double *x, double *y, double u,
        double  coeff[], int n, struct xycoord p[])

      /* Return coordinates for current 'u' */
{
int     i;
double b;

  *x = *y = 0;
  for (i = 0; i <= n; i++) {
    b = blend (i, n, u, coeff [i]);
    *x = *x + (b * p[i].xcoord);
    *y = *y + (b * p[i].ycoord);
  }
} /* ----------------------- */


void far drawBezier (struct xycoord p[], int npts, int segments)

      /* Draw a Bezier curve */
{
int     i, oldx, oldy;
double u, x, y;
double coeff [20];      /* should be big enough for any curve */

  for (i = 0; i < npts; i++)      /* compute binomial coeffs */
    coeff [i] = c (npts-1, i);
  for (i = 0; i <= segments; i++) {
    u = (double) i / segments;
    bezierFcn (&x, &y, u, coeff, npts-1, p);
    if (i == 0) {
      _moveto (x, y);
      oldx = x, oldy = y;
    } else {
      _lineto ((int) x, (int) y);
      oldx = x, oldy = y;
    }
  }
} /* ----------------------- */
```

The segments argument passed to **drawBezier()** is the basis for u in the calculations. It defines how many line segments make up the complete curve. The **drawBezier()** function controls curve-drawing with the loop

```
for (i  =  0;  i  <=  segments;  i++) {  . . .
```

and calculates u as i / segments. Therefore 0.0 u 1.0, representing a percentage of the complete transit from origin to destination.

Three of the five subroutines in **BEZIER.C** are directly useful to application programs. The **drawBezier()** function is probably the only one you'll ever call, but it's conceivable that you might want to call **bezierFcn()** for purposes such as marking points on the curve—say every 10 percent of its length, or its midpoint. Given the desired point in terms of u, **bezierFcn()** will return the coordinates. The other one, **fact()**, is a general mathematical function that returns the factorial of an integer.

Putting It to Work

You've already seen the output from the demonstration program in Listing 13.3, **BEZCURVE.C**. It's the curlicue shown in Figure 13.1. This program uses the Bezier library to draw the curve in a virtual coordinate space.

You can make this program from the command line with

```
QCL bezcurve.c vcoords.c exgraph.c bezier.c
```

Listing 13.3 **A program to draw a Bezier curve.**

```c
/* BEZCURVE.C: Draws a Bezier curve and its hull */

#include <graph.h>
#include <conio.h>
#include <stdio.h>
#include "vcoords.h"
#include "exgraph.h"
#include "bezier.h"
#define DOTTED_LINE 0xCCCC
#define SOLID_LINE  0xFFFF

#define NPOINTS 7

struct xycoord pt[] = {
{400, 270}, {400, 120}, {100, 120}, {100, 540},
{510, 480}, {475, 270}, {700, 270}
};
int order[] = {0, 1, 2, 3, 4, 5, 6};

void main ()
{
int n;
```

Listing 13.3 *(continued)*

```
/* Set up screen in graphics mode, virtual coords */
if (_setvideomode (bestmode())) {
  setvcoords (800, 600);

  /* Convert virtual coords in vector array to device */
  for (n = 0; n < NPOINTS; n++) {
    pt[n].xcoord = dx (pt[n].xcoord);
    pt[n].ycoord = dy (pt[n]]ycoord);
  }

  /* Draw the hull outline */
  _setlinestyle (DOTTED_LINE);
  _setcolor (2);
  _polyline (6, pt, order);

  /* Draw the Bezier curve */
  _setlinestyle (SOLID_LINE);
  _setcolor (3);
  drawBezier (pt, NPOINTS, 40);

  /* Hold image for keypress, then quit */
  getch ();
  _setvideomode (_DEFAULTMODE);
} else
  puts (""Unable to enter graphics mode'');
}
```

The program itself is quite simple and self-explanatory. It puts the display adapter into the best graphics mode available, initializes the virtual coordinate system, and converts the hull array (pt[]) into device coordinates. After that it outlines the hull in one color and draws the Bezier curve in another. The program then waits for a keypress and terminates.

Joining Curves

The nature of Bezier curves is such that a change in any hull vertex changes the path of the entire curve. If you're working on a complex shape, it's usually easiest to decompose the object into a number of smaller curves and join them together. That way you can tweak individual parts of the shape without introducing undesired side effects elsewhere.

In order to achieve a smooth joint between curves, there are two rules: They're the same as for joining conic splines. First, make the end points of the adjacent curves coincident. That is, one curve ends at exactly the same point where the next begins. The second is to create continuity in the adjoining hulls across the joint.

Figure 13.3 **Joining two curves.**

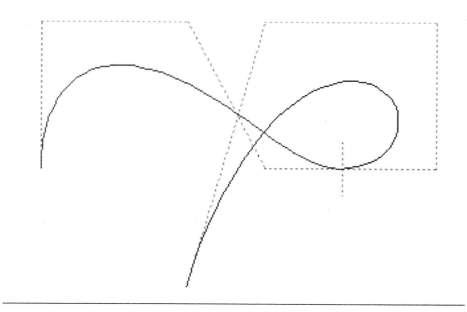

Say, for example, that you have two hulls called A and B, and that A, which flows into B, has six control points. To achieve continuity, A[4], A[5] (coincident with B[0]), and B[1] must all lie on the same plane, so that a straight line passes through all of them. The span from A[4] through B[1] should be fairly long, so that the curves have room to sweep gracefully to their coincident end points. This avoids an abrupt kink that would disrupt the flow.

Figure 13.3 illustrates this. Both hulls are outlined in dotted lines. A vertical line marks the joint, which is in the bottom center of the right-hand polygon. Curve A sweeps up from the left side of the screen and down to the end point, where curve B picks up and crosses back over A. If you study and run the **TWOCURVS.C** program in Listing 13.4, you'll see that curve A is drawn in one color and curve B in another. This is to identify more clearly that you're looking at two curves and where, in their smooth transition, one ends and the next begins.

The command line to make this is

    QCL twocurvs.c bezier.c exgraph.c

Listing 13.4 **Program to draw the adjoining curves in Figure 13.3.**

```
/* TWOCURVS.C: Draws two joined curves on the CGA */

#include <graph.h>
#include <conio.h>
```

Listing 13.4 *(continued)*

```c
#include <stdio.h>
#include "bezier.h"
#include "exgraph.h"

#define NPOINTS   5
#define SEGMENTS 40
#define DOTTED_LINE 0xCCCC
#define SOLID_LINE  0xFFFF

struct xycoord a[] = {              /* hull for first curve */
{ 10, 110}, { 10,   0}, {120, 0}, {180, 110}, {240, 110}
},
    b[] = {                        /* ... and for second */
{240, 110}, {310, 110}, {310, 0}, {180,   0}, {120, 199}
};
int order[] = {0, 1, 2, 3, 4};

void main ()
{
  if (_setvideomode (_MRES4COLOR)) {

    /* Draw the first hull */
    _setlinestyle (DOTTED_LINE);
    _setcolor (1);
    _polyline (4, a, order);

    /* Mark the joint */
    _moveto (a[4].xcoord, a[4].ycoord-20);
    _lineto (a[4].xcoord, a[4].ycoord+20);

    /* Draw the second hull */
    _polyline (4, b, order);

    /* Draw the first curve */
    _setlinestyle (SOLID_LINE);
    _setcolor (2);
    drawBezier (a, NPOINTS, SEGMENTS);

    /* ... and the second */
    _setcolor (3);
    drawBezier (b, NPOINTS, SEGMENTS);

    /* Hold for keypress and quit */
    getch ();
    _setvideomode (_DEFAULTMODE);
  } else
    puts ("Unable to enter graphics mode");
}
```

The program in Figure 13.5 carries the idea of joining curves a little further. The output looks like balloons on a string. Four are above the string and three

below. This program alternates between two Bezier curves that are identical
except for their orientations. Both curves are based on the vertical center of
the virtual display, which provides a plane for achieving smooth joints.

As the main loop of the program reiterates, it relocates each curve by calling the **advance()** function, which adds the fixed **INTERVAL** to the X coordinates. The curves occupy 110 virtual X units along the base plane, so the
downward hull is initialized with X values 110 greater than the upward
array. Thus, one iteration moves each alternating curve right by 220 virtual X
units, which is the value of **INTERVAL**.

The **fill()** function finds the middle of the closed circular object formed by
the Bezier curve. It does this by calculating the X and Y coordinates midway
between the second and fourth points, which are opposite corners of the hull
defining the curlicue. This point is the origin for a **_floodfill()** that gives each
"balloon" its color.

Make this program from the command line with:

QCL balloon.c bezier.c vcoords.c exgraph.c

Listing 13.5 **A series of joined Bezier curves.**

```
/* BALLOON.C: Draws balloons with joined Bezier curves */

#include <graph.h>
#include <conio.h>
#include "bezier.h"
#include "vcoords.h"
#include "exgraph.h"

#define NPOINTS    6
#define SEGMENTS   30
#define INTERVAL 220

struct xycoord up[] = {                      /* upward balloon */
    {  0, 300}, {140, 300}, {140, 480},
    {-30, 480}, {-30, 300}, {110, 300}
},
    dn[] = {                                 /* downward balloon */
    {110, 300}, {250, 300}, {250, 120},
    { 80, 120}, { 80, 300}, {220, 300}
};

void main ()
{
int  n;
void advance (struct xycoord m[]),
     fill (struct xycoord m[]);

  if (_setvideomode (bestmode())) {
    setvcoords (800, 600);
    _setcolor (3);
```

Listing 13.5 *(continued)*

```
        /* Convert points to device coords */
        for (n = 0; n < NPOINTS; n++) {
          up[n].xcoord = dx (up[n].xcoord);
          up[n].ycoord = dy (up[n].ycoord);
          dn[n].xcoord = dx (dn[n].xcoord);
          dn[n].ycoord = dy (dn[n].ycoord);
        }

        /* Draw first curve */
        drawBezier (up, NPOINTS, SEGMENTS);
        fill (up);
        advance (up);

        /* Draw two more of each curve */
        for (n = 0; n < 3; n++) {
          drawBezier (dn, NPOINTS, SEGMENTS);
          fill (dn);
          advance (dn);
          drawBezier (up, NPOINTS, SEGMENTS);
          fill (up);
          advance (up);
        }

        /* Hold for keypress */
        getch ();
        _setvideomode (_DEFAULTMODE);
      } else
        puts ("Unable to enter graphics mode");
} /* ----------------------- */

void advance (struct xycoord m[])
      /* Advance the X coords by fixed interval */
{
int  i;

  for (i = 0; i < NPOINTS; i++)
    m[i].xcoord += dx (INTERVAL);
} /* ----------------------- */

void fill (struct xycoord m[])
      /* Fill each balloon with color */
{
  _floodfill ((m[1].xcoord + m[3].xcoord) / 2,
             (m[1].ycoord + m[3].ycoord) / 2, 3);
}
```

Art with Bezier Curves

Because the Bezier algorithm was developed chiefly to help in the design of
automobiles, it lends itself to forms of artistic expression that would other-

Figure 13.4 **A vase constructed from Bezier curves.**

wise be difficult or impossible with a computer. We live amidst irregular, complex curves, and since art imitates life, the Bezier algorithm gives us a means of replicating the visual world around us.

Figure 13.4 provides an example. It depicts an amphora, a graceful urn shape much in favor in the ancient Mediterranean and still popular for flower vases. This picture consists entirely of repetitions of the same basic Bezier curve. The stripes of alternating color give a sense of form and depth to the vase, making it appear higly realistic. Although an amphora is itself a complex object, the application of a Bezier curve makes the writing of a program to draw it surprisingly easy.

The most important step in writing this program was to design the Bezier curve outlining the right side of the vase; it forms the basis for the entire amphora. A bit of experimentation produced a five-point hull with the following vertices expressed in virtual coordinates:

        100, 500
       −80, 420
        220, 300
        180, 100
         40, 100

Figure 13.5 shows the hull as dotted lines and its resulting curve.

Figure 13.5 **Hull and curve for right side of amphora.**

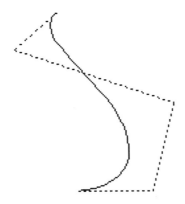

So now that we have the curve, what do we do with it? The trick is to "rotate" the Bezier hull around a reference point—the horizontal center of the display—redrawing the curve at regular intervals. Trigonometry enables us to do this. If a circle is R units from its center, then the X coordinate where a line at angle theta intersects with it is found by the equation

$$X = R \cos theta$$

The variable R is, of course, the radius of the circle.

What is the radius in this case? The X coordinates of the hull points. Each point is a different distance from the center. Therefore, rotating the hull involves applying the equation to each points with a given theta. This has the effect of swinging the right side toward the viewer.

Because the center of the vase is assumed to be 0 (the left edge of the screen), it's necessary to add the center X of the display to each derived X. This relocates the curve to a position relative to the middle of the display.

The left-hand curve is a mirror image of the right-hand one, so we can calculate its X's with the expression

```
leftx  =  cx  -  rightx  +  cx;
```

Say cx = 160 and rightx = 190. Then

```
leftx  =  160  -  190  +  160  =  130
```

Listing 13.6 **Program to draw a vase with a Bezier curve.**

```c
/* VASE.C: Draws a vase using Bezier curves */

#include <graph.h>
#include <math.h>
#include <conio.h>
#include <stdio.h>
#include "vcoords.h"
#include "bezier.h"
#include "exgraph.h"

#define NPOINTS  5                    /* number of points in hull */
#define SEGMENTS 25                   /* segments in Bezier curve */
#define DEG2RAD  3.1415927 / 180.0         /* degrees to radians */

struct xycoord ref[] = {             /* reference points for curve */
{100, 500}, {-80, 420}, {220, 300}, {180, 100}, {40, 100}
};

void main ()
{
int    n, angle, cx, color = 1, topy, basey, step = 6;
double cosine;
struct xycoord rside[5], lside[5];
struct videoconfig video;

  /* Set up to run */
  if (_setvideomode (bestmode())) {
    setvcoords (800, 600);
    _getvideoconfig (&video);
    _setcolor (color);
    cx = video.numxpixels / 2;    /* vertical centerline */

    /* Double image width if CGA */
    if (video.mode == _MRES4COLOR) {
      _selectpalette (0);
      for (n = 0; n < NPOINTS; n++)
        ref[n].xcoord *= 2;
    }

    /* Convert reference coords to device coords */
    for (n = 0; n < NPOINTS; n++) {
      ref[n].xcoord = dx (ref[n].xcoord);
      rside[n].ycoord = lside[n].ycoord = ref[n].ycoord
        = dy (ref[n].ycoord);
    }

    /* Get Y for top and base */
    topy  = ref[0].ycoord;
    basey = ref[4]

    /* Draw the edges of the vase (too narrow for fill) */
```

Listing 13.6 *(continued)*

```
for (angle = 0; angle < 21; angle += step) {
  cosine = cos (DEG2RAD * angle);
  for (n = 0; n < NPOINTS; n++) {
    rside[n].xcoord = dx ((int)(cosine * ref[n].xcoord)) + cx;
    lside[n].xcoord = cx - rside[n].xcoord + cx;
  }
  if (step > 1) --step;
  drawBezier (rside, NPOINTS, SEGMENTS);
  drawBezier (lside, NPOINTS, SEGMENTS);
}

/* Draw the body of the vase */
for (angle = 20; angle < 90; angle += 20) {
  color = (color == 1) ? 2 : 1;
  _setcolor (color);
  drawBezier (rside, NPOINTS, SEGMENTS);       /* right curve */
  drawBezier (lside, NPOINTS, SEGMENTS);        /* and left */
  _moveto (lside[0].xcoord, topy);
  _lineto (rside[0].xcoord, topy);             /* close mouth */
  _moveto (lside[4].xcoord, basey);
  _lineto (rside[4].xcoord, basey);             /* and base */
  _floodfill (cx, dy(300), color);                /* fill */
  cosine = cos (DEG2RAD * (angle + 20));
  for (n = 0; n < NPOINTS; n++) {         /* compute next curve */
    rside[n].xcoord = dx((int)(cosine * ref[n].xcoord)) + cx;
    lside[n].xcoord = cx - rside[n].xcoord + cx;
  }
}

/* Hold image for keypress, then quit */
getch ();
_setvideomode (_DEFAULTMODE);
} else
  puts ("Unable to enter graphics mode");
}
```

Listing 13.6 lists **VASE.C**, which draws the amphora. Make it from the command line with

QCL vase.c vcoords.c bezier.c exgraph.c

Here's how the program works. The extreme edges of the vase are very narrow since the viewer is seeing them at an acute angle. At the widest point, these stripes are only half a dozen pixels in breadth. Consequently the program draws them as a series of curves. The interval between curves begins at six degrees (the step variable) and decreases by one degree for each curve drawn, to a fixed floor of one degree. This is a fill/optimization trick; no sense drawing lots of curves when we can see only a few of them. The drawing method changes when the extreme edges have been produced.

Each color stripe traverses 20 degrees of arc. They appear in alternating colors: red and green on the CGA, blue and green on high-resolution devices. Consequently we can perform a loop that steps by 20 degrees and toggles the color each time. Here are the steps performed by the loop:

- Toggle to the alternate color.
- Draw the right and left curves in the new color.
- Close off the mouth and base in the same color.
- Fill the area thus enclosed.
- Rotate the curve to the next increment of 20 degrees.

This loop repeats at angles of 20, 40, 60, and 80 degrees. The filled area between the curves grows narrower each time, thus creating the stripes.

It's difficult to imagine how one could draw an amphora—or any other such complex object from the real world—without Bezier curves.

It usually takes some experimentation to get a curve the way you want it, but the Bezier method gives you a powerful means for describing complex shapes with a few data points that have an intuitive feel about them. Because Bezier curves were developed in response to the need for CAD tools to design cars, they're eminently well suited to computer art, and a fascinating object of study as well.

So far our discussion of graphics has concentrated on drawing objects of various kinds. The next chapter introduces text in graphics displays.

CHAPTER **14**

Using Quick C Fonts

A new feature with Quick C 2.0 is selectable fonts for producing varied typography in graphics. Earlier releases of Quick C relied exclusively on the graphics adapter's default font, which meant that you had no choice about how text would look, and also that text positioning—even in graphics—was tied to the same coordinate space as in non-graphics modes. That's all changed now. Let's see how.

The term *font* refers to the way characters are formed. The graphics arts business employs many different fonts, each carefully selected for particular reasons. You can see examples of that in this book, where one font is used for normal text and another, embedded within the text, indicates variable names, keywords, and other elements of C programs.

Quick C 2.0 comes with six fonts. Their names are Courier, Helvetica, Times Roman, Modern, Script, and Roman. Additionally, of course, there's the font built directly into your video adapter, though it's not truly a graphics font. You can purchase additional fonts. Also, the Quick C fonts are the same as for Microsoft Windows, so if you have Windows on your system you already have access to more fonts. My copy of Windows has 13.

Graphics artists generally divide fonts into two broad categories, *serif* and *sans serif*. Serifs are little embellishments that make a font more readable. The small right angles at the ends of the rays in the letter E are serifs. Among the Quick C fonts, Helvetica and Modern are sans serif fonts, and Courier, Times Roman, and Roman have serifs. (Script, which emulates handwriting, is a class by itself.)

There's a second way to categorize fonts in computer graphics: bit-mapped and scaled. A bit-mapped font is one in which an *m* x *n* matrix of bits exists to define the configuration of pixels forming each character. The CGA's built-in font is a good example; it's an 8-bit x 8-row array of pixels representing each fixed-size character. A scaled font is an entirely different way of defining and forming character images. Scaled (or "stroked" or "vector") fonts consist of data structures which are transformed into images by drawing Bezier curves. A scaled font is therefore infinitely variable in size (within the resolution of the display). Thus you can fill the entire screen with one character, or reduce the same character to a single pixel.

Table 14.1 is a table showing the Quick C fonts and their characteristics. Note that bit-mapped fonts include two serif faces and one sans serif, and scaled fonts include a serif and sans serif, plus script.

Table 14.1 **The Quick C Fonts**

Name	Type	Serif	Height x width	Spacing
Courier	Bit	Y	10x8, 12x9, 15x12	Fixed
Helvetica	Bit	N	10x5, 12x7, 15x8, 18x9, 22x12,28x16	Proportional
Times Roman	Bit	Y	10x5, 12x6, 15x8, 16x9, 20x12,26x16	Proportional
Modern	Vector	N	Scaled	Proportional
Script	Vector	N/A	Scaled	Proportional
Roman	Vector	Y	Scaled	Proportional

The spacing of a font governs the amount of room required for a character. The fixed font, Courier, is like the default hardware font in that every character occupies the same physical space on the display, regardless of its actual width. Thus, i and W take equal numbers of pixels. By contrast, the spacing between characters in a proportional font is uniform, but the characters themselves claim only as much room as their individual widths demand. If you compare the same string displayed in fixed and proportional fonts of the equal type size, the proportional string takes less room.

The trade-off between mapped and scaled fonts is this: Bit-mapped fonts are easier to draw and thus write to the screen faster, but scaled fonts are more flexible in terms of proportion and size. However, both kinds can be positioned relative to a pixel (instead of a character cell as with the default font).

Each font is contained within a disk file having the suffix .**FON**. A Quick C program treats a font as a special kind of exernal data file, and the **GRAPHICS** library furnishes half a dozen functions and a data structure for working with fonts from within a program. The .**FON** files should be in the same directory as the program; if not, your program must specify the path to find them. We'll get to that in more detail shortly.

The general procedure for using one or more fonts is:

1. Register the font(s).
2. Select the desired one.
3. Output text in graphics mode.

To register a font is to open the .**FON** file and automatically load its characteristics into a hidden data structure accessible to the graphics library. Your program thus knows of a font's existence, but it doesn't yet have access to it.

For that, you have to set the active font through a rather complex function call. Once selected, the font is available for producing output. Let's discuss details.

Registering Fonts

The font registration function is _registerfonts(). This library function takes a string as its argument, where the string contains a .FON filename. For example, to register the Helvetica font from the current directory, the call is

    _registerfonts ("HELVB.FON");

If the .FON file is in another directory—say \QC2\FONTS—you must specify the full path, as in

    _registerfonts ("\\QC2\\FONTS\\HEVLB.FON");

Because Helvetica comes in six different sizes, _registerfonts() returns 6. If unsuccessful, it returns −1. Fonts can be indexed by a number between 1 and the returned value, where 1 is the largest version and so on toward the smallest; this is useful later when you select the font.

You can issue wildcards in the call to _registerfonts(). To open all fonts in the current directory, write

    nfonts = _registerfonts ("*.FON");

When all supplied .FON files are in the directory, nfonts receives the value 18, which is the total number of fonts and sizes thereof.

It's advisable always to check the returned value from _registerfonts() so that, at a miminum, you can take the appropriate action if 0 comes back indicating failure. Here is an example:

    if (_registerfonts ("HELVB.FON")) {
            /* succeeded, so do font stuff */
                } else
                    puts ("Unable to register fonts");

Registering one or more fonts makes them available to the program, but then you have to select which one you want.

Selecting a Font

The _registerfonts() function places a set of font descriptors into an array. Via the _setfont() function, the Quick C library furnishes several different ways of picking a font from the array. Only one font can be active at a time. When you select a font, disk activity occurs in order to load the .FON file contents into memory. Thus, if you're using more than one font, it makes for better performance if you write all the output for one font, then change fonts and write everything using it, and so on, rather than flipping back and forth.

The _setfont() function takes a command string as its argument. This string can contain any of the following codes:

Table 14.2 **Codes found within command strings.**

Code	Means
t'fontname'	Select a font by name, where the possibiliies are one of these: courier　　modern helv　　script tms rmn　　roman
hm	Height of a character in pixels, where m is a decimal number.
wn	Width of a character in pixels, where n is a decimal number.
b	Select the best fit for height and width from among the registered fonts. Always picks one of the indicated size or the next smaller if none exactly fulfill the h and w specifications.
nd	Select a font by index number relative to the value returned by _registerfonts(), where d is a decimal number. The first element is 1. Within the range of sizes for a given bit-mapped font, the lowest-numbered is the largest.
f	Select a font with fixed spacing.
p	Select a font with proportional spacing.
v	Select a vectored (scaled) font.
r	Select a raster (bit-mapped) font.

As an example, let's say you've registered Courier and you want the middle of its three sizes. You can do this with

    _setfont ("n2");

Later you need to fit 18 characters into a space 150 pixels in width. You could figure out and manually code which font to pick, or you can let the system do it for you automatically. 150 / 18 = 8.33, so you need a font size with a width of eight. You can then get the appropriate font with

    _setfont ("bw8");

which says, in effect, "pick the best font for a character width of eight." In this case, then, the function selects the smallest Courier font (10 high by 8 wide) and returns three, its index. If you passed a width smaller than any available font, _setfont() would return 0 to indicate lack of success in honoring the request.

Now let's say you've registered all the fonts, and you want to select the Helvetica size closest to 20 pixels in height. The call is

    _setfont ("T'HELV' H20,B");

This time _setfont() limits its choices to Helvetica and automatically picks the 18 high by 9 wide font.

There's something you should note about this call. The command string can specify codes in any order and in either upper- or lowercase. You can also separate codes with spaces and other noncode delimiters such as the comma.

Note that one combination of codes in the command string is mutually exclusive. This is "fv," which calls for a fixed-point scaled font: There is no such thing.

When a selected font is scaled, the width and height codes establish the proportions of its characters. In the absence of one of these factors, the graphics library makes assumptions in order to scale the other dimension. The default ratio of width to height ranges from 0.65 to 0.8 depending on the font.

If you've asked _setfont() to automatically pick a font for you, how do you determine its vital statistics?

Inquiring about the Current Font _____

It's often necessary to know things about the current font, particularly its character size. For that, the library furnishes the function _getfontinfo() and an associated data structure called _fontinfo. When you call _getfontinfo(), the function fills in the structured variable whose address is passed as an argument.

This structure is defined in GRAPH.H as

```
struct _fontinfo {
int    type;           /* b0 set = vector,clear = bit map*/
int    ascent;         /* pix dist from top to baseline      */
int    pixwidth;       /* character width in pixels, 0=prop */
int    pixheight;      /* character height in pixels         */
int    avgwidth;       /* average character width in pixels */
char   filename[81];   /* file name including path           */
char   facename[32];   /* font name                          */
};
```

Some of these fields merit explanation. The **ascent** field is one. A font needs to reserve some space for descenders, the tails that hang below characters such as p and q. The baseline is the imaginary line along which the bottoms of nondescender characters are placed. The **pixheight** field tells the overall height of a character in pixels; ascent gives the distance from the baseline to the top. By subtraction, you can determine the amount of space reserved for descenders.

All the Quick C fonts except Courier are proportional; that is, they use less horizontal space for characters such as l and i than for m and w. The **pixwidth** value is thus meaningful only for Courier. In all other cases, this field contains 0. You can determine the average width of a character by checking the **avgwidth** field. There is also a function **_getgtextextent**(), discussed later, that returns the actual width of a string in pixels.

The rest of the fields are self-explanatory in light of the previous discussion of fonts.

Text Output Using Fonts

The purpose of all this is, of course, to get text onto the graphics display using something besides the default hardware font. To do this, use the combination of the two functions **_moveto**() and **_outgtext**().

_moveto() is familiar from other chapters. It places the graphics pen at a specified pixel position, and a subsequent line is drawn from that point. Text also proceeds from there. The pixel position specified by **_moveto**() represents the upper left corner of the first character to be produced. For example, if you write

```
_moveto (320, 180);
```

and then write the word "Font," the northwest corner of F will be at {320, 180} and text will proceed downward and to the right from there. The pen comes to rest at the top left of the next available graphics character position, much as it is advanced by **_lineto**().

The function that writes text in the current font is **_outgtext**(). This is like **_outtext**() except that it utilizes the current font instead of the default hardware character set. **_outgtext**() accepts only preformatted strings. Thus, if you want to show the current value of a variable starting at graphics coordinates {18, 29}, you might write something like

```
sprintf (string, "Loop count = %d", counter);
_moveto (18, 29);
_outgtext (string);
```

If you find yourself coding such sequences often, consider writing a stretched function **_outgtextf**() modeled on **_outtextf**() in EXGRAPH.C.

Releasing Fonts

Font information is stored in dynamic memory. This doesn't steal data work-space from the program, but it does take up heap space that you might need for other things. (Part IV of this book covers dynamic memory—the heap—in detail.) Each registered font takes up 140 bytes of memory; for bit-mapped fonts, 140 bytes are needed for each size. Consequently, if you register all fonts you'll gobble up 2520 bytes of dynamic memory (140 * 18). When you don't need the fonts any more, you might as well release the space.

You can do this with _unregisterfonts(), which takes no arguments. The function is analogous to free() or _ffree() in that it releases the space. It also parallels fclose() by disconnecting access to the fonts.

Looking at the Fonts

Now that we've discussed font control to within an inch of its life, let's actu-ally see what the fonts included with Quick C 2.0 look like. SHOFONTS.C (Listing 14.1) creates a display showing the default hardware font and all six software fonts. Each line is written in a different font and tells what it is. An example is

This is Courier from file COURB.FON

The exact appearance of the display depends on the video adapter. On an EGA, the text is all in the upper left quadrant, whereas it occupies most of the screen on the CGA. Pixel size accounts for the wide variations; fonts are merely graphics objects in the same sense as circles and other things we've drawn in previous chapters, and are thus subject to the same rules and hard-ware limitations.

Build the program from the command line with

QCL shofonts.c exgraph.c

Listing 14.1 **A font sampler.**

```
/* SHOFONTS.C: Shows the six fonts that come with Quick C 2.0 */

#include <graph.h>
#include <conio.h>
#include <stdio.h>
#include "exgraph.h"

char fontname[][8] = {                    /* internal font names */
  {"courier"}, {"helv"}, {"tms rmn"},
  {"modern"}, {"script"}, {"roman"}
```

```
};

void main()
{
short fontsreg, n, y = 20;
char   spec[25];
struct _fontinfo font;

  /* Register all the fonts at once */
  fontsreg = _registerfonts ("*.FON");
  if (fontsreg == -1) {
    puts ("No fonts are available\n");
    puts ("Put the .FON files into your working directory,\n");
    puts ("or else set a path to them in _registerfonts()\n");
    exit (-1);                                /* end program */
  }

  /* Switch to graphics mode, show default font */
  if (_setvideomode (_MRES4COLOR)) {
    _outtext ("This is the default font");

    /* Display fonts */
    for (n = 0; n < 6; n++) {
      sprintf (spec, "t'%s' w9 h14 b", fontname[n]);
      _setfont (spec);                        /* select font */
      _getfontinfo (&font);                      /* get info */
      _moveto (1, y);                  /* set output location */
      y += 20;                             /* next text row */
      _outgtext ("This is ");
      _outgtext (font.facename);        /* tell which font */
      _outgtext (" from ");
      _outgtext (font.filename);        /* and font file */
    }

    getch();                             /* wait for keypress */
    _unregisterfonts();                      /* release fonts */
    _setvideomode (_DEFAULTMODE);
  } else
    puts ("Cannot enter graphics mode");
}
```

This program implements many of the principles already covered: registration, selection/scaling according to specifications, inquiry, positioning, output.

The program output reveals that fonts vary as to legibility. At the low end is script (use it sparingly; it's hard to read and too unprofessional for most applications). The upper end among the software fonts is probably Courier, the same font produced by many typewriters. The drawback of Courier is that it's the only nonproportional font, thus requiring more space, on average, than the others.

Now let's solve some specific problems of programming graphics fonts.

Scaling and Placement

One advantage in using scaled fonts is that you can make text of any size appropriate to the application, and you can place it on the display with fine precision.

The application we'll consider here is light-hearted—a program to wish your favorite computer user a happy birthday—but it illustrates scaling and placement. BIRTHDAY.C appears in Listing 14.2. Make this program from the command line with

    QCL birthday.c exgraph.c curve.c

Listing 14.2 **Scaling and placing graphics text.**

```
/* BIRTHDAY.C: Displays a happy birthday message */
/*             using the Script font               */
/* Illustrates scaling and placing a font          */

#include <graph.h>
#include <stdio.h>
#include <conio.h>
#include "exgraph.h"
#include "curve.h"

#if !defined TRUE
#define FALSE 0
#define TRUE  !FALSE
#endif
#define HAPPY "Happy"
#define BDAY  "birthday!"

void main()
{
int toobad = TRUE, width, x;
struct videoconfig video;

  if (_setvideomode (_MRES4COLOR)) {
    _getvideoconfig (&video);

    /* Register the script font */
    if (_registerfonts ("SCRIPT.FON") != -1)
      toobad = FALSE;

    /* Draw a happy face */
    if (!toobad) {
```

```
     _setbkcolor (_BLUE);
     _curve (115, 100, 160,  50, 115,  50);     /* outline */
     _curve (160,  50, 205, 100, 205,  50);
     _curve (205, 100, 160, 150, 205, 150);
     _curve (160, 150, 115, 100, 115, 150);
     _curve (140, 120, 180, 120, 160, 140);       /* mouth */
     _curve (145,  85, 155,  85, 150,  75);       /* eyes */
     _curve (165,  85, 175,  85, 170,  75);

     /* Select and scale the font */
     _setfont ("t'script' h30 w20");

     /* Write the birthday greeting */
     width = _getgtextextent (HAPPY);  /* width of string */
     x = (video.numxpixels - width) / 2;/* for centering */
     _moveto (x, 10);                          /* top line */
     _outgtext (HAPPY);
     width = _getgtextextent (BDAY);  /* ditto for bottom */
     x = (video.numxpixels - width) / 2;
     _moveto (x, 160);
     _outgtext (BDAY);

     /* Wait for keypress */
     getch();
     _unregisterfonts();
   }
   _setvideomode (_DEFAULTMODE);
 }

 if (toobad) {
   puts ("Can't draw you a picture,\n");
   puts ("but happy birthday anyway!");
 }
}
```

This program uses a series of conic splines to draw a happy face against a blue background in CGA four-color mode. The face occupies the area between Y coordinates 50 and 150, leaving 50 pixels each at the top and bottom. These open spaces are where we'll center the happy birthday message, one word above, the other below.

In order to achieve pleasing proportions, let's make the scaled text 30 pixels high, thus leaving spaces of ten pixels above and below each word. In general, the ratio of width to height in scaled text should be around 2/3. Since the height is 30, the width assigned via the _setfont() call is 20.

We have two words of dissimilar length using a proportional text and we need to center each one. That means we need to find out the width of each in pixels. The graphics library furnishes the function _getgtextextent() to help us do this.

At first glance, this function's name seems to make no sense. It would have been more readable had Microsoft broken it up with underscores, as in _get_ gtext_extent(). At any rate, given a string, the function returns its length in pixels for the current font.

To calculate the starting X for A_STRING, first find its length in pixels with a call such as

        width = _getgtextextent (A_STRING);

Then subtract the returned value from the screen width and divide by two, as in

        start_x = (video.numxpixels − width) / 2;

Finally, _moveto (start_x, y) and write the output with _outgtext (A_STRING). That's how the program writes the birthday greeting, leaving ten pixels of space above and below the happy face.

Labeling Graphical Objects

A picture might be worth a thousand words, but sometimes a few words help to understand the picture, too. Examples are business charts, scientific/mathematical graphs, and mechanical drawings. Without labels, it's often difficult to know what such graphics mean.

Effective labeling of graphical objects requires some planning, but it's not difficult. The font management routines help by calculating string lengths in pixels, fetching critical values from the _fontinfo structure, and so on.

As an example, say you have a rectangle and you want to place a label above it, located such that three pixels of height separate the bottoms of the characters from the top of the rectangle. The value you need, then, is the Y for the starting text position relative to the rectangle's top. Having loaded a variable of type struct _fontinfo, your program can calculate the vertical position as

        text_y = rect_top − font.pixheight − 3;

Let's say you also want to center the label with respect to the rectangle. It's necessary to know the X coordinates of the rectangle's left and right sides—call them lx and rx—and to obtain the label width in pixels. The expression then becomes

        text_x = lx + ((rx − lx − width) / 2);

For example, if the rectangle runs from 200 to 300 and the label width is 50, then

        text_x = 200 + ((300 − 200 − 50) / 2) = 225

You can then _moveto (x, y) and output the label text.

Now let's say you want to place a label to the left of an object, with five
pixels between the last character and the object's left side. In this case,

text_x = obj_left_x − width − 5;

Assuming that the object's X is 100 and the label width is 45, this expression
furnishes a starting X of 50, which is intuitively correct.

Listing 14.3 produces a mechanical drawing showing the cross-section of a
footing for a brick wall. FOOTING.C contains several examples of labeling
graphical objects in different ways.

Listing 14.3 **Labeling graphical objects.**

```
/* FOOTING.C: Mechanical drawing of a footing */
/*   Shows labeling objects with a font */

#include <graph.h>
#include <stdio.h>
#include <conio.h>

char concrete[] = {                     /* fill pattern for concrete */
  0x88, 0x22, 0x88, 0x22, 0x88, 0x22, 0x88, 0x22
};

void main ()
{
int x, y, width;
struct _fontinfo font;

if (!(_registerfonts ("HELVB.FON"))) {        /* font unavailable */
   puts ("Helvetica font cannot be registered");
   exit (-1);
  }

  /* Use CGA 640 x 200 mono graphics */
  if (_setvideomode (_HRESBW)) {
   _setfillmask (concrete);                    /* set fill pattern */

   /* Draw the footing */
   _moveto (220, 170);
   _lineto (420, 170);  _lineto (420, 130);  _lineto (360, 115);
   _lineto (360, 100);  _lineto (280, 100);  _lineto (280, 115);
   _lineto (220, 130);  _lineto (220, 170);
   _floodfill (320, 160, 1);                   /* fill with pattern */

   /* Draw the brick wall */
   _rectangle (_GBORDER, 270, 52, 370, 77);
   _rectangle (_GBORDER, 270, 75, 370, 100);
   _moveto (270, 52); _lineto (270, 45);
   _moveto (370, 52); _lineto (370, 40);
```

Listing 14.3 *(continued)*

```
/* Show ground level */
_moveto (70, 100); _lineto (570, 100);

/* Draw the drainage tiles */
_ellipse (_GBORDER, 440, 140, 465, 150);
_ellipse (_GBORDER, 175, 140, 200, 150);

/* Set the graphics font */
_setfont ("h12, w7");                           /* 12 x 7 Helvetica */

/* Label the footing itself */
width = _getgtextextent ("Poured concrete");
x = (640 - width) / 2;                           /* for centering */
_moveto (x, 172); _outgtext ("Poured concrete");

/* Label the wall */
_moveto (390, 50); _outgtext ("Brick");
_moveto (390, 60); _outgtext ("wall");

/* Label ground level with 2 rows between ltrs and line */
/*      and 75 X's right and left of wall */
_getfontinfo (&font);
y = 100 - font.pixheight - 2;
x = 270 - _getgtextextent ("Ground") - 100;     /* to left */
_moveto (x, y); _outgtext ("Ground");
x = 370 + 100;                                   /* to right */
_moveto (x, y); _outgtext ("level");

/* Label drainage tiles */
width = _getgtextextent ("Drainage");
x = 175 - width - 5;                             /* to left */
_moveto (x, 135); _outgtext ("Drainage");
width = _getgtextextent ("tile");
x = 175 - width - 5;
_moveto (x, 145); _outgtext ("tile");
_moveto (470, 135); _outgtext ("Drainage");     /* to right */
_moveto (470, 145); _outgtext ("tile");

/* Label the drawing in the largest size */
_setfont ("n1");
width = _getgtextextent ("Footing for Wall");
x = (640 - width) / 2;
_moveto (x, 5); _outgtext ("Footing for Wall");

/* Wait for keypress and quit */
getch();
_setvideomode (_DEFAULTMODE);
} else
puts ("CGA Graphics not available");
}
```

Shadowing Effects _____

While working in the Quick C environment, you've no doubt noticed that dialog boxes appear to float in front of the overlaid display. This visual effect is created by shadowing: darkening the area below and to the left of the box. This kind of optical illusion makes for distinctive screens not only in text, but in graphics as well. And not only can objects such as rectangles cast shadows, but so can font-based text.

The illusion of a raised object is created by making it appear that there's a light source over the viewer's shoulder. The light shines down and to the right in the case of the Quick C dialog boxes. That is, the light source is over your left shoulder. It can also shine the other way, as we'll see shortly.

The CGA offers very limited shadowing capabilities due to its meager four colors. Nevertheless, you can create some interesting effects using black, the default background color, as a shadow.

For example, let's say we have a white rectangle that we want to raise in front of a cyan backdrop. The image must be built toward the viewer from the distance, so first we fill the screen with cyan. This provides the backdrop against which to cast a shadow. Next, we determine where the raised rectangle is to appear. But before we draw it, we have to draw its shadow since that's farther in the distance.

When a light source is over the viewer's right shoulder, the shadow is cast downward and to the left. The way to make the shadow, then, is to draw a dark rectangle the same size as the object casting the shadow, but shift it downward and away from the light source some number of units. For example, if the lower left corner of the raised object is at {100, 100}, we might draw its shadow as a black box with the lower left corner at {90, 90}. Finally, we draw the shadow-casting in its color.

We can also cast shadows using font-based text. Say we want to make it appear that some characters are floating in front of a colored surface. First we shift the graphics pen down and away from the light source and write the text in black, then we change colors and write the text again where it belongs.

And that's exactly what **SHADOWCG.C** in Listing 14.4 does. Using CGA four-color graphics, it creates the illusion of magenta text floating in front of a white panel, which in turn stands up from a cyan backdrop. The imaginary light source is over the viewer's right shoulder.

Listing 14.4 **Casting shadows with the CGA.** _____

```
/* SHADOWCG.C: Shadowing effects on CGA */

#include <graph.h>
#include <conio.h>
#include <stdio.h>
#define SHX -5
#define SHY  5
```

Listing 14.4 *(continued)*

```c
void main()
{
int x, y, width;
struct videoconfig video;

  /* Register Roman (scaled) font */
  if (!(_registerfonts ("ROMAN.FON"))) {
    puts ("Roman font not available");
    exit (-1);
  }

if (_setvideomode (_MRES4COLOR)) {        /* use CGA 4-color */
    _getvideoconfig (&video);

    /* Fill screen with color 1 */
    _setcolor (1);
    _rectangle (_GFILLINTERIOR, 0, 0, 319, 199);

    /* Make a shadow on it */
    _setcolor (0);
    _rectangle (_GFILLINTERIOR, 40+SHX, 40+SHY,
                279+SHX, 150+SHY);

    /* Draw the raised box throwing the shadow */
    _setcolor (3);
    _rectangle (_GFILLINTERIOR, 40, 40, 279, 150);

    /* Set the font size */
    _setfont ("w30 h45");

    /* Set the string size and position */
    width = _getgtextextent ("Shadow");
    x = (video.numxpixels - width) / 2;
    y = (video.numypixels - 45) / 2;

    /* First print the shadows of the characters */
    _setcolor (0);
    _moveto (x+SHX, y+SHY); _outgtext ("Shadow");

    /* Now print the raised letters */
    _setcolor (2);
    _moveto (x, y); _outgtext ("Shadow");

    /* Hold for keypress and quit */
    getch();
    _setvideomode (_DEFAULTMODE);
  }
}
```

The richer color sets of the EGA and VGA offer much more effective potential for shadowing. In particular, the VGA's virtually unlimited shading permits shadowing and texturing that surpasses TV quality. But even the EGA is capable of remarkably subtle shadowing effects.

The EGA's 16-color mode is really two different intensity levels of eight default colors, as discussed in Chapter 10. That being the case, we can draw a surface in a bright color, then cast a shadow on it using the lower intensity. This is more realistic than the black shadows of the CGA. It parallels the real world, where colors are still discernible when a shadow blocks some of the light from reaching them.

Listing 14.5 lists SHADOWEG.C, an EGA version of the shadowing program. The image is the same for both, but the EGA version uses high and low intensities to create the illusion of shadows.

Listing 14.5 Casting more subtle shadows with the EGA.

```
/* SHADOWEG.C: Shadowing effects on EGA */

#include <graph.h>
#include <conio.h>
#include <stdio.h>
#include "textscrn.h"              /* for color palette names */
#define SHX -5
#define SHY  5

void main()
{
int x, y, width;
struct videoconfig video;

  /* Register Roman (scaled) font */
  if (!(_registerfonts ("ROMAN.FON"))) {
    puts ("Roman font not available");
    exit (-1);
  }

if (_setvideomode (_ERESCOLOR)) {          /* use EGA 16-color */
    _getvideoconfig (&video);

    /* Fill screen with light cyan */
    _setcolor (LTCYAN);
    _rectangle (_GFILLINTERIOR, 0, 0, 619, 349);

    /* Make a shadow on it */
    _setcolor (CYAN);        /* darker shade of background */
    _rectangle (_GFILLINTERIOR, 80+SHX, 80+SHY,
              559+SHX, 269+SHY);

    /* Draw the raised box throwing the shadow */
    _setcolor (WHITE);
    _rectangle (_GFILLINTERIOR, 80, 80, 559, 269);
```

Listing 14.5 *(continued)*

```
    /* Set the font size */
    _setfont ("w30 h45");

    /* Set the string size and position */
    width = _getgtextextent ("Shadow");
    x = (video.numxpixels - width) / 2;
    y = (video.numypixels - 45) / 2;

    /* First print the shadows of the characters */
    _setcolor (LTGRAY);
    _moveto (x+SHX, y+SHY); _outgtext ("Shadow");

    /* Now print the raised letters */
    _setcolor (MAGENTA);
    _moveto (x, y); _outgtext ("Shadow");

    /* Hold for keypress and quit */
    getch();
    _setvideomode (_DEFAULTMODE);
  }
}
```

You can achieve similar real-world effects by reverse-shadowing text; that is, "engraving" the text into a surface so that the light source casts the characters themselves into shadow, while reflecting off the edges opposite the light source. An example is a control button with its legend engraved. In this case, if the light comes from over your right shoulder, it will cast the interior of the engraving into shadow while reflecting brightly off the right and lower edges of the inset characters.

BUTTON.C listed in Listing 14.6 creates a realistic three-dimensional power button such as one sees on control panels of various kinds. The button consists of three shades of red: the surfaces struck directly by the light source (top and right), one partially in shadow (face of the button), and those in deep shadow (left and lower).

Listing 14.6 **Reverse shadowing in EGA 16-color mode.**

```
/* BUTTON.C: Using shadowing to create a power button */
/* Light source is above and right of viewer */
/* This program runs only on EGA and VGA */

#include <graph.h>
#include <conio.h>
#include <stdio.h>
#include "textscrn.h"   /* for default palette color names */

#define R1   0x15L                        /* Three hues of red */
#define R2   0x2AL
```

```
      #define R3  0x3FL
      #define RED1 1                        /* Names for palette regs */
      #define RED2 2
      #define RED3 3

      void main()
      {
      int width, x, y;
      struct _fontinfo font;
      void fill (int, int, int, char*);

        /* Register Modern font */
        if (!(_registerfonts ("MODERN.FON"))) {
          puts ("Modern font unavailable");
          exit (-1);
        }

        /* Use EGA 16-color graphics mode */
        if (_setvideomode (_ERESCOLOR)) {

          /* Load palette regs with custom colors */
          _remappalette (RED1, R1);
          _remappalette (RED2, R2);
          _remappalette (RED3, R3);

          /* Draw button */
           setcolor (LTGRAY);
          _rectangle (_GBORDER, 240, 115, 400, 235);
          _rectangle (_GBORDER, 210,  85, 430, 265);
          _moveto (210,  85); _lineto (240, 115);      /* corners */
          _moveto (430,  85); _lineto (400, 115);
          _moveto (430, 265); _lineto (400, 235);
          _moveto (210, 265); _lineto (240, 235);

          /* Set button colors */
          _setcolor (RED2);                    /* center is med red */
          _floodfill (320, 175, LTGRAY);
          _setcolor (RED3);        /* top and right are light red */
          _floodfill (320, 100, LTGRAY);
          _floodfill (415, 175, LTGRAY);
          _setcolor (RED1);        /* bottom and left are dark red */
          _floodfill (225, 175, LTGRAY);
          _floodfill (320, 250, LTGRAY);

          /* Set the scaled font size */
          _setfont ("w20 h30");
          _getfontinfo (&font);

          /* Produce the label as indented inscription */
          width = _getgtextextent ("POWER");
          x = (640 - width) / 2;          /* vertical centering */
          y = (350 - font.ascent) / 2;        /* and horizontal */
          _setcolor (LTGRAY);                 /* reflective edges */
```

Listing 14.6 *(continued)*

```
    fill (x, y, 2, "POWER");
    _setcolor (RED1);                /* indented inscription */
    fill (x, y, 1, "POWER");

    /* Hold for keypress and quit */
    getch();
    _setvideomode (_DEFAULTMODE);
  }
} /* ----------------------- */

void fill (int x, int y, int n, char *text)
        /* fill a 2 x 2 area relative to x, y with text */
        /* where n is the number of pixels below, left  */
{
int xoff, yoff;

  for (xoff = -n; xoff <= 0; xoff++)
    for (yoff = n; yoff >= 0; yoff--) {
      _moveto (x+xoff, y+yoff);
      _outgtext (text);
    }
}
```

The inscription **POWER** is centered vertically, and also horizontally with respect to its ascent (the entire word is above the base line with no descenders, revealing a use for the ascent field in the _fontinfo structure).

The reflectivity of the edges exposed to light are as important to the realistic text display as the shadows within the engraved letters. The fill() function accomplishes the effect by repetitively drawing the characters in the prevailing color. The first call fills all possible text pixels with the reflected color, and the second with the shadow color. The shadows replace the reflections where appropriate, leaving only the reflecting edges opposite the light source and casting the rest of each character image into darkness. The result is a strikingly realistic depiction of a three-dimensional power on/off button.

Armed with the technique presented in the past several chapters, you can program highly effective graphics in Quick C 2.0. Now let's wrap up our coverage of graphics programming with perhaps the most important area of computer graphics: business charts.

CHAPTER 15

Presentation Graphics

New with Quick C 2.0 is an entire subsytem devoted to presentation graphics or, more descriptively, business charts. This subsystem is similar to the libraries developed in this book in that it adds functionality to the Quick C graphics library discussed in the past few chapters. Its purpose is to enable you to describe and produce professional quality business charts with a minimum of effort.

The presentation graphics package consists of several data structures and a couple of dozen functions formanipulating them, all defined in **PG-CHART.H**. A program that creates business charts must include this file and **GRAPH.H**, and it must link with the **PGCHART** and **GRAPHICS** libraries (unless you combined them with the run-time libraries at installation).

The package produces five basic kinds of business charts:

- Pie
- Line
- Bar
- Column
- Scatter

By setting fields within the descriptor data structures prior to drawing a chart, you can achieve a great deal of flexibility in tailoring the result to your needs. The package is largely device-independent, doing the best it can with the current video mode; this means that a business graphics application written in Quick C will—without modification—produce reasonably similar results on any machine that offers one of the modes supported by the graphics library. That's good news for commercial and corporate software developers.

The quality of the results depends, of course, on the graphics adapter. If you run exactly the same program on a CGA and an EGA, the EGA output will be much more pleasing. The **PGCHART** library attempts to compensate for the CGA's limited capabilities through the use of fill patterns that aren't necessary when a wider range of colors is available. The **PGCHART** library also downscales graphics elements to make room for the larger characters on the CGA. These and other adjustments are made automatically, relieving you of the need to worry about them. The overall thrust of the presentation graphics subsystem is to allow you to concentrate on the problem rather than on the pesky details surrounding this or that video adapter.

Chapter 13 of the Quick C manual, *C For Yourself*, discusses the basics of presentation graphics and presents several simple applications along with pictures of their results. Consequently, after a brief review of fundamentals, our thrust here will be to cover some of the more complex issues and to explore aspects left unmentioned in the documentation. The objective is to get you to a comfortable level in using the presentation graphics package.

Working with the PGchart Library

Programs that produce business charts using the **PGCHART** package must follow a fixed sequence of steps and conform to certain conventions expected by the library. The steps are:

1. Include **GRAPH.H** and **PGCHART.H**, in addition to other header files as required.
2. Enter a graphics mode using _setvideomode().
3. Initialize the presentation graphics subsystem with a call to _pg_initchart().
4. Initialize a chart environment data structure using _pg_defaultchart().
5. Change environment structure fields to tailor the chart.
6. Display the chart.
7. Wait for a keystroke or time-out.
8. Restore the default adapter mode.

Steps 4 and 5 are the easiest way to set up a chart. Alternatively, you could load all the chart environment structure fields yourself and go directly to step 6. A glance at the structure definitions in **PGCHART.H** will convince you that the way shown here is better. The _pg_defaultchart() function constructs a default chart based on the chart type specified in its argument list. In Step 5 you override the default selections to get the options you want.

The options provide for great flexibility in controlling the chart's appearance. List **PGCHART.H** and study it to see the kinds of things you do by tweaking the contents of the environment structure. It's a good idea to keep this listing handy as you write presentation graphics programs.

The whole idea of a chart is, of course, to depict two or more data values graphically so that the eye can compare them. A chart showing only one data value is pointless, because no comparison is possible. This brings us to the concept of a series: a group of related data values to be compared. Examples are earnings by quarter, the daily Dow-Jones Industrial Average, and income by age group. These are data series that become proportionally scaled visual objects on the display, such as pie slices or bars whose relative sizes represent their value relationships.

The **PGCHART** package imposes some conventions on data series. First, the data must be of type **float**. This is the only data type accepted. Second, the series must be in an array, with values sequenced according to order of output. For example, when building a column chart, the package makes the first series element the leftmost column and proceeds to the right, element by element. Finally, when displaying two or more series on the same chart (a comparison of budget to actual, for example), the series must be in a two-dimensional array. We'll deal with this requirement in more detail later in the chapter.

Naturally your program has to acquire the data series from some source. The simplest, but least flexible, way is to build the data directly into the program by initializing an array of type **float**. The disadvantage is that, if the data change, you have to modify and recompile the program. You can achieve much more flexibility by storing the data in a disk file and reading the file with the chart program; a simple loop places sequential input items into the series array. There are other data acquisition methods as well, such as asking the user to type the values at the keyboard, or accepting remote data via a serial port. Our interest in this chapter is seeing how to use presentation graphics, so we'll opt for the simplest method and build the data series into source programs.

The concept of logical ordering also applies to other chart elements. For example, categories are text strings describing the way the data are broken down. The word "by" is operative in identifying categories, as in "sales by quarter." In this case, the categories are quarters, so the text strings should identify them as such in logical sequence: "1Q89," "2Q89," and so on. The chart package then figures out where to place the category strings on the display so as to establish the context of the graphics.

Listing 15.1 illustrates this discussion with a simple column chart displaying a quarterly sales forecast. The **periods** variable is an array of string pointers indicating the data categories, and the **sales** variable holds the data series: that is, the forecast itself, whose elements are ordered by category. Note that a variable of type **chartenv** is always required in a **PGCHART** program; this data structure contains a complete specification for the chart.

The programs in this chapter use the **EXGRAPH** library developed earlier. The command line for making the **FORECAST** program is

    QCL forecast.c exgraph.c

The other programs in this chapter require a similar command line in order to incorporate **EXGRAPH**.

Figure 15.1 **A simple column chart program.**

```c
/* FORECAST.C: Displays a sales forecast as column chart */

#include <stdio.h>
#include <pgchart.h>
#include <graph.h>
#include <stdlib.h>
#include "exgraph.h"

#define QUARTERS 4
#if !defined TRUE
#define FALSE 0
#define TRUE  !FALSE
#endif

char far *periods [QUARTERS] = {
  "1Q", "2Q", "3Q", "4Q"
};
float far sales [QUARTERS] = {
   21.2, 26.3, 29.5, 19.0
};

void main()
{
chartenv env;
short result;

  /* Initialize for column chart */
  if (!_setvideomode (bestmode())) {
    puts ("Graphics not available");
    exit (EXIT_FAILURE);
  }
  _pg_initchart ();
_pg_defaultchart (&env, _PG_COLUMNCHART, _PG_PLAINBARS);

  /* Set up the chart particulars */
  strcpy (env.maintitle.title, "Sales Forecast by Quarter");
  env.maintitle.titlecolor = 4;
  env.yaxis.grid = TRUE;               /* horiz grid lines */
  env.xaxis.axiscolor = 3;                    /* colors */
  env.yaxis.axiscolor = 3;
  env.chartwindow.bordercolor = 2;

  /* Display the chart and hold for keypress */
  result = _pg_chart (&env, periods, sales, QUARTERS);
  if (result != 0) {
    _setvideomode (_DEFAULTMODE);
    puts ("Error drawing chart");
    exit (EXIT_FAILURE);
  } else {
    getch();
    _setvideomode (_DEFAULTMODE);
  }
}
```

The call to _pg_defaultchart() initializes the chartenv structure with default values. The second argument specifies the chart type (column in this case), and the third argument gives additional information about the chart. Here we have a choice of plain bars (each by itself) or stacked bars.

After initializing, we modify the default values to reflect the particulars of the chart. This program sets a chart title, which is centered by default, and specifies some colors for various elements. It also sets up grid lines on the Y (vertical) axis, which run horizontally across the chart at regular intervals. Grid lines help the viewer measure the actual values of columns.

With the setup complete, the program calls _pg_chart(), passing the environment, categories, data series, and number of items in the series. This produces the actual chart, which remains on the display until the user presses a key.

Multiple Data Series

Much can often be learned by visually comparing two or more related sets of numbers on the same chart. The scenario we'll use here is comparing actual sales results with the forecast. In this case we want to place two columns side by side in each quarter: one representing the forecast, the other the actual for that period. The forecast and the actuals are related but logically distinct sets of values. Therefore they're two series.

The PGCHART package requires that multiple series be placed into a two-dimensional array of type float. The first dimension of the array defines the number of series it contains: two in this case. The second dimension reflects the number of elements in the series, which is four here. Thus, to represent the forecast and actuals, we need a two x four array of type float. The forecast logically precedes the actuals, so the first (or 0th) series contains the quarterly forecast numbers and the second contains the sales results. (Note: All sets must be of equal length when using multiple series.)

This ordering of series tells the chart package to group two columns—one from each series—into each quarter, with the forecast column on the left and the actual on the right. The package automatically assigns a distinctive appearance to each series: on the EGA, solid bars of one color for the forecast and another color for the actuals; on the CGA and other less-capable devices, different colors and/or fill patterns. The library makes these decisions based on the capabilities of the video hardware.

Multiple series usually require an additional set of text elements to label each grouping. In this case, the labels are "Forecast" and "Actuals," specified in the same order as the series along the first dimension of the data array. When you pass a pointer to the labels as an argument to the chart-drawing routine, the graphics package creates a cross-reference legend located, by default, in the upper right corner of the chart. This legend shows the color/pattern assigned to the series and its associated label.

Listing 15.2 lists ACTUAL.C, which translates this discussion into working code. The program is similar to FORECAST.C (Listing 15.1), except that it compares two data series. Note how the sales array is initialized in two rows reflecting the two series: forecast first, actuals last. Following that, the labels array provides descriptive text elements for the chart legend.

Listing 15.2 **Comparing two data series.**

```c
/* ACTUAL.C: Displays forecast vs actuals as column chart */
/* Two data series in same chart */

#include <stdio.h>
#include <pgchart.h>
#include <graph.h>
#include <stdlib.h>
#include "exgraph.h"

#define QUARTERS 4
#define FDATA "FORECAST.DAT"
#if !defined TRUE
#define FALSE 0
#define TRUE  !FALSE
#endif

char far *periods [QUARTERS] = {
  "1Q", "2Q", "3Q", "4Q"
};
float far sales [2][QUARTERS] = {
   { 21.2, 26.3, 29.5, 19.0 },
   { 23.6, 22.4, 27.3, 18.7 }
};
char far *labels[] = {"Forecast", "Actuals"};

void main()
{
int mo;
chartenv env;
char amt [10];
short result;

  /* Initialize for column chart */
  if (!_setvideomode (bestmode())) {
    puts ("Graphics not available");
    exit (EXIT_FAILURE);
  }
  _pg_initchart ();
  _pg_defaultchart (&env, _PG_COLUMNCHART, _PG_PLAINBARS);

  /* Set up the chart particulars */
  strcpy (env.maintitle.title,                    /* title */
          "Forecasts vs Actuals by Quarter");
  env.yaxis.grid = TRUE;                          /* horiz grid lines */
```

```
    env.maintitle.titlecolor = 4;                          /* colors */
    env.xaxis.axiscolor = 3;
    env.yaxis.axiscolor = 3;
    env.chartwindow.bordercolor = 2;

    /* Display the chart and hold for keypress */
    result = _pg_chartms (&env, periods, (float far*) sales,
                          2, QUARTERS, 2, labels);
    if (result != 0) {
      _setvideomode (_DEFAULTMODE);
      puts ("Error drawing chart");
      exit (EXIT_FAILURE);
    } else {
      getch();
      _setvideomode (_DEFAULTMODE);
    }
}
```

The main difference in this program is the chart-drawing call. All presenta-tion graphics functions have the prefix _pg_. Those that work with multiple series also have the suffix ms. Thus, to draw a column chart using a multiple series, you call _pg_chartms(). The function takes different arguments than its simpler counterpart.

The first three are the same for both: the chartenv structure, the categories, and the data series. To the latter, apply the cast float far*; the program works fine if you don't, but the compiler issues a warning. The remaining argu-ments are as follows:

- The number of series.
- The number of data elements per series.
- The number of series again.
- A far pointer to the labels.

This calling sequence differs from that specified in my prerelease version of the Quick C 2.0 documentation (which doesn't work as given).

Pie Charts

By definition, a pie chart can only represent a single series of data. There is no such thing as a multiple-series pie chart. This is because the pie shows the relative sizes of the components (slices) that form a whole.

Some kinds of data are applicable to pie charts and others are not. Ordinarily, time-sequenced data, such as quarterly figures, are better displayed on a col-umn, bar, or line chart, all of which have an implicit time line. A pie chart show-ing quarterly earnings would only be meaningful if you wanted to illustrate the relative sizes of each quarter's contribution to the entire year's earnings.

A pie chart, then, is a way of showing percentages visually, where the sum of all slices always equals 100 percent. Such data are usually a "snapshot" as of a given moment, and not strung out over time. An example is the ethnic composition of a company's workforce as of a certain date: so many blacks, whites, Hispanics, Asians, etc.

Lising 15.3 is ETHNICS.C, which implements this example. The data series gives the headcount for each racial category. The _pg_chartpie() function then computes the size of each slice as a percentage of a full circle and draws the pie accordingly, with each slice visually differentiated from the others.

Listing 15.3 A pie chart shows the components of a whole.

```
/* ETHNICS.C: Pie chart showing ethnic mix of a community */

#include <pgchart.h>
#include <graph.h>
#include <conio.h>
#include <stdio.h>
#include <string.h>
#include <stdlib.h>
#include "exgraph.h"
#define CATEGORIES 5

char far *races [CATEGORIES] = {
  "Black", "White", "Hispanic", "Asian", "Other"
};
float far headcount [CATEGORIES] = {
    153.0,    336.0,    117.0,    80.0,    22.0
};
short far explode [CATEGORIES] = {0};

void main()
{
chartenv env;

  /* Initialize for pie chart */
  if (!_setvideomode (bestmode())) {
    puts ("Graphics mode not available");
    exit (EXIT_FAILURE);
  }
  _pg_initchart();
_pg_defaultchart (&env, _PG_PIECHART, _PG_PERCENT);

  /* Give the chart a title */
  strcpy (env.maintitle.title, "Ethnic Mix of Employees");

  /* Draw the chart and hold for keypress */
  if (_pg_chartpie (&env, races, headcount,
                    explode, CATEGORIES)) {
    _setvideomode (_DEFAULTMODE);
    puts ("Error drawing pie chart");
    exit (EXIT_FAILURE);
```

```
    } else {
      getch();
      _setvideomode (_DEFAULTMODE);
    }
  }
```

When you want to emphasize a particular slice for some reason, an effective visual technique is to "explode" it from the pie: That is, move it away from the center so that it is physically separate. The _pg_chartpie() function accepts an array of Booleans—one element per item in the series—indicating which slices to explode. A 0 (FALSE) means no, and TRUE (nonzero) means explode the corresponding slice. For example, if we wanted to explode the Hispanic slice in ETHNICS.C, we could set the array element explode[2] to a nonzero value.

If you know that a program must always explode the slice with the largest (or smallest) value, you can build in the smarts to do it automatically. That's what BESTRGN.C in Listing 15.4 does. This program finds the sales region with the best results and pulls out its slice for emphasis. By inspecting the data series visually, we can see that Southwest has the best results. The program's bestregion() function behaves similarly, scanning the results and saving the index of the highest achiever, which it returns. The returned value (1) is used to set the corresponding explode[] entry to TRUE, thus causing the slice to be exploded.

Listing 15.4 Exploding the largest pie slice automatically.

```
/* BESTRGN.C: Pie chart showing sales results by region */
/* Automatically explodes the best region's slice */

#include <pgchart.h>
#include <graph.h>
#include <conio.h>
#include <stdio.h>
#include <string.h>
#include <stdlib.h>
#include "exgraph.h"
#define REGIONS 5
#if !defined TRUE
#define FALSE 0
#define TRUE  !FALSE
#endif

char far *regions [REGIONS] = {
  "Northwest", "Southwest", "Central",
  "Southeast", "Northeast"
};
float far results [REGIONS] = {
    70.63, 90.15, 50.11, 65.92, 81.25
};
short far explode [REGIONS] = { FALSE };
```

Listing 15.4 *(continued)*

```c
void main()
{
chartenv env;
int bestregion (void);

  /* Initialize for pie chart */
  if (!_setvideomode (bestmode())) {
    puts ("Graphics mode not available");
    exit (EXIT_FAILURE);
  }
  _pg_initchart();
_pg_defaultchart (&env, _PG_PIECHART, _PG_PERCENT);

  /* Give the chart a title and subtitle */
  strcpy (env.maintitle.title, "Best Sales Region");
  strcpy (env.subtitle.title, "Third Quarter Results");

  /* Set up to explode best region's slice */
  explode [bestregion()] = TRUE;

  /* Draw the chart and hold for keypress */
  if (_pg_chartpie (&env, regions, results,
                    explode, REGIONS)) {
    _setvideomode (_DEFAULTMODE);
    puts ("Error drawing pie chart");
    exit (EXIT_FAILURE);
  } else {
    getch();
    _setvideomode (_DEFAULTMODE);
  }
} /* ----------------------- */

int bestregion (void)    /* find region with highest sales */
{
int rgn, best;
float highest = 0.0;

  for (rgn = 0; rgn < REGIONS; rgn++)        /* scan results */
    if (results [rgn] > highest) {
      highest = results [rgn];               /* get new highest */
      best = rgn;                                /* and who */
    }
  return best;
}
```

Controlling the Size and Location of Charts _____

The chart environment contains a number of data structures whose fields, as we have already seen to some extent, can be manipulated to control the chart's appearance. One of these structures is called **chartwindow**. By modifying its **x2** and **y2** fields, you can override the default full-screen size of the chart.

When **_pg_defaultchart()** finishes initializing the environment, the chartwindow **xn** and **yn** fields all contain 0. The chart drawing routines take these values to mean that the chart should occupy the entire display, and so during the drawing process they set **x2** and **y2** to the lower right corner. The inner windows (data and legend) are automatically adjusted to fit within the overall chart window.

To override the default size, change **x2** and **y2** to something besides 0. For example, say you want the chart to occupy 2/3 of the display area. First call getvideoconfig() to obtain the screen dimensions, then set the chart window size with expressions such as

```
env.chartwindow.x2  =  (video.numxpixels  *  2)  /  3;
env.chartwindow.y2  =  (video.numypixels  *  2)  /  3;
```

Now when you call a drawing function, the chart is downsized accordingly. Its upper left corner coincides with the upper left corner of the screen.

If you want to relocate the chart elsewhere on the display, you have to change the screen's logical origin. This has the effect of moving coordinates {0, 0} to a new point. The reason is that the **PGCHART** drawing routines always originate the chart window at home position, regardless of the value you place in **chartwindow.x1** and **y1** (and despite what the Quick C documentation says to the contrary).

Change the logical origin with **_setlogorg()**, which takes absolute X and Y coordinates as its arguments. For example, to move the logical origin to the center of the CGA screen, write

```
_setlogorg  (160,  100);
```

Thereafter any graphics instruction involving coordinates will offset from the center of the display rather than from the upper left corner.

In the case of the 2/3-sized chart, say you want it to appear in the lower right corner of the display. Move the logical origin with an expression such as

```
_setlogorg  (video.numxpixels/3,  video.numypixels/3);
```

and then issue the appropriate chart drawing call. The **2CHARTS.C** program in the next section provides working examples of resizing and relocating charts.

Displaying Multiple Charts _____

Now let's return to the best sales region problem to see how you can display more than one chart at a time. Rerunning the **BESTRGN** program reveals a weakness of pie charts: it's hard to eyeball the relative sizes of the slices, especially when they're all fairly close as in this case. Southwest might be the winner, but Northeast looks to be about the same size in the pie chart. This is a case where you might want to produce a companion bar chart that more clearly reveals how the five regions compare with one another.

To do this, we'll revise BESTRGN, calling it 2CHARTS.C (Listing 15.5). Much of the program operates just as before. A minor change occurs at line 38, where we eliminate percentages from the pie chart specification. The main change to the pie chart begins just below the explosion decision. As described in the previous section, the window for the pie chart is limited to 2/3 of the display. Its origin remains fixed at the upper left corner of the screen. Then we draw the chart.

But instead of waiting for a keypress as before, we then prepare to draw a bar chart on the same screen, using the same data. A good deal of space is wasted in the pie chart window, so the bar chart will partially overlap it. By looking at the **datawindow** structure in the environment, we can find out where the drawing routine located the data window's right edge (field **x2**). The left edge of the new chart will occur 10 pixels inside the pie chart's data window. The top of the new chart will be at the screen's vertical center. We assure this placement by changing the logical origin.

Now we can begin constructing the bar chart. First we initialize its environment by calling _pg_defaultchart(). The lower right corner of the chart window must be computed so as to fall just inside the display area, which is the purpose of the next two statements. After giving the chart a title and turning off the legend, which isn't needed, we draw the bar chart. The display then freezes awaiting a keypress.

Listing 15.5 Drawing two charts on the same display.

```
/* 2CHARTS.C: Pie chart showing sales results by region, */
/*      and bar chart with same data  */
/* Automatically explodes the best region's slice */

#include <pgchart.h>
#include <graph.h>
#include <conio.h>
#include <stdio.h>
#include <string.h>
#include <stdlib.h>
#include "exgraph.h"
#define REGIONS 5
#if !defined TRUE
#define FALSE 0
#define TRUE  !FALSE
#endif

char far *regions [REGIONS] = {
  "NW", "SW", "MW", "SE", "NE"
```

```
};
float far results [REGIONS] = {
    70.63, 90.15, 50.11, 65.92, 81.25
};
short far explode [REGIONS] = { FALSE };

void main()
{
chartenv env;
int bestregion (void), x, y;
struct videoconfig video;

  /* Initialize for pie chart */
  if (!_setvideomode (bestmode())) {
    puts ("Graphics mode not available");
    exit (EXIT_FAILURE);
  }
  _pg_initchart();
_pg_defaultchart (&env, _PG_PIECHART, _PG_NOPERCENT);

  /* Give the chart a title and subtitle */
  strcpy (env.maintitle.title, "Best Sales Region");
  strcpy (env.subtitle.title, "Third Quarter Results");

  /* Set up to explode best region's slice */
  explode [bestregion()] = TRUE;

  /* Limit pie chart window to upper left 2/3 of screen */
  _getvideoconfig (&video);          /* screen dimensions */
  env.chartwindow.x2 = (video.numxpixels * 2) / 3;
  env.chartwindow.y2 = (video.numypixels * 2) / 3;

  /* Draw the pie chart */
  if (_pg_chartpie (&env, regions, results,
                    explode, REGIONS)) {
    _setvideomode (_DEFAULTMODE);
    puts ("Error drawing pie chart");
    exit (EXIT_FAILURE);
  }

  /* CHART #2: BAR CHART IN LOWER RIGHT QUADRANT */
  x = env.datawindow.x2 - 10;        /* X origin of chart */
  y = video.numypixels / 2;               /* and Y origin */
  _setlogorg (x, y);      /* change display logical origin */

  /* Initialize column chart */
  _pg_defaultchart (&env, _PG_BARCHART, _PG_PLAINBARS);
  env.chartwindow.x2 = video.numxpixels - x - 1;   /* size */
  env.chartwindow.y2 = video.numypixels - y - 1;
  strcpy (env.maintitle.title, "Results by region");
  env.legend.legend = FALSE;                  /* no legend */

  /* Draw the column chart */
```

Listing 15.5 *(continued)*

```
  _pg_chart (&env, regions, results, REGIONS);

  /* Wait for keypress, quit */
  getch();
  _setvideomode (_DEFAULTMODE);
} /* ---------------------- */

int bestregion (void)    /* find region with highest sales */
{
int rgn, best;
float highest = 0.0;

  for (rgn = 0; rgn < REGIONS; rgn++)       /* scan results */
    if (results [rgn] > highest) {
       highest = results [rgn];            /* get new highest */
       best = rgn;                              /* and who */
    }
  return best;
}
```

By now you should be comfortable enough with the presentation graphics package to begin undertaking your own projects with a reasonably good chance of success. We haven't covered all its possibilities, nor even all its functions, but those things should now come to you quite easily.

This concludes our coverage of graphics programming in Quick C 2.0. So far, most of this book has dealt with the "foreign relations" of C programs—files, user interface, graphics—all of which influence the way programs interact with the outside world. The next section turns inward, exploring the unseeable, but no less important subject of dynamic memory management, which is key to advanced programming.

PART IV

Dynamic Memory

Many C applications deal with large amounts of data whose format is known in advance but whose quantity is not. Here are a couple of examples:

1. In a windowing environment, it's necessary to save the current screen before writing a new window, so that you can later restore the display to its previous appearance. We saw cases of this in Part II. It's often impossible to predict how many screen images you might have to save when the user is capable of popping up menus, dialog boxes, help panels, and so forth. The problem is solved by building an image stack in dynamic memory.
2. An effective method for gaining instant access to any given record within a file is to index the file on a key value. When you want to fetch a specific record, you look up its key in the index, and an associated field tells you where the record is within the file so that you can use direct access to get to it. It is usually impossible to know in advance how many records a file contains. Therefore a dynamic index structure is appropriate.

There are plenty of other uses for dynamic memory as well. These two examples give a flavor for its importance.

This part of the book begins with a discussion of the concepts and tools for dynamic memory allocation. Chapter 17 covers singly linked lists, which embody many of the basic principles that serve as the foundation for the more complex structures later. Chapter 18 examines doubly linked lists, queues (FIFO structures), stacks (LIFO structures), and circular lists. Chapter 19 looks at binary trees, which offer extremely efficient means for organizing and searching large quantities of data. Finally, Part IV concludes with a discussion of irregular data structures.

These five chapters are not intended as a comprehensive treatment of dynamic data structures, but rather as an introduction to the most common ones. Weighty tomes have been written on the subject. Perhaps the best known, and an excellent resource if you want exhaustive coverage, is *The Art of Computer Programming*, by Donald E. Knuth (Addison-Wesley, 1973). This multivolume series is known among software engineers simply (and affectionately) as Knuth.

Another caveat: Most of the program examples in this book are workaday functions that you can apply directly to your own projects. Those in this part of the book are instead conceptual in nature. This is because operations on linked lists are highly application-dependent; we search on specific criteria, develop structures for defined purposes, etc. Therefore, you must adapt the concepts to suit your own objectives.

Having said that, let's get on with it.

CHAPTER 16

Dynamic Allocation

Dynamic memory is the portion of the computer's memory that belongs to your program, but is not committed to any specific purpose such as code or static data. This uncommitted memory, often called the "heap," is dynamically available because a program can grab and release pieces of it as needed.

DOS itself is memory-resident, and on the IBM PC and compatibles, there are often other TSRs (Terminate and Stay Resident programs) as well: Sidekick, ProKey, device drivers of one kind and another, etc. The running program takes up some additional memory, and it needs a stack for calling subprograms and passing parameters. The sum of committed memory might add up to a couple of hundred K. All the rest (total installed main memory on the machine less committed memory) is available to the program through dynamic allocation. For example:

Total main memory		640K*
Less:		
DOS	35	
TSR's	85	
Running program	56	
Stack segment	64	
Subtotal		240K
Available for dynamic allocation		400K

* Note that expanded/extended memory (EMS) is not included in "main memory" since it takes special techniques to use addresses beyond 640K. The last chapter of this book discusses EMS in detail.

In other words, about two-thirds of memory (400/640) is uncommitted in this case and is available to the program as dynamic space. That's a lot of memory that you can use for dynamic data workspace.

The default size of the accessible heap varies according to which of the five Quick C memory models you use. The small data configurations (small and medium models) use near pointers by default, meaning that the heap is lim-

291

ited to 64K of data space. The large data configurations (compact, large, and huge) employ far pointers that make all the unclaimed memory available.

The standard C function **malloc()** is the primary means for obtaining ("allocating") heap space to the program. Its opposite is **free()**, which releases the space associated with a pointer.

You can override the small-data limitation by declaring far pointers to heap space and using the Quick C library functions **_fmalloc()** and **_ffree()** to claim and release space. I recommend this for programs that will only ever run on the IBM PC; it's not ANSI-standard C (which doesn't support the concept of far pointers at all), but it guarantees that your programs will have access to the full heap no matter which memory model you select.

Pointers are perhaps the most confusing aspect of C, and the segmented-memory architecture of the Intel chips used on the IBM PC and compatibles muddies the waters even more. If you're a bit shaky on these concepts, you might wish to read the following section. Otherwise, I'll meet you at the section entitled Dynamic Memory Allocation.

Of Addresses and Pointers

The Intel processor family, which includes the 8088, 8086, 80286, and 80386 (the latter two running in real mode), uses two 16-bit words to represent a memory address. This scheme is called segmented addressing. The first word is the segment, which is a 16-byte paragraph computed as

actual address mod 16

The second word is the data offset, a value that offsets from the segment paragraph address to find the location of the variable in question. The notation is:

Segment	: Offset
0120	: 00C3 (in hex)
0288	: 0195 (in decimal)

The upshot of all this is that any memory address on the IBM PC and compatible machines is a 32-bit value. However, only 20 of the full 32 bits are needed to gain access to a memory location. This is because of an 80×86 architectural concept known as segment registers.

There are four segment registers, as follows:

Register	Points to
CS	Code segment
DS	Data segment
SS	Stack segment
ES	Extended segment

Each register gives the starting paragraph address of its relevant 64K segment.

When a small-model program begins to run, DOS loads the CS register with the start of the code segment, DS with the start of the data segment, and SS with the start of the stack segment. The default near heap exists in the stack segment and can use all the space not occupied by the stack. The size of all three segments is fixed at 64K each, which means that these registers never change during program execution.

Consequently, the only part of the address that you need to locate any program element is the 16-bit offset. The processor adds this to the appropriate segment register to derive actual addresses. For a static data value, the CPU adds the offset to the DS register; to jump to an executable location, it adds the offset to the CS register; etc.

These 16-bit offsets are all that the small-code group needs to locate anything fixed within the domain of the program. They are called *pointers*, or more precisely within the context of Quick C, *near pointers*. A near pointer is a 16-bit offset from a segment register whose content is fixed for the duration of the program's execution.

The heap is separate from the stack segment in the large data models. Since it's an area of more than 64K, you must use far pointers to locate objects within it. The same is true when overriding the default near heap in the small data models. The difference is, of course, that in the large models far pointers are implicit, whereas in small models you must explicitly declare pointers as far or huge. The following discussion should help clear up any confusion over these qualifiers.

A program written for the small memory model might have the following declarations:

```
OBJTYPE  *nearptr;
OBJTYPE  far  *farptr;
```

Both pointers point to an object of type **OBJTYPE**, but the first is a 16-bit entity that will offset from the SS register on the near heap, while the second is a 32-bit pointer giving the full address of an object on the far heap. The far modifier overrides the default pointer size for the compilation model.

The Quick C compiler automatically develops pointers of the appropriate size—16 or 32 bits—depending on the memory model. In the large model, for example, pointers to static data are 16 bits offset from DS while pointers to executable code are 32 bits.

You might wish to override the default pointer size the other way; i.e., making a near code pointer within the large model, thus forcing the compiler to generate a 16-bit pointer where it would normally create one of 32 bits. Such a declaration might read

```
void     near  somefcn (void)
```

In this case, **somefcn()** takes no arguments, returns no value, and is accessed via a 16-bit pointer offset from the current CS register. The effect is to make **somefcn()** callable only within the current 64K code segment; it is not accessible from outside the segment, since other segments will have different settings for the CS register. Why do this? To reduce overhead. It takes fewer machine cycles to handle a 16-bit offset ("short jump") than a 32-bit address ("long jump"). This is particularly useful for recursive functions, and can significantly improve program performance.

Quick C has two kinds of 32-bit pointers called far and huge. Both contain segment and offset portions and can be used interchangeably. The difference is that huge pointers are normalized. A far pointer contains a paragraph address in the segment portion and any value up to 64K in the offset; by contrast, a huge pointer's offset is limited to values in the range 0 through 16, while the nearest lower paragraph address appears in the segment. In other words, a normalized pointer has as much of the address information as possible packed into the segment portion, and only a value ranging from 0 through 0Fh in the offset portion.

This suggests a trade-off. Because far pointers are not normalized, you cannot compare them and expect reliable results. The following two hex addresses are equivalent:

```
093B : 0011
093C : 0001
```

However, they are not equal. Thus, if you compare them with

```
if (ptra == ptrb)
```

the comparison will fail even though the pointers indicate the same memory location.

Normalization forces all 32-bit huge pointers to contain the nearest paragraph in the segment. The second pointer above is normalized. As a result, if **ptra** and **ptrb** are both declared as huge, the comparison will return valid results. The trade-off is overhead. Normalization of huge pointers executes additional compiler-inserted code every time a huge pointer is modified.

One way to get the best of both worlds is to use far pointers as a matter of course and cast them to huge prior to a comparison, as in

```
OBJTYPE far *ptra, *ptrb;
{
    ptra = (OBJTYPE huge*) ptra;
    ptrb = (OBJTYPE huge*) ptrb;
     if (ptra == ptrb)...
}
```

Indirection

Indirection is a technique used in C and other languages such as Pascal to get at a data object indirectly; i.e., through the use of a pointer rather than by direct reference.

The notation for pointers and addresses frequently confuses C programmers. Some reading tricks help to alleviate these problems.

When you declare the variable

```
int  count;
```

you tell the compiler to assign a memory location symbolically referred to as count, which will hold a 16-bit value of type int. There is no ambiguity about this matter; count is an integer variable that you can manipulate directly with instructions such as

```
count+ +;
```

Now suppose you declare the variable

```
int  *count;
```

Here count is a pointer to an integer. In other words, count is the symbolic name for a variable that contains a pointer to an integer, and not the integer itself. The expression

```
*count+ +;
```

can be read "increment the integer pointed to by count," or more concisely, "increment count's referent." Similarly, you can use the referent in more complex expressions, such as

```
fpcount  =  (double)  *count;
mod2  =  *count  %  2;
if  (*count)  .  .  .
```

Read these statements as

"fpcount becomes count's referent cast as a double"

"mod2 becomes count's referent modulo 2"

"if count's referent is not equal to 0"

The if() statement above has a very different meaning if you don't include the asterisk. The statement

```
if  (!count)  .  .  .
```

means "if count points to nothing" or, equivalently, "if count is a null pointer."

A pointer usually acquires a value through assignment. Three kinds of pointer assignments are appropriate. Given that count and another are declared as pointers and var as a variable of a compatible type, then:

Null assignment   count = 0;

Pointer-to-pointer   count = another;

Address-to-pointer   count = &var;

In the first case, count (and not its referent) is being initialized to a null value to indicate that the pointer is not currently in use; i.e., count points to nothing. (NOTE: A pointer declared as static is automatically initialized to NULL. An auto pointer—i.e., one declared in a function and thus existing on the stack—must *always* be initialized to NULL unless something is assigned to it before its first reference in the function.) In the second case, another is also a pointer to an integer, and the address it contains is being transferred to count. In the last case, the address or offset of var is being loaded into count, such that var becomes count's referent. After this instruction executes (and as long as nothing further is done to count), the following two instructions are exactly equivalent:

```
var      + =  2;
*count   + =  2;
```

This should help clear up another confusion about C notation. The * operator means "the referent of" whereas & means "the address of."

Dynamic Memory Allocation

The prototypes for the Quick C dynamic allocation functions are in the header file malloc.h. If your program uses memory from the heap, place the following line near the top of the source listing:

```
#include  <malloc.h>
```

Dynamic allocation is the process of acquiring and using heap space. The process is:

1. Request the amount of memory you need.
2. Store the returned value in a pointer bound to the appropriate data type.

Thereafter, you can use the pointer to access the data much as you access any other variable.

As an example, suppose you're working with cubes, which have the attributes of length, width, and height. You might declare a structure type to describe them as follows:

```
typedef  struct {
     int    length, width, height;
} CUBETYPE;
```

For any object placed on the heap, there must be a pointer available to the program so that it can locate the object. In this case, you might declare the pointer as

```
CUBETYPE    *cube;
```

meaning that "cube is a pointer to an object of CUBETYPE."

There are two options for acquiring the heap space for the object: malloc() and calloc(). While they take different arguments, the chief difference is that malloc() does not initialize the allocated space, while calloc() does (i.e., sets the allocated space to all zeros). Thus, space acquired with malloc() is guaranteed to contain garbage, but it's slightly faster than calloc(). On the other hand, calloc() is more suited for allocating array space on the heap.

Both malloc() and calloc() operate within the defined memory model. Thus these functions work on the far heap and return far pointers when a large data model is in use, and they work on the near (64K) heap and return near pointers in small models. Later we'll see how to override these defaults.

Only one argument is passed to malloc(), which is the size in bytes of the space requested. It works fine in this case, where you only want to set aside space for one object of CUBETYPE, and as long as you don't care if the space is uninitialized. Given the declarations above:

```
cube  =  malloc (sizeof (CUBETYPE));
```

or

```
cube  =  malloc (sizeof *cube);
```

NOTE: sizeof is not a function, but instead a C keyword. To take the size of a data type, you must surround the typename with parentheses. It is not necessary to surround a variable name with parentheses, however, as these examples show.

This instruction computes the size of the CUBETYPE object and passes it to malloc(). When malloc() returns the pointer, which is of type void, the compiler binds it to CUBETYPE (the declared data type of the receiving variable) and assigns it to cube.

The call to calloc() entails two arguments: the number of objects to allocate, and the size of each. Obviously, all objects must be of the same type in a given call to calloc(), suggesting an array. The call is

```
cube  =  calloc (1, sizeof (CUBETYPE));
```

which accomplishes the same thing as the call to malloc(). If you wanted to set aside space for three CUBETYPE structures, you would substitute "3" for "1" in the argument list.

Both malloc() and calloc() return a pointer to the allocated space if successful, and NULL (a pointer containing all zeros) when not. It's good practice to check the results after each allocation request with a statement such as

```
if (cube  = =  NULL) . . .
```

If this test proves true, about the only thing you can do is gracefully end the program, unless you want to go to heroic ends to keep it running.

Whichever function you use and assuming a NULL pointer isn't returned, you can now store values in the allocated structure. Once again, there are two alternatives in the notation. To place 3 into the length member, you can write either

```
(*cube).length  =  3;
```

or

```
cube − >length  =  3;
```

The choice is one of personal preference; mine is the second, and thus the arrow notation appears in this book.

Once the structure members have been assigned values, you can use them in expressions like normal variables, e.g.,

```
volume  =  cube − >length  *  cube − >width  *  cube − >height;
```

and

```
partial  =  cube − >height  *  factor;
```

Releasing Heap Space

Dynamically allocated space is automatically released when the program ends. If a program runs for a while, though, you might wish to release space when it's no longer needed, thus making that memory available for future allocation requests and preventing the heap from filling up with forgotten junk. The free() function exists for that purpose.

To use free(), simply pass to it the pointer of the object you want to discard. Continuing the example from the previous discussion, you can release the space occupied by the structure with

```
free (cube);
```

Overriding the Default Heap

The malloc(), calloc(), and free() functions work with the heap and pointer size implicit in the current memory model: that is, near heap and 16 bits for small data models, far heap and 32 bits for large data models.

To ensure that any program, regardless of memory model, uses the far heap, declare pointers with the type modifier far, and replace malloc() and free() with _fmalloc() and _ffree(), respectively.

Similarly, you can override the default far heap in the large data models by declaring pointers as near, and using the allocation functions _nmalloc() and _nfree().

Thus, to request space for ten structures of type CUBETYPE on the far heap and assign to fcube the pointer to the first one, declare a pointer such as

        CUBETYPE far *fcube;

and request the space with

        fcube = _fmalloc (sizeof (CUBETYPE) * 10);

or

        fcube = _fmalloc (sizeof *fcube * 10);

Thereafter, (unless _fmalloc() returns NULL), you have space for an array of ten structures of type CUBETYPE. You can gain access to them using notation such as

        fcube[n] − >height = 5;

The effect of this expression is to find the nth structure and assign five to its height field.

Later you can free the far heap space occupied by the ten structures with

        _ffree (fcube);

The following several chapters provide practical applications of this material.

CHAPTER 17

Singly Linked Lists

This chapter covers singly linked lists, which are the simplest kind of dynamic data structure. The basic building block of any linked list is an object called a *node*, so we begin by discussing what a node is, and then proceed into the structure and manipulation of singly linked lists.

The term *node* crops up all over computer science. Its meaning is "a definable entity." In the context of dynamic memory, a node is one complete data object placed on the heap. Chapter 16 defined a structure type called **CUBETYPE** and showed how to allocate heap space for it and how to use it in various ways. In the strictest sense, an object of **CUBETYPE**, placed on the heap, is a node.

The trouble with **CUBETYPE** is that it doesn't lead anywhere. It is one thing, period. As Chapter 16 noted, there must be a pointer to every object on the heap, lest the software be unable to locate it. We can allocate some number of objects at one time, thus effecting an array, and access them via arithmetic with the common pointer, as in

```
fcube[n] – >member
```

However, this is an unsatisfactory method when the number of nodes is unknown in advance, as when building a dynamic list from keyboard input or a disk file.

A better method is to build the dynamic list naturally, as it grows, where each node points to its successor so that a logical chain develops: This node leads to the next, which leads to the next, and so on to the end of the list. In an alphabetic context:

AA leads to

AB leads to

AC leads to

. . .

ZY leads to

ZZ which is the end of the list

That is what a linked list does. Minimally, it furnishes a static pointer which points to the head (entry node) of a list, and each node thereafter provides a pointer to its successor, so that software can pursue the chain throughout the entire list and detect when it has reached the end.

Why is this important? For three reasons. First, only one pointer needs to be stored in the data segment to gain access to the entire list. Second, the size of the list can vary dynamically from one access to the next—i.e., nodes can be inserted, appended, or deleted—and the only external effect is the time it takes to pass through the list. Finally, different node types can be placed in succession on the heap depending on the order of dynamic allocation requests. You might have three lists—A, B, and C—intermingled on the heap, and each with a different node size. The order could be A[0], C[0], B[0], B[1], A[1], C[1], A[2], B[2], and so on. If the order is properly constructed via pointers, each A node leads to the next A node, each B to the next B, etc., irrespective of their physical arrangement in memory.

The essential element of a linked list node, therefore, is that it contain a pointer to the next node in succession. Singly and doubly linked lists, queues, stacks, circular lists, and binary trees all adhere to this principle. They furnish a single static pointer as a gateway to the list and a mechanism for following a path through related nodes.

Singly Linked Lists: Background

The least versatile, but most understandable form of dynamic data structure is the Singly Linked List (SLL). We say "singly linked" because there is one and only one path through the nodes, leading from the head to the tail. In other words, a single link—a pointer—joins each node to the next in the list.

It is possible to have a list consisting of nodes that contain only a pointer to the next node. However, this is not very practical inasmuch as the purpose of a linked list is to store data, and the pointers are merely a means for getting at that data. For that reason, the minimal node in an SLL consists of two components: a data field, and a pointer field. Figure 17.1 depicts such a node.

For the sake of illustration, let's say that each node occupies ten bytes of storage and the SLL is on the near heap, thus using 16-bit pointers. In that case, then, the list might appear conceptually as shown in Figure 17.2. Each node's offset appears to the left, thus showing how the pointer field provides a path from one node to the next. Note that the last node's pointer field is set to NULL. That's because it leads nowhere, or in other words it signifies the end of the list.

Figure 17.1 **Minimal node for a singly linked list.**

Data	Pointer

Now suppose that another object not belonging to this list is placed on the heap. This "foreign object" begins at offset 1,050 and occupies some amount of space: let's say 32 bytes from 1,050 through 1,081. What happens if you then add a new node to the tail of the SLL? The **NULL** pointer in the old tail is changed to point to the new node. Thus, while the foreign object exists physically, it is not a barrier to expansion; as far as traversing the list is concerned, it effectively does not exist at all. The link pointer allows a program to jump over the intervening node as though it weren't there. Figure 17.3 illustrates this and shows how differing objects can be placed on the heap without interfering with each other.

The only declared data element that absolutely must exist outside the list is a pointer to the head, so that the software can find where the path through the list begins. In this example, the head pointer contains the offset 1,000. To traverse the list, the software first acquires the value of the head pointer and uses it to locate the first node, then uses a loop or a recursive call to access successive nodes. In each iteration, the list-traversal routine grabs the pointer field from the current node to find the next node. We will deal with this in more concrete terms when we get to the discussion of operations on singly linked lists.

Traversal of the list ends when the pointer field contains **NULL**. This is a signal to the program that there are no more nodes. For example, if you had a loop to print out all the data components, the loop would terminate when it fetched the pointer to the next node and found that it was **NULL**. As another

Figure 17.2 **Conceptual diagram of a singly linked list.**

1000	Data	Pointer 1010
1010	Data	Pointer 1020
1020	Data	Pointer 1030
1030	Data	Pointer 1040
1040	Data	Pointer NULL

example, if you're adding a new node, it's necessary to update the old tail's pointer so that it points to the new member of the list. Therefore, you follow the path until you hit a **NULL** pointer, allocate the new node, stuff its address into the pointer field of the old tail, and then use that pointer to initialize the new node.

Very long lists require a time-consuming traversal to find the old tail each time a new node is added. You can save traversal time by keeping an external pointer not only to the head, but also to the current tail. That way you can go directly to the tail without having to look for it. It's also easier to load data into the new SLL node with a tail pointer. We will illustrate this in the next section.

Declaring a Node Type

Let's define a node on which to base a working example. We'll build an SLL containing the first names of some people. First names are relatively short, so the data component is a ten-character string. The other field is the mandatory linkage pointer.

The pointer must be bound to the data type of the node, thus requiring a recursive definition. We can accomplish this in C using the optional tag field in a structure definition, as follow:

Figure 17.3 **Adding a node beyond a foreign object.**

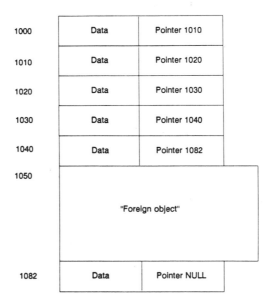

```
typedef struct      {
ntag
    char            name  [10];
struct  ntag        *next;
}  SLNODE;
```

Now we can begin building and manipulating a singly linked list.

Operations on Singly Linked Lists

SLL's are analogous to sequential disk files; there is only one direction through the data (top to bottom), and the data elements appear in the order acquired and can't be easily rearranged. The chief advantage of an SLL over a sequential disk file is that it's much faster to work with.

It's also relatively simple, and for those reasons SLL's are frequently used for lookup tables of unpredictable size. As an example, most compilers use SLL's to construct symbol tables built and frequently referred to during the compilation process. Each node contains a variable's name, its data type, its dimensions if an array, and other information, along with a pointer to the next node. Because there is no way to anticipate the number of symbols a given source program might contain, a dynamic data structure such as an SLL is a perfect solution to the problem of accumulating everything so that it's readily accessible on the heap. You'll probably never write a compiler, but chances are that your programs often need to build and refer to tables.

Building an SLL

The one essential data element external to a linked list is a pointer to the head. This is ordinarily a global pointer variable bound to the node type. When the program begins execution, the linked list does not exist. Therefore the head pointer should be immediately initialized to **NULL**. It's easiest to do this at declaration, as in

```
main()
{
SLNODE  *head  =  NULL;
 .  .  .
```

Any other pointers to the linked list should also be "born" initialized. For example, if you plan to maintain a tail pointer, code something like this:

```
SLNODE  *head  =  NULL, *tail  =  NULL;
```

An even easier way to accomplish the same thing is to declare the SLL pointers at the top of the program, before **main()** and outside the scope of any function. This makes them static variables, which the compiler automatically initializes. Here is an example:

```
SLNODE  *head,  *tail;
main()
{  .  .  .
```

Initialization of the SLL pointers, if followed through by testing for **NULL** pointers in the code, helps to guarantee that the program won't malfunction because of a pointer containing garbage.

The SLL comes into existence with the allocation of its first node. In this case, the head pointer must be reset to indicate the starting node and the tail pointer (if it exists) must also be set to the same value. Adding a node to an existing list is a similar process, the chief difference being that the head pointer remains unchanged. The steps are:

1. Allocate the new node.
2. If a tail node already exists, update its pointer field to indicate the new node.
3. Set the tail pointer to the new node, and set the head pointer to the same value if it is **NULL**.
4. Set the new node's pointer field to **NULL**.

You can then load the data component using the tail pointer.

Because adding nodes to SLLs is an operation you might want to perform at different points in a program—possibly involving more than one list—this procedure lends itself to a subprogram. Using double indirection, the function can automatically alter the head and tail pointers appropriately, thus relieving the caller of the responsibility for maintaining its own pointers.

The addsl() function in Listing 17.1 implements this discussion. Because it updates pointers, addsl() requires the addresses of the head and tail pointers (using the & operator) as its arguments. It returns a pointer to the new node.

Thus you see that with one algorithm, you can start the SLL and build it by adding new nodes at the tail. The addsl() function is sufficiently generalized that it could control the growth of several independent lists all using the same node type, merely by passing it different pointers.

Traversing an SLL

Traversal of an SLL is not usually an end unto itself, unless you're merely seeking the tail in the absence of a specific tail pointer. Ordinarily you pass through the nodes performing some operation on each one: searching for a data value, listing the node's contents, etc. Whatever, the basic process is always the same. Here it is expressed in C:

```
SLNODE *np;      /* local pointer */

    np  =  headptr;
    while (np != NULL) {
        /* perform the operation */
        np  =  np->next;
    }
```

The local pointer np is necessary since you don't want to corrupt any static pointers such as headptr. In the first step, np is pointed to the head of the list. The loop executes only as long as np is not NULL; it will not execute at all if the list doesn't exist, i.e., if headptr is NULL. The first part of the loop does whatever you want to do with the node currently pointed to by np. The key part of the loop is the instruction

```
    np  =  np->next;
```

The np pointer advances to the next node by grabbing the pointer field from the current node. Using Figure 17.3 as an example, if np contains 1,020, it acquires the pointer field from the node at 1,020 and thus advances to 1,030. This is the value that np contains when the loop reiterates. When np points to 1,082, it grabs NULL from the next field and the loop does not repeat because its exit condition is true.

Listing 17.1 includes the function freelist(), which releases all the space occupied by an SLL. In this case, the argument is a pointer to the head of the list, and the operation performed during the traversal is to free each node in succession. In effect, freelist() erases the SLL from memory.

Application: Building, Listing, and Deleting an SLL

Now let's look at a complete program that demonstrates an SLL. This program (SLLDEMO1.C in Listing 17.1) builds a linked list of five nodes, asking you to type a person's first name into the data field of each one. As it runs, it reports the amount of memory left on the near heap and the values of the head and tail pointers. When you have furnished the five names, the program displays them by traversing the list, and then erases the list from the heap with another traversal. It ends by reporting the amount of memory left on the heap. Note that the showlist() and freelist() functions differ only in the single operation each performs.

Listing 17.1 **Demonstration of SLL operations.**

```
/* SLLDEMO1.C: Builds and traverses a SLL in near heap */

#include <stdio.h>
#include <malloc.h>

typedef struct ntag {                    /* SLL node structure */
  char               name [10];
  struct ntag near *next;
} SLNODE;

SLNODE near *head, near *tail;     /* static list pointers */
/* ------------------------------------------------------ */

void main ()
{
int  i;
void showlist (SLNODE near*), freelist (SLNODE near*),
        addsl (SLNODE near**, SLNODE near**);

  for (i = 0; i < 5; i++) {
    addsl (&head, &tail);
    printf ("\nMemory left = %u", _memavl());
    printf ("\nhead = %p, tail = %p", head, tail);
    printf ("\nEnter a name... ");
    gets (tail->name);
  }
  showlist (head);
  freelist (head);
    printf ("\nMemory left after freeing = %u\n", _memavl());
} /* ----------------------- */

void addsl (SLNODE near **h, SLNODE near **t)
     /* Add node to tail of SLL */
```

Listing 17.1 *(continued)*

```
{
SLNODE near *new;
  new = _nmalloc (sizeof *new);
  if (*t != NULL)
    (*t)->next = new;   /* update old tail's pointer field */
  if (*h == NULL)
    *h = new;                /* set head pointer if necessary */
  *t = new;                             /* update tail pointer */
  (*t)->next = NULL;     /* blank new tail's pointer field */
} /* ----------------------- */

void showlist (SLNODE near *h)
     /* Traverse list and display names */
{
SLNODE near *n;
  puts ("\n\nList of names in nodes:");
  n = h;                           /* point to head of SLL */
  while (n != NULL) {              /* until end of list... */
    printf ("\n%s", n->name);         /* display name and */
    n = n->next;                       /* go to next node */
  }
} /* ----------------------- */

void freelist (SLNODE near *h)
     /* Delete list from heap */
{
SLNDE near *n;
  n = h;                           /* point to head of SLL */
  while (n != NULL) {              /* until end of list... */
    _nfree (n);                        /* free current node */
    n = n->next;                       /* go to next node */
  }
} /* ----------------------- */
```

Searching an SLL

This is another traversal operation, but with one important difference: It returns a pointer to the node in which the match is found, or NULL if there is no match.

As mentioned earlier, one of the chief uses of SLL's is in lookup tables. There are two basic things we do with tables:

- Determine if a key value is valid.
- Find out additional information about a key value.

An example of the first case might be validation of keyboard entries. Suppose you're writing a payroll system in which the key value is the employee

Social Security number. Each time the operator types a new timecard entry, it's necessary to determine if the Social Security number is valid. Consequently, your program could search an SLL containing all employee Social Security numbers. If there is no match in the list, the operator has made an error. This is detected by a **NULL** pointer being returned from the search routine. Detecting it, the program can request re-entry.

We can also draw an example of the second case from business applications: getting additional information about a key value. The SLL nodes might contain customer account numbers, billing and shipping addresses, and credit ratings. When the order entry operator types the account number, a search of the SLL automatically fills in the billing and shipping addresses and verifies that the customer has a credit rating sufficient for the terms of sale. If no match is found for the account number, the operator made a mistake.

We could present numerous other examples, but you get the idea. By checking the pointer to the node matching the key value, your program can determine validity and other information from the lookup table. A **NULL** pointer indicates an error.

An SLL search function requires two arguments: a pointer to the head of the list, and the key value to be matched with a data element within the nodes. The key value must be of the same data type as the node's data element, or else the search results will be unreliable. The search function must return a pointer to the matching node or **NULL**, depending on the outcome.

An example is validating keyboard entries of people's first names. If the operator types Susan and there is no Susan in the SLL, the lookup routine returns **NULL**. On the other hand, a non-**NULL** return indicates a valid entry. You might do this with a function such as:

```
SLNODE *findsl (SLNODE *h, char *key)
{
SLNODE *n;
  n = h;
  while (n != NULL) {
    if (strcmp (key, n->name) == 0)
     break;
    n = n->next;
  }
  return (n);
}
```

Deleting a Node

Just as lists grow, sometimes they also shrink, as in removing entries from a lookup table when they're no longer useful. This is trickier than traversal, because we not only follow pointers, but rearrange them. Further complicat-

Figure 17.4 **Deleting a node within a list.**

Before

1000	Alice	1010
1010	Bob	1020
1020	Cathy	NULL

After

1000	Alice	1020
1020	Cathy	NULL

ing matters is the possibility that the node being deleted is either the head or the tail of the list, thus requiring update of the involved static pointer.

Normally a deletion involves a search: "Delete the node whose data field contains the name Bob." First you have to find the node, then you can delete it. It would appear that you can use the function listed above for this, but alas, there's a catch; you have to be able to locate the node preceding the one to be deleted. Here's why.

Let's say you have a list containing three nodes, as shown in the "Before" part of Figure 17.4, and you're going to delete the one containing Bob. You begin searching the list at the head. No match, so you save the address of this node and follow its pointer field to the next node, where you find what you're looking for.

The deletion itself is simple. You take the pointer field from Bob's node and copy it into Alice's (which explains why you have to keep track of the last node you checked). Though not necessary, it's good practice to deallocate Bob's deleted node.

The "After" portion of Figure 17.4 shows the effect. Within the scope of the list, Bob's node has ceased to exist because Alice's pointer field now links to Cathy's node, thus bypassing Bob's. Note that the list is physically the same size as before, since Cathy hasn't moved. It's just that Bob's former node is now dead space.

You can tell if you're about to delete the head of the list by comparing the node's pointer with the head pointer. If they're equal, you're deleting the head of the list.

Figure 17.5 **Deleting head of list.**

Before   **After**

Head→ 1000	Alan	1010
1010	Beth	1020
Tail → 1020	Carl	NULL

| Head→ 1010 | Beth | 1020 |
| Tail → 1020 | Carl | NULL |

Two possible conditions arise when deleting the head: Either there are other nodes, or it's the only remaining one. Whichever, you're going to have to change the head pointer. The question is, to what?

If another node follows the head, it becomes the new head of the list, so copy the next field from the node into the head pointer. Figure 17.5 depicts this situation before and after the deletion.

When the node to be deleted is the only one remaining, the list will cease to exist as a result of the deletion. In that event, set the head pointer to **NULL**. These alternatives can be handled with the C expression

```
nead = (head->next != NULL) ? this->next : NULL;
```

Deleting the tail is similar. Again, you can find out if the deleted node is at the end of the list by comparing its pointer with the tail pointer. If they're equal, change the preceding node's pointer field to **NULL** and put the address of the preceding node into the tail pointer, or change the tail and head pointers to **NULL** if deleting the only node left in the list.

Figure 17.6 shows deletion of the tail when there is still another node left to assume its position at the end of the list.

The length of this discussion might make it seem that deleting a node is a process of bewildering complexity, but in fact there are only four circumstances:

Figure 17.6 **Deleting tail of list.**

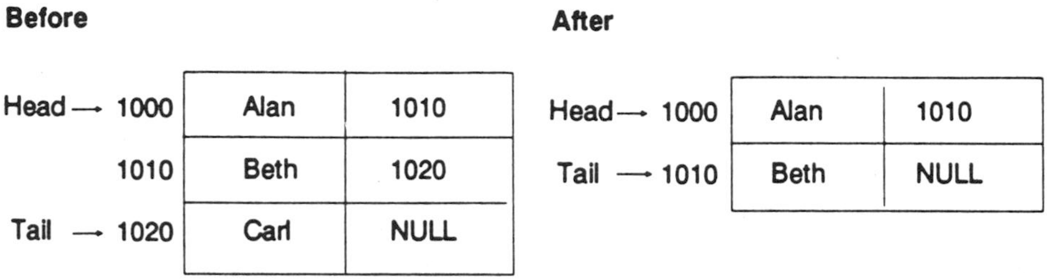

Before

Head → 1000 | Alan | 1010
1010 | Beth | 1020
Tail → 1020 | Carl | NULL

After

Head → 1000 | Alan | 1010
Tail → 1010 | Beth | NULL

- Deleting a node inside the list.
- Deleting the head.
- Deleting the tail.
- Deleting the only remaining node.

Because C is a terse language, the actual code to accomplish the task is quite brief, as the delsl() function in Listing 17.2 shows.

Tying It Together

Figure 17.2 lists **SLLDEMO2.C**, which implements all the operations on SLLs discussed in this chapter. This program builds on the one in Listing 17.1. The chief difference is that, once the SLL is complete, the program prompts you for a name to delete from the list. If you type a valid name, the program removes the node, and otherwise it reports **NOT FOUND**. After each attempt, the current list contents are displayed. You can end execution by pressing Enter in response to the name prompt.

Listing 17.2 **SLL operations including search and delete.**

```
/* SLLDEMO2.C: Builds a SLL, then selectively deletes    */
/*      based on key entered by user                      */
```

```
/* Uses Quick C near heap                              */

#include <stdio.h>
#include <malloc.h>
#include <string.h>

typedef struct ntag {                    /* SLL node structure */

  char              name [10];
  struct ntag near *next;
} SLNODE;

SLNODE near *head, near *tail;     /* static list pointers */
/* ------------------------------------------------------- */

void main ()
{
int  i;
char name [10];
void showlist (SLNODE near*), freelist (SLNODE near*),
        delsl (SLNODE near**, SLNODE near**, char*),
        addsl (SLNODE near**, SLNODE near**);

  for (i = 0; i < 5; i++) {
    addsl (&head, &tail);
    printf ("\nMemory left = %u", _memavl());
    printf ("\nhead - %p, tail = %p", head, tail);
    printf ("\nEnter a name... ");
    gets (tail->name);
  }
  showlist (head);

  do {
    printf ("\n\nName to delete? ");
    gets (name);
    if (name [0] != 0) {
      delsl (&head, &tail, name);
      puts ("\n");
      showlist (head);
    }
  } while (name [0] != 0);

  printf ("\nhead = %p, tail = %p\n", head, tail);
  freelist (head);
} /* ----------------------- */

void addsl (SLNODE near **h, SLNODE near **t)
      /* Add node to tail of SLL */
{
SLNODE near *new;

  new = _nmalloc (sizeof (SLNODE));
  if (*t != NULL)
```

Listing 17.2 *(continued)*

```
      (*t)->next = new;   /* update old tail's pointer field */
   if (*h == NULL)
      *h = new;                   /* set head pointer if necessary */
   *t = new;                              /* update tail pointer */
   (*t)->next = NULL;      /* blank new tail's pointer field */
} /* ----------------------- */

void showlist (SLNODE near *h)
      /* Traverse list and display names */
{
SLNODE near *n;

   puts ("\n\nList of names in nodes:");
   n = h;                              /* point to head of SLL */
   while (n != NULL) {                 /* until end of list... */
      printf ("\n%s", n->name);          /* display name and */
      n = n->next;                       /* go to next node */
   }
} /* ----------------------- */

void freelist (SLNODE near *h)
      /* Delete list from heap */
{
SLNODE near *n;

   n = h;                              /* point to head of SLL */
   while (n != NULL) {                 /* until end of list... */
      _nfree (n);                        /* free current node */
      n = n->next;                       /* go to next node */
   }
} /* ----------------------- */

void delsl (SLNODE near **h, SLNODE near **t, char *key)
      /* Delete node indicated by key from SLL */
{
SLNODE near *this, near *last = NULL;

   /* First find node to be deleted */
   this = *h;
   while (this != NULL) {
      if (strcmp (this->name, key) == 0)        /* if found */
         break;                     /* break out of while loop */
      last = this;                   /* else remember this node */
      this = this->next;                    /* and go to next */
   }
   if (this == NULL) {                          /* no match */
      puts ("\nNOT FOUND");                     /* so tell 'em */
      return;                                   /* and quit */
   }

   /* Node is found, so delete it */
```

```
    if (this != *h)                           /* not deleting head */
       last->next = this->next;       /* so bypass deleted node */
    else                              /* maybe we are deleting head */
       *h = (this->next != NULL)
               ? this->next : NULL;    /* if so update head ptr */
    if (this == *t)                              /* deleting tail */
       *t = last;                           /* so update tail ptr */
    _nfree (this);                          /* deallocate space */
} /* ------------------------ */
```

Singly linked lists are simple dynamic data structures analogous to sequential disk files, but much faster because of being in memory. SLL's lend themselves nicely to applications such as small lookup tables, where the order of data is relatively unimportant. Because of their simplicity, SLL's are not as useful for more complex requirements as their bigger siblings, doubly linked lists, which we discuss in the next chapter.

CHAPTER 18

Doubly Linked Lists

If a singly linked list is analogous to a one-way street, then a doubly linked list (DLL) is comparable with a two-way street. That is, it provides two parallel paths through the node structure, one from the head to the tail, the other from tail to head. While the structure of a DLL is more complex than a SLL, the ability to traverse bidirectionally and to find out where any node's neighbors are allows you to create much more versatile, efficient dynamic data structures.

Each node in a DLL contains two pointers to its own type, one pointing to the next node in sequence, the other to the one previous. This effects a two-way street, as the following list shows:

In the node named	Prev points to	Next points to
D	C	E
E	D	F
F	E	G
G	F	H

If you're in node E and you want to move down the list, you follow the **Next** pointer to get to node F. Conversely, you can follow the **Prev** pointer to move up the list to Node D.

This bidirectional capability is important in creating and searching ordered lists, i.e. lists that are sorted according to their data content. A common example is alphabetic ordering, as in:

Alice

Bill

Charlie

. . .

Xavier

Figure 18.1 **Node for a doubly linked list.**

char name[15];	mnode *prev;	mnode *next;

Yvette

Zeke

The nodes of this list might contain other data elements, such as sales figures, phone numbers, and so forth, but the nodes are arranged by alphabetic order of names. The field that determines the order—the name field in this case—is called the key.

SLLs lend themselves nicely to static lists that are ordered by some principle, such as time of arrival or key sequence, then searched linearly each time a lookup is done. DLLs, on the other hand, are better suited for applications in which nodes are constantly being added to and deleted from the list, and/or in which the list must either be maintained without searching, or searched in either direction from the most recently visited node. Examples are circular lists, stacks, and queues, which we'll discuss later in this chapter.

DLL Nodes

The minimal practical node for a DLL consists of:

- At least one data-conveying component.
- At least two pointers to its own node type.

The two pointers are for the upward and downward paths to neighboring nodes. We say "at least two," since a node can contain other pointers as well, even to other node types. Figure 18.1 depicts a minimal node for a DLL containing 15-character strings.

As with the SLL nodes covered in the last chapter, the physical order of fields within the node doesn't matter.

You can define this node in Quick C using a **typedef** as follows:

```
typedef  mnode {
      char              name  [15];
      struct  mnode     *prev,  *next;
} MINNODE;
```

From this definition you can declare pointer variables such as

```
MINNODE      *head,  *tail,  *new;
```

that allow you to manipulate lists.

The Circular DLL Model

Like an SLL, a DLL can have a head and tail that are the extremes of the list. In this case, the upward path is terminated when head − >prev = = NULL and the downward path when tail − >next = = NULL, using C notation. To simplify matters, though, this chapter focuses on a type of DLL called a circular list.

Life is easier inside a circular DLL than in a list with terminal nodes for several reasons. Chiefly, the processes for insertion are virtually identical whether the new node is at the head, the tail, or in between. Also, one simple test tells when you've traversed the list no matter which direction you're moving: no need to look for different NULL pointers depending on direction.

Conceptually, a circular list wraps around on itself and has no definable start and end. The list grows and shrinks dynamically, with its "circumference" defined by the number of nodes it contains at any given moment. The program needs only to remember the address of one node somewhere in the circular list (we'll call it "head") to gain access to the entire structure. If the list contains three nodes, its pointer arrangement is as follows:

Node name	Prev points to	Next points to
A	C	B
B	A	C
C	B	A

Thus a search in either direction from any node will always bring you back to the starting point. The list is circular because it wraps around on itself.

When searching, you have to compare pointers to determine when you've completely traversed the list. Otherwise you'll end up in the deadly embrace of an infinite loop, forever running in circles through the list with no exit.

What about the situation in which a circular DLL consists of only one node? In that case, the pointers are as follows:

Node name	Prev points to	Next points to
A	A	A

Here an attempt to traverse the list immediately brings you back to the point of origin.

Now say you add a node. The pointers rearrange as follows:

Node name	Prev points to	Next points to
A	B	B
B	A	A

No matter which way you go, you'll move to the other node and from there back to the origin.

It doesn't matter in any dynamic data structure where the nodes are located physically on the heap. They might be contiguous or scattered all over the place in random physical order. The computer doesn't take longer to jump over 30,000 bytes than over three. Thus, by dealing with pointers, we work in concepts of order rather than in physical arrangement. In effect, we don't care where the nodes are as long as we have reliable pointers to them.

Now let's consider the question of where one inserts a new node in a circular list. The answer is that that depends. There are three general forms of list management that govern the placement of new nodes:

- LIFO (Last In First Out) or stack organization makes the most recently added item the first available. This is the in-basket concept, in which the most recently delivered letter gets taken off the pile first and the old stuff gets older. In this case, the new node always becomes the head of the list and when an item is removed, the head shifts to the next-older node.
- FIFO (First In First Out) or queue organization is analogous to standing in line at the bank. You join the end of the line and work your way to the front. In a circular FIFO list, new nodes are inserted above the head, or in other words at the tail. When a node is removed, the whole line moves forward one position.
- Ordered lists pay no attention to the time of arrival, but instead to the collating sequence of keys. In this case, it's necessary to search the list and determine where the new node belongs, then rearrange the pointers to accommodate it.

Each of these list disciplines has practical applications in software. LIFO keeps track of interrupted tasks so that you always return to successively lower levels. FIFO queues up events in their order of arrival, so that all events have an equal chance for service. Ordered lists are primarily applicable to lookup tables.

Operations on DLLs

In discussing operations on DLLs, we'll use ordered lists as the example since they are the most flexible form of list discipline. You can adapt the algorithms to other DLL concepts.

Starting the List

To manage a circular DLL, you need only one pointer to the node type; we'll call it head in this discussion, and it points to some node that is an entry point to the list. Since we're dealing here with ordered lists, head should point to the node containing the key lowest in sequence ("Alice" in the example given earlier). Head thus remains fixed unless we insert a lower-order node: Aaron, for example.

As a practical matter, it's advisable to declare the entry to the list as a global variable in Quick C, i.e., a static outside any function and ahead of main(). Example:

```
typedef  ntype  {...}  NTYPE;
NTYPE  *head;
main()
{
        .  .  .
}
```

This assures that the head is initialized to NULL before you ever use it, and that local functions can refer to the pointer directly, saving the trouble and overhead of passing it as an argument. An alternative when the head is a local variable declared inside a block is

```
main  ()
{
NTYPE  *head  =  NULL;
        .  .  .
}
```

The thrust is that you must initialize the pointer to NULL. That way you have a reliable value to test in order to determine if the list exists; garbage is a false indicator.

When you allocate the first node in the list (or any other node, for that matter), you have to fetch its pointer from the return value of malloc() (or _fmalloc() or whatever other allocation routine you use). Thus, if you have declared

```
NTYPE      *new;
```

assign the returned pointer to new with

    new = malloc (sizeof *new);

After that you can store a value in the node with

    *new = someval;

As a general rule, list-building routines should assign any new node's address to a working pointer such as new, store data in the node, and then check to see if this is the first node in a list. If so, assign the value of new to head, as in

    if (head = = NULL)
       head = new;

That way the head of the list is automatically set by the routine.

Once this process completes, you have the beginnings of a list that you can expand either by appending nodes to the tail, or by inserting between two existing nodes. In circular lists, there's not much difference. A new node at the tail goes between the old tail and the head, whereas a node inserted elsewhere goes between nodes at a position determined by the order of keys. Let's discuss these two methods in order.

Appending a Node at the Tail

It's simplest to grow a list by inserting new elements immediately above the head: i.e., between the head and the old tail. The result is, of course, an "unordered" list. (In fact, it's ordered by the sequence of arrival rather than by key values, which is sometimes what you want, as in the queues and stacks discussed later in this chapter.)

The process for doing this is as follows:

1. Allocate the new node, assigning the resulting pointer to "new."
2. Put data into the new node.
3. Copy head–>prev to new–>prev.
4. Set head–>prev to the new pointer.
5. Copy new–>prev–>next to new–>next.
6. Set new–>prev–>next to the new pointer.

Steps 3 through 6 rearrange the pointers to effect insertion of the new node between the head and the old tail. Figure 18.2 depicts this process with before and after views of the lists (where parentheses around a name indicate "pointer to the node containing that person's name").

Figure 18.2 **Appending a new tail to a DLL.**

Before:

Data	Prev	Next
Zeke	(Yvette)	(Alice)
Alice	(Zeke)	(Bob)

After:

Data	Prev	Next
Zeke	(Yvette)	(Carla)*
Carla	(Zeke)	(Alice)
Alice	(Carla)*	(Bob)

*Pre-existing pointers changed by the insertion

Now if the list is traversed from the head back to the head, Carla is the last key encountered. That's appropriate, since she arrived most recently and is therefore at the tail.

Inserting a Node Based on Key Value

This method has the effect of sorting data, since it inserts each incoming node into the list based on the relative values of keys. The steps are as follows:

1. Allocate the **new** node and assign the returned pointer to "**new**."
2. Put the data into the **new** node.
3. Determine where to insert the **new** node by traversing the list comparing keys.
4. Rearrange the pointers to effect insertion.

Step 3 is what differentiates this process from the one described previously. Step 4 is the same as steps 3 through 6 above.

Data often come into a program in random order; the person doing data entry types names or numbers; a measurement device propagates values, or whatever, without regard to sequence. Insertion based on a key value is a sensible way to order data as they arrive.

Step 2 puts the data into the new node. To find the proper position of the node, then, simply traverse the list starting at the head and compare keys. Usually you sort data into ascending order. Thus, when

new − >key > compared − >key

(as in C › B), keep looking. When

new − >key < compared − >key

the search is over and you have found the point of insertion; it's between the compared node and the one preceding. At that point:

1. Copy compared − >prev into new − >prev.
2. Set compared − >prev to the new pointer.
3. Copy new − >prev − >next into new − >next.
4. Set new − >prev − >next to the new pointer.

Note that this differs from the algorithm in the previous section only in that 'compared' is substituted for "head."

In searching a circular list for the insertion point, you have to be alert to one other possibility: That no element in the existing list has a higher value than the new key. If you don't watch for this, you'll run in circles forever inside the list. You can detect this condition by checking the compared node's pointer against head. If the two are the same, you've completely traversed the list without finding a higher key than that of the new node. Therefore, re-encountering the head is the same as finding the point of insertion, and the new node belongs at the tail.

Similarly, it's possible that the new node has a key lower in order than the existing head, as when the present head's key is Alice and the new node's is Abel. In that case, the new node goes between the former head and the current tail, but it becomes the new head. Rearrange the pointers as already discussed, but also update the global head pointer to point to the new node. You can detect this condition by checking "compared" against "head": If the same, compare keys. If the new node's key is less than that of the head, change the global head pointer.

Application: Building an Ordered List

Now let's tie this discussion together with a demonstration program. We'll call it MAKEDLL.C, and Listing 18.1 lists it. The purpose of this program is to accept last and first names from the keyboard and organize them into an ordered list sorted by last name. Each time you finish typing a name, the list appears in sorted order on the screen, as in

Last name?   Perez
First name? Dennis

Ellsworth, Don
Hoffman, Doug
Needham, Nancy
Perez, Dennis
Randall, Peggy

Last name?

You can signal the program that the input is finished by pressing the Enter key in response to the "Last name?" query. At that point, the entire list appears on the screen, and the program saves the list in alphabetic order by last name into a text file called **NAMES.DLL**.

As you'll see in the next section, it saves programming complexity to sort the data on entry, as we've done in Listing 18.1. When you read the file or load it into a DLL, as we do later, it's already in order.

If you need test data, here are the names in the order I typed them into **MAKEDLL**. Later examples use these names for table searching. As in the real world, the names follow no particular order.

Ellsworth, Don
Needham, Nancy
Randall, Peggy
Hoffman, Doug
Perez, Dennis
Quion, Nadine
MacDonald, Laureen
Cady, Frank
Katz, Michael
Marcus, Larry
Irvine, Ed
Austin, Avis
Wallis, Angela
Lindho, Joe
Chow, Doris

Listing 18.1 **Demonstration: building an ordered list.**

```
/* MAKEDLL.C: Build DLL from keyboard input. On receiving   */
/*    blank last name, save list in file NAMES.DLL          */

#include <stdio.h>
#include <malloc.h>
#include <string.h>

#define  MAXSTR  15
```

```
      #ifndef   TRUE
      #define   TRUE   1
      #define   FALSE  0
      #endif
      #pragma pack(1)

      typedef struct dnode {
        char            LastName[MAXSTR], FirstName[MAXSTR];
        struct dnode    *prev, *next;
      } DNODE;

      /* LOCAL FUNCTION PROTOTYPES */
      DNODE   *GetData (void);
      DNODE   *FindInsert (DNODE *new);
      void    InsertNode (DNODE *new);
      void    ShowList (void);
      void    BuildList (void);
      void    StoreList (void);
      void    ShowList (void);

      /* GLOBALS */
      DNODE   *head;
      /* ------------------------- */

      void main ()
      {
        BuildList();
        StoreList();
      } /* ------------------------- */

      void  BuildList (void)            /* Build DLL from kbd input */
      {                                /* Done when GetData returns NULL */
      DNODE   *new;

        do {
          new = GetData ();
          if (new != NULL)
            InsertNode (new);
          ShowList ();
        } while (new != NULL);
      } /* ------------------------- */

      DNODE *GetData (void)       /* Capture data from kbd, put in */
                          /* new node. Return node address or NULL */
      {                          /* if nothing was entered by user */
      char  name[MAXSTR];
      DNODE *new = NULL;

        printf ("\nLast name?  ");
        gets (name);                                /* get last name */
        if (name[0]) {
          new = (DNODE*) malloc (sizeof (DNODE));   /* alloc node */
          strcpy (new->LastName, name);       /* put in last name */
```

Listing 18.1 *(continued)*

```
    printf ("First name? ");
    gets (new->FirstName);                    /* get first name */
  }
  return (new);                        /* return pointer or NULL */
} /* ----------------------- */

DNODE *FindInsert (DNODE *new)
                           /* Find point where new->key fits */
{                /* into list, or quit on re-encountering head */
char   found = FALSE;
DNODE  *this;

  this = head;
  do {
    if (strcmp (new->LastName, this->LastName) < 0)
      found = TRUE;                    /* found insertion point */
    else
      this = this->next;                    /* try the next node */
  } while (!found && this != head);
  return (this);
} /* ----------------------- */

void  InsertNode (DNODE *new)
{                                /* Insert new node into list */
DNODE  *ins = NULL;

  if (head == NULL) {                  /* If first node in list */
    head = new;                             /* set head pointer */
    head->prev = head->next = head;      /* point to itself */
  } else {
    ins = FindInsert (new);            /* Find insertion point */
    new->prev = ins->prev;                /* Rearrange pointers */
    ins->prev = new;
    new->next = new->prev->next;
    new->prev->next = new;
    if (strcmp (new->LastName, head->LastName) < 0)
      head = new;                      /* If new head, change head */
  }
} /* ----------------------- */
void  ShowList (void)      /* Display list as entered so far */
{
DNODE  *this;

  if (head != NULL) {
    this = head;
    do {
      printf ("\n%s, %s", this->LastName, this->FirstName);
      this = this->next;
    } while (this != head);
    putchar ('\n');
  }
```

```
} /* ------------------------- */
void   StoreList (void)          /* Store DLL in file NAMES.DLL */
{
FILE   *f;
DNODE  *this;

  if (head != NULL) {
    f = fopen ("NAMES.DLL", "w");
    this = head;
    do {
      fputs (this->LastName, f);
      fputc ('\n', f);
      fputs (this->FirstName, f);
      fputc ('\n', f);
      this = this->next;
    } while (this != head);
    fclose (f);
  }
} /* ------------------------- */
```

Searching a DLL

Search an unordered DLL the same way you would an SLL: top to bottom following the "next" pointers and comparing each node's key with the value
sought (the "argument"). Alternatively, you could go the other way in the
chain furnished by the "prev" pointers. Neither direction has an advantage
over the other since an unordered list is random by definition. On average, a
search passes through half the list to discover the object it's seeking. The
head of an unordered circular list is merely an arbitrary, known entry point,
and you know that you've completely but fruitlessly traversed the list when
the chain of pointers takes you back to the head.

The search of an ordered list is more intelligent. Assuming the keys are in
ascending order and you're following the "next" pointers, each key comparison produces one of three possible outcomes that form the basis for deciding
what to do next. These are:

1. Argument > node's key. Continue the search.
2. Argument = node's key. The search is successful.
3. Argument < node's key. Abandon the search.

A fourth condition is returning to the head. This happens when the argument
is greater than any key in the list. It has the same effect as item three.

Listing 18.2 illustrates this algorithm using the **DNODE** structure defined
in Listing 18.1. It is a function that returns the address of the node containing
the argument, or **NULL** if unsuccessful, and can be used as a model for your
applications.

Listing 18.2 **Model function to search an ordered list.**

```
DNODE *match (char *arg, DNODE *head)
{
DNODE *this;
int    result;
char   found = FALSE;

  this = head;
  do {                                              /* traverse list */
    result = strcmp (arg, this->LastName)      /* comp keys */
    if (result > 0)              /* if arg lower in alpha order */
      this = this->next;                     /* continue searching */
    else
      if (result == 0)
        found = TRUE;                              /* found match */
      else
        return (NULL);                           /* else abandon */
  } while (!found && (this != head));
  return (this);
} /* -------------------------------- */
```

Deleting a Node

Before deleting a node, of course, you have to know where it is. A common way is to search the list for the key value you want to delete, using a routine similar to Listing 18.2 to get the pointer to the node. If the returned pointer isn't **NULL**, you merely rearrange adjacent pointer fields and free the heap space; this is exactly the opposite of inserting a node. Figure 18.3 illustrates the effect on adjacent pointers when a node is removed.

Described in C notation, the pointer shuffling is:

$$del->next->prev = del->prev;$$
$$del->prev->next = del->next;$$

In other words, from the deleted node, drop the prev pointer to the next node and lift the next pointer to the previous node.

Note that the list doesn't physically close up when a node is deleted; nothing actually moves, but the pointers instead bypass the removed node, effectively forgetting that it ever existed.

Now let's consider two special cases: You're deleting the only node in the list, and you're deleting the head when other nodes still exist. Both cases, in fact, involve deleting the head, which requires an update to the global head pointer. In the first instance, the deletion erases the list altogether, so you set the head pointer to **NULL**. In the second, you promote the next node to be the head. You can find out which case you're dealing with by comparing del->next (or del->prev) with del itself. If the two are equal, the node is the

Figure 18.3 **Pointer rearrangements for deleting a node.**

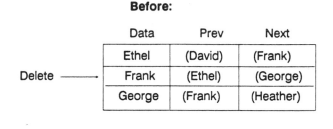

Before:

Data	Prev	Next
Ethel	(David)	(Frank)
Frank	(Ethel)	(George)
George	(Frank)	(Heather)

Delete ⟶ (points to Frank row)

After:

Data	Prev	Next
Ethel	(David)	(George)*
George	(Ethel)*	(Heather)

* Changed pointers

last on the list. You can bypass pointer rearrangements in that event, resetting the head pointer to **NULL** and freeing the node's space.

If **del** equals head, and **del** − >next and **del** are not equal, you're deleting the head of a list containing at least two nodes. Therefore, rearrange pointers, advance the global head pointer to **del** − >next, and free the old node space.

Listing 18.3 lists a model function **delnode()** that summarizes this discussion. Note the use of double indirection in passing the head parameter; this is so that you can pass a change to the head pointer's value back to the caller. The double-indirection argument ****head** passes the address of the pointer to the head node. Therefore the single-indirection statement

    *head = del − >next;

changes the pointer itself.

Listing 18.3 **Function for deleting a node.**

```
void delnode (DNODE *del, DNODE **head)
{
  if (del == NULL) return;                    /* already deleted */
  if (del == *head)                     /* then deleting head node */
    if (del == del->next) {             /* if the only node... */
      *head = NULL;                            /* erase the list */
      free (del);
      return;                                 /* and quit */
```

Listing 18.3 *(continued)*

```
    } else
      *head = del->next;       /* else promote next to head */
   del->next->prev = del->prev;        /* rearrange pointers */
   del->prev->next = del->next;
   free (del);                              /* deallocate space */
} /* ------------------------- */
```

Call this function after using match() or some equivalent function to locate the node you want to delete. For example, to remove the node containing the last name Jones, write:

```
delete = match ("Jones", head);
delnode (delete, &head);
```

Let's put these techniques to work in a program.

Application: Finding and Deleting Nodes in an Ordered DLL

Listing 18.1 presented the program MAKEDLL.C, which put names typed at the keyboard into a circular DLL and later saved them in the disk file NAMES.DLL. This application—Lsiting 18.4—uses that file in a somewhat opposite manner; it's a seek and destroy mission that loads the file into a DLL, then locates the nodes containing your keyboard entries and removes them from the DLL (though not from the disk file itself).

The program asks you for a last name. After finding the associated node, it displays the person's full name and asks if that's the node you want to delete. Type Y for yes and anything else for no. The program then deletes the node if appropriate and redisplays the entire list as it now stands.

Listing 18.4 **Demonstration: finding and deleting DLL nodes.**

```
/* DELDLL.C: Demos searching and deleting nodes in a DLL */

/* INCLUDED FILES */
#include <stdio.h>
#include <malloc.h>
#include <string.h>
#include <conio.h>
#include <graph.h>

/* CONSTANTS */
#define   MAXSTR   15
#ifndef   TRUE
#define   TRUE  1
#define   FALSE 0
#endif
```

```
#pragma pack(1)

/* TYPES */
typedef struct dnode {                        /* DLL node structure */
  char          LastName[MAXSTR], FirstName[MAXSTR];
  struct dnode  *prev, *next;
} DNODE;

/* LOCAL FUNCTION PROTOTYPES */
void    BuildList (void);
void    ShowList (DNODE*);
void    InsertNode (DNODE*);
DNODE   *FindInsert (DNODE*);
void    Delete (void);
DNODE   *match (char*, DNODE*);

/* GLOBALS */
DNODE     *head;
/* -------------------------- */

void main ()
{
  BuildList ();
  Delete ();
} /* -------------------------- */

void  BuildList (void)           /* Build DLL from disk file */
{
FILE    *f;
DNODE   *new;
char    last[MAXSTR], first[MAXSTR];

  f = fopen ("NAMES.DLL", "r");                    /* Open file */
  if (f == NULL) {                                 /* error */
    puts ("Unable to open NAMES.DLL");
    exit (1);
  }
  while (!feof (f)) {              /* while not end of file */
    fscanf (f, "%s%s", last, first);         /* get data */
    if (!feof (f)) {
      new = (DNODE*) malloc (sizeof (DNODE));
      strcpy (new->LastName, last);
      strcpy (new->FirstName, first);
      InsertNode (new);                       /* put into list */
    }
  }
  fclose (f);                               /* close file at end */
} /* -------------------------- */

void  InsertNode (DNODE *new)      /* Insert node into DLL */
{
DNODE   *ins = NULL;
```

Listing 18.4 *(continued)*

```
  if (head == NULL) {                    /* First node in list */
    head = new;                              /* set head pointer */
    head->prev = head->next = head;      /* point to itself */
  } else {
    ins = FindInsert (new);    /* else find insertion point */
    new->prev = ins->prev;                /* rearrange pointers */
    ins->prev = new;
    new->next = new->prev->next;
    new->prev->next = new;
    if (strcmp (new->LastName, head->LastName) < 0)
      head = new;      /* change global pointer if new head */
  }
} /* ----------------------- */

DNODE  *FindInsert (DNODE *new)
{                                /* Find where new->key fits */
char   found = FALSE;
DNODE *this;

  this = head;
  do {
    if (strcmp (new->LastName, this->LastName) < 0)
      found = TRUE;                  /* found insertion point */
    else
      this = this->next;            /* else try the next node */
  } while (!found && this != head);
  return (this);
} /* ----------------------- */

void ShowList (DNODE *head)          /* Show list on screen */
{
DNODE  *this;

  this = head;
  do {
    printf ("\n%s, %s", this->LastName, this->FirstName);
    this = this->next;
  } while (this != head);
  putchar ('\n');
} /* ----------------------- */

void   Delete (void)     /* Sub to delete nodes on request */
{
char   reply = 'N', name[MAXSTR];
DNODE  *del = NULL, *start;

  do {
    _clearscreen(_GCLEARSCREEN);
    puts ("\nCURRENT CONTENTS OF LIST:");
    ShowList (head);
    start = head;
```

```
            printf ("\n\nName to delete? ");
            gets (name);                    /* get name from keyboard */
            while (name[0] && reply != 'Y') {
               del = match (name, start);   /* find node with name */
               if (del) {
                  printf ("\nFound %s %s", del->FirstName,
                            del->LastName);
                  printf ("\nDelete this one? (Y/N)... ");
                  reply = getche();
                  reply = toupper (reply);
                  if (reply == 'Y') {
                     del->prev->next = del->next;     /* remove node */
                     del->next->prev = del->prev;
                     if (del == head)        /* if deleting head node */
                        head = del->next;            /* repoint head */
                     free (del);
                  } else
                     if (del->next != head)  /* if not wrapping back */
                        start = del->next;      /* resume at next node */
                     else
                        start = NULL;                /* else stop search */
               } else {
                  printf ("\nUnable to find %s", name);
                  puts ("\n\nPress any key to continue... ");
                  getch();
                  break;                       /* to stop while() loop */
               }
            }
            reply = 'N';                    /* to re-enable while() loop */
         } while (name[0]);
      } /* ------------------------- */



DNODE *match (char *name, DNODE *list)
                                           /* find name in list */
{
DNODE   *this;
int     found = 0;


   if (list != NULL) {
      this = list;
      do {
         if (strcmp (name, this->LastName) == 0)
            found = 1;
         else
            this = this->next;
      } while ((this != head) && !found);
   }
   if (!found)
      this = NULL;
   return this;
} /* ----------------------- */
```

Stacks and Queues

Stacks and queues differ from other linked lists not in their structure and mechanics, but in the way they're used. So far we've considered unordered and key-sorted lists. In stacks and queues, the organizing principle is order of arrival in and retrieval from the list. Thus they represent two alternative forms of list management.

A queue is like a conveyor belt: Things go in one end and come out the other. Another analogy is a line of people waiting at the grocery checkout; you join at the end and eventually you get your turn to pay.

In software, queues are often used to hold requests for service until it's convenient to service them. An example is an interrupt from an external device. The interrupt arrives while the system is busy doing other things, so it puts a record of the interrupt into a queue ("enqueues" it) and goes on about its business. Later it gets around to servicing interrupts, of which there might be several. The software pulls the oldest off the queue first ("dequeues" it), takes care of it, then gets the next, and so on until the queue is drained or some distraction arises.

Consequently, a queue lines things up in order of arrival, and furnishes them to the software in the same order. Queues are also called FIFO buffers, short for First In, First Out.

You effect a queue by always adding new nodes to the tail, and always fetching and deleting the head when you take a node out of the list. The program in Listing 18.5 illustrates this.

A stack works on the opposite principle; the last item added is the first to be retrieved. An analogy is the in-basket on your desk at work. Everything goes on top of the existing contents, and when you want something to do you take off the most recently arrived thing first. If you always pulled from the bottom of the pile, you'd be maintaining a queue, but that's not the way it usually works. Stacks also go by the name LIFO, for Last In, First Out.

Stacks are essential for retracing the path back out of a sequence of events, and are thus used throughout software. An example close to C programmers is retreating from a series of subroutine calls. The main() function calls fcn1(), which calls fcn2(). When fcn2() completes, it returns to fcn1(), and eventually fcn1() returns to main(). The program maintains a stack where it places the return address each time your C code calls a function. The return() statement or the closing curly brace of a subroutine pulls the return address from the top of the stack so that execution can resume where it left off when you called the function.

Stacks are so common that there is a vocabulary surrounding them. Placing an item on the stack is called "pushing." Thus, in the example above, you push a return address onto the stack before calling a subroutine. Taking it off the stack later is called "popping," as in "pop the return address off the stack."

There are several ways to manage a stack. We saw one method using SLLs in the TEXTSCRN and EXGRAPH libraries (Chapters 7 and 11, respectively). In the context of this chapter, you can operate a stack by always pushing and popping the head node. Conceptually the stack grows upward and shrinks downward by activity at its top.

Popping and dequeueing are the same thing, since the object at the head is removed and the list shrinks toward its "lower" end. The distinction is that in popping from a stack, you get the most recent item, while in dequeueing you fetch the oldest thing.

Listing 18.5 lists a program called STAQUE.C. It's an entertaining demonstration of queue and stack operations. As you key in a line of text, the program enqueues and pushes each character in separate dynamic structures. When you press Enter, the program dequeues the characters to reconstruct your input in the order of arrival. After that, it pops characters and writes them to the screen in the reverse order that characterizes a stack. The queue- and stack-affecting subprograms (enqueue(), dequeue(), push(), and pop()) implement the discussion.

Note that this program also proves a point mentioned early in the chapter: that two or more linked lists can be physically intermingled on the heap without fear of confusion. Examining the flow of Listing 18.5, you can see that stack and queue nodes alternate. Yet they don't confound each other since proper pointer management keeps the lists separate and uncorrupted.

Listing 18.5 Demonstration: stack and queue operations.

```
/* STAQUE.C: Queue and stack operations */

#include <stdio.h>
#include <malloc.h>
#include <conio.h>
#include <graph.h>

#define ENTER 13
#define BKSPC  8

typedef struct chnode {
  char         ch;
  struct chnode *prev, *next;
} CHNODE;

/* Globals */
CHNODE  *stack, *qhead, *qtail;

/* Prototypes */
CHNODE *enqueue (char, CHNODE*);
CHNODE *dequeue (char*, CHNODE*);
CHNODE *push (char, CHNODE*);
CHNODE *pop (char*, CHNODE*);
```

Listing 18.5 *(continued)*

```
/* ------------------------- */

void main ()
{
char   ch;

  /* Get the data, put into queue and stack */
  _clearscreen(_GCLEARSCREEN);
  puts ("Queues and stacks\n");
  puts ("Type something:");

  /* NOTE: following is not a complete keyboard processor */
  do {
    ch = getche ();                        /* get char and echo */
    if (ch != ENTER) {          /* until Enter is pressed... */
      qtail = enqueue (ch, qtail);         /* enqueue char */
      if (qhead == NULL)
        qhead = qtail;              /* set queue head if first */
      stack = push (ch, stack);            /* push char */
    }
  } while (ch != ENTER);

  /* Read from the queue */
  puts ("\n\n- Your input taken from the queue:");
  while (qhead != NULL) {
    qhead = dequeue (&ch, qhead);     /* dequeue next char */
    if (qtail == NULL)                /* reset head if last */
      qhead = NULL;
    putchar (ch);                            /* print char */
  }

  /* Read from the stack */
  puts ("\n\n- Your input taken from the stack:");
  while (stack != NULL) {
    stack = pop (&ch, stack);              /* pop next char */
    putchar (ch);                            /* print it */
  }
  putchar ('\n');
} /* ------------------------- */

CHNODE *enqueue (char c, CHNODE *tail)
  /* add node to end of queue, return pointer to new tail */
{
CHNODE *newtail;

  newtail = malloc (sizeof (CHNODE));    /* allocate node */
  newtail->ch = c;                            /* save char */
  if (tail) tail->next = newtail;       /* update old tail */
  newtail->prev = tail;              /* set new tail's pointers */
  newtail->next = NULL;
  return newtail;
```

```
} /* ------------------------ */

CHNODE *dequeue (char *c, CHNODE *head)
            /* remove node from head of queue, return next */
{
CHNODE *newhead = NULL;

  if (head) {                              /* if queue exists... */
    *c = head->ch;                           /* give back char */
    newhead = head->next;
    newhead->prev = NULL;          /* update backward pointer */
    free (head);                         /* deallocate space */
  } else
    *c = NULL;                      /* else no char to return */
  return newhead;
} /* ------------------------ */

CHNODE *push (char c, CHNODE *top)
          /* push char onto stack, return new top of stack */
{
CHNODE *newtop;

  newtop = malloc (sizeof (CHNODE));     /* allocate space */
  newtop->ch = c;                           /* save char */
  if (top) top->prev = newtop; /* update old top of stack */
  newtop->next = top;          /* set new node's pointers */
  newtop->prev = NULL;
  return (newtop);
} /* ------------------------ */

CHNODE *pop (char *c, CHNODE *top)
                    /* pop char from stack, return new top */
{
CHNODE *newtop = NULL;

  if (top) {                              /* if stack exists... */
    *c = top->ch;                           /* send back char */
    newtop = top->next;
    newtop->prev = NULL;          /* update backward pointer */
    free (top);                             /* free space */
  } else
    *c = NULL;                      /* else no char to return */
  return newtop;
} /* ------------------------ */
```

This chapter has explored some of the possibilities that doubly linked lists offer for creating highly flexible dynamic data structures. We've touched on unordered lists, but most of our attention has been focused on three types of ordered structures: sorted by key, queues, and stacks. DLLs lend themselves to ordered sequences of nodes much more readily than SLLs, since insertion of a node between two that already exist are painless. Therefore, as a practical matter, if your data is inherently unorganized and you don't care, use an SLL for it; otherwise, use a DLL.

The circular lists covered here are much easier to use in organizing a key-ordered list than are DLLs with terminal nodes. It's probably a little easier to use terminal-node lists with queues and stacks, but the circular model erects few inconveniences in any case and is a workable solution for most DLL applications.

The trouble with both SLLs and DLLs is that searches must always proceed in a sequential manner. Ordered DLLs offer the option of bailing out early when you detect that the key you're looking for isn't in the list. Still, in both types of lists, if the list contains n items, it takes n/2 comparisons on average to find what you want. In very large lists, this can potentially consume a significant amount of time. So can the problem of ordering a DLL, which is not ordered unless you specifically undertake to make it so.

Let's move on now to binary trees, dynamic structures those nodes resemble those of DLLs, but which are inherently ordered and offer a dramatically faster search path.

CHAPTER **19**

Binary Trees

The nodes of a binary tree look the same as those of a doubly linked list in that they include two pointers, one to a "higher" node and the other to one that is "lower." The similarity ends there. A linked list is sequential, much like a string of pearls where one follows another. A binary tree, on the other hand, has a hierarchical branching structure, such that the path divides into two at each node. The import of this difference will become apparent as we proceed.

A binary tree is inherently ordered according to its key, making the concept of sorting implicit in the organization. Every time you add a new element, the node is inserted into its proper position within the hierarchy and the overall structure of the tree adjusts accordingly. The tree also changes its structure when you delete a node. And because searches traverse the tree—not sequentially as in a linked list, but along paths that are continually dividing—movement through a binary tree is blazingly fast. Binary trees are perfectly suited to organizing and searching very large amounts of data.

There are many practical applications for binary trees. One example is a spelling checker, which has to order huge numbers of words and find any one in the bat of an electronic eye. Another is a database management system, which organizes records indexed by key fields. Your programs might use binary trees to arrange customer ledgers by account number, phone lists by name, mailing labels by ZIP code, or a library's card catalog by accession number. The uses for ordering data by a key are limitless.

Paradoxically, the concept of a binary tree is fairly simple and the algorithms extremely efficient, but the underlying details are difficult unless you are thoroughly indoctrinated in the self-defining world of recursion. We'll cover some concepts first, and then get into details and some working applications.

Organization of a Binary Tree _____

A binary tree takes its name from its resemblance to a biological tree turned upside down. Turn over Figure 19.1 and you'll see it clearly. Some of the tax-

Figure 19.1 **A typical binary tree.**

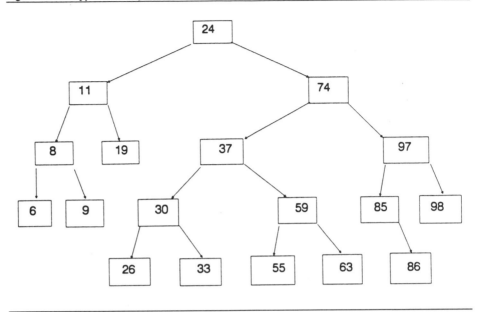

onomy associated with binary trees also comes from the biological model: root, branch, and leaf.

Each of the nodes in Figure 19.1 shows its key value so that you can see how keys order the structure. The topmost node contains key 24; it's called the "root," and it serves as the point of entry to the tree much as the "head" does in linked lists.

Two branches flow from the root. The subtree to the left contains keys that are all less than the root's key, while those in the right-hand subtree are greater than the root's.

The subtrees follow the same ordering principle. Taking the left subtree as an example, the nodes to the left of its root all have keys less than 11, while the nodes to the right have keys greater than 11 but less than 24, the value of the tree's main root. The sub-subtree beginning at 8 is similarly organized, as are all structural components of a binary tree.

Terminal nodes (6, 9, 19, 26, etc.) are called "leaves" because, like the leaves on a tree, they are the ends of the paths and lead nowhere beyond. Unlike a linked list, a binary tree has no definite end or "tail." Instead, its many paths all culminate eventually in leaf nodes. A leaf can be detected by both its linkage pointers being **NULL**.

The term "binary" comes, in this case, from the less-than/greater-than organization. From any given node, the path to subsequent nodes depends on whether the sought key is less than or greater than the current node's key. It might also be equal, in which case the search ends successfully.

Efficiency of Binary Trees

The tree in Figure 19.1 contains 18 nodes. If these same nodes were in a linked list, on average it would take nine compares per search to find a given value. This is based on the assumption that all nodes have an equal chance of being selected, so the "average" node would be in the middle of the list. Therefore, 18 / 2 = 9 searches on average.

The computation is somewhat more complex in a binary tree. It also depends on the structure of the individual tree; if the tree in Figure 19.1 had different key values, the tree would have a different structure. This leads to the general observation that every binary tree is unique, and because it is a dynamic data structure that automatically adjusts its own configuration to accomodate the insertion and deletion of nodes, uniqueness extends down to the level of any given moment in a particular tree's existence. Still, since we know how this tree is organized, we can compute the average number of compares to reach a specific node.

Typical Case

Figure 19.2 illustrates that the tree consists of five levels. The level number is equivalent to the number of compares it takes to reach that level. That is, if the argument is 24, the first compare finds a match at the first level. Similarly, if the argument is 26, we have to compare it with 24, 74, 37, 30, and finally 26 to find a match; 26 is on level 5, and it takes five compares to get there.

Therefore we can estimate a weighted average based on the number of nodes per level times the level number. The righthand column in Figure 19.2 shows the number of nodes at each level. The total number of compares to reach all nodes is:

$$(1*1) \ + \ (2*2) \ + \ (3*4) \ + \ (4*6) \ + \ (5*5) \ = \ 66$$

Since there are 18 nodes, the average number of compares to find any given node is 66/18 = 3.67.

In other words, searching this binary tree is almost three times as efficient as searching for the same key in a linked list. And this is a small tree. As the amount of data increases, the average number of compares rises very slowly in contrast to linked lists, where it grows at exactly half the rate of increase in the number of nodes. For example, adding two nodes at level 4—say keys of 17 and 21—would increase the average number of compares from 3.67 to 3.7, while in a linked list it would go from 9 to 10. Thus you can see that the search efficiency for a binary tree is dramatically better even for a small amount of data, and it keeps getting better as the amount of data increases.

Computer scientists such as Knuth have devoted a great deal of mathematical energy to this subject. The general conclusion is that it takes something on

Figure 19.2 **Levels of the binary tree.**

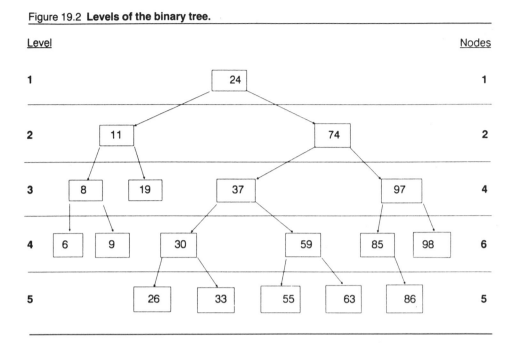

the order of $[LOG^2 2N] - 1$ searches to find a node within the average tree, where N is the total number of nodes. The point is that reasonably balanced binary trees are well-suited for organizing large amounts of data.

Best Case

The best case in the organization of a tree is illustrated by the subtree beginning at node 37 in Figures 19.1 and 19.2 Here every possible path reaches a leaf at the same level. In other words the subtree is perfectly symmetrical or "balanced."

Unfortunately, most binary trees aren't perfectly balanced. We'll consider some extreme cases of imbalance in a moment. A reasonable degree of balance occurs when keys arrive in random order, so that the tree grows more or less uniformly along all possible paths. Usually this is "good enough." There are techniques for forcing a tree into symmetry. The best-known is the AVL method, named for two Russian mathematicians—G.M. Adelson-Velski and E.M. Landis—who developed it in 1962. Such techniques go far beyond the scope of this book, but they're worth investigating if you're faced with a humongous tree problem. Knuth covers them, and heavyweight programming magazines such as *Dr. Dobbs' Journal* regularly report new methods.

Figure 19.3 **Degenerate trees.**

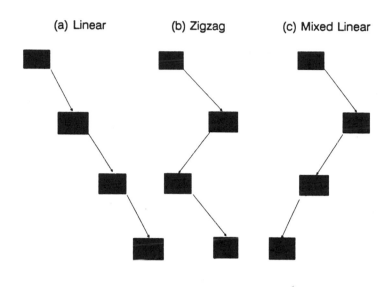

    (a) Linear   (b) Zigzag   (c) Mixed Linear

    In this book we'll assume that keys arrive in random order and achieve a fairly balanced tree that will deliver better performance than an equivalent linked list.

Worst Case

    Figure 19.3 shows three trees exhibiting the worst possible binary structures, which we call linear, zigzag, and mixed linear. In all cases, each node has only one path away from it. Such trees are said to be "degenerate," as though they were somehow morally reprehensible. As for performance, they are no different than ordinary linked lists, and their efficiency is exactly equal.

    From this you can conclude that, in the worst case, a binary tree will deliver the same search performance as a linked list. Sadly, it's quite easy to build a worst-case binary tree. The secret of reasonable balance is random arrival of keys; a binary tree built from previously ordered data inevitably results in a worst-case structure.

    Later we'll cover a method called preorder traversal that enables us to save and rebuild a binary tree, thus potentially avoiding the construction of a worst-case organization.

    Now let's consider the building blocks of binary trees.

Figure 19.4 **Conceptual structure of a node.**

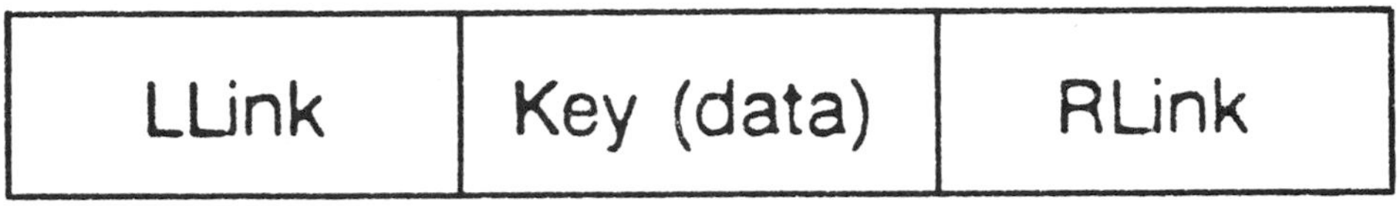

LLink	Key (data)	RLink

Node Structure

The nodes of a binary tree are identical to those of a doubly linked list; i.e., the minimal node consists of:

- A data element that can serve as a key.
- Two pointers bound to the node type.

The node can, of course, contain nonkey data elements as well. The difference between binary tree and DLL nodes is in how we employ the pointers.

By convention, the pointers are referred to as LLink and RLink, where LLink points to the "left" (a node whose key is of lesser value) and RLink points to the "right" (greater key). In the root of Figures 19.1 and 19.2, LLink leads to the node containing 11, and RLink leads to 74. Figure 19.4 shows a convenient visualization of the node structure.

In C, you could define this node as follows:

```
typedef  struct  binnode  {
    int              key;
    struct  binnode *LLink,  *RLink;
} BINNODE;
```

Figure 19.5 **Starting the binary tree.**

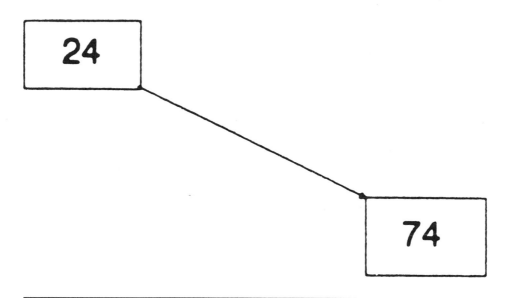

As in the other node types discussed in the preceding chapters, the order of fields doesn't matter. Thus the node format defined here has the same content as, but a different order of elements than, the node depicted in Figure 19.4.

Building a Binary Tree

The first data presented to a routine that builds a new binary tree become the root node. Say we're building the tree depicted in Figure 19.1. In that case, the first data value—hence key—is 24, which becomes the "splitting value" of the tree that ensues.

Maybe the next key that comes to the tree is 74. It's greater than 24, so the root's RLink is set to point to the node containing 74, and the tree takes the form shown in Figure 19.5.

Perhaps the next value to arrive is 11. To find its rightful place, we begin searching the tree at the root. Because 11 < 24 and the root's LLink is NULL, we set root->LLink to point to the new node, with the result that appears in Figure 19.6. Now we get the key value 37 and things become more interesting as we search for its home. Starting at the root, 37 > 24, so we follow RLink to key 74. There we discover that 37 < 74. This node's LLink is NULL, so we set it to point to the new node and a tree takes shape as in Figure 19.7.

Figure 19.6 **Adding a third node to the tree.**

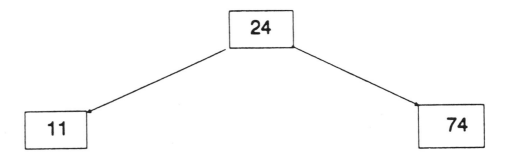

The next incoming value is 59. Again starting at the root, 59 > 24, 59 < 74, and 59 > 37. Because the RLink at 37 is **NULL**, the tree takes the new shape in Figure 19.8.

This process continues along the same lines for as long as new nodes keep arriving. Each new node falls into the LLink or RLink path from its "parent" (higher-level node), and is added to the tree as a leaf.

Duplicate Keys

Conceivably an application could have duplicate keys in a binary tree. An example is a system that tracks daily sales orders using the customer account number as the key; the same customer might place two or more orders in the same day, resulting in duplication of the key in the tree.

Binary trees are capable of dealing with this problem, but it's not a good idea. Why? Because searches will always stop at the first encounter with the key being sought. You have to introduce considerable overhead to look at secondary criteria and decide whether or not to continue the search. This might cancel out the benefits of using binary trees.

A better approach is to use a key that you're confident is unique in all cases. In this example, organize and search on the customer purchase order number instead of the internal account number. It might be unlikely that any given customer will place two or more separate orders using the same PO

Figure 19.7 **A tree begins to form.**

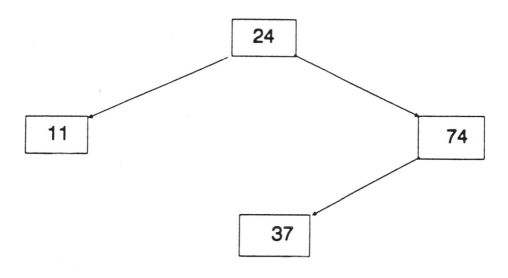

Fig 19.8 **The tree continues to grow as nodes arrive.**

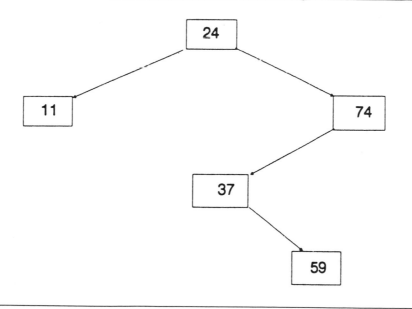

number, and statistically improbable that two different customers will generate the same PO number in any given day.

Binary trees work best when all keys are unique.

Traversing a Tree

As with lists, the process of moving through a tree and accessing each of its
nodes is called "traversing." This is a purely sequential operation in a list;
it's considerably more complicated in a tree, which has a complex organization.

There are three ways to traverse a binary tree: in-order, pre-order, and post-
order, referring to the sequence in which the contents of individual nodes are
accessed. Each has application to real-world programming problems, and
we'll discuss some of those applications as we cover the three methods.

In-Order Traversal

In-order traversal follows the tree according to the collating sequence of its
keys (A through Z or whatever). A common usage is in printing out a sorted
listing of node contents. For example, if the tree is keyed on employee names,
in-order traversal will automatically produce an alphabetized list of
employees. In-order traversal of the tree in Figure 19.1 follows the order

```
        6
        8
        9
       11
       19
       24
        ⋮
       86
       97
       98
```

The LLink pointer of every node points either to another node having a
lower key value, or it is NULL. If you enter at the root and follow the chain of
LLinks until you encounter a NULL pointer, you have reached the lowest-val-
ued leaf in the tree. The in-order algorithm, then, always strives to the left
until it can go no further. At that point it reports the data, then follows RLink
and begins striving to the left again. When all RLinks have been followed in a

subtree, the process backs up to the next higher level and follows its RLink to a node where it again strives to the left. This continues until all RLinks have been exhausted, or in other words until there's nowhere left to go. In Figure 19.1, this happens at the node whose key is 98.

While this and the other traversal algorithms sound complex, it takes only three lines of code to do it using the mysterious magic of recursion. We'll cover the "how" later in the chapter.

Pre-Order Traversal

The most important value in a binary tree is its root key. Secondary in importance are the root keys of subtrees. These pivotal values, if preserved in the proper order with respect to all other keys, enable us to save a binary tree's contents in a disk file and later reconstruct the tree in its present form. That's what pre-order traversal is all about: preserving the tree's contents for later reconstruction.

Why would you want to save the tree's structure as well as its data? Suppose you have a large, reasonably well-balanced table that is used by several applications, or is called in from disk once a day for updates and reference. If you save it with in-order traversal, you end up with an ordered list. The next time you bring it in, you will build a degenerate tree whose performance is no better than a linked list. In other words, the balance, and thus the advantage of the tree are destroyed by saving it in-order. That's why saving it pre-order is important.

Like in-order, pre-order tends to the left and only faces to the right when its leftward path dead-ends in a NULL LLink. The difference is the order in which it accesses the data as it traverses. In-order processes the node's data contents whenever it switches from the LLink path to the RLink. On the other hand, pre-order processes the contents when it first enters a node, and *then* it attempts to move left. When it runs into a NULL LLink, it grabs the first RLink it can find and against strives leftward. For the tree in Figure 19.1, the pre-order is:

24

11

8

6

9

19

74

⋮

97

85

86

98

If you take these values and manually reconstruct the tree, you will build a
configuration exactly like that shown in Figure 19.1.

Post-Order Traversal

Post-order is most commonly employed when traversing a tree to dispose of
its elements, i.e., when deleting the tree from the heap. You might do this to
free up heap space for other uses when the tree is no longer needed ("garbage
collection").

In post-order, the action associated with the traversal (disposal, output, or
whatever) occurs when you leave the node for the final time to move upward
in the tree. Thus, the post-order traversal of Figure 19.1 operates on the nodes
in this order:

6

9

8

19

11

26

33

30

$\vdots$

98

97

74

24

Traversal Summary

In all three traversal algorithms, a transition occurs between LLink and RLink at some point in every node. The terms pre-, in-, and post- refer to the time when data processing occurs with respect to this transition.

- In pre-order, the action occurs before the transition. Thus pre-order accesses a parent node first, then all its left-hand children, then all on the right.
- In-order takes action during the transition, as the algorithm moves from LLink to RLink. Consequently, in-order accesses all the left-hand children, then the parent, then all the right-hand children.
- Post-order operates on the data after the transition, accessing all the left-hand children, all the right-hand children, and finally the parent. As a result, when deleting a tree with post-order, the root node is the last to go.

Later we will translate this discussion into C code.

Searching the Binary Tree _____

As mentioned earlier, a search path in a binary tree tends to be very short because it follows a hierarchy that divides continuously. In a perfectly balanced tree of 65,536 nodes, for example, it would take no more than 16 attempts to locate any given key.

Searching a binary tree is a matter of comparing the key value sought (argument) against the current node's key. There are three possible outcomes:

1. Argument = key—The search succeeds and ends.
2. Argument < key—Follow LLink.
3. Argument > key—Follow RLink.

A fourth outcome results when the argument is not in the tree; i.e., you're looking for a key that doesn't exist. You know that's the case when the search is barred by a **NULL** pointer.

Perhaps the first argument you search for in Figure 19.1 is 37. Entering the tree at the root, you find that 37 > 24, so you follow RLink. There, 37 < 74, so you follow LLink. The next node contains a match, so the search ends successfully.

Next you look for 18. Since 18 < 24, you follow LLink. In the next node, 18 > 11, sending you by RLink to the node containing 19. Following the determination that 18 < 19, your progress is halted since LLink is **NULL** in this node. Therefore, the key sought is not in the tree.

The process, then, is to compare values and, if not equal, to move left or right depending on the outcome until you either find a match or come to a dead end.

Since searching is the most common operation in binary trees, it's clear that the search procedure needs some way to report results back to the caller. There are two possible outcomes: found and not found. If found, you usually want to do something else, such as printing or otherwise using nonkey data items from the node; if not found, you need to know that too, so that you can display a "no match" message or take some contingency action.

This suggests a function returning a pointer to the found node, or **NULL** if the search was unsuccessful.

Our thoughts are now turning from the theoretical to the practical, so let's translate this discussion into code.

Binary Trees in Action _____

First we need to establish a context for the following examples since, like linked lists, binary trees are application-dependent with respect to details. Let's say you're accumulating a database that relates part numbers to their descriptions. For instance, if the part number is 5432, the database furnishes the description "Resistor, 4 ohm." Part names in this application consist of strings up to 20 characters in length. The key field is the part number, which might be a character field with a length of six.

We can define the node structure in C as follows:

```
typedef struct {
     char      nbr[6];      /* part #, key field */
     char      name[20];
} DATAPART;
typedef struct partnode {
     DATAPART      part;
     struct partnode   *LLink, *RLink;
} PARTNODE;
```

Note that we've developed two structures here, in which **DATAPART** becomes a substructure within **PARTNODE**. Why? Because later we might want to save the **DATAPART** on disk without also storing the pointers from **PARTNODE**. The use of nested structures lets us refer to the substructure and its members in an intuitive manner. The whole substructure can be referred to as **node − >part**, while the part number field is **node − >part.nbr**. Figure 19.9 visualizes the structure defined by **typedef DATAPART**.

Perhaps the most important variable in the program is

```
PARTNODE *root   =   NULL;
```

Figure 19.9 **Visualizing the PARTNODE structure.**

nbr[6]	name[20]	*LLink	*RLink

which will eventually point to the root of the binary tree.

Having defined the major elements, we can implement a binary tree. First, though, let's review recursion, which is essential in understanding how to traverse binary trees.

Of Recursion

Recursion in software means that a function calls itself ("recurs"). This might seem a strange thing for a function to do, but in fact it's merely a variation on the theme of looping. Because it uses the stack for storing and passing information from one invocation to the next, recursion is particularly well-suited to navigation within a complex structure such as a binary tree.

Here we'll look at a simple example that does nothing useful except to illustrate how recursion works. Later in the chapter you'll have plenty of exposure to practical applications.

When one function calls another, it places its arguments on the stack, followed by some control information and the return address at which execution is to resume after the called routine completes. A recursive call acts in exactly the same way. If eight bytes of data go on the stack each time the function is called, and the function calls itself recursively three times, then it places a total of 24 bytes on the stack. Each time the function resumes recursively, it can fetch the arguments from the stack that were placed there by the most recent call, using them as it would if called from outside. In effect, the function doesn't know it's been called by itself. Therefore there's nothing peculiar about its operation.

Since recursion is like looping, the same rule applies to both: You must have some condition that stops the recursion. When that happens, the function returns to its prior invocation, which in turn returns to its predecessor, and so on, each time removing the data placed on the stack before it was called. Eventually it returns to a caller outside itself, thus ending the recursion.

A simple recursive function is

```
void  recur  (int  n)
{
    if  (n  !=  0)
       recur  (n-1);
}
```

Say you call this function with

```
recur  (2);
```

The if() condition is true, so recur() calls itself passing n − 1, which is now 1. This is the second invocation, and again the if() test succeeds and recur() calls itself, this time passing 0 as the argument.

Now the terminating condition is satisfied. The function is at the second level of recursion; i.e., it called itself with 1, then with 0 as an argument. It must now back out of the levels. The return address for the first-level call is effectively at the closing curly brace, to which the second level returns. This causes the first level to return, and now the highest level, which was called from outside, reverts control to the original caller. And that's how it works.

Other conditions can also terminate the recursive calling sequence. Later we'll see functions that stop calling themselves on hitting a NULL pointer.

This example, of course, doesn't do anything except call itself. Real recursive functions do something before invoking themselves, afterwards, or both, and some that work on binary trees call themselves more than once.

Building a Binary Tree

Ideally the routine that controls the acquisition of data and the building of the binary tree should be short, relying on a function elsewhere in the program to handle the details of structuring the tree. Listing 19.1 contains an example.

Listing 19.1 **Controlling data capture and tree building.**

```
do {                                    /* repeat the following... */
  puts ("\n--------------------------------------\n");
  puts ("Part number? (ENTER to end data entry) ");
  gets (number);
  if (strlen (number) > 0) {
    puts ("\nPart description? ");
    gets (name );
    if (root == NULL)
      root = newnode (number, name, root, root);
    else                                         /* ignore result */
      newnode (number, name, root, root);
  }
} while (strlen (number) > 0);
```

This fragment of code keeps getting inputs from the keyboard until the user presses Enter in lieu of a part number, thus signalling the end of input. When the root pointer is NULL—i.e., the tree doesn't yet exist—the routine calls the newnode() function, whose return value is assigned to the root pointer. This establishes the existence of the tree. Thereafter, the routine calls newnode() for each new entry, but ignores the pointer it returns by not assigning it to anything. The if() block within the loop prevents the creation of an empty node when the user signals end of input.

Having defined a context and role for the tree-building function newnode(), we can proceed to develop it. The reason for passing the address of the root node twice as an argument in Listing 19.1 will become clear later.

The function heading reads

```
PARTNODE *newnode (char *arg, char *name,
                     PARTNODE *parent, PARTNODE *node)
```

where arg is a pointer to the key value (part number) of the node to be added and name points to the new part name. The function returns a pointer of type PARTNODE, pointing to the node it added to the tree.

The first order of business is to determine where the node belongs. For this we can use a recursive search:

```
if (strnicmp (arg, node->part.nbr, KEYLEN) < 0)
  node = newnode (arg, name, node, node->LLink);
else
  node = newnode (arg, name, node, node->RLink);
```

Each time we enter a node, we compare the argument with its key. If less than, we proceed to the left by passing this node's LLink, and otherwise we go right by passing RLink to the next invocation of newnode(). Note that the call passes the current node's address to the next invocation's parent argument; that's because this node is the parent of the next we visit. In this manner, by comparing the argument against successive keys and passing on to

LLink or RLink as appropriate, the process intelligently follows branching paths to the place where the new node belongs.

The recursive search algorithm above is not yet complete, though, because it has two problems:

1. It doesn't recognize an empty tree, i.e., one in which no root node exists.
2. There's no way to end the search.

The second is of paramount concern in recursive functions in general, lest the function keep calling itself until the program crashes from running out of stack space. A recursive function with no exit, or with exit conditions that can never be satisfied, is conceptually like an endless loop: bad news. Because recursive exits are usually less intuitively obvious than loop terminations, you have to code them carefully. In this case, the recursion must stop when the linkage pointer passed as the node argument is **NULL**. That happens automatically on the first call to **newnode()**, since the **NULL**-initialized value of root is passed. Thereafter, when a tree of at least one node exists, the node argument becomes **NULL** when we pass along a **NULL** LLink or RLink from the parent. This signifies the end of the search path.

The body of the recursive function **newnode()**, then, must be able to recognize when the search has ended, so that it can create and connect the new leaf in its proper place. The condition is whether or not the node parameter is **NULL**. Expressed in C notation, the overall logic of the function is

```
if (node != NULL)
  /* continue recursive search */
else
  /* make and connect the new node */
```

Listing 19.2 lists the implementation of this logic within the context of the parts data base.

Listing 19.2 **Adding a new node to a binary tree.**

```
PARTNODE *newnode (char *arg, char *name,
                   PARTNODE *parent, PARTNODE *node)
{                                     /* insert new node into tree */

   if (node != NULL)       /* find location for node in tree */
     if (strnicmp (arg, node->part.nbr, KEYLEN) < 0)
       node = newnode (arg, name, node, node->LLink);
     else
       node = newnode (arg, name, node, node->RLink);
   else {                          /* new leaf's position found */
     node = (PARTNODE *) malloc (sizeof (PARTNODE));
     node->LLink = NULL;        /* leaf ptrs are always NULL */
     node->RLink = NULL;
```

```
        strncpy (node->part.nbr, arg, KEYLEN);     /* init leaf */
        strncpy (node->part.name, name, NAMELEN);
        if (strnicmp (arg, parent->part.nbr, KEYLEN) < 0)
          parent->LLink = (PARTNODE *) node;
        else
          parent->RLink = (PARTNODE *) node;
    }
    return (node);
} /* ----------------------- */
```

Tree Traversal Algorithms

Tree traversal is the process of moving through an entire binary tree in an orderly fashion and doing something with each node's contents. The three methods, discussed earlier, are in-order, pre-order, and post-order. Traversal entails a lot of up-and-down movement along complex paths; you have to keep track of where you came from so that you can retreat from lower levels. Were it not for recursion, which uses the stack to store this information, traversal routines would be impossibly complicated. With recursion, it's simple.

The following three figures are templates that you can adapt to your own tree-following projects. The output and free() statements are the only application-dependent portions of the functions. The rest you can use directly, without modification.

In-Order

In-order traversal produces the contents of the tree sorted into ascending order by key: the field part.nbr in this case. Listing 19.3 shows an inOrder() function that lists the node contents in key order to an output device.

Listing 19.3 **Function to output a tree in key order.**

```
void inOrder (FILE *dev, PARTNODE *node)
{                                /* print tree in sorted order */

  if (node != NULL) {
    inOrder (dev, node->LLink);            /* keep going left */
    fprintf (dev, "\n%.bs     %s",            /* output data */
          node->part.nbr, node->part.name);
    inOrder (dev, node->RLink);                 ow go right */
  }
} /* ----------------------- */
```

Refer to Figure 19.1 to follow how this function works. The call that initiates the ordered output process is

inOrder (root);

which passes a pointer to the root of the tree (24). Because the node pointer is not **NULL**, the first recursive call passes **node − >LLink** from node 24, which leads to node 11. Successive calls keep passing LLink from the current node, eventually arriving at node 6.

This node is a leaf, so its LLink is **NULL**. Therefore on the next invocation, node is **NULL** and the if() test fails, causing the invocation to return to node 6. The return address for that level points to the **fprintf()** statement, so the contents of node 6 go to the output device. Now the function calls itself passing RLink. Because RLink in node 6 is also **NULL**, the newly-called level returns immediately, enabling the level that points to node 6 to return also. Having returned to the next-higher level, the data from node 8 goes to the output device and the process repeats passing node 8's RLink.

This goes on through all the left-hand subtree, processing 6, 8, 9, 11, and 19, and finally returning to the root, where the data associated with key 24 is output. Now the function moves to the right-hand subtree using **root − >RLink**. Because of the tendency to strive left, the next node is key 26, and so it goes in the same manner until we finally reach node 98. There are no RLinks left to follow, so all recursive levels return, each to its caller, until the top-level call returns control to the program.

The thrust of this process is that the contents of any given node are processed only when all lesser values (to the left) have been processed, and before moving on to the greater values to the right. The result is ordering by key.

Pre-Order

In contrast to key sequence, pre-order produces nodes based on their position within the hierarchy. It does this by following the tree in the same order, but processing contents as soon as it enters a node rather than waiting until it returns to the node from its left-hand children. Consequently it processes the contents of the present node, then all its children to the left, then all those to the right. This is simply a matter of resequencing the statements, as Listing 19.4 shows.

A common use of pre-order traversal is to save a tree in a disk file so that it can be reconstructed later with the same hierarchy, and that's how we use it here. Needless to say, the file must already be open and ready to receive data before calling the function for the first time.

Listing 19.4 **Function to save a tree in hierarchical order.**

```
void preOrder (FILE *file, PARTNODE *node)
{                                         /* save file in tree order */

  if (node != NULL) {
    fprintf (file, "%s\n%s\n", node->part.nbr,
      node->part.name);                        /* write to file */
    preOrder (file, node->LLink);              /* now go left */
    preOrder (file, node->RLink);           /* and then right */
  }
} /* ----------------------- */
```

Post-Order

Post-order defers action on a given node until it has visited all the children both left and right. Thus it doesn't do anything with the current node until it's ready to return to the parent. As with pre-order, this is a matter of changing the sequence of statements. Here we put the work-performing statement after the two recursive calls.

Listing 19.5 performs the task most commonly associated with post-order traversal: removing an entire binary tree from the heap and freeing the space. If this is not clean-up work at the end of a program run, it's advisable to reinitialize the root pointer so that you can't later use it to barge into corrupted space and cause the program to go haywire. The sequence

```
postOrder (root);
root  =  NULL;
```

effectively disarms the root pointer.

Listing 19.5 **Function to delete an entire tree from memory.**

```
void postOrder (PARTNODE *node)
{                                         /* deletes tree from heap */
  if (node != NULL) {
    postOrder (node->LLink);                  /* do all to left */
    postOrder (node->RLink);               /* then all to right */
    free (node);                        /* then free this node */
  }
} /* ----------------------- */
```

Sample Application _____

It's time to tie together the discussion with a working program that is the first of a pair implementing binary trees. This program (MAKETREE.C in Listing 19.6) does the following:

1. Captures data from the keyboard and builds a binary tree from it.
2. When data entry is done (hit Enter instead of typing a part number), lists the nodes in key order.
3. Writes the data in hierarchical order to a disk file named BINARY.TRE.

The subsequent program (DELNODES.C in Listing 19.8) will fetch the data from disk, rebuild the tree, and let you search for and delete selected nodes by key.

Here are the records I entered into the database:

3730	Aquarium tank
3026	Gravel
5955	Floating thermometer
6359	Aquarium pump
3330	Air distributor
5563	Tank cover
2630	Underwater filter

Listing 19.6 **Sample program to create, list, and save a tree.**

```
/* MAKETREE.C: Builds a binary tree, lists it, and saves   */
/*             to a file                                    */
/* ------------------------------------------------------- */
/* INCLUDES */
#include <stdio.h>
#include <io.h>
#include <fcntl.h>
#include <string.h>
#include <malloc.h>
#include <conio.h>
#include <graph.h>

/* CONSTANTS */
#define EJECT    12                    /* printer page eject */
#define KEYLEN    6                    /* length of key string */
#define NAMELEN  21                    /* length of descr field */
#define TREEFILE "BINARY.TRE"          /* output filename */

/* TYPES */
#pragma pack(1)
typedef struct {                                    /* substructure */
  char       nbr [KEYLEN];   /* part #, key field for node */
  char       name [NAMELEN];          /* part description */
} DATAPART;
typedef struct partnode {            tree node definition */
  DATAPART         part;
  struct partnode  *LLink, *RLink;
} PARTNODE;

/* LOCAL FUNCTION PROTOTYPES */
```

```
        PARTNODE *newnode (char *arg, char *name,
                           PARTNODE *parent, PARTNODE *node);
        void inOrder (FILE *dev, PARTNODE *node);
        void preOrder (FILE *file, PARTNODE *node);
        void postOrder (PARTNODE *node);

        /* -------------------------- */

        void main ()
        {
        PARTNODE   *root = NULL;
        char       number [KEYLEN];
        char       name [NAMELEN];
        FILE       *output = stdout; /* change to stdprn for paper */

        /* GET DATA AND BUILD LIST */
          _clearscreen(_GCLEARSCREEN);
          do {
            puts ("\n---------------------------------------\n");
            printf ("Part number? (ENTER to end data entry) ");
            gets (number);
            if (strlen (number) > 0) {
              printf ("\nPart description? ");
              gets (name );
              if (root == NULL)
                root = newnode (number, name, root, root);
              else                                /* ignore result */
                newnode (number, name, root, root);
            }
          } while (strlen (number) > 0);

        /* PRINT OUT ALL NODES IN ORDER BY KEY */
          fputs ("\r\nAll nodes in key order:", output);
          inOrder (output, root);              /* list tree in order */
          if (output == stdprn)
            fputc (EJECT, output);           /* eject page if printer */

        /* SAVE TREE IN HIERARCHICAL ORDER IN DISK FILE */
          output = fopen (TREEFILE, "w");              /* open file */
          preOrder (output, root);                     /* save tree */
          fclose (output);                             /* close file */

        /* DELETE TREE FROM HEAP */
          postOrder (root);
          root = NULL;
        } /* ---------------------- */

        PARTNODE *newnode (char *arg, char *name,
                           PARTNODE *parent, PARTNODE *node)
        {                                   /* insert new node into tree */

          if (node)              /* find location for node in tree */
```

Listing 19.6 *(continued)*

```
      if (strnicmp (arg, node->part.nbr, KEYLEN) < 0)
        node = newnode (arg, name, node, node->LLink);
      else
        node = newnode (arg, name, node, node->RLink);
    else {                          /* new leaf's position found */
      node = malloc (sizeof (PARTNODE));
      node->LLink = NULL;           /* leaf ptrs are always NULL */
      node->RLink = NULL;
      strncpy (node->part.nbr, arg, KEYLEN);   /* init leaf */
      strncpy (node->part.name, name, NAMELEN);
      if (parent)
        if (strnicmp (arg, parent->part.nbr, KEYLEN) < 0)
          parent->LLink = (PARTNODE *) node;
        else
          parent->RLink = (PARTNODE *) node;
    }
    return (node);
} /* ----------------------- */

void inOrder (FILE *dev, PARTNODE *node)
{                                   /* print tree in sorted order */

  if (node != NULL) {
    inOrder (dev, node->LLink);          /* keep going left */
    fprintf (dev, "\r\n%.6s    %s",          /* output data */
        node->part.nbr, node->part.name);
    inOrder (dev, node->RLink);           /* now go right */
  }
} /* ----------------------- */

void preOrder (FILE *file, PARTNODE *node)
{                                   /* save file in tree order */

  if (node != NULL) {
    fprintf (file, "%s\n%s\n", node->part.nbr,
      node->part.name);                     /* write to file */
    preOrder (file, node->LLink);           /* now go left */
    preOrder (file, node->RLink);          /* and then right */
  }
} /* ----------------------- */

void postOrder (PARTNODE *node)
{                                   /* deletes tree from heap */
  if (node != NULL) {
    postOrder (node->LLink);               /* do all to left */
    postOrder (node->RLink);              /* then all to right */
    free (node);                        /* then free this node */
  }
} /* ----------------------- */
```

Searching A Binary Tree

A search commences at the root and proceeds to successively lower levels in the tree, following branches until it either finds a match or doesn't. The sought key doesn't exist when further searching is blocked by a **NULL** pointer. Because movement is strictly downward, searching isn't a recursive process.

Comparison is the basis for searching. In every node there are three possible outcomes:

Argument $=$ key	Successful	
Argument $<$ key	Go left	
Argument $>$ key	Go right	

A fourth is no match, detected by a **NULL** pointer blocking the way.

There is no point in searching unless you do something as a result. If a match exists, you output the data, plug a field into a computation, or take some other action. The search function should consequently return a pointer to the matching node, or **NULL** if there is no match. That way you can use the returned pointer to access the matching node or undertake recovery action, whichever is appropriate.

You might use this function (**search**() in Listing 19.7) as follows:

```
gets (key);
this = search (key, root);
if (this == NULL)
    /* not found */
else
    /* it was found */
```

Listing 19.7 **Searching a binary tree.**

```
PARTNODE *search (char *arg, PARTNODE *node)
{                                  /* find matching node */
  while (strnicmp (arg, node->part.nbr, KEYLEN) != 0)
    if (node == NULL)
      return (NULL);
    else
      node = (strnicmp (arg, node->part.nbr, KEYLEN) < 0) ?
             node->LLink : node->RLink;
  return (node->active ? node : NULL);
} /* ---------------------- */
```

Deleting a Binary Tree Node _____

Algorithms exist for deleting nodes from binary trees. One of the most common is to "promote" the nearest-valued leaf to replace a deleted parent. The problem is that such algorithms must be able to rearrange the entire tree if necessary, and that entails great complexity.

A simpler solution, given here, is to flag a deleted node and thereafter simply ignore its data content in output operations. This doesn't actually remove the node, of course, but it gives you an indicator to test. The node's key is still available for traversal comparisons.

You can do this by adding the field

```
char     active;
```

to the node structure and initializing it as TRUE. Later, to effectively delete the node, you change the field to FALSE. Functions such as inOrder() can test it, as in

```
if  (node − >active)
    printf  (.  .  .);
```

and find out whether to list the node's content or not. Similarly, the exit statement of the search() function can be written as

```
return  (node − >active  ?  node  :  NULL);
```

which returns a pointer to the found node if it's active and NULL if marked as deleted.

This solution has the disadvantage that it adds overhead to tree traversals and searches. The overhead, however, is trivial compared with the saving in complexity obtained by using a simple method for deleting nodes.

Moreover, you can use the deleted nodes to construct an audit trail at the end of processing, producing a report that shows which items were deleted from the database. An audit trail is often mandatory in tightly controlled applications such as finance. The audit trail routine simply reverses the check in inOrder(), printing deleted nodes and ignoring those still active with the test

```
if  (!(node − >active))
    printf  (.  .  .);
```

Now let's see how this discussion of searching and deleting tree nodes fits into a working program.

Sample Application, Part Two _____

This application continues the exercise begun above with Listing 19.6. There we created and saved a data base in disk file **BINARY.TRE**. Now we'll read that file back into a binary tree and list the contents by key order, then do selective deletions of entries.

The program contains a function **stripnl()** to overcome a problem introduced by **preOrder()** in Listing 19.6, which wrote the file. It uses **fprintf()** to embed newline characters ("\n") in the text. The objective is to make it easy to distinguish individual strings when reading **BINARY.TRE**. The problem is that **fgets()** retains these newlines, and since they weren't present in the original data, we have to take them out. The **stripnl()** function does this by replacing the newline with a null terminator, or setting the last valid character position to null if the data completely fill the available space, thus preventing a runaway string on output.

Using **DELNODES.C** in Figure 19.8, you can select a key to delete by answering the questions on the display. The program always precedes the Q&A session by displaying all non-deleted nodes on the basis of the **node →active** field's status. Before doing the deletion, the program finds the node and verifies that it's the item you want to delete; answer with Y or N. The program also tells you if you've typed a key that doesn't exist or that has been deleted, which are effectively the same thing.

This process continues until you press Enter without any preceding data in response to the request for a key to delete. The program then displays an audit list of deleted items and quits. It does not save the changes in **BINARY.TRE**; if you want it to, add a **preOrder()** routine that checks the status of **node →active** before writing the data back to the file.

Listing 19.8 Sample program to find and delete nodes in a binary tree.

```
/* DELNODES.C: Search and delete nodes from binary tree */

/* INCLUDES */
#include <stdio.h>
#include <string.h>
#include <conio.h>
#include <ctype.h>
#include <malloc.h>

/* CONSTANTS */
#define EJECT    12                      /* printer page eject */
#define KEYLEN    6                    /* length of key string */
#define NAMELEN  22                   /* length of descr field */
#define FNAME    "BINARY.TRE"            /* input filename */
#define BAR      "\n--------------------------------"
#ifndef TRUE
#define FALSE    0
#define TRUE     !FALSE
```

Listing 19.9 *(continued)*

```
#endif

/* TYPES */
#pragma pack(1)
typedef struct {                     /* substructure for data */
  char    nbr[KEYLEN];        /* part #, key field for node */
  char    name[NAMELEN];               /* part description */
} DATAPART;

typedef struct partnode {          /* tree node definition */
  DATAPART        part;
  struct partnode *LLink, *RLink;
  char            active;
} PARTNODE;

/* LOCAL FUNCTION PROTOTYPES */
PARTNODE  *newnode (char *arg, char *name,
                    PARTNODE *parent, PARTNODE *node);
void inOrder (PARTNODE *node);
void auditTrail (PARTNODE *node, FILE *device);
PARTNODE *search (char *arg, PARTNODE *node);
void delete (PARTNODE *node);
void stripnl (char *str, int maxlen);
/* ------------------------- */

void main ()
{
FILE      *file;                                    /* input file */
PARTNODE *root = NULL, *this;    /* pointers to tree nodes */
char      key[KEYLEN];                           /* input key */
char      name[NAMELEN];                   /* part descriptor */
char      reply;                        /* keyboard interaction */
FILE      *audit = stdout;   /* change to stdprn for paper */

/* OPEN INPUT FILE AND BUILD TREE */
  if ((file = fopen (FNAME, "r")) == NULL) {
    printf ("\nUnable to open input file %s", FNAME);
    exit (-1);
  }
  do {                                    /* until eof... */
    fgets (key, KEYLEN, file);         /* get part number */
    if (!feof (file)) {
      stripnl (key, KEYLEN);               /* remove newline */
      fgets (name, NAMELEN, file);       /* get part name */
      stripnl (name, NAMELEN);           /* remove newline */
      if (root == NULL)                       /* start tree */
        root = newnode (key, name, root, root);
      else                               /* else add to it */
        this = newnode (key, name, root, root );
    }
  } while (!feof (file));
```

```
      fclose (file);                    /* then close input file */

  /* SEARCH AND DELETE SELECTED NODES */
    do {
      puts (BAR);
      puts ("Items currently in tree:");
      inOrder (root);                        /* list entire tree */
      putchar ('\n');
      puts ("Key of item to delete? (Enter if done) ");
      gets (key);
      if (strlen (key) != 0) {
        this = search (key, root);     /* find match in tree */
        if (this == NULL) {
          puts ("\nItem not found");
          puts ("\nPress any key to continue... ");
          getch ();
        } else {
          printf ("\nItem name is %s\n", this->part.name);
          cputs ("Delete this item? (y/n) ");
          reply = getche();
          reply = toupper (reply);
          if (reply == 'Y')
            delete (this);
        }
      }
    } while (strlen (key) != 0);

  /* PRODUCE AUDIT TRAIL */
    fputs (BAR, audit);
    fputs (
        "\r\nAudit trail: Following items removed from tree:",
        audit);
    auditTrail (root, audit);
    if (audit == stdprn)
      fputc (EJECT, audit);
    putchar ('\n');
  } /* ------------------------ */


PARTNODE *newnode (char *arg, char *name,
                   PARTNODE *parent, PARTNODE *node)
{                                 /* insert new node into tree */
  if (node)               /* find location for node in tree */
    if (strnicmp (arg, node->part.nbr, KEYLEN) < 0)
      node = newnode (arg, name, node, node->LLink);
    else
      node = newnode (arg, name, node, node->RLink);
  else {                          /* new leaf's position found */
    node = malloc (sizeof (PARTNODE));
    node->LLink = node->RLink = NULL;     /* leaf pts NULL */
    node->active = TRUE;               /* mark node as active */
    strncpy (node->part.nbr, arg, KEYLEN);   /* init leaf */
    strncpy (node->part.name, name, NAMELEN);
    if (parent)
```

Listing 19.9 *(continued)*

```
        if (strnicmp (arg, parent->part.nbr, KEYLEN) < 0)
          parent->LLink = (PARTNODE*) node;
        else
          parent->RLink = (PARTNODE*) node;
    }
  return (node);
} /* ----------------------- */

void inOrder (PARTNODE *node)
{       /* output list of non-deleted nodes in key order */
  if (node != NULL) {
    inOrder (node->LLink);
    if (node->active)
      printf ("\n%.6s       %s", node->part.nbr,
              node->part.name);
    inOrder (node->RLink);
  }
} /* ----------------------- */

void auditTrail (PARTNODE *node, FILE *device)
{            /* output list of deleted nodes in key order */
  if (node != NULL) {
    auditTrail (node->LLink, device);
    if (!(node->active))
      fprintf (device, "\r\n%.6s       %s", node->part.nbr,
              node->part.name);
    auditTrail (node->RLink, device);
  }
} /* ----------------------- */

PARTNODE *search (char *arg, PARTNODE *node)
{                                    /* find matching node */
  while (strnicmp (arg, node->part.nbr, KEYLEN) != 0)
    if (node == NULL)
      return (NULL);
    else
      node = (strnicmp (arg, node->part.nbr, KEYLEN) < 0) ?
              node->LLink : node->RLink;
  return (node->active ? node : NULL);
} /* ----------------------- */

void delete (PARTNODE *node)      /* mark node as deleted */
{
  node->active = FALSE;
} /* ----------------------- */

void stripnl (char *str, int maxlen)    /* remove newline */
{
int   length;

  length = strlen (str);
```

```
   if (length > maxlen)
     str [maxlen] = '\0';
   else
     str [length-1] = '\0';
}  /* ----------------------- */
```

Binary trees provide a sophisticated technique for ordering large amounts of data and performing lightning-fast searches. Recursion simplifies the complexity of traversals in hierarchical structures. While less intuitive than lists, reasonably balanced trees deliver many times the performance, and have the added benefit that they automatically sort the data into order by key.

Now let's wrap up our coverage of dynamic data structures by considering lists in which the nodes are of inconsistent sizes.

CHAPTER 20

Irregular Dynamic Data Structures

The preceding chapters have given the impression that dynamic data structures must always consist of nodes that have a uniform size. In fact that's not so, but for the sake of understanding we've let the impression stand. Now that you're well indoctrinated in handling lists and trees, we can deal with one of the realities of software, which is that requirements seldom pay much attention to tidy rules.

There are numerous situations in which dynamic structures must have the flexibility to deal with variable-length data. A typical example, which we'll use as the case study in this chapter, is a queue. What might we place in a queue? Anything from individual characters typed at the keyboard up to data streams of several hundred or even several thousand bytes arriving from disk or over a serial port. A queue, you'll recall from Chapter 18, is a place where we stick things that we want to put off until later. Therefore, almost by definition, a queue is a list of data objects whose sizes are infinitely variable and cannot possibly be anticipated in advance.

There are other examples. For example, DOS itself manages all of the computer's transient memory—the space where programs and their associated data areas live—as a giant singly linked list whose nodes vary in size. For a discussion, see *Advanced MS-DOS* by Ray Duncan, Microsoft Press, Redmond, WA, pp. 179–181. This approach differs from the one discussed here, but it bears study if you're interested in investigating the subject further.

The method we present in this chapter involves two dynamic structures. One is a queue consisting of predefined nodes that manages undefined—i.e., variable-length—nodes also located on the heap. Each fixed-length "directory" node points to the variable-length data node it controls. The two node types are physically mingled on the heap, but because the entire structure relies on pointers, we don't care where the actual nodes are located in memory.

370

Figure 20.1 **Visualization of a directory node.**

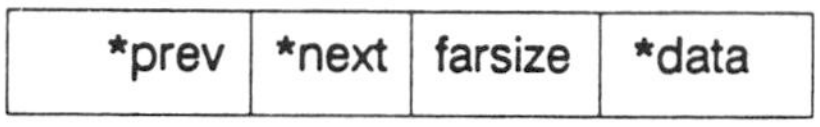

*prev	*next	farsize	*data

The Big Picture

We're going to queue keyboard entries for deferred processing. The keyboard entries arrive at random times, go into the queue, and are pulled from it at your convenience to be printed in the order entered. The random times occur whenever you choose to respond to a query from the program. The variability is the number of characters you key, which can be from one to 80 characters. The deferred processing is a listing of the strings, which appears whenever you press Enter (without typing any data) in response to a query. A simple application, perhaps, but one whose elements are readily understandable, and which you can adapt to your own more complex requirements.

Each time you finish typing a line of text at the keyboard, two objects come into existence. The first is the fixed-length directory node whose constituent parts appear in Figure 20.1. This node goes into a circular DLL managed as a queue—FIFO buffer—as the new tail. (Recall that in a queue, we always add to the tail and draw from the head.) The objective here is to create a list that is easy to manage, and fixed-length objects are always easier to deal with than those of variable length. The queue itself serves as a directory to the more complex variable-length objects.

We'll define this node template as

```
typedef struct obj {
     struct obj   *prev, *next;
     unsigned     strsize;
     char         *data;
} OBJ;
```

The prev and next fields are pointers to other nodes of the same format, and used customarily in the management of the circular DLL. The strsize field gives the number of bytes—up to 64K—in the data string, and the data field is a pointer to the string itself.

Figure 20.2 **Relationships of the two dynamic structures.**

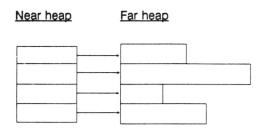

The data string is, of course, the variable-length object, whose sheer cuss-edness demands that we go to these lengths to manage it.

When you've entered several strings and enqueued them using this approach, you might have a directory/data combination that looks something like Figure 20.2.

Each fixed-length directory entry points to a variable-length object in one-to-one correspondence. Because the program uses the directory entries to manage the variable-length objects, it need only refer to the involved directory node. The purpose of using a separate directory is, after all, to simplify management of the variable-length data elements.

Building the List Structures

Here is the algorithm for constructing the two parallel data structures, expressed in pseudocode:

```
repeat
    get data from keyboard;
    if datalength > 0
    begin
        put new directory node in queue;
        update queue head pointer if first node;
        store size of data in directory node;
        allocate data object;
        store pointer in directory node;
        copy input data to data object;
    endif;
while datalength > 0;
```

Listing 20.1 expresses this high-level algorithm in C notation.

Listing 20.1 **Creating the parallel structures.**

```
do {
  puts ("\n\nEnter a string (Enter to quit)");
  gets (string);
  if ((datasize = strlen (string)) != 0) {
    new = enqueue (queue, datasize, string); /* allocate */
    if (queue == NULL)               /* set queue if first */
      queue = new;
    printf ("\n   Fixed-length node is at %p", new);
    printf ("\n   String node is at  %p", new->data);
    printf ("\n   Copied %d characters to string node",
      new->strsize);
  }
} while (datasize > 0);
```

The **enqueue()** function holds no surprises; it's like enqueue operations we've seen in Chapter 18, with the exception that it sets up the new tail node with the datasize argument and creates the variable-sized data node.

Listing the Queue

After several keyboard entries, you'll have a directory-to-data relationship something like Figure 20.2. That is, the heap contains a circular DLL consisting of a number of fixed-length directory nodes, each controlling a corresponding variable-length data node. Continued construction of these two related lists ends when you press Enter in response to a prompt from the keyboard.

At that point, deferred processing occurs in the form of listing the strings you've entered in chronological—i.e., FIFO—order. In pseudocode, this algorithm is

```
while queue is not empty do
begin
    print the next data string from the queue;
    remove head of queue;
    update queue pointer;
enddo;
```

This is implemented under the heading **DATA OUTPUT SECTION** in Listing 20.2 (**VARLIST.C**), which illustrates how an ordinary linked list can manage the more complex aspects of implicitly unordered, variable-length data.

Listing 20.2 **Mixing dynamic structures on the heap.**

```
/* VARLIST.C: Dynamic data structs with variable-sized nodes */

/* INCLUDES */
#include <stdio.h>
#include <malloc.h>
#include <dos.h>
#include <string.h>

/* TYPES */
typedef struct obj {
  struct obj *prev, *next;              /* local node pointers */
  unsigned   strsize;                   /* size of string object */
  char       *data;                     /* pointer to string object */
} OBJ;                                  /* directory object definition */

/* LOCAL FUNCTION PROTOTYPES */
OBJ *enqueue (OBJ*, int, char*);
void allocstr (OBJ*);
void copy2far (OBJ*, char*);
void copy2near (OBJ*, char*);
void shownext (OBJ*);
OBJ *drain (OBJ*);
/* ------------------------------------------------------------ */


void main ()
{
char string[80];                        /* string I/O variable */
int  datasize;                          /* size of input string */
OBJ  *queue = NULL, *new;               /* ptrs to directory objects */

/* DATA ENTRY SECTION */
  do {
    puts ("\n\nEnter a string (Enter to quit)");
    gets (string);
    if ((datasize = strlen (string)) != 0) {
      new = enqueue (queue, datasize, string);      /* allocate */
      if (queue == NULL)                   /* set queue if first */
        queue = new;
      printf ("\n   Fixed-length node is at %p", new);
      printf ("\n   String node is at  %p", new->data);
      printf ("\n   Copied %d characters to string node",
          new->strsize);
    }
  } while (datasize > 0);

/* DATA OUTPUT SECTION */
  puts ("\n\n\nStrings in order typed:");
```

```
      while (queue) {                         /* while queue is not empty.. */
        printf ("\n%s", queue->data);                    /* show next item */
        queue = drain (queue);                     /* remove head of queue */
      }
      puts ("\n\n");
    } /* ------------------------ */


OBJ *enqueue (OBJ *q, int strsize, char *str)
{                                 /* place new directory entry in queue */
OBJ *this;

      this = malloc (sizeof (OBJ));                            /* allocate */
      if (q == NULL)                              /* if first in queue */
        this->prev = this->next = this;           /* points to itself */
      else {                                      /* insert as new tail */
        this->prev = q->prev;                     /* in circular queue */
        this->next = this->prev->next;
        this->prev->next = this->next->prev = this;
      }
      this->strsize = strsize + 1;         /* add one for null termin */
      this->data = malloc (this->strsize);       /* get string space */
      strcpy (this->data, str);                  /* copy string to it */
      return (this);
    } /* ------------------------ */


OBJ *drain (OBJ *q)                          /* remove head of queue */
{
OBJ  *next;

      free (q->data);                     •        /* release string space */
      if (q == q->next) {                       /* if last entry in queue... */
        free (q);
        return (NULL);
      } else {                                  /* remove node from head */
        q->next->prev = q->prev;
        next = q->prev->next = q->next;
        free (q);
        return (next);                          /* return next node */
      }
    } /* ------------------------ */
```

Conclusion _____

This part of the book has covered a number of techniques for dealing with
unpredictable quantities and sizes of data using dynamic data structures. The

purpose has not been to provide exhaustive coverage, but rather to lay a solid foundation on which you can build with informed experience.

We've come a long way in these 20 chapters. The final part of the book covers several advanced aspects of MS-DOS programming.

PART V

Using the DOS Environment in Quick C

MS-DOS/PC-DOS, the disk operating system of the IBM PC and equivalents, furnishes a number of services to application programs. We've already used many of them: dynamic allocation, the DTA, low-level calls using int86(). Indeed, most of the standard library functions are merely DOS services "sugar-coated" in C syntax.

This final part of the book deals with some of the more complex and exotic features that DOS programmers can use. After covering some background material—useful and interesting in its own right—we'll delve into matters such as interrupts, calling other programs from within a Quick C application, and using EMS.

The techniques given here, coupled with those already covered, will enable you to write powerful advanced software.

CHAPTER 21

Understanding .EXE
Files

T he machine language programs produced by Quick C are in .EXE format, one of the two kinds of executable files under DOS. An understanding of the .EXE format is essential to the rest of the material in this book, so this chapter explains how they work.

As you're well aware, the primary way to start a program in DOS is to type its name at the command level. You may not be aware of what DOS does to execute that command, or of the important role played by a system-level data structure called the *Program Segment Prefix*.

How DOS Loads Command Files

Three types of files, in addition to the **COMMAND.COM** shell, contain DOS commands: .BAT, .COM, and .EXE. DOS handles each one differently, and follows a present sequence in attempting to process the command.

Let's say you type the command

    SKLRGX

in response to the system prompt (normally **C:** on a machine with a hard disk). Command lines are inputs to the command interpreter shell **COM-MAND.COM**, which gets loaded as a memory-resident program whenever the machine boots. **SKLRGX** is not a built-in command, so the shell, having determined this, begins a series of activities to locate a disk file whose base name is **SKLRGX**. The disk search begins in the current directory, and goes in order through all other directories specified by the most recent **PATH** command.

The shell first searches for **SKLRGX.COM**. A .COM file is the memory image of an executable program in machine language. That is, a .COM file can be loaded anywhere in memory and executed without further modification (subject to a bit of setup described later). A .COM file is somewhat limited: Its code and data segments cannot exceed 64K apiece, and there are other constraints as well. It's intended chiefly for small programs such as DOS utilities.

Failing to locate SKLRGX.COM, the shell next searches for SKLRGX.EXE. Like a .COM, an .EXE file (usually pronounced "eksey") contains executable machine language, but in a different form. DOS has to do more work to load and start an .EXE file; more on this later. The size of an .EXE file's data and code segments can equal all of memory, which makes it suitable for large software systems.

If neither SKLRGX.COM nor SKLRGX.EXE exists along the search path, DOS looks for SKLRGX.BAT. A .BAT file is not directly executable, but instead contains one or more commands to be processed in sequence. It is thus a "batch" file, and the shell performs the actions it specifies as though each command had been typed at the DOS prompt.

When all searches prove fruitless, the shell responds with the familiar message

```
Bad command or file name
```

which means, "I give up."

The shell works directly with the contents of .BAT files, treating each entry as though it had just been typed from the keyboard (with the exception that it fills in numerically sequenced placeholders such as %1 and %2 with corresponding command-line arguments). For .COM and .EXE files, the shell builds the environment block, loads the contents into memory starting at the next available segment, and fills in the Program Segment Prefix, a data structure accompanying each executable program.

DOS also performs some other setup steps For .EXE files. The linker embeds instructions in the .EXE file's header record (described later) so that the DOS program loader knows what to do. Chiefly, this entails resolving addresses using a process called *segment fix-ups*. A single chunk of executable code cannot exceed 64K in size, so a large .EXE file contains several such chunks. The DOS program loader pulls the chunks apart and aligns each one on the next segment (16-byte paragraph) boundary. Using data in the header record, the loader also resolves the addresses of far pointers in the code so that they become absolute segment/ offset memory references, sets the heap and stack locations, and performs other setup tasks required by a complex program.

The Program Segment Prefix (PSP), common to both .COM and .EXE files, contains information that either DOS or the program itself needs. DOS fills it in as it loads the program, then passes control to the program's entry point and starts it running. When the program terminates, DOS uses information from the PSP to restore the environment.

Contents of the PSP

The PSP is a 256-byte reserved area with a fixed format. In general, the first 92 (5Ch) bytes are inviolable; you can read them, but don't change anything lest you crash the machine. The remaining 164 bytes might or might not contain useful information. They contain two default file control blocks (not used by Quick C programs) and the command line. Programmers sometimes use this area, whose location is known via the PSP pointer, to pass data between processes that have no common data space.

So what's in those first 92 bytes? The following is a list of the officially documented contents by hex offset:

Offset:	Contains:
00–01	Int 20h, DOS call for program termination. Of no practical value to Quick C programs.
02–03	Segment address of the end of available memory.
04	Reserved byte
05–09	Long call to Int 21h, the primary entry to the DOS functions. Of no value to Quick C programs.
0A–0D	Address of the routine to get control when this program terminates, taken from the vector for Int 22h. Normally this is a **COMMAND.COM** routine, but a program can stuff its own routine in the vector, then start ("spawn") another program. This field in the spawned program's PSP contains the address of the first program's routine, which will gain control when the spawned process completes. When the original program completes, DOS grabs this value and stuffs it back into the interrupt vector so that control reverts to the next-higher level's termination routine.
0E–11	Address of the Ctrl-Break routine in use before this program began, obtained from the vector for Int 23h. A program can set its own Ctrl-Break routine, so DOS uses this value to make sure the vector is properly restored on exit.
12–15	Address of the critical error handler in use before this program began, obtained from the vector for Int 24h.
16–2B	Reserved for DOS.
2C–2D	Segment address of the environment block. Chapters 22 and 23 cover the environment block.
2E–5B	Reserved for DOS.
5C–6B	A file control block for the first file specified on the command line (empty if none). Quick C doesn't use this FCB, so the memory is available for your program to use, if necessary.
6C–7F	File control block for the second file specified on the command line. As above.
80	Length in bytes of the command line arguments, if any.
81–FF	Command line arguments, if any. (80-FF are also shown in some DOS references as the default DTA. Quick C programs allocate their own DTA.) You can use C's standard **argc/argv[]** method to fetch command line arguments (also called the "command tail") out of this area more conveniently than by accessing the PSP directly.

Listing 21.1 contains a C structure defining the PSP, which you can place in a file **PSP.H.**

Listing 21.1 **Program segment prefix structure.**

```
/* PSP.H: Defines the program segment prefix structure */

#pragma pack(1)
typedef struct {
    unsigned  int20h,               /* pgm term call (no value) */
              topofmem;             /* segment of top of memory */
    char      res1,                       /* reserved by DOS */
              int21h [5];               /* no value in Quick C */
    long      oldtermvec,     /* old int 22h interrupt vector */
              oldcbvec,          /* old Ctrl-Break int vector */
              oldcritvec;   /* old critical error int vector */
    char      res2 [22];                    /* reserved area */
    unsigned  envblock;      /* segment of environment block */
    char      res3 [46],                    /* reserved area */
              avail [36],       /* FCB's: open memory */
              cmdtaillen,         /* length of command tail */
              cmdtail [127];          /* command tail text */
} PSPSTRUC;
```

Getting the Address of the PSP

There are two methods for obtaining the PSP's address. Quick C's **STDLIB.H** file defines the global variable **_psp**, which automatically acquires the PSP segment address when your application starts running. The PSP is always at offset 0 within its segment, so you can construct a far pointer to it with a statement such as

> mypsp = MK_FP (_psp, 0);

This method requires inclusion of the **MK_FP.H** file presented in Chapter 6.

DOS 3.0 and above furnish function 62h under Int 21h, which returns the PSP's segment address as an unsigned integer in Register BX. This is more work than referring to the **_psp** variable without any additional payoff, so there's no point in Quick C programmers using the DOS call.

Listing 21.2 is a program that reads a few items of interest from its own PSP and lists them on the display.

Listing 21.2 **Fetching information from the PSP.**

```
/* PSP.C: Displays information from the PSP */

#include <stdio.h>
#include <stdlib.h>
#include <graph.h>
#include "mk_fp.h"
#include "psp.h"
```

Listing 21.2 *(continued)*

```
void main ()
{
PSPSTRUC far *psp;

  _clearscreen(_GCLEARSCREEN);
  psp = MK_FP (_psp, 0);
  printf ("PSP Contents for This Program:\n\n");
  printf ("Top of memory                       %04X:0000\n",
          psp->topofmem);
  printf ("Environment block                   %04X:0000\n",
          psp->envblock);
  printf ("Old int 22 vector                   %lp\n",
          (void far*) psp->oldtermvec);
  printf ("Old ctrl-break vector               %lp\n",
          (void far*) psp->oldcbvec);
  printf ("Old critical error vector           %lp\n\n",
          (void far*) psp->oldcritvec);
  printf ("PSP is located at %04X:0000\n", _psp);
}
```

Much of the interaction with the PSP occurs in connection with TSR (Terminate and Stay Resident) and spawned programs, the latter of which we discuss in Chapter 24. In other programs, the PSP's upper, uncommitted areas are useful when you need some free memory, as in saving the results of an interrupt.

Getting Information About .EXE Files

As mentioned earlier, the linker stores loading information in a complex structure at the start of the .EXE file. This structure, called the *header record*, consists of a 14-word fixed portion followed by a variable-length relocation table.

There's seldom any reason to snoop around the relocation table, but it's instructive and sometimes useful to read the fixed-length data at the start of the .EXE's header record. This record contains the following information, given hex offsets:

Offset	Content
00	.EXE file signature, always 5A4Dh. Identifies the file as an .EXE.
02	File length MOD 512: the remainder after dividing the file into 512-byte pages.
04	Number of 512-byte pages in the file, plus one.
06	Number of entries in the relocation table.
08	Number of 16-byte paragraphs in the header record.
0A	Minimum number of paragraphs required for the heap and stack.
0C	Maximum number of paragraphs desired for the heap and stack.
0E	Segment displacement of the stack module.

10	Initial setting of the Stack Pointer (SP).
12	Word **checksum**. Used internally by the loader to make sure the file is complete.
14	Initial setting of the IP register. This is the program's entry point.
16	Segment displacement of the entry point. Used to set the CS register.
18	Byte offset of the relocation table.
1A	Overlay number. Zero if this is a stand-alone program or the root of an overlay system.

The segment displacement fields give a paragraph offset from the originating segment of the program. For example, if the field at record offset 16h contains 1Ah and the loader decides to start the program space at segment 200h, then the initial setting of the CS register will be 21Ah.

Listing 21.3 lists EXEINFO.C, which inspects the header record of any .EXE file. It lists some fields directly and calculates values from others, such as the number of bytes in the header and in the module as a whole. The program accepts a filename on the command line, and if you don't furnish one, it asks for it. You must furnish the .EXE suffix when typing the filename. EXEINFO.C also checks the signature to make sure the file is an .EXE. If not, it tells you so and quits with no further action.

Listing 21.3 Listing information about an .EXE file.

```
/* EXEINFO.C: Displays contents of any .EXE header record */

#include <stdlib.h>
#include <conio.h>
#include <io.h>
#include <string.h>
#include <fcntl.h>
#include <errno.h>
#include <stdio.h>
#include <graph.h>

#define   EXESIG 0x5A4D        /* fixed .EXE file signature */

#pragma pack(1)
typedef struct {
  unsigned
    signature,                 /* Fixed at 5A4Dh for .EXE */
    modSize,                          /* size mod 512 */
    nPages,                     /* number of 512-byte pages */
    relocItems,            /* number of relocation table items */
    headerSize,           /* header size in 16-byte paragraphs */
    minHeap,               /* minimum number of paras in heap */
    maxHeap,                  /* max number of paras in heap */
    stackDispl,             /* segment displacement of stack */
    initSP,                  /* initial value of SP register */
    checksum,                /* internal checksum for module */
    entryPoint,            /* setting of IP register to begin */
    codeSeg,                    /* code segment displacement */
    relocTable,             /* offset of reloc table in file */
```

Listing 21.3 *(continued)*

```
    overlayNbr;                    /* overlay number, 0 if root */
} HEADREC;

void main (int argc, char *argv[])
{
int      handle, nbytes = sizeof (HEADREC);
char     filepath [80];
HEADREC header;

  /* Get file path from command line or console */
  _clearscreen (_GCLEARSCREEN);
  if (argc < 2) {
    puts ("\nFilename (include .EXE extension)... ");
    gets (filepath);
  } else
    strcpy (filepath, argv[1]);

  /* Open the file */
  handle = open (filepath, O_RDONLY - O_BINARY);
  if (handle == -1) {
    puts ("\n\nERROR: ");
    switch (errno) {
      case ENOENT:  puts ("Path or filename not found");
                    break;
      case EMFILE:  puts ("Too many open files"); break;
      case EACCES:  puts ("Permission denied");   break;
    }
    puts ("\nProgram terminated");
    exit (-1);
  }

  /* Get the header record */
  read (handle, (char*) &header, nbytes);

  /* Show its contents */
  if (header.signature != EXESIG) {
    printf ("\n%s is not an .EXE file", filepath);
    puts   ("\nProgram terminated");
  } else {
    printf ("\nInformation about file %s:\n", filepath);
    printf ("\nOverlay number                    %u",
      header.overlayNbr);
    printf ("\nModule size: in pages             %u",
      header.nPages);
    printf ("\n             in bytes             %lu",
      (long) ((header.nPages-1) * 512L) + header.modSize);
    printf ("\nRelocation: number of items       %u",
      header.relocItems);
    printf ("\n            table offset          %04Xh",
      header.relocTable);
    printf ("\n.EXE header: in paragraphs        %u",
```

```
        header.headerSize);
    printf ("\n                   in bytes            %lu",
        (long) (header.headerSize * 16L));
    printf ("\nHeap/stack: min paragraphs            %u",
        header.minHeap);
    printf ("\n             max paragraphs            %u",
        header.maxHeap);
    printf ("\nStack: segment displacement           %04Xh",
        header.stackDispl);
    printf ("\n         initial SP offset            %04Xh",
        header.initSP);
    printf ("\nProgram code segment displacement     %04Xh",
        header.codeSeg);
    printf ("\n             entry point offset       %04Xh",
        header.entryPoint);
    }
  putchar ('\n');
}
```

Now that we understand some of the basics of how DOS structures, loads, and controls executable programs, let's see how programs find out about their environment.

CHAPTER 22

Environment Variables

D OS has a feature that's like Rodney Dangerfield: It don't get no respect. At least not from users. But those who develop more than casual software for DOS learn to appreciate this little-known corner of the operating system. Since the purpose of this book is to lead you toward advanced programming, it's appropriate to discuss it here.

The feature is the *environment block*. It's a group of text strings buried in the operating system's memory space. These text strings are called *environment variables*, and they're used for several purposes:

- To provide running programs with general information about the system, such as the directory search path.
- To pass specific information from one program to another.
- To tell a program how its installation was configured, so that it can find its support files and learn about other selections the user made at set-up time.

The original source of environment strings is the **AUTOEXEC.BAT** file, which usually contains several commands that place information in the environment block: **SET**, **PATH**, and **PROMPT**, among others. You can also enter these commands at the DOS prompt, or issue equivalent environment-affecting calls from within a program written in Quick C.

The **AUTOEXEC.BAT** file on my computer is an example of how environment strings come into existence. It reads as follows:

```
QUIKBUF2  AT  256  E  P
PATH = \DOS;\MOUSE;\QC2\BIN;\BIN;\BRIEF;
set  bpath = ;c:\brief\macros
set  bhelp = c:\brief\help
set  bpackages = prg:r
set  bflags = -i120k1l78M57t  − mKP  − Dega
mouse  2
menu
click
```

```
dos_edit
prompt $p$g
ng\ng
```

Some of these statements start up memory-resident programs: **QUIKBUF2** (an EMS-based print spooler), **MOUSE**, **MENU**, and **CLICK** (supporting the Logitech Mouse), **DOS_EDIT** (a public-domain DOS shell), and **NG** (the Norton Guides). The rest set environment variables.

I can list the contents of my environment block by typing the **SET** command and pressing Enter. Here's what I get:

```
COMSPEC=C:\COMMAND.COM
PATH=\DOS;\MOUSE;\QC2\BIN;\BIN;\BRIEF;
BPATH=;c:\brief\macros
BHELP=c:\brief\help
BPACKAGES=prg:r
BFLAGS=-i120k1l78M57t  −mKP  −Dega
PROMPT=$p$g
```

The **COMSPEC** variable gives the path to the command interpreter (usually **COMMAND.COM**). It's automatically set by DOS at start-up. All the rest are the results of statements in **AUTOEXEC.BAT**, a command file that DOS processes whenever I power up or reset the machine. **PATH** gives the sequence of directories that DOS searches when I type a command that isn't in the current directory. **PROMPT** determines the appearance of the DOS prompt; **pg** tells DOS to display the current directory path. For example, while writing this book I usually see the prompt

```
C:\QC2\QCBOOK>
```

The rest of the environment strings pass specific information to applications.

In particular, note **BHELP** and **BFLAGS**. Both pertain to **BRIEF**, a program editor. **BHELP** tells **BRIEF** where to find the **HELP** files. **BFLAGS** looks like gibberish, but it tells **BRIEF** which installation options I've selected. The point is that environment variables are to be used by programs, not by people.

This example illustrates the format of environment variables, which is

```
NAME  =  <variable information as text>
```

The name of each string must be unique. If you want to add a new variable to the environment, it has to have a name that doesn't already exist. Reusing a variable name has the same effect as in a program. For example, say you type

```
SET BFLAGS = xyz
```

and later on you start **BRIEF**. It won't recognize the text string, which is now "xyz," so the installation options you selected are no longer operative since the original setting of **BFLAGS** has been replaced.

STDLIB.H defines the global variable environ, which gives the segment of the program's environment block. Its value is the same as the corresponding entry in the PSP. The environment block always begins at offset 0 within its segment. The environ variable is of little use to programs, however, since we're usually interested in specific strings within the block, and Quick C provides two functions for operating on them.

Getting Environment Variables

The getenv() function searches the environment for a specific variable name. Its argument is a string containing the environment variable name you want to look for. Wildcard characters such as "*" are not valid, so you have to be specific. getenv() returns a pointer to the environment string matching the argument, or **NULL** if the environment block doesn't contain a variable so named.

GETPATH.C in Listing 22.1 illustrates the use of getenv() in searching the environment for the string set by the DOS **PATH** command.

Listing 22.1 **Getting the** PATH **environment string.**

```
/* GETPATH.C: Fetch PATH from environment */

#include <stdio.h>
#include <stdlib.h>

void main()
{
char *path;

  if ((path = getenv ("PATH")) != NULL)
    puts (path);
  else
    puts ("No PATH in your environment");
}
```

On my system, the program's output is

       \DOS;\MOUSE;\QC2\BIN;\BIN;\BRIEF;

which corresponds to the **PATH** command in **AUTOEXEC.BAT**. If I type **PATH** at the DOS prompt level, I get a similar response, except that it's prefixed by "**PATH**=." The Quick C function assumes that you knew what variable name you were looking for when you issued **getenv()**, and so doesn't feed it back in the response.

The search path contains a couple of symbols that have special meanings. The backslash (\) means "another directory," while the semicolon says "stop here and go back to the root." The root is the main directory of the disk; it's where you go when you type

    CD\

Thus, the sequence "\DOS;\MOUSE" means "look in the \DOS directory and if you don't find it there, go back to the root and then to the \MOUSE directory."

Adding a String to the Environment _____

The **putenv()** function is the opposite of **getenv()**; it adds a new string to the environment, and it can also modify or delete an existing environment variable. Its argument is a string containing the variable's complete text in the form

    VNAME = text

For example,

    putenv ("HOMEDIR = \\APPS");

sets the environment variable as shown (the double backslash resolves to a single character). If you decide to delete this variable later, you can issue the statement

    putenv ("HOMEDIR =");

This removes all reference to **HOMEDIR** from the current environment.

putenv() returns 0 if successful and −1 if not. The main reasons for failure are an improperly formatted string (no equals sign) and running out of environment space.

Listing 22.2 lists **CHENV.C**, which illustrates manipulation of an environment variable called **TEST_STRING**. The program declines to run if **TEST_STRING** is a legitimate environment variable. Otherwise, it sets up a string by this name with **putenv()**, fetches it with **getenv()**, changes it to something else with another **putenv()** and fetches the new string, and finally deletes it from the environment. At each stage, it reports what it's done.

Listing 22.2 **Manipulating an environment string.**

```c
/* CHENV.C: Set/change/delete an environmental variable */

#include <stdio.h>
#include <stdlib.h>
#include <graph.h>
#define  STR "TEST_STRING"

void main ()
{
char   *vbl, new [80];

  /* See if the variable already exists */
  _clearscreen (_GCLEARSCREEN);
  if ((vbl = getenv (STR)) == NULL)
    printf ("Variable %s does not currently exist", STR);
  else {
    printf ("Current contents of %s = %s", STR, vbl);
    puts
      ("\nProgram ended to avoid corrupting environment\n");
    exit (-1);
  }

  /* Set the new environment */
  sprintf (new, "%s=new environment string", STR);
  if (putenv (new) == -1) {
    puts ("\nUnable to add new string. Program ended.\n");
    exit (-1);
  }

  /* Check for new string */
  if ((vbl = getenv (STR)) == NULL)
    puts ("\n\nNew variable not found");
  else
    printf ("\n\nNew variable is %s=%s", STR, vbl);

  /* Change environment string */
  sprintf (new, "%s=different string", STR);
  putenv (new);

  /* Get changed string */
  if ((vbl = getenv (STR)) == NULL)
    puts ("\n\nChanged variable not found");
  else
    printf ("\n\nChanged string is %s=%s", STR, vbl);

  /* Remove string from environment */
  sprintf (new, "%s=", STR);
  if (putenv (new) == -1)
    puts ("\n\nUnable to remove string from environment");
  else
    puts ("\n\nRemoved string");
}
```

Passing Information Via the Environment

When DOS starts a .COM or .EXE file running, it copies the current environment into a new memory space and sets a pointer to it in the PSP. Thus, the running program owns its own copy of the environment, and any changes the program makes with putenv() are to this copy and not to the caller's. This prevents a program from altering the system environment and possibly causing the computer to suddenly start acting in unexpected ways.

As we'll discuss in Chapter 23, a process that starts another program running is a "parent," and the job it starts is a "child." The DOS shell program COMMAND.COM is therefore the ultimate parent of all processes on a PC. However, Program A (a child of DOS) can start Program B running, in which case A becomes a parent, B is its child, and COMMAND.COM is—metaphorically—the grandparent of B.

In this scheme, DOS passes a copy of its environment to A. Perhaps A changes the environment, then initiates B via a call to the appropriate Quick C routine (spawn() or exec(), discussed in Chapter 24). At start-up, B acquires a copy of A's modified environment. In this way, A can pass information to B, which B obtains with getenv() and acts on.

Note that this is a one-way communication path: parent to child only. The child has a copy of the environment and doesn't know where its parent's is. Any changes the child makes are to its own environment. They cease to exist when the child terminates, since DOS releases the memory occupied by the child's environment. Thus the parent's environment is unaffected by the activities of its child (unlike a human parent's).

This is both good and bad. It's good because it keeps the system environment from getting cluttered with old and potentially hazardous stuff. It's bad because you can't run a program that tailors the environment for a bunch of other programs, unless they're all children of the first one. However, there is a way to set environment variables globally and make them a permanent part of the system. That's what we discuss next.

Setting Global Environment Variables

The only way to set an environment variable that's globally available is at the DOS prompt level with the SET command. The variable then becomes a part of DOS' environment as long as the system remains powered up, and it's automatically passed to all children.

It's impractical, of course, to expect a user to type a SET command every time he or she wants to run your software. However, there's a way around this. Lines in .BAT files are treated as DOS commands, so if you add SET commands to a .BAT file and then run that .BAT file, they have the same effect as if typed manually. The one .BAT file that is guaranteed to run every time you start the computer is AUTOEXEC.BAT.

Consequently, you can place SET commands into AUTOEXEC.BAT, and the contents of those SET commands become a permanent part of the DOS environment.

The names of environment variables should be unique enough that there's little chance someone else has already claimed them, and that they don't conflict with keywords such as PATH, COMSPEC, and PROMPT. The contents of the strings can be anything you like, so long as it's text and doesn't contain an embedded null terminator (ASCII 0).

A Working Example

A common use of environment strings in commercial software packages is to pass configuration information to the application's program(s). This can include directory paths specified by the user, as well as installation parameters such as BFLAGS shown earlier. Run an install program that appends SET commands to AUTOEXEC.BAT, then have the user reboot the computer to put those commands into effect. Thereafter, the variables are always part of the system environment. The program they configure can then read the appropriately named variables with getenv() and adapt itself accordingly.

The programs in Listings 22.3 and 22.4 illustrate this idea by simulating an application (APP.C) and its installation program (APPINST.C). Run APP.C first, without doing the "installation." The program checks for an environment string called APPPARMS to find out what the screen colors are. If it fails to find the string (because the installation hasn't yet been performed), it refuses to run and tells the user what needs to be done to earn its cooperation.

This program uses the TEXTSCRN library developed in an earlier chapter. To make it from the command line, type

        QCL app.c textscrn.c

Listing 22.3 **A simple application requiring configuration information from environment strings.**

```
/* APP.C: Application stub: reads installation info from  */
/*        global environments set by AUTOEXEC.BAT         */
/* APPINST.C must be run before this program can work     */
/* ----------------------------------------------------- */

#include <stdio.h>
#include <stdlib.h>
#include <graph.h>
#include "textscrn.h"
```

```
void main ()
{
char   fore, back, *string, parms[] = "APPPARMS",
       path[] = "APPPATH";

  /* Get screen installation choices */
  if ((string = getenv (parms)) == NULL) {
    puts ("First run APPINST to install this application");
    puts ("\n(You must reboot the computer afterwards)");
    puts ("\nProgram ended");
    exit (1);
  }

  /* Set up screen with installed colors */
  fore = string [0];
  back = string [1];
  _settextcolor (fore - '0');
  _setbkcolor ((long) back - '0');
  _clearscreen (_GCLEARSCREEN);

  /* Label screen */
  _settextposition (1, 27);
  _outtext ("* * APPLICATION SCREEN * *\n");

  /* Show configuration info */
  _outtextf ("\n\nForeground color = %c", fore);
  _outtextf ("\n\nBackground color = %c", back);
  string = getenv (path);
  _outtextf ("\n\nPath to application is %s", string);

  /* Wait for keypress and end */
  _outtext ("\n\n\nPress any key to end . . .");
  getch ();
  _settextcolor (LTGRAY);
  _setbkcolor ((long) BLACK);
  _clearscreen (_GCLEARSCREEN);
}
```

After the installation is completed, **APP** sets up the screen with the configuration choices, shows what they are, and displays the other configuration information. It waits for a keypress, then restores the default screen and quits. But first you have to do the installation, which is what **APPINST.C** in Listing 22.4 handles.

This program asks the user to furnish three installation options: the directory path to the application, and the screen foreground and background colors. First, though, it makes a backup copy of **AUTOEXEC.BAT** (or creates a new file by that name if one doesn't exist). The backup is made by renaming the file **AUTOEXEC.OLD**, then creating a new **AUTOEXEC.BAT** and copying everything from .OLD into it. The new .BAT file is left open and ready for the **SET** statements that the program will add.

The program does nothing to ensure that the application path is reasonable (this is just a "pretend" installation, after all). A real installation program should make sure the path actually exists and give the user guidance if not. Here it simply writes a SET command to the new .BAT file.

The acquisition of colors is a little smarter. It makes sure the user enters valid choices. When that's done, the program adds another SET command, closes the file, and quits. Observe the notice to reboot; that part's not "pretend," but instead required to implement the new environment strings.

Like APP.C in Listing 22.3, APPINST relies on the TEXTSCRN library. Make the program from the command line with

     QCL appinst.c textscrn.c

Listing 22.4 An installation program that modifies the AUTOEXEC.BAT **file.**

```
/* APPINST.C: Sample installation program */
/* Writes installation options into AUTOEXEC.BAT */

#include <stdio.h>
#include <stdlib.h>
#include <errno.h>
#include <graph.h>
#include "textscrn.h"

void main ()
{
FILE *old, *new;
char fore = 'x', back = 'x', c, path [80],
     cmd [100];
int  n, col = 49, row = 12, p;
struct rccoord text;

  /* Identify the program */
  _clearscreen (_GCLEARSCREEN);
  _settextposition (1, 26);
  _outtext ("* * INSTALLATION PROGRAM * *\n");

  /* Make a backup copy of AUTOEXEC.BAT */
  if (rename ("\\AUTOEXEC.BAT", "\\AUTOEXEC.OLD") != 0) {
    switch (errno) {
      case ENOENT:
        _outtext ("\nAUTOEXEC.BAT being created");
        new = fopen ("\\AUTOEXEC.OLD", "a");
        break;
      case EACCES:
        _outtext ("\nUnable to continue");
        _outtext ("\nFile access error");
        _outtext
          ("\nPossible conflict with existing AUTOEXEC.OLD");
        _outtext ("\nProgram ended");
        exit (-1);
```

```
        break;
    }
  } else {                           /* Copy contents to new file */
    _outtext
      ("\nYour AUTOEXEC.BAT has been saved in AUTOEXEC.OLD");
    old = fopen ("\\AUTOEXEC.OLD", "r");
    new = fopen ("\\AUTOEXEC.BAT", "a");
    while (!feof (old)) {
      c = fgetc (old);
      fputc (c, new);
    }
    fclose (old);
  }


  /* Get application path, put into file */
  _outtext ("\n\nName of directory containing application? ");
  gets (path);
  sprintf (cmd, "\nSET APPPATH=%s", path);
  fputs (cmd, new);
  _outtextf ("\n\nAdded command: %s", cmd);


  /* Get color combo for APP screen */
  _outtext ("\n\n\nColor selection:");


  /* First build a box showing colors */
  text = _gettextposition();              /* note position */
  _textbox (row, col, row+5, col+10, 2);
  for (n = 0; n < 8; n++) {                /* display colors */
    _settextcolor (LTGRAY);                 /* digit color */
    _settextposition (row+n+1, col+1);
    _outtextf ("%d", n);
    _settextcolor (n);                      /* bar color */
    for (p = 0; p < 2; p++)
      _outch (219);
    if (n == 3)
      col += 6, row -= 4;
  }
  /* Now get color choice from user */
  _settextcolor (LTGRAY);                 /* default foreground */
  _settextposition (text.row, text.col);
  _outtext ("\n\nForeground color? ");
  do {
    fore = getche();
    if ((fore < '0') || (fore > '7')) /* verify selection */
  _outtext ("\nInvalid choice - try again: ");
  } while ((fore < '0') || (fore > '7'));
  _outtext ("\n\nBackground color? ");
  do {
    back = getche();
    if ((back < '0') || (back > '7'))
      _outtext ("\nInvalid choice - try again: ");
  } while ((back < '0') || (back > '7'));
```

Listing 22.4 *(continued)*

```
/* Add to file */
sprintf (cmd, "\nSET APPPARMS=%c%c", fore, back);
fputs (cmd, new);
_outtextf ("\n\nAdded command: %s\n\n", cmd);

/* Close and quit */
fclose (new);
_outtext ("Press Ctrl-Alt-Del to complete installation\n");
}
```

Now you can run **APP** and see how it adapts itself to the configuration parameters in the new environment strings. After you've completed this exercise, copy **AUTOEXEC.OLD** back to **AUTOEXEC.BAT** to undo the changes made by **APPINST**. The strings do no harm, but they'll continue to occupy memory needlessly unless you get rid of them.

Environment variables can add a lot of power and flexibility to your software, and quite painlessly. We'll use them in the next chapter, where we see how to run child processes from within Quick C programs.

CHAPTER 23

Running One Program From Another

As application programs increase in complexity and sophistication, it's sometimes necessary for one program to run other programs. An example is giving your user the ability to leave the application temporarily in order to operate at the DOS-prompt level, then return to the application (as in the File/DOS shell menu selection of the QuickC environment). Other examples are executing DOS commands from within programs, using overlays or other programs in the manner of overlays (as in running a test program from within the QuickC environment), and chaining two or more programs to form a jobstream.

Quick C furnishes three functions for executing other programs from within your applications:

- **system()** is the simplest. It executes any DOS command.
- The **spawn...()** functions invoke and run another program as a child process. Depending on the mode argument, **spawn...()** works either like **system()** or like **exec()**, described next.
- The **exec...()** functions chain to another program, thus overlaying the memory space occupied by the invoking application. There is no return to the parent.

Thus, the three functions furnish two different strategies for invoking another program: with and without return. This chapter describes the alternatives.

Using system()

If you don't intend to port your applications to other C compilers, **system()** is the easiest call to use for invoking child processes that are to return to the parent. A child process can be any DOS command: one built into the COMMAND.COM shell, a .BAT file, or an executable program in the .COM or .EXE format. You can also use it to drop into the DOS environment and return to the application with the **EXIT** command.

The ability to call on DOS intrinsic commands (those built into **COM-MAND.COM**) can save you a lot of work. If you want to give your software users a listing of the files on the A: drive, you can write the statement

```
system ("DIR A:");
```

and the program, when it comes to this statement, executes the quoted command as though typed at the DOS prompt level. Similarly, if you want to copy all the .**EXE** files from drive A to the current subdirectory (as in an installation program), the statement is

```
system ("COPY A:*.*");
```

This is much simpler than writing unique routines to list the directory, copy files from one drive to another, and so on.

The downside of this method is that the commands behave exactly the same as if typed at the DOS level. For example, the copy command lists on the screen all files copied. A way around this is to redirect the normal screen output to a disk file, as in

```
system ("COPY A:*.*  ›  JUNK.XYZ");
```

The output is thus written to **JUNK.XYZ** in the current directory.

Another potential problem is that you can lose the current directory for the application. Consider the following sequence of statements:

```
system ("md \\NEWAPP");
system ("cd \\NEWAPP");
system ("COPY A:*.*");
```

This leaves the system in subdirectory **\NEWAPP**. That can be a real problem if the application subsequently creates and manipulates other files that it expects to be located in its own subdirectory.

The solution is to use **getcwd()** to load the current directory into a variable before initiating the sequence above. Afterwards, you can use **chdir()** to return to the proper directory:

```
char  direc [64];

     getcwd (direc, 64);
     system ("md \\NEWAPP");
     system ("cd \\NEWAPP");
     system ("COPY A:*.*");
     chdir (direc);
     .  .  .
```

The system() function invokes a copy of COMMAND.COM using the COM-SPEC environment variable. As a result, it behaves exactly like COM-MAND.COM at the DOS prompt level, including the execution of intrinsic commands plus .BAT, .EXE, and .COM files. The executable files (.EXE and .COM) can be in the current directory or in any other directory that is along the PATH environment string. For example, say your program is running from directory \MYAPP and PATH = \DOS;\SYSTEM, with CHKDSK residing in \SYSTEM. If your program issues the statement

```
system ("CHKDSK /F");
```

the CHKDSK program will be executed, since COMMAND.COM searches the directory path for it. Note also that it's valid to pass command line arguments such as /F in system() calls.

The system() function returns an integer indicating its status, where 0 = success. You can check the status, as in

```
if (system (cmd)  = =  0)
     /* operation was successful */
else
     /* it wasn't */
```

Unfortunately, the returned status doesn't indicate whether the DOS command itself was successful. If you send an invalid command as an argument to system(), the message

```
Bad command or file name
```

appears on the display, but system() returns 0 anyway. Therefore the returned status isn't of much use, and you can safely ignore it most of the time.

The one situation in which it's advisable to check the return code from system() is at its first invocation in the program. A nonzero value probably means that there isn't enough memory to load and execute the command interpreter. The upshot is that if the first invocation doesn't work, none will and the program must therefore either take defensive action or notify the user of the problem.

Opening a Doorway to the DOS Command Level

In programs with a user interface environment, it's a considerate touch to furnish a doorway to the DOS command level. This enables the user to run programs and execute commands at will, then return to the application by typing the EXIT command. EXIT is an intrinsic command that tells COMMAND.COM to quit and restore control to its parent; it has no effect if COMMAND.COM is not functioning as a child process.

A simple **system()** call takes the user to the DOS prompt level from a program:

```
system  ("C:\\COMMAND");
```

This loads a copy of COMMAND.COM from the C drive's root directory and passes control to it. COMMAND.COM signals that it's alive by displaying a copyright notice and presenting the normal DOS prompt. The parent program remains in memory in a state of suspended animation while COMMAND.COM has control. The user proceeds as though the parent program had ended. However, when the user types EXIT, the copy of COMMAND.COM relinquishes control and the parent program resumes running at the statement following the **system()** call. The memory occupied by COMMAND.COM returns to the general memory pool and is thus available for other use.

The difference between this and executing a command via **system()** is that the command is passed through the interpreter for execution, while this approach takes the user into the interpreter itself. The similarity is that, in both cases, COMMAND.COM is the parent of the running application, which is the parent of a second copy of COMMAND.COM, which in its turn may be the parent of a process executed in response to a command.

Graceful Exits and Returns

Before invoking a child process that will return, it's usually advisable to save the parent's visual context (i.e., current display), then give the new program a clean slate to work on by clearing the screen. On return, you can restore the visual context and resume execution of the parent. Running an external program doesn't affect the parent's data, but it does corrupt the display. This simple way of handling the visual context provides intuitive boundaries between parent and child.

Demonstration: A DOS Shell

Listing 23.1 is a simple DOS shell that illustrates the points covered so far. While it lacks some of the glitzy features of commercial DOS shells such as XTREE, the program is a complete and useful utility.

It lists ten common intrinsic DOS commands on a menu. The other two menu selections are for command-line mode and to quit the program. You select a choice by typing its associated number and pressing Enter. In most cases, the program then prompts for the command-line arguments and executes the completed command via a **system()** call. If you select 11 (command line), the program takes you into COMMAND.COM and you operate at the DOS prompt level until you type EXIT.

Most of this program's work is done in the processCommand() function. Four of the menu choices don't require a separate display, working instead in the background without visual effects; these are CHDIR, DEL, MKDIR, and RENAME. The rest entail switching to a fresh screen while they run, then restoring the shell's visual context upon a keypress.

Note the showdir() function also. It displays the current drive and directory in a box near the top of the display. This function is initially called from main() during the setup phase. processCommand() also calls it if the user changes directories with menu selection 1 or returns from command-line mode, in which he or she might have changed directories. showdir() dynamically sizes the directory window and its surrounding text box according to the length of the current directory path.

DOSSHELL has a lot of visual appeal on a color monitor, since it uses colors liberally. The program relies heavily on techniques and routines for managing pop-up windows, which were covered in earlier chapters. For that reason, you need to include POPUP.C and TEXTSCRN.C in your program list.

Listing 23.1 **A DOS shell utility.**

```
/* DOSSHELL.C: A simple DOS shell program */

#include <stdlib.h>
#include <stdio.h>
#include <conio.h>
#include <dos.h>
#include <direct.h>
#include <string.h>
#include <graph.h>
#include "textscrn.h"
#include "popup.h"

/* Application screen descriptor */
POPUP scrn = {1, 1, 25, 80, 0, YELLOW, MAGENTA, BLACK, CYAN};

/* DOS screen descriptor */
POPUP dos = {1, 1, 25, 80, 0, LTGRAY, 0, BLACK};

/* Popup descriptor for command line arguments */
POPUP arg = {22, 2, 22, 79, 1, RED, 0, BLACK, 0};

/* POPUP descriptor for current directory */
POPUP dir = {3, 1, 3, 1, 2, MAGENTA, 0, BLACK, 0};

/* List of commands */
char cmd [][16] = {
{"CHDIR"},  {"COPY"},   {"DATE"},           {"DEL"},
```

Listing 23.1 *(continued)*

```c
{"DIR"},    {"MKDIR"}, {"RENAME"},         {"SET"},
{"TIME"},   {"TYPE"},  {"Command line"}, {"Quit"}
};

/* Local functions */
void buildScreen (void);
void processCommand (int);
char *getargs (int);
char *noargs (int);
void showdir (void);

/* -------------------------------------------------- */

void main ()
{
int   curdrive, choice, n;
char  curdir [64], oldpath [67], entry [3];

  /* Get current drive and directory */
  _dos_getdrive (&curdrive);
  getcwd (curdir, 64);

  /* Set up screen */
  buildScreen ();
  showdir ();

  /* Loop for DOS commands */
  do {
    _settextposition (22, 30);
    _cleareol();
    _outtext ("Select by number . . . ");
    gets (entry);               /* string input from keyboard */
    choice = atoi (entry);              /* convert to number */
    if ((choice > 0) && (choice < 13))
      processCommand (choice);
  } while (choice != 12);

  /* Restore entry drive and path, then quit */
  _dos_setdrive (curdrive, &n);
  sprintf (oldpath, "CD %s", curdir);
  system (oldpath);
  _settextcolor (LTGRAY);
  _setbkcolor ((long) BLACK);
  _clearscreen (_GCLEARSCREEN);
} /* ---------------------- */

void buildScreen (void)              /* Build display and menu */
{
int  row = 7, col = 23, n;

  _clearscreen (_GCLEARSCREEN);
```

```
      popShow (&scrn);
      popCenter (&scrn, 1, "* * *  D O S    S H E L L  * * *");
      popHilite (&scrn, 1);
      _settextcolor (GREEN);
      _textbox (5, 20, 19, 60, 2);
      _settextposition (5, 35);
      _outtext (" COMMANDS ");
      _settextcolor (scrn.normal);

      /* Show list of commands */
      for (n = 0; n < 12; n++) {
        if (n == 6) col += 19, row -= 12;          /* column break */
        _settextposition (row+(n*2), col);         /* next position */
        _settextcolor (scrn.hilite);
        _outtextf ("%2d ", n+1);
        _settextcolor (scrn.normal);
        _outtext (cmd [n]);
      }
    } /* ----------------------- */

void processCommand (int choice)
                         /* Execute command selected by user */
  {
char    *command;

    popKeep (&scrn);                          /* save screen state */
    switch (choice) {
      case  1:
      case  4:
      case  6:
      case  7: command = getargs (choice);
               system (command);
               break;
      case  2:
      case  3:
      case  5:
      case  8:
      case  9:
      case 10: command = getargs (choice);
               _savescrn (0);
               popShow (&dos);
               system (command);
               puts (
                 "\nPress any key to return to shell . . .");
               getch();
               _restscrn (0);
               break;
      case 11: _savescrn (0);
               popShow (&dos);                  /* Go to COMMAND.COM */
               system ("\\COMMAND");
               _restscrn (0);
               break;
    }
```

Listing 23.1 *(continued)*

```
   popUse (&scrn);
   if ((choice == 1) ||              /* if changed directories */
       (choice == 11))         /* or went to DOS command level */
     showdir ();
} /* ---------------------- */


char *noargs (int choice)
                    /* Build command line without arguments */
{
char cmdline [5];

   sprintf (cmdline, "%s", cmd [choice-1]);
   return cmdline;
} /* ---------------------- */


char *getargs (int choice)
                     /* Build command line with arguments */
{
static char cmdline [80];
char arglist [80];

   _savescrn (0);
   popShow (&arg);
   _outtextf ("%s ", cmd [choice-1]);
   gets (arglist);
   sprintf (cmdline, "%s %s", cmd [choice - 1], arglist);
   _restscrn (0);
   return cmdline;
} /* ---------------------- */


void showdir (void)                   /* Show current directory */
{
char  path [64];
int   i;

   popKeep (&scrn);                  /* save current window state */
   _settextwindow (1, 1, 25, 80);        /* full screen mode */
   for (i = dir.top; i <= dir.bottom; i++) {
     _settextposition (i, 1);
     _cleareol();                  /* clear old dir display area */
   }
   getcwd (path, 64);                       /* get current dir */
   i = strlen (path) + 14;
   dir.left = ((80 - i) / 2);          /* size new window */
   dir.right = 80 - dir.left;
   popShow (&dir);                            /* show it */
   _outtextf ("  Directory: %s", path);
   popUse (&scrn);                    /* restore old window */
} /* ---------------------- */
```

Using spawn...()

The Quick C manual explains the **spawn**...() family of functions in considerable detail, so we won't give much space to them here. In general, the spawn functions require one to three suffixes selected from these four: l, v, p, and e. These suffixes specify methods for passing arguments to the child, the search path, and the child's environment. There are eight possible combinations of suffixes. The same is true of the **exec**...() functions covered later.

One of the most important things to note about the **spawn** functions is the modeflag *parameter*. There are three, defined in **PROCESS.H**:

1. **P_WAIT** suspends the parent's activity until the child completes. This mode makes **spawn**...() equivalent to the **system**() function, except when passing a new environment (discussed below).
2. **P_NOWAIT** ostensibly keeps the parent running while the child executes. This is a UNIX and OS/2 mode. Don't use it with DOS, which can't support multiprocessing.
3. **P_OVERLAY** brings the child process into the memory space occupied by the parent. You can't return to the parent from a child called in **P_OVERLAY** mode. This mode is equivalent to the **exec**...() functions discussed later in this chapter.

Because the **spawn**...() functions in **P_WAIT** mode are more complicated than **system**(), there usually isn't much point in using them. The exception is when passing a new environment to the child.

Communicating with a Child Process

It's frequently necessary for a parent to pass information to the child process it invokes. This information might be quite simple, such as the name of a file containing data to be processed, or as complicated as the data itself along with instructions as to what's to be done. It depends on the application. The environment can be as large as 32K, which allows a good deal of information to be passed.

As discussed in Chapter 22, the environment consists of a set of null-terminated text strings, each having the form

    VARNAME = <text>

A program can obtain the address of a specific variable name's string using the **getenv**() function.

If you want to pass the parent's environment to the child without modification, use the **system**() function. It has no provision for altering the environment, so the child simply inherits the same environment as the parent has.

On the other hand, if you want to pass your own environment strings, you have to use one of the **spawne..()** (or **exece..()**) functions. The e-suffixed functions take an argument that is an array of character pointers, with each element pointing to a null-terminated environment string. A **NULL** pointer in this array indicates the end of the list. The pointed-to strings need not be in contiguous memory; before initiating the child program, DOS collects them all in the child's environment block and sets the PSP pointer.

How the Child Obtains Information from the Parent

When the child gets control, it can fetch environment strings with **getenv()**. Because **getenv()** searches the environment for the variable whose name appears as an argument, the child process must be conditioned to "know" the names of the strings it needs.

Similarly, the parent invoking the child through a **spawn** or **exec** call can pass simulated command-line arguments. The *l* (literal) and *v* (vectored) suffixes govern how the arguments are passed: separately or as an array of pointers similar to the environment argument, respectively. This is another way of sending information to the child. The child must know which method (*l* or *v*) the parent uses, so that it can process the command line appropriately. The examples in this chapter use the *v* method.

Listing 23.2 is a program called **CHILD.C**, which we'll use twice in this chapter. The first time we'll call it with the **spawnvpe()** function in **P_WAIT** mode. When the child runs to completion, the parent regains control, thus treating **CHILD.C** as a sort of glorified subroutine. The second time we'll call it with **execvpe()**. In that case, there is no return since the child overlays and thus replaces the parent.

Listing 23.2 **A child process.**

```
/* CHILD.C: Child process                                  */
/* This program is invoked by a spawn...() or exec...()     */
/*   call. Lists arguments passed and the environment       */
/*   strings COMSPEC, PROMPT, PATH, and XYZ                 */

#include <stdlib.h>
#include <stdio.h>

void main (int argc, char *argv[])
{
int    n;
char   *estr, *var[] = {"COMSPEC", "PROMPT", "PATH", "XYZ"};

  puts ("\n\nIn child process, arguments are:");
  for (n = 0; n < argc; n++)
    printf ("  argv [%d] = %s", n, argv [n]);
```

```
    puts ("\n\nChild's environmental strings are:");
    for (n = 0; n < 4; n++) {
      estr = getenv (var [n]);
      printf ("  %s = %s\n", var [n],
              estr == NULL ? "(nonexistent)" : estr);
    }
    exit (EXIT_SUCCESS);
}
```

CHILD.C expects to find an array of vectors pointing to the command-line arguments. It also expects its environment to contain the three "standard" strings COMSPEC, PATH, and PROMPT, plus a fourth unique string XYZ, which presumably contains control information passed from the parent via the environment. The program simply outputs the information from the parent and quits, but it illustrates the fetching of command-line arguments and environment strings in a child process. It also gives us a real program to call in the following exercises.

If you run the program from the DOS prompt or the Quick C environment, the output looks something like this:

```
In child process, arguments are:
  argv [0]  =  C:\QC\MYDIR\CHILD.EXE

Child's environmental strings are:
  COMSPEC  =  C:\COMMAND.COM
  PROMPT  =  $p$g
  PATH  =  \DOS;\MOUSE;\BIN;\BRIEF;
  XYZ  =  (nonexistent)
```

There are actually no command-line arguments, but a program always receives a 0th argument from DOS giving the complete path that invoked it (only in DOS 3.0 and later). That's what argv[0] is. Among the environment strings, the one to notice on this printout is XYZ. There is no such string in the current environment, so the program reports it as nonexistent. Later, when the programs in Listings 23.3 and 23.4 invoke CHILD, they'll pass an XYZ environment string, so CHILD will report its value.

Preparing to Invoke a Child Process

It's necessary to do some setup before invoking a child process with the spawn and exec functions. Often you can make all the preparations with initialized variable declarations; the Quick C manual's treatment of these two functions shows examples. It takes more work if you want to pass along certain of the parent's environment strings and others of your own.

The getenv() function returns the variable associated with an environment string, but not the string name and equals sign. Consequently, you have to reconstruct each full string. The easiest way to do this is with sprintf():

```
char path [80], prompt [80], comspec [80],
     xyz[]  =  "XYZ=7890", *envp [5];


     sprintf (path, "PATH=%s", getenv ("PATH"));
     sprintf (prompt, "PROMPT=%s", getenv ("PROMPT"));
     sprintf (comspec, "COMSPEC=%s", getenv ("COMSPEC"));
```

These statements build properly formatted environment strings that can be passed along to the child.

Once the strings are built, put pointers to them into an array of character pointers such as *envp[]:

```
envp [0]  =  comspec;
envp [1]  =  path;
envp [2]  =  prompt;
envp [3]  =  xyz;
envp [4]  =  NULL;
```

Note that the string pointers need not be in the same order as that of declaration. Also, xyz is an initialized variable that we're adding to the child's environment. The list *must* end with a NULL pointer, hence envp[4]. The variable envp (without subscripts) then becomes a pointer to an array of environment pointers passed with a spawne..() or exece..() call. DOS uses it to build the child's environment block.

SPAWN.C in Listing 23.3 illustrates the setup and calling of CHILD (Listing 23.2). First the program displays its own environment, then it performs the steps just described to construct a new environment for the child. SPAWN also passes command-line arguments via the vector of pointers declared in *args[].

Listing 23.3 Calling a child and returning from it.
_____

```
/* SPAWN.C: Passes modified environment to child process */

#include <stdio.h>
#include <stdlib.h>
#include <process.h>
#include <dos.h>
#include <errno.h>
#include <graph.h>

void main ()
{
char  newvar[] = "XYZ=7890",     /* New environment string */
```

```
        *envp [5],                    /* pointers to env strings */
        childpath[] = "CHILD.EXE",            /* path to child */
        *args[] = {"CHILD.EXE",    /* command line arguments */
                "A1", "A2", NULL},
        comspec [64], path [64], prompt [64];
    int   status;

    /* Show current environment */
    _clearscreen (_GCLEARSCREEN);
    puts ("In parent, original environment is:\n");
    system ("SET");

    /* Get current environment strings for child */
    sprintf (comspec, "COMSPEC=%s", getenv ("COMSPEC"));
    sprintf (path, "PATH=%s", getenv ("PATH"));
    sprintf (prompt, "PROMPT=%s", getenv ("PROMPT"));

    /* Load pointer array for environment strings */
    envp [0] = comspec;
    envp [1] = path;
    envp [2] = prompt;
    envp [3] = newvar;
    envp [4] = NULL;

    /* Spawn the child */
    status = spawnvpe (P_WAIT, childpath, args, envp);
    printf ("\n\nIn parent, spawn status = %d", status);

    /* Check for, report error */
    if (status != EXIT_SUCCESS) {          /* child exit status */
      puts ("\nError occurred:\n");
      switch (errno) {
        case E2BIG:   puts ("Argument list too long"); break;
        case EINVAL:  puts ("Invalid argument"); break;
        case ENOENT:  puts ("Bad path or filename"); break;
        case ENOEXEC: puts ("Exec format error"); break;
        case ENOMEM:  puts ("Not enough memory"); break;
      }
    } else
      puts (" (Successful)");
} /* ----------------------- */
```

Because SPAWN invokes the child process using spawnvpe() in P_WAIT mode, termination of the child restores control to the parent. You see this happen when the program reports the spawn status. An error message only appears if spawnvpe() indicated failure by returning a value other than EXIT_SUCCESS (from STDLIB.H). In that case, the child process will not have run, and the message explains why.

The amount of memory not claimed by the parent program constrains the size of a child. For example, say you have 500K of available memory (after claims by DOS and TSRs), and the aggregate total memory requirement of the parent program is 300K: code, data, stack, and heap. That leaves 200K available for all the memory requirements of the child. If that's not enough, **spawn** in **P_WAIT** mode returns − 1 and **errno** is set to **ENOMEM**, indicating insufficient memory to load and run the child.

The alternative in that case is to allow the child to overlay the parent. You can do it either by setting a spawn function to **P_OVERLAY** mode, or by using an **exec** function.

Using exec...()

Almost everything we've said about the **spawn** functions applies equally to the **exec** functions: same suffixes, methods for passing information to the child, error conditions. There's only one major difference: Child processes called with **exec** always overlay the parent.

There's good news and bad news about child processes that overlay their parent. The good news is that they're less memory-constrained; the child receives the same helping of memory as its parent. The bad news is that you can't return to the parent when the child runs to completion. Once the child has control, there's no going back. Thus this method of invoking child processes is more properly called *chaining*.

A chain is a one-way sequence of programs, each invoking the next, which replaces its parent. Taken as a whole, the chain constitutes what they call a jobstream in the mainframe world: A series of related programs that follow a logical progression.

If a return to the original parent is necessary, you can construct a circular chain. For example, A calls B, which calls C, which calls A. And because the **exec** functions allow each parent along the line to pass information to its child, via both command-line arguments and the environment, it's possible (though tricky) to make the reinvoked parent appear to resume running where it left off. That's software engineering stuff well beyond the scope of this book, but it should serve to open your imagination to the enormous power available in program chaining.

On a less grandiose scale, let's see an **exec** function in action. EXEC.C in Listing 23.4 is very similar to Listing 23.3 (SPAWN.C). Because an exec function doesn't return unless there's a problem, this program omits the status variable and, right after the **execvpe()** call, goes into error reporting. The exec functions support a few error conditions that spawn doesn't, so they've been added here. And, finally, there's a goodbye message announcing that the program is chaining to a child process. Note that after the child finishes running, the chain ends and the system reverts to the DOS prompt. That's because there's no return from an overlay.

Listing 23.4 **Chaining to a child process.**

```
/* EXEC.C: Uses exec() to invoke a child process */

#include <stdio.h>
#include <stdlib.h>
#include <process.h>
#include <dos.h>
#include <errno.h>
#include <graph.h>

void main ()
{
char   newvar[] = "XYZ=7890",      /* New environment string */
       *envp [5],                  /* pointers to env strings */
       childpath[] = "CHILD.EXE",           /* path to child */
       *args[] = {"CHILD.EXE",     /* command line arguments */
                  "A1", "A2", NULL},
       comspec [64], path [64], prompt [64];

   /* Show current environment */
   _clearscreen (_GCLEARSCREEN);
   puts ("In parent, original environment is:\n");
   system ("SET");

   /* Get current environment strings for child */
   sprintf (comspec, "COMSPEC=%s", getenv ("COMSPEC"));
   sprintf (path, "PATH=%s", getenv ("PATH"));
   sprintf (prompt, "PROMPT=%s", getenv ("PROMPT"));

   /* Load pointer array for environment strings */
   envp [0] = comspec;
   envp [1] = path;
   envp [2] = prompt;
   envp [3] = newvar;
   envp [4] = NULL;

   /* Chain to the child */
   puts ("\nChaining to child process\n");
   execvpe (childpath, args, envp);

   /* This code runs only if there was an error */
   puts ("\nError occurred:\n");
   switch (errno) {
     case E2BIG:   puts ("Argument list too long"); break;
     case EACCES:  puts ("File access denied");     break;
     case EMFILE:  puts ("Too many open files");    break;
     case ENOENT:  puts ("Bad path or filename");   break;
     case ENOEXEC: puts ("Exec format error");      break;
     case ENOMEM:  puts ("Not enough memory");      break;
   }
} /* ------------------------ */
```

Despite the somewhat daunting appearance of the Quick C manual's coverage of **spawn** and **exec** functions, it's not particularly difficult to invoke one program from another. Yet this capability adds great power and flexibility to your applications.

The next chapter peels away another layer of the mystery surrounding advanced programming by examining interrupts.

CHAPTER **24**

Writing Interrupt Service Routines

The ability to service and otherwise manipulate interrupts opens the door to great power and flexibility. It allows your software to take control—and tailor the operation—of the machine to suit its purposes.

Writing interrupt service routines is not the simplest programming task, but neither is it the product of smoke and mirrors. You need plenty of documentation before you take it on, because to tinker with interrupts is to perform surgery on the delicate innards of the system. The *DOS Technical Reference* is a good place to start. Ray Duncan's *Advanced MS-DOS* and Bob Jourdain's *Programmer's Problem Solver* both contain excellent advice. So does a book by Michael Hyman with the verbose title *Memory Resident Utilities, Interrupts, and Disk Management with MS & PD DOS* (MIS Press, Portland, OR 1987). All three commercial books provide step-by-step guides for handling interrupts. Thus equipped, writing an interrupt service routine ("ISR" or simply "handler") becomes a matter of fleshing it out with specifics.

This chapter is not a comprehensive treatment of the subject. Rather, it serves as an introduction to interrupts and furnishes some simple working examples. For more information, see one of the works cited, or any other indepth coverage of DOS systems programming.

What Is an Interrupt? _____

An interrupt is an event that demands the immediate attention of the processor. When an interrupt occurs, the processor stops what it's doing, branches to a routine that services the interrupt, and then resumes where it left off. An ISR is thus a special kind of subroutine.

There are two kinds of interrupts—classified as hardware and software—and they're very different. A hardware interrupt is typically generated by

413

some system element outside the control of the running program. Examples are a keypress, a character arriving at a serial port, a tick of the system clock, and an intolerable error such as division by zero. In contrast, a software interrupt is generated on purpose by the running program. The most common example is when a program requests service from DOS. The calling program loads information into registers, generates an interrupt, and (usually) receives a returned value that it uses subsequently. A software interrupt handler is therefore a kind of subroutine that belongs to one software element (e.g., an operating system) and is available to other software elements (e.g., application programs).

The vast majority of handlers written into C programs service hardware interrupts, and consequently we'll confine our discussion to them. In the unlikely event that you find it necessary to write a software interrupt service routine, use the ROM BIOS listings in your hardware documentation as a guide, and write the handler in Assembly Language.

Hardware interrupts occur at unpredictable intervals, and the running program doesn't know when one has occurred. A hardware ISR usually takes the minimal actions of saving incoming data if necessary, and setting a switch to indicate that the interrupt has occurred. It's the responsibility of other parts of the program to process the results of the interrupt at their convenience.

DOS tends to cluster most of its hardware interrupts in Int 0 through Int 1F, and to tie some undocumented interrupts to Int EEh through Int FFh.

What do these hex numbers mean? They identify the interrupt, and also serve as an index to a special system data structure called the *interrupt vector table*.

The Interrupt Vector Table

The steps that occur in response to an interrupt are intimately tied to the computer's processor. In fact, they're built into the silicon so that the processor doesn't have to follow a program in order to know what to do.

The processors that propel the PC family of machines all handle interrupts in a consistent way. When an interrupt occurs, the CPU saves the current context (i.e., all the registers), then uses the interrupt number to find the address of the handler associated with that interrupt. It loads the address into its CS and IP registers, so the next instruction to be executed is the entry point of the handler. The handler itself is software somewhere in the machine's address space (either in RAM or ROM). This software runs until the processor encounters an IRET instruction, which tells it to return from the interrupt. The processor then reloads the context of the interrupted process, which restores control at the point where the interrupt occurred.

The processor finds the address of the handler by using the interrupt number to index into the interrupt vector table. This is a list of 256 far pointers ("vectors") beginning at memory address zero. Since a far pointer occupies four bytes, the table is 1,024 bytes in length, running from 0:0 through 0:03FFh. The processor multiplies the interrupt number by four to calculate the appropriate offset. For example, the vector for Int 0 is at 0:0, and for Int 1 at 0:4. When Int 1 occurs, the processor grabs the vector at 0:4 and branches to that address.

By implication, the existence of 256 vectors limits the PC to 256 possible interrupts numbered 0 through FFh. That's a lot of interrupts. DOS, the ROM BIOS, and assorted TSRs and device drivers take up about a hundred, leaving some 150 vacant slots in the table. If you write your own interrupt handler, you can take over any vacant vector as your own.

The problem is identifying an unclaimed vector.

Inspecting the Interrupt Vector Table

The interrupt vector table is initialized during machine start-up, partially by the ROM BIOS and partially by the DOS bootstrap program. Therefore the disposition of unused vectors is up to the implementor. Some PCs I've worked on—notably those running DOS 2.n and an early ROM BIOS—left the unused vectors as NULL pointers, or, in other words, as zero values. Others, including my present AT clone, point the unclaimed vectors at an IRET buried somewhere in memory.

The latter approach makes more sense. That way, a spurious or misdirected interrupt simply returns without doing anything. A NULL pointer, on the other hand, can send the machine into never-never land. However, an unused pointer initialized to an IRET is indistinguishable from one that points to a real routine, unless you know for sure that it's unclaimed. One way to do this is to physically inspect the table. If there are scads of vectors all having the same value, they're the unused ones.

Quick C furnishes the function _dos_getvect() for fetching an interrupt vector. This function returns the far pointer plucked from the specified vector. You can use it to determine the address of the handler associated with the interrupt number passed as its argument.

Listing 24.1 illustrates the use of getvect() and also furnishes the useful utility SHOWVECS.C. This program lists the entire interrupt vector table, showing 64 vectors per panel. There are thus four panels, and the program steps through the interrupts in sequence. You can press Q to quit, or advance to the next panel with any other keystroke.

Make this program from the command line with

```
QCL  showvecs.c  textscrn.c
```

Listing 24.1 **A utility for inspecting the interrupt vector table.**

```
/* SHOWVECS.C: Lists contents of interrupt vector table */

#include <graph.h>
#include <dos.h>
#include <ctype.h>
#include <stdlib.h>
#include "textscrn.h"

#define ICOLOR YELLOW
#define VCOLOR GREEN

void drawBoxes (void);
void showVectors (int);

void main ()
{
int  screen;
char reply;

  _clearscreen (_GCLEARSCREEN);
  drawBoxes ();
  for (screen = 0; screen < 4; screen++) {
    _settextcolor (ICOLOR);
    _settextposition (1, 23);
    _outtext ("CONTENTS OF INTERRUPT VECTOR TABLE");
    showVectors (screen * 64);
    _settextposition (24, 20);
    _cleareol();
    _settextcolor (ICOLOR);
    if (screen != 3) {
      _outtext ("Q to quit, any other key to continue...");
      reply = getch();
      reply = toupper (reply);
      if (reply == 'Q') {
        _settextcolor (LTGRAY);
        _setbkcolor ((long) BLACK);
        _clearscreen (_GCLEARSCREEN);
        exit (EXIT_SUCCESS);
      }
    } else {
      _outtext ("          Press any key to end");
      getch();
    }
  }
  _settextcolor (LTGRAY);
  _setbkcolor ((long) BLACK);
  _clearscreen (_GCLEARSCREEN);
} /* ---------------------- */

void drawBoxes (void)
                    /* Draw boxes around the vector lists */
```

```
{
int  col = 4, box;

  _settextcolor (VCOLOR);
  for (box = 0; box < 4; box++) {
    _textbox (3, col, 20, col+17, 1);
    col += 18;
  }
} /* ----------------------- */

void showVectors (int start)
                    /* List 64 vectors beginning at start */
{
int  inter, row = 4, col = 6, listed = 0;
void far *vect;

  for (inter = start; inter < start+64; inter++) {
    _settextposition (row++, col);
    _settextcolor (ICOLOR);
    _outtextf ("%02Xh ", inter);

    vect = _dos_getvect (inter);
    _settextcolor (VCOLOR);
    _outtextf ("%04X:%04X", FP_SEG (vect), FP_OFF (vect));

    if (++listed == 16) {
      col += 18;
      row -= 16;
      listed = 0;
    }
  }
} /* ----------------------- */
```

As you run this program, note that there's a lot of vacant real estate past the middle of the vector table, especially around Int A0h. If you need a vector, it's probably safe to claim one somewhere in this vicinity, but check first. Load up every TSR (memory-resident program, such as Sidekick) that you can lay your hands on, then run **SHOWVECS** and pick an unused vector.

An alternative to using an unclaimed vector is interrupt chaining—that is, calling the handler that owns a vector—which we'll discuss later.

Vector Management

Once you've identified the vector you want to use, you can put a pointer to your routine in it. But first, *save the current vector.* Fetch it with **_dos_getvect()** and tuck it into a safe place: preferably a global variable.

Why? Because it's absolutely essential that you restore the old vector before terminating the program. If you fail to do this, the vector will continue to point at where your handler used to be; the next time that interrupt fires, the system will probably crash. Restoring changed vectors puts the original handler back into service.

For a normal program (not a TSR), a good way to ensure orderly termination with restoral of the changed vector(s) is to use the QuickC atexit() or onexit() function (the two are identical). These functions register up to 32 subroutines that are automatically called when the program ends. For example, say you declare the global variables

```
void  interrupt  (*oldvec)();
int  myvec;
```

and load the pointer with

```
oldvec  =  _dos_getvect (myvec);
```

(where myvec has been set to the interrupt number you've claimed). Your program then includes a function such as:

```
void  endofjob  (void)
{
        _dos_setvect (myvec, oldvec);
}
```

Early in main(), register the function using the statement

```
atexit (endofjob);
```

Then, even if you have multiple termination points in the program (using exit() calls, plus normal termination at the end of main()), the endofjob() function will gain control and restore the changed vector to its original state.

Dos and Don'ts of ISRs

Interrupt service routines are, in effect, extensions of DOS and thus don't behave like normal programs. They have many dos and don'ts that the works cited earlier describe in detail. Here we'll cover a few of the important ones.

Use the Interrupt Keyword

An ISR has special characteristics that normal functions don't have. The Quick C compiler knows to assign these characteristics to a function when it is defined using the keyword *interrupt*, as in

```
void  interrupt  myint  (void)
{
    /*  do  interrupt  stuff  */
}
```

An interrupt function comes equipped with machine code that automatically saves all registers before its enclosed code gets control, and restores them on completion. The last statement of an interrupt function is IRET, which restores the system context and resumes execution where the interrupt occurred.

An interrupt function is by definition a far function, regardless of the QuickC memory model in use. A reference to its address generates a 32-bit segment: offset value.

Do the Minimum Possible

An interrupt steals time from the running application. Therefore, the less time it takes to do its job, the better. If you look at the ROM BIOS listing in the Technical Reference Manual for your machine, you'll see that the ISRs there are typically a dozen or two lines of assembly code. One or two lines of C code can easily generate the equivalent amount of machine language.

Say you're writing an ISR that accepts incoming data from a remote device attached to a serial port. An effective ISR in this case wakes up when a character is at the port, gets it, stuffs it into a buffer, and sets a flag to indicate that data are awaiting processing. Elsewhere, your application can check the flag periodically and, if it's on, flush the buffer by copying its contents elsewhere. The ISR's only responsibility is to save the data and tell somebody that it's done so.

User-written ISRs are highly application-dependent, of course, and they vary widely in their purposes. The point is that they should do the absolute minimum required to service the interrupt, in order to avoid stealing too much time from the task they've interrupted.

Use Volatile External Variables

If an ISR sets a flag and saves data someplace, those variables have to be accessible to the host software. An ISR can declare local variables just like a normal subprogram, but they're allocated on the stack and cease to exist when the ISR returns. Consequently, local variables are not externally visible, and they're perishable.

This means that when an ISR needs to pass information to the running program, it has to use an external variable that is global to the host software. Quick C furnishes a special declaration modifier volatile for this purpose.

The volatile keyword indicates that the variable can be modified by some element outside the program's direct control: an interrupt in this case. Always tag global variables that are affected by ISR's as volatile, and declare them in the heading of the program that contains the ISR. The program in Listing 24.2 later in this chapter contains an example.

Don't Do Any I/O

The business of an ISR is to service interrupts, not generate them. By definition, an I/O operation generates other interrupts. This can upset DOS so much that it crashes.

The reason is that DOS is a single-user, single-tasking operating system, and thus its routines are not re-entrant. With certain exceptions, only one interrupt can be in process at a time. If your interrupt is the one that's active and it tries to generate other interrupts, the machine stack can become corrupted and critical variables overlaid, causing the operating system to lose its way. When DOS gets confused, the machine either goes berserk or locks up.

Chain Interrupts

Any time you grab an interrupt vector, you potentially inhibit activation of the ISR that's normally accessible through that vector. Sometimes you do this deliberately, as when replacing a built-in system ISR with one of your own. In most cases, however, the ISRs you write merely enhance existing system services by adding functionality. For example, TSR utilities usually watch for their activating "hot key" by inserting some process into the keyboard interrupt handling sequence. The keyboard handler operates normally except when the hot key is pressed.

In such cases, your ISR must chain to the process it replaced when it seized the interrupt vector. Depending on how it fits into the interrupt handling sequence, it can chain either before or after it performs its job. (It might also decide not to chain at all if special circumstances arise, such as the arrival of a hot key.)

Since you must save the old vector anyway, you can accomplish chaining by using that pointer as a function variable. Here is an example:

```
void  far  *oldvec;                          /* global for old vector */

void  main()
{
   oldvec  =  _dos_getvect (INT);                      /* get old */
   _dos_setvect (INT, myrtn);                       /* install new */
   ...                                            /* do other stuff */
```

```
}                                              /* end of main */

void interrupt myrtn (void)                         /* ISR */
{
    ...                                    /* do the routine's job */
    if (oldvec)
      _chain_intr (oldvec);                         /* chain */
}
```

Here main() gets the old vector and installs the new handler myrtn() in the interrupt vector table. Whenever the associated interrupt occurs, myrtn() performs its job and then chains to the ISR it displaced from the table. The if test prevents the handler from chaining to a NULL pointer.

The next section implements this discussion with a working example.

Using the System Timer Tick

PCs furnish software access to the system timer via Int 1Ch. This vector normally points to an IRET, but you can take control of it if your software needs a real-time clock.

Note that Int 8 is also associated with the system timer. It's not advisable to monkey with this interrupt. The ROM BIOS relies on it to maintain the master time-of-day clock and calendar, to synchronize disk operations, and for other purposes. The system may go to sleep, or at least forget to do things, if you take control of Int 8. Always use Int 1Ch instead, which exists specifically for application program use (Int 8 chains to it).

The system timer ticks 18.2044 times per second. This seems like an insane interval, but there's a reason. An hour is 3,600 seconds, and 18.2044 x 3600 = 65,536, the maximum number obainable in a 16-bit word. The system counts ticks and knows that an hour has passed when the counter reaches its terminal value.

Listing 24.2 is a program TICKER.C that illustrates an application of the timer tick interrupt. Each time the interrupt fires, the program's handler increments the ticks variable. That's all it does, consistent with the general rule that an ISR should remain active for the absolute minimum amount of time possible.

Listing 24.2 **Harnessing the timer tick interrupt.**

```
/* TICKER.C: Uses system timer ticks (Int 1Ch) to measure */
/*     how long a process runs                             */

#include <dos.h>
#include <math.h>
#include <stdlib.h>
#include <graph.h>
```

Listing 24.2 *(continued)*

```
#define ITER 1000

/* Globals */
void far *oldvec;                            /* old vector */
volatile long ticks;                         /* used by ISR */

/* Prototypes */
void interrupt far tickisr (void);
void install (void);
double elapsed (void);
/* -------------------------------------------------------- */

void main ()
{
double v, x = 2.13579e+123, etime;
int    n;

  _clearscreen (_GCLEARSCREEN);
  install();                            /* install the handler */

  printf ("Finding %d natural logarithms\n", ITER);
  ticks = 0L;                           /* reset the timer */
  for (n = 0; n < ITER; n++)
    v = log (x);
  etime = elapsed();
  printf ("\n  Total duration was %1.6Lf seconds", etime);
  printf ("\n  Average per operation was %1.6Lf seconds",
          etime / (double) ITER);

  printf ("\n\nFinding %d square roots\n", ITER);
  ticks = 0L;
  for (n = 0; n < ITER; n++)
    v = sqrt (x);
  etime = elapsed();
  printf ("\n  Total duration was %1.6Lf seconds", etime);
  printf ("\n  Average per operation was %1.6Lf seconds",
          etime / (double) ITER);

  _dos_setvect (0x1C, oldvec);    /* restore old vector */
} /* ----------------------- */

void interrupt far tickisr (void)
      /* This ISR runs every time the system timer ticks */
{
  ticks++;                              /* update tick counter */
  if (oldvec)
    _chain_intr (oldvec);               /* chain interrupt */
} /* ----------------------- */

void install (void)
        /* This routine installs the tick ISR in Int 1Ch */
```

```
{
  oldvec = _dos_getvect (Ox1C);            /* save old vector */
  _dos_setvect (Ox1C, tickisr);                /* install new */
} /* ----------------------- */

double elapsed (void)
    /* This routine returns elapsed time of nticks in sec */
{
  return ((double) ticks / 18.2044);
} /* ------------------------------------------------------ */
```

After installing the tickisr() routine in the interrupt vector table, this program calculates 5,000 natural logarithms and 5,000 square roots, reporting
the total elapsed time and the average time for each test. It begins a test by
zeroing the ticks variable. As the ensuing loop executes, it is interrupted 18.2
times per second by the timer tick, but because a tick is a hardware interrupt,
the loop resumes each time where it left off. At the end of the loop, the program uses the value in ticks to compute and report the elapsed time in
seconds and fractions. At completion, TICKER unhooks the local ISR from
the vector, restoring the old pointer.

Now let's wrap up the book with a discussion of EMS.

CHAPTER 25

Using Expanded Memory in Quick C

Parkinson's Law states that work expands to fill the available time. A variant of that rule seems to apply to computers: Software expands to fill available memory. When the present microcomputer era began with the IBM PC and MS-DOS, 640K seemed like an enormous amount of memory. After all, the previous generation of small machines had a maximum of 64K, and many large mainframes at that time ran with half a meg or even less. So although the 8088 chip that powered early PCs had a larger potential address space, the DOS limit of 640K seemed more than generous.

Within a couple of years, Parkinson's Law had taken effect and 640K was decried as woefully inadequate. No one had figured on the new generation of software with vast amounts of code to manage the user interface, nor had anyone foreseen that PCs would become workhorses largely replacing the mainframe.

The 640K barrier became an insurmountable wall, and users demanded a solution. Thus was born EMS, the *Expanded Memory Specification*, which Lotus announced in 1985. Intel and Microsoft quickly jumped on the bandwagon, seeing EMS as a way around the 640K barrier until a new operating system with a greater addressing range could be developed. That operating system is, of course, OS/2, which is now in use but will probably not become the standard PC operating system for several more years. Thus, EMS promises to remain with us for a while longer.

The basic premise of EMS is that a computer can be equipped with several megabytes of memory beyond the reach of DOS. A combination of dedicated hardware and firmware, coupled with some software, can manage this memory, shuttling data back and forth between expanded and conventional memory via a buffer. The net result is that EMS makes an enormous amount of memory available to a program.

Naturally, this data-shuttling doesn't happen by magic (although part of it seems to). It requires some special programming techniques. Those techniques, along with a discussion of how EMS works, are the subject of this chapter.

Extended Versus Expanded Memory, Compounded by EEMS

Let's begin by clearing up some confusing terminology. Extended memory is any memory that goes beyond 1MB (segment FFFFh, or absolute address 1,048,575). *Expanded* memory is a specific implementation of *extended* memory. We'll explain the implementation in a moment. Meanwhile, let's discuss some basics of extended memory addressing.

The address range controlled by DOS is segment 0 through segment 9FFFh (absolute addresses 0 through 655,359). A program can place code or data anywhere within this range, and DOS will be able to access it.

The PC has more active memory areas at or above segment A000h, but this is reserved for hardware use. For example, the video buffers are in this high region, as are the ROM BIOS code, the machine identification byte, and other hardware-related things that must occupy memory but needn't be managed by DOS. As we'll see shortly, EMS grabs an uncommitted piece of this high memory as a transfer buffer.

All PCs have memory above segment A000h regardless of the amount of main memory they possess. Say a machine has 512K of main memory. This memory occupies segments 0 through 7FFFh. The hardware memory still begins at A000h or above. In between—say segments 8000h through 9FFFh— is a gap.

Extended memory thus begins at or above segment 10000h (absolute address 1,048,576 or greater). This memory is not addressable by the machine's CPU, because segment addresses of more than four hex digits require a register wider than 16 bits. (NOTE: The 80286 and 80386 running in protected mode can directly address extended memory, but the hows and whys are beyond the scope of this book.)

In general, extended memory resides on one or more separate boards installed in the computer's card cage. Each board has its own microprocessor acting as an embedded controller and running under firmware to control the memory and communicate with the host system.

Some software packages, such as Framework, can utilize extended memory directly by communicating with the controller(s). This is highly advanced stuff, and we won't cover it here because there's an easier way to access extended memory. That's through the implementation known as *expanded* memory.

Expanded memory relies on a software unit called a *device driver*. A device driver is a special kind of interrupt handler that DOS installs in low memory during a cold start. There are a number of default device drivers built into DOS, for handling the printer, the serial ports, the keyboard, and other hardware units. Installable—i.e. optional—device drivers are specified in the **CONFIG.SYS** file, which is located in the root directory of the boot disk. The **CONFIG.SYS** entry is

DEVICE = drivername

During start-up, DOS checks **CONFIG.SYS** and loads any such specified device drivers. The installation process includes hooking the driver into one or more interrupt vectors.

The usual name for the EMS device driver is **EMM.SYS**. The letters **EMM** stand for Expanded Memory Manager. The .SYS suffix is the customary extension for device drivers. **EMM.SYS** is not a guaranteed name, however; many board manufacturers ship a special EMS device driver with a different name. For convenience, we'll refer to it here as **EMM**, and if yours goes by a different name you can make the substitution. The **CONFIG.SYS** entry for installing this driver, then, is

DEVICE = EMM.SYS

So what does **EMM** do? In short, it allows programs to specify how the extended memory is allocated and managed, and it handles the transfer of information to and from the extended memory. Because this memory is under the control of a specific discipline imposed by **EMM**, it is called the *expanded* memory system, or EMS.

EMM, then, is the device driver itself, and EMS is the expanded memory it controls. **EMM** behaves much like Int 21h, the gateway to most of the DOS services. You place a function code and parameters in registers, then execute software interrupt 67h. **EMM** takes it from there. We'll talk more about this shortly.

Confounding this alphabet soup is EEMS, a competing and similar standard put forth by a different set of vendors. EEMS stands for *Enhanced Expanded Memory Specification*. It hasn't gained the popularity of the LIM (Lotus/Intel/ Microsoft) EMS version, and so we won't discuss it further.

There are several versions of EMS. The most recent (as of this writing) is LIM EMS 4.0, introduced late in 1987. All earlier versions have a major number of 3, with the minor number indicating tweaks in the revision level. LIM 4.0 supports all of the 3.n functions and significantly expands the number of operations, chiefly to support multiprocessing, to allow code to be executed from expanded RAM, and to allow for up to 32MB of EMS memory (LIM 3.n provides up to 8MB). To date, LIM 4.0 has not attracted as much enthusiasm as the earlier versions.

Because this chapter is an introduction to EMS, it concentrates on the 3.n functions. Once you've covered the material here, you'll have the concepts necessary to delve into the new 4.0 functions, if you're so inclined.

Determining if EMM is Present

Before you can use EMS, the EMM device driver must be present in the system. Your program should check for it. Here's how.

Every DOS device driver has a fixed-format header containing certain information about the driver and the nature of the device it controls. DOS places the start of the header at a segment boundary. Somewhere within that segment is the entry point that gains control when Int 67h fires. Therefore the vector for Int 67h contains the driver's segment and an offset that is beyond the header.

Commencing at offset 10 (decimal) within the header is the name of the driver. A valid EMS device driver, regardless of its filename on disk, contains the embedded driver name EMMXXXX0 (that's a zero character at the end, followed by a null terminator). This is a name guaranteed by convention and included by all vendors.

Therefore, to determine if an EMS device driver is alive and well in the system, do the following:

1. Fetch the vector for Int 67h.
2. Form a far pointer consisting of the fetched segment and offset 10 decimal.
3. Compare the eight characters indicated by the pointer with the literal string EMMXXXX0.

If they're the same, EMS is active, and otherwise it's not.

Listing 25.2 later in this chapter furnishes the function isEMS() to do this.

How EMS Works

Somewhere within the memory above the 640K mark, there is an uncommitted 64K segment. The exact whereabouts of this RAM depends on the hardware configuration, and EMM knows how to find it.

This 64K piece of memory serves as the EMS frame buffer, which is a two-way communications area between conventional and expanded RAM. Your program can find out where it is by issuing Int 67h, Function 41h; EMM returns the segment address in register DX.

To save data in EMS, your program merely copies the data to the frame buffer. EMM watches the frame buffer and, whenever it's changed, automatically moves the new data into EMS. To read data from EMS, you issue an Int 67h function to tell EMM what you want to read, and EMM copies it into the frame buffer. Your program can then fetch the data from the frame buffer, copying it into normal variables or a heap node. Conceptually, then, the frame buffer is a window giving a view of some portion of the EMS memory space.

It's actually four windows, because **EMM** divides the frame buffer into four pages of 16K each. The EMS documentation generally refers to these as *physical pages*. Similarly, the entire EMS RAM is divided into 16K pieces, which are called *logical pages*. Any logical page can be associated with any physical page in the frame buffer, thus giving access to that portion of EMS memory. The association of a logical to a physical page is made via *mapping*, an important **EMM** function.

There are some parallels between EMS and disk files. Before you can use a file, you have to open it and acquire an identifier such as a handle. Similarly, it's first necessary to allocate some number of EMS logical pages and acquire a handle for them. Most EMS functions require passing the EMS handle, which identifies to **EMM** which set of pages you mean, just as a file handle specifies a particular file.

Mapping says, in effect, "Associate logical page L belonging to handle H with physical page P." Thereafter, until the next remapping, physical page P in the frame buffer will contain an image of handle H's logical page L.

Why handles? Well, you might have several disk files open at the same time, and similarly you might have several storage areas allocated in EMS simultaneously. A handle identifies which allocation group you're talking about. It's how **EMM** keeps track of files in EMS RAM.

Because there are four pages in the frame buffer, you can access up to four different EMS files simultaneously. You can also access four pages from the same file in any logical-to-physical mapping order. Or you can have a combination. For example, this might be the mapping:

PP	LP	Handle
0	3	C
1	0	A
2	1	A
3	7	B

Here three EMS files are mapped to four physical pages in the frame buffer. Physical pages 1 and 2 map to consecutive logical pages associated with handle A. Therefore, you could copy up to 32K bytes to or from physical page 1 at one time and be assured that you're working with truly consecutive data. In the other two pages, you can only safely deal with up to 16K at a time.

EMS is volatile memory; that is, when the power goes out, its contents are gone. Therefore, a program that uses EMS for data storage must retrieve anything valuable and store it to disk before terminating. A program can, however, pass an open EMS handle to a child process; consider using a command-line argument. This is an alternative and generally better way of passing along data than the environment.

When you're done using a handle, close it using **EMM** function 45h. Closing releases the logical pages and makes the handle available for other uses.

Implementing the Basic EMS Functions

EMS 3.n furnishes sixteen functions, of which seven are essential to working with expanded memory. These seven are furnished by the **EMS.H** library (Listing 25.1) and its source listing (**EMS.C** in Listing 25.2), plus an eighth that returns the EMM version number. If you want to know more, see Duncan, Hyman, or the EMS spec itself, which you can obtain from Intel, Lotus, or Microsoft.

Listing 25.1 **Foundation routines for EMS.**

```
/* EMS.H: Basic functions for Expanded Memory (3.n) */

#define PP0 0                   /* frame physical page offsets */
#define PP1 0x4000
#define PP2 0x8000
#define PP3 0xC000

int isEMS (void);
    /* Returns TRUE if EMS is installed, FALSE if not */

void EMSerror (int code);
     /* Print explanation of EMS error code */

int EMSstatus (void);          /* Returns EMS device status */

int EMSframe (unsigned *segment);
     /* Gets segment of 64K page frame used by EMS */
     /* Returns segment in argument */
     /* Returns success code directly */

int EMSpages (unsigned *totalPages, unsigned *freePages);
     /* Gets total EMS pages available, number of free */
     /*   pages (not already allocated), returns them   */
     /*   to the arguments (page is 16K)                */
     /* Returns success code directly.                  */

int EMSversion (unsigned *major, unsigned *minor);
      /* Returns the EMS version number via arguments */

int EMSopen (unsigned *handle, int npages);
      /* Allocates npages 16K pages to an EMS handle */
      /* Handle is returned via argument and must be */
      /*   used for all EMS I/O's                    */

int EMSmap (unsigned handle, int lpage, unsigned ppage);
      /* Ties EMS logical page associated with handle  */
      /*   to physical (frame) page so that the logical */
      /*   page can be accessed by the caller           */

int EMSclose (unsigned handle);
      /* Releases space allocated to handle and frees */
      /*   the handle for reassignment                */
```

Listing 25.2 **EMS library source.**

```
/* EMS.C: Basic functions for Expanded Memory (3.n) */

#include <dos.h>
#include <string.h>
#include <stdio.h>
#include "mk_fp.h"
#include "ems.h"

union REGS inreg, outreg;

#define EMS 0x67
#define callEMS() int86 (EMS, &inreg, &outreg)
#ifndef TRUE
#define FALSE 0
#define TRUE  !FALSE
#endif
/* ------------------------------------------------------- */

int isEMS (void)
    /* Returns TRUE if EMS is installed, FALSE if not */
    /* Checks device driver name to find out */
{
void far *driver;
char far *ident;
char id [8];
int n;

  driver = _dos_getvect (EMS);                    /* driver addr */
  ident = MK_FP (FP_SEG (driver), 10);    /* point to name */
  for (n = 0; n < 8; n++)      /* get device name into auto */
    id[n] = ident[n];    /* to avoid memory model problems */
  return ((strncmp (id, "EMMXXXX0", 8) == 0)
          ? TRUE : FALSE);
} /* ----------------------- */

void EMSerror (int code)
    /* Print explanation of EMS error code */
{
  puts ("\n\nEMS error: ");
  switch (code) {
    case   0: puts ("None"); break;
    case 128: puts ("Software malfunction"); break;
    case 129: puts ("Hardware malfunction"); break;
    case 131: puts ("Invalid handle"); break;
    case 143:
    case 132: puts ("Invalid function call"); break;
    case 133: puts ("No handles left"); break;
    case 134: puts ("Page mapping error"); break;
    case 135:
    case 136: puts ("Not enough pages"); break;
    case 137: puts ("Can't allocate 0 pages"); break;
    case 138: puts ("Too many pages requested"); break;
```

```c
      case 139: puts ("Invalid page"); break;
      case 140: puts ("Device driver out of memory"); break;
      case 141: puts ("Duplicate handle"); break;
      case 142: puts ("Used unopened handle"); break;
   }
   puts ("\n\n");
} /* ----------------------- */

int EMSstatus (void)            /* Returns EMS device status */
{
   inreg.h.ah = 0x40;                       /* EMS function */
   callEMS ();                              /* call driver */
   return (outreg.h.ah);                    /* return status */
} /* ----------------------- */

int EMSframe (unsigned *segment)
     /* Gets segment of 64K page frame used by EMS */
     /* Returns segment in argument */
     /* Returns success code directly */
{
   inreg.h.ah = 0x41;
   callEMS ();
   *segment = outreg.x.bx;             /* segment is in BX */
   return (outreg.h.ah);               /* return success */
} /* ----------------------- */

int EMSpages (unsigned *totalPages, unsigned *freePages)
     /* Gets total EMS pages available, number of free */
     /*   pages (not already allocated), returns them   */
     /*   to the arguments (page is 16K)                */
     /* Returns success code directly.                  */
{
   inreg.h.ah = 0x42;
   callEMS ();
   *freePages =  outreg.x.bx;
   *totalPages = outreg.x.dx;
   return (outreg.h.ah);
} /* ----------------------- */

int EMSversion (unsigned *major, unsigned *minor)
     /* Returns the EMS version number via arguments */
{
   inreg.h.ah = 0x46;
   callEMS ();
   *major = outreg.h.al >> 4;       /* break out components */
   *minor = outreg.h.al & 0x0F;
   return (outreg.h.ah);
} /* ------------------- HANDLE FUNCTIONS --------------- */

int EMSopen (unsigned *handle, int npages)
     /* Allocates npages 16K pages to an EMS handle */
     /* Handle is returned via argument and must be */
     /*   used for all EMS I/O's                    */
```

Listing 25.2 *(continued)*

```
{
  inreg.h.ah = 0x43;
  inreg.x.bx = npages;
  callEMS ();
  *handle = outreg.x.dx;
  return (outreg.h.ah);
} /* ----------------------- */

int EMSmap (unsigned handle, int lpage, unsigned ppage)
      /* Ties EMS logical page associated with handle  */
      /*    to physical (frame) page so that the logical */
      /*    page can be accessed by the caller           */
{
  inreg.h.ah = 0x44;
  inreg.h.al = (unsigned) ppage / PP1;        /* digit 0-3 */
  inreg.x.bx = lpage;
  inreg.x.dx = handle;
  callEMS ();
  return (outreg.h.ah);
} /* ----------------------- */

int EMSclose (unsigned handle)
      /* Releases space allocated to handle and frees */
      /*    the handle for reassignment               */
{
  inreg.h.ah = 0x45;
  inreg.x.dx = handle;
  callEMS ();
  return (outreg.h.ah);
} /* ----------------------- */
```

Now let's examine the library source file. The **REGS** objects are registers used in calling the device driver via the EMS interrupt, and the **callEMS()** macro is shorthand for the actual call. **PP0** through **PP3** define the offsets for the four physical pages within the frame buffer. The remaining definitions ensure the existence of Boolean values. As for the functions:

- **isEMS()** checks to see if an **EMM** device driver is present in the system and hooked into Int 67h. It returns **TRUE** if so and **FALSE** otherwise. Always call this function first, before you begin issuing EMS calls. (NOTE: Because **strncmp()** is sensitive to the memory model and cannot compare near and far strings, the routine copies the device name into an auto variable before performing the comparison.)
- **EMSerror()** doesn't deal with **EMM** itself, but instead translates EMM error codes into English statements displayed on the screen. Call this function whenever **EMM** returns a non-zero result. You might wish to modify **EMSerror()** in some way to prevent it from corrupting the display.

- EMSstatus() checks the status of the EMM driver, returning 0 when the device driver is functioning properly and one of the codes shown in EMSerror() when there's a problem. It's advisable to call this function immediately after isEMS() to make sure that the driver is not only installed, but operational.
- EMSframe() gets the segment address of the 64K frame buffer used by EMM. The function loads the segment into the unsigned variable indicated by the pointer passed as an argument, and returns a success code directly. You must call this function in order to determine where the frame buffer is; afterwards, use the returned segment to build far pointers to the physical pages.
- EMSpages() tells the total number of 16K logical pages in the EMS address space, and how many are free for allocation. It loads the results into the variables pointed to by the arguments, and returns a success code directly. This function is handy for finding out in advance if there will be enough pages to satisfy an EMS allocation request.
- EMSversion() reports the EMM major and minor version numbers. The main reason for calling it is to find out if LIM 4.0 services are available, in the event that you want to use them.
- EMSopen() allocates the indicated number of 16K logical pages in the EMS address space, and assigns an EMS handle to that hunk of EMS memory. Via the parametric pointer, it passes back the handle, which is required for all operations affecting the allocated space. This is analogous to creating a disk file, except that the amount of space is fixed.
- EMSmap() maps one of the logical pages associated with the given handle into one of the four physical pages in the frame buffer. In other words, it makes the physical page a window into the logical page. Note that EMM expects the physical page to be identified by a digit 0–3, but the Quick C function's ppage argument is the page's frame buffer offset. This is a deliberate effort to make the function call more intuitive by using the constants PP0 through PP3. For example,

      EMSmap (handle, 3, PP2);

  maps logical page 3 to physical page 2. Because PP1 is not only an offset but also the size of one page, the expression that loads register AL resolves the page offset down to a digit 0–3. A call to EMSmap() is necessary each time you want to move the window to a new EMS logical page.
- EMSclose() deallocates the EMS logical pages associated with the handle, and returns both the EMS memory space and the handle itself to the available pool. This is analogous to closing a disk file, but with one important difference. If you forget to close a disk file, the normal termination of a program will close it for you. That's not so with EMS. The EMM driver has no way of knowing when your program has ended, so if you've neglected to call EMSclose(), the space remains unavailable, the data within it are unchanged, and the handle is still active. This is useful

when spawning a child process, but potentially catastrophic if you've simply ended the program without calling EMSclose(). Therefore, you must *always* call EMSclose() when you have no further use for the EMS space allocated to the handle.

A Demonstration

The EMSTEST.C program in Listing 25.3 checks the EMS subsystem, and also puts each of the functions in the EMS library to work. It reports what it's doing at each step, and whether the test was successful.

After reporting the general status of EMS, the version number, and so on, the program allocates one logical page to a handle and maps that page to physical page 0 in the frame buffer. It then copies a 16K array of integers into the physical page, which stores the array in EMS. Having done that, it remaps logical page 0 to physical page 2. Thus, PP2 becomes a window into EMS, and it should contain the same data copied earlier to PP0.

To prove this, the program copies from PP2 into a different array, then compares the arrays. If they're the same, the test succeeds, and otherwise it fails.

Regardless of the outcome, if EMM is alive and healthy, space will have been allocated to a handle, so the program calls EMSclose() to release it, then quits.

If your system doesn't have EMS, the program simply reports "EMS not detected" and ends. Otherwise, it produces a full screen of information derived from the test.

The comments in the program explain what each step does. You can refer to it as a model for interfacing to EMS. You can make this program from the command line with

    QCL emstest.c ems.c

Listing 25.3 **An EMS test program.**

```
/* EMSTEST.C: Tests EMS routines */

#include <dos.h>
#include <string.h>
#include <stdio.h>
#include <stdlib.h>
#include <process.h>
#include <graph.h>
#include "mk_fp.h"
#include "ems.h"

#define PAGESIZE 16384
#define NELEM    PAGESIZE / 2
```

```c
int y [NELEM], z [NELEM];

void main ()
{
unsigned a1, a2, status, frameSeg, handle;
int  n, far *frame;

  _clearscreen (_GCLEARSCREEN);

  /* Find out if the EMS is installed and alive */
  puts ("Checking EMS board:");
  if (!(status = isEMS ()))
    puts ("  EMS not detected");
  else {
    puts ("  EMS is active");
    status = EMSstatus ();
    printf ("  Initial status is %d", status);
    if (status)
      EMSerror (status);
    else
      puts ("  (No error)");

    /* Get the EMS version number */
    if ((status = EMSversion (&a1, &a2)) == 0)
      printf ("  Version number is %d.%02d", a1, a2);
    else EMSerror (status);

    /* Find out where the communications frame is */
    if ((status = EMSframe (&frameSeg)) == 0)
      printf ("\n  Frame is at segment %04X", frameSeg);
    else EMSerror (status);

    /* Determine the number of logical 16K pages */
    if ((status = EMSpages (&a1, &a2)) == 0) {
      printf ("\n  Pages: total = %u", a1);
      printf ("\n          free  = %u", a2);
    }
    else EMSerror (status);

    /* NOW GET READY TO TEST THE EMS I/O */
    puts ("\n\nEMS write/read test:");

    /* First get one page and assign to a handle */
    puts ("  Opening a handle");
    if ((status = EMSopen (&handle, 1)) != 0) {
      EMSerror (status);
      exit (EXIT_FAILURE);
    }

    /* Map the handle's page to physical frame 0 */
    printf ("  Mapping handle %X to frame page 0",
            handle);
    if ((status = EMSmap (handle, 0, PP0)) != 0) {
```

Listing 25.3 *(continued)*

```
      EMSerror (status);
      exit (EXIT_FAILURE);
   }
   EMSpages (&a1, &a2);
   printf ("\n  Free pages now = %d", a2);

   /* Initialize an array to be stored in the EMS */
   for (n = 0; n < NELEM; n++)
     y [n] = n;

   /* Now store it in EMS */
   frame = MK_FP (frameSeg, PP0);  /* destination pointer */
   for (n = 0; n < NELEM; n++)        /* copy array to dest */
     frame [n] = y [n];

   /* Remap handle to frame page 2 */
   printf ("\n  Remapping handle %X to frame page 2",
           handle);
   if ((status = EMSmap (handle, 0, PP2)) != 0) {
     EMSerror (status);
     exit (EXIT_FAILURE);
   }

   /* Copy the saved data back to a different array (z) */
   frame  = MK_FP (frameSeg, PP2);
   for (n = 0; n < NELEM; n++) /* copy array from source */
     z [n] = frame [n];

   /* Check to make sure both arrays are the same */
   if (strncmp ((char*) y, (char*) z, PAGESIZE) == 0)
     puts ("\n\n  ** Test passed **");
   else
     puts ("\n\n  ** Test failed **");

   /* Regardless of outcome, close the EMS handle */
   printf ("\nClosing handle %X", handle);
   if ((status = EMSclose (handle)) != 0)
     EMSerror (status);
   EMSpages (&a1, &a2);
   printf ("\nFree pages now = %d", a2);
   puts ("\nTest completed");
   }
}
```

A Graphics Application Using EMS

If it's fair to regard EMS as a sort of high-speed file store, it's just as reasonable to consider it an alternative to the heap. You can save and retrieve any sort of data there, including screen images. So let's consider an application in which EMS helps to achieve graphics animation.

The image we'll develop is a fairly simple one: A hoop rotating about its vertical axis. The real-world analogy is a radio direction finder's antenna. This is a loop of wire that turns, detecting radio signals and reporting the bearings to their sources. Navigators on ships and airplanes use such a device to compute the craft's position. What we'll see is the antenna rotating continuously through 360 degrees.

Rotation of a circle about a vertical axis results in a series of ellipses. When the hoop is perpendicular to the viewing axis, it forms a full circle, and when parallel to the viewing axis, a vertical line. In between these extremes are ellipses whose Y dimension is invariant, but whose X dimension varies.

When viewed from above, the rate of rotation is constant. Seen edge-on, however, it is not if we're to simulate realistic rotation. The changes are relatively slow when the hoop is fairly perpendicular to the viewing axis and become increasingly faster as the circle approaches the parallel perpective. Using trigonometry, the aspect of each ellipse is given by

$$X \ \ radius \ = \ R \ cos \ theta$$

where R is the radius of the circle and theta is the angle of rotation (where the angle is measured in radians for the Quick C cos() function).

The conversion from degrees to radians is straightforward. A circle is 360 degrees or 2*pi radians. Therefore a half-circle is 180 degrees or pi radians, so one degree equals pi/180 radians. It's more intuitive for people—i.e., programmers—to work in degrees, so we can apply this as a factor in converting degrees to radians.

If we consider the problem, we can see that it's only necessary to represent a circle through one-quarter of its full rotation. When played forward and then backward, the image appears to move through a 180-degree turn about its axis. Two repetitions simulate a complete rotation.

Suppose we select an image size that is between 2K and 4K. We can then store four images in one 16K EMS page. To achieve relatively smooth motion from one angle to the next, the granularity of angles has to be fairly close together. Given four images per page through a 90-degree rotation, if we select 32 images, the requirement is eight EMS pages to contain them.

The EMS frame buffer maps to four pages maximum. Therefore, if the 32 images are saved in consecutive pages, we can map 16 at a time into the frame buffer and use putimge() to store them and getimage() to fetch them. The exercise becomes one of calculating a pointer offset from the start of the frame buffer for each image.

Say we call the first 16 images "low EMS" and the second 16 "high EMS." Then to save the 32 consecutive images we do the following for a 180-degree rotation:

```
allocate 8 pages to an EMS handle;
set step to 90 degrees / 32 images;
map low EMS;
for image = 0 to 32 {
    convert image angle to radians;
    find cosine;
    draw ellipse at angle;
    if image == 16
        map high EMS;
    calculate pointer offset into frame buffer;
    save image;
}
```

Having done this, we can fetch the images back for a 180-degree rotation with

```
map low EMS;
for image = 1 to 32 {
    if image == 16
        map high EMS;
    calculate frame pointer for image;
    copy to display;
}
for image = 32 to 1 {
    if image == 15
        map low EMS;
    calculate frame pointer for image;
    copy to display;
}
```

This discussion provides an overview of the program HOOP.C in Listing 25.4. The program first draws and saves 32 ellipse images in EMS, then plays them back ten times. Given all that this book has developed, the details should become apparent by examining the listing and running the program.

Make the program from the command line with

```
QCL hoop.c ems.c
```

Listing 25.4 **Graphics animation using EMS.**

```
/* HOOP.C: Uses 8 pages of EMS to simulate animation */

#include <dos.h>
#include <graph.h>
#include <math.h>
#include <stdio.h>
#include <process.h>
#include <stdlib.h>
#include "ems.h"
#include "mk_fp.h"
```

```
/* DEFINES */
#define IMAGES    32                      /* number of images */
#define PI        3.1415927
#define RADPERDEG PI / 180.0           /* radians per degree */
#define STEPSIZE  90.0 / (IMAGES-1)    /* step size in deg */
#define STEP      STEPSIZE * RADPERDEG   /* and in radians */
#define YRADIUS   55                   /* y radius of ellipse */
#define XRADIUS   60                   /* and max x radius */
#define CX        160                  /* center X of ellipse */
#define CY        100                     /* and center Y */
#define LEFT      CX - XRADIUS         /* image area extremes */
#define TOP       CY - YRADIUS
#define RITE      CX + XRADIUS
#define BOTTOM    CY + YRADIUS
#define NODESIZE  4096                 /* size of an image node */
#define LPAGES    8                      /* EMS pages */
#define NTIMES    10               /* number of playback times */

/* GLOBAL VARIABLES */
unsigned handle;                       /* EMS file handle */
unsigned frame;               /* pointer to EMS frame buffer */
unsigned picsize;                    /* size of screen area */

/* Local functions */
void eoj (void);
void initEMS (void);
void saveImages (void);
void playback (int);
void mapLowEMS (void);
void mapHighEMS (void);
void far *frameaddr (int);

/* ----------------------------------------------------- */

void main ()
{
int  status;

  /* Set up to run */
  initEMS ();                              /* prepare EMS */
  if (!_setvideomode (_MRES4COLOR)) {
    puts ("Cannot run this program without graphics");
    exit (EXIT_FAILURE);
  }

  /* Ready to run. Get actual image size and EMS space */
  picsize = _imagesize (LEFT, TOP, RITE, BOTTOM);
  status = EMSopen (&handle, LPAGES);
  if (status != 0) {
    eoj ();
    EMSerror (status);
    exit (EXIT_FAILURE);
  }
```

Listing 25.4 *(continued)*

```
   atexit (eoj);                        /* register exit procedure */
   saveImages ();                  /* build images and store in EMS */
   playback (NTIMES);            /* play back the rotating hoop */
} /* ----------------------- */

void initEMS (void)                      /* Initialize EMS */
{
unsigned n, freepages;
int      status;

   if (!isEMS()) {                /* if EMS not present... */
     puts ("Cannot run this program without EMS");
     exit (EXIT_FAILURE);
   } else {
     status = EMSstatus ();              /* check EMS status */
     if (status != 0) {                  /* if not OK... */
       EMSerror (status);                /* show problem */
       exit (EXIT_FAILURE);              /* and quit */
     } else {
       EMSpages (&n, &freepages);        /* get free pages */
       if (freepages < LPAGES) {    /* if not enough... */
         puts ("Not enough EMS pages available to run");
         exit (EXIT_FAILURE);
       }
     }
   }
   EMSframe (&frame);             /* get frame buffer address */
} /* ----------------------- */

void eoj (void)              /* Exit processing for program */
{
   EMSclose (handle);
   _setvideomode (_DEFAULTMODE);
} /* ----------------------- */


void saveImages (void)
                 /* Build 32 hoop images and save in EMS */
{
unsigned n, xrad;
double   angle;
void far *frameloc;

   mapLowEMS ();                  /* map Lpages 0-3 to frame */
   for (n = 0; n < IMAGES; n++) {
     _clearscreen (_GCLEARSCREEN);         /* fresh screen */
     _setcolor (2);
     _moveto (CX, TOP); _lineto (CX, BOTTOM);
     _setcolor (3);
     angle = STEP * n;                 /* angle in radians */
     xrad = cos (angle) * XRADIUS;  /* X radius of ellipse */
     _ellipse (_GBORDER, CX-xrad, TOP, CX+xrad, BOTTOM);
```

```
      /* save image in EMS frame buffer */
      if (n == IMAGES / 2)              /* if frame is full... */
        mapHighEMS ();                        /* remap to high EMS */
      frameloc = frameaddr (n);          /* get frame location */
      _getimage (LEFT, TOP, RITE, BOTTOM, frameloc);
   }
} /* ----------------------- */


void playback (int times)     /* Play back the saved images */
{
int       t, n;
void far *frameloc;

   for (t = 0; t < times; t++) {
     mapLowEMS ();                      /* start with low images */
     for (n = 0; n < IMAGES; n++) {           /* play forward */
       if (n == (IMAGES / 2))           /* if frame used up... */
         mapHighEMS ();                       /* remap to high EMS */
       frameloc = frameaddr (n);        /* get frame location */
       _putimage (LEFT, TOP, frameloc, _GPSET);     /* copy */
     }
     for (n = (IMAGES - 1); n >= 0; n--) {   /* play backwd */
       if (n == ((IMAGES / 2) - 1))
         mapLowEMS ();
       frameloc = frameaddr (n);
       _putimage (LEFT, TOP, frameloc, _GPSET);
     }
   }
} /* ----------------------- */


void far *frameaddr (int image)
                          /* Compute frame address for image */
{
void far *addr;
unsigned offset;

   if (image < (IMAGES / 2))
     offset = NODESIZE * image;
   else
     offset = NODESIZE * (image - (IMAGES / 2));
   addr = MK_FP (frame, offset);
   return (addr);
} /* ----------------------- */


void mapLowEMS (void)
                  /* Map low logical pages to frame buffer */
{
  EMSmap (handle, 0, PP0);
  EMSmap (handle, 1, PP1);
  EMSmap (handle, 2, PP2);
  EMSmap (handle, 3, PP3);
} /* ----------------------- */
```

Listing 25.4 *(continued)*

```
void mapHighEMS (void)
                 /* Map high logical pages to frame buffer */
{
  EMSmap (handle, 4, PP0);
  EMSmap (handle, 5, PP1);
  EMSmap (handle, 6, PP2);
  EMSmap (handle, 7, PP3);
} /* ----------------------- */
```

Farewell

Quick C provides an extremely powerful and flexible tool for developing highly advanced applications for the IBM PC and related machines. This book has exploited many of its potentials and developed numerous tools in the form of libraries that you can adapt to meet your needs. Along the way, I hope you have picked up some useful techniques and become a more sophisticated C programmer, for teaching has been my intent as much as tool-building. No single book can tell you everything you ever need to know about anything, least of all about programming a thing as complex as a computer: the most pliable, challenging machine devised by Man. Programmers are like lawyers; given any problem, either will come up with at least seven solutions, all of which are workable and passionately defensible. Therefore some—perhaps including you—will differ with the approach I've taken to specific problems in these pages. And that's fine, because it proves the point that there's no one right way to do anything.

If this book furnishes one workable solution to each of the problems it presents, it accomplishes a goal. And if it teaches you how to solve a difficult problem and makes you a better programmer in the process, then it succeeds.

I hope this book helps you succeed as a programmer, for that is its only purpose.

Happy programming.

Software Tools Developed in This Book

In keeping with its "stretching" theme, this book has developed a number of libraries and other tools that extend the capabilities of Quick C 2.0. These are useful tools that you can apply to your own programming projects. You might wish to extend them even further, for one of the great strengths of the C language is its extensibility via libraries of functions and macros. They allow you to do as we have done here, tailoring the language to suit your needs.

Because the tools are scattered throughout the book, presented where appropriate, we believe you will appreciate having a concise reference to them all in one place. Hence this appendix, which lists their header files.

By convention, C programmers usually place the header (.H) files that come with the language package in a separate directory, then set an environment string telling the compiler where to find them. Source programs surround the standard header filenames with angle brackets, as in

```
#include  <stdio.h>
```

Programmers also develop header files for their own libraries and macros, as we have done here, and in that case they customarily place them in the directory for a given application. The convention for including a user-developed header file is to surround the name with quotes, as in

```
#include  "textscrn.h"
```

That is the practice observed throughout this book, and I encourage you to continue it.

Here are the header files from *Stretching Quick C 2.0*, with descriptions and the chapters where they were originally presented.

Chapter 1: BOOTSEC.H _____

This file defines the data structure of a disk boot sector.

```
- - - - - - - - - - - - - - - - - - - - - - - - - - - - - - - - - - - - - - - - - - -
/* BOOTSEC.H: Header file describing DOS boot sector        */
/*        (track 0, head 0, sector 1) on any formatted disk  */
/* - - - - - - - - - - - - - - - - - - - - - - - - - - - - - - - - - - - - - - */
#pragma pack(1)

typedef struct {
  unsigned char signature;              /* E9h or EBh if formatted */
  unsigned      skip;                             /* no value */
  char          oem [8];                       /* OEM identifier */
  unsigned      byPerSec;          /* start of BPB: bytes/sector */
  char          secPerClus;              /* sectors per cluster */
  unsigned      resSecs;                    /* reserved sectors */
  char          nFats;           /* # of FATs retained on disk */
  unsigned      nRootEnts;              /* # of root dir entries */
  unsigned      totSec;                /* # of sectors in volume */
  unsigned char mediaDescr;           /* media descriptor byte */
  unsigned      secPerFat;               /* sectors per FAT */
  unsigned      secPerTrack;            /* sectors per track */
  unsigned      nHeads;               /* # of heads (surfaces) */
  unsigned      nHidden;              /* # of hidden sectors */
  char          loader [482];          /* bootstrap loader area */
} BOOTSEC;

#pragma pack()
- - - - - - - - - - - - - - - - - - - - - - - - - - - - - - - - - - - - - - - - - - -
```

Chapter 3: FILEMISC.H _____

Functions for changing the attributes of any file, and for converting file time and data stamps.

```
- - - - - - - - - - - - - - - - - - - - - - - - - - - - - - - - - - - - - - - - - - -
/* Library FILEMISC.H: Miscellaneous file service func-      */
/*    tions that extend QuickC                                */
/* - - - - - - - - - - - - - - - - - - - - - - - - - - - - - - - - - - - - - - */
/* _chmod(): Stretched version of QuickC chmod function     */
/* Changes a named file to any attribute except label       */
/*    and directory.                                          */
/* Returns 0 if successful, -1 if not, and sets global       */
/*    variable errno when unsuccessful.                       */

int _chmod (char far *path, int new_attrib);
```

```
/* ---------------------------------------------------------- */
/* timestamp(): Converts the DOS file time stamp into:        */
/*      1. A formatted string of 12 chars (hh:mm:ss ?m)       */
/*      2. Its hour, min, and sec numeric components          */
/* For any component not to be converted, pass NULL arg       */

void timestamp (unsigned field,
        char *string, unsigned *hour,
        unsigned *min, unsigned *sec);

/* ---------------------------------------------------------- */
/* datestamp(): Converts the DOS file date stamp into:        */
/*      1. A formatted string of 11 chars (mm/dd/yyyy)        */
/*      2. Its month, day, and year numeric components        */
/* For any component not to be converted, pass NULL arg       */

void datestamp (unsigned field,
        char *string, unsigned *year,
        unsigned *month, unsigned *day);
-------------------------------------------------------------
```

Chapter 6: MK_FP.H

A macro for forming a far pointer from the segment and offset portions of an address.

```
-----------------------------------------------------------
/* MK_FP.H: Macro to form a far pointer */

#pragma check_pointer(off)
#define MK_FP(seg, off) ((void far *) \
        (((unsigned long)(seg) << 16) + (unsigned)(off)))
-----------------------------------------------------------
```

Chapter 6: BIOSAREA.H

Definition of the ROM BIOS data area's contents.

```
-----------------------------------------------------------
/* biosarea.h: ROM BIOS data area at 0x0040:0 in memory */

#ifndef byte
#define byte    unsigned char            /* define byte as a type */
#endif
#pragma pack(1)
```

```c
/* BIT FIELDS USED IN ROM BIOS DATA AREA */
typedef struct {
    unsigned    hasFloppies : 1     /* 1 = system has floppy drives */
                nu1 : 1,                             /* not used */
                mbRAM : 2,               /* motherboard RAM size */
                initVideo : 2,              /* initial video mode */
                nDisks : 2,               /* nbr of floppy drives */
                nu8 : 1,                             /* not used */
                nSerialPorts : 3,      /* nbr of serial ports attached */
                gamePort : 1,           /* 1 = game port attached */
                nu13 : 1,                            /* not used */
                nLPT : 2;                     /* number of printers */
} EQFLAGS;            /* this is the equipment flags structure */


typedef struct {
    unsigned    riteShiftDown : 1,      /* 1 = right shift key is down */
                leftShiftDown : 1,       /* 1 = left shift key is down */
                ctrlShiftDown : 1,      /* 1 = ctrl-shift combo is down */
                altShiftDown : 1,       /* 1 = alt-shift combo is down */
                scrollLockOn : 1,       /* 1 = scroll lock mode is on */
                numLockOn : 1,          /* 1 = num lock mode is on */
                capsLockOn : 1,         /* 1 = caps lock mode is on */
                insOn : 1,              /* 1 = ins mode is on */
                unused : 3,                          /* spare bits */
                ctrlNumLockOn : 1,     /* 1 = ctrl-numLock mode on */
                scrollLockDown : 1,    /* 1 = scroll lock key is down */
                numLockDown : 1,       /* 1 = num lock key is down */
                capsLockDown : 1,      /* 1 = caps lock key is down */
                insDown : 1;            /* 1 = ins key is down */
} KBDFLAGS;              /* this is the keyboard flags structure */


typedef struct {
    unsigned    serialPortAddr[4];
    unsigned    parallelPortAddr[4];
    EQFLAGS     eqptFlags;
    byte        mfgrTestFlags;
    unsigned    mainMem;
    unsigned    expRAM;
    KBDFLAGS    kbdStat;
    byte        keypad;
    unsigned    kbdBuffHead;
    unsigned    kbdBuffTail;
    char        kbdBuff[32];
    byte        seekStat;
    byte        motorStat;
    byte        motorCnt;
    byte        diskErr;
    byte        NECStatus[7];
```

```
    byte        videoMode;
    unsigned    scrnWidth;
    unsigned    vidBuffSz;
    unsigned    vidBuffOfs;
    byte        cursPos[8][2];
    byte        cursBottom;
    byte        cursTop;
    byte        activeDispPage;
    unsigned    activeDispPort;
    byte        CRTModeReg;
    byte        palette;
    unsigned    dataEdgeTimeCount;
    unsigned    CRCReg;
    char        lastInputValue;
    unsigned    tick;
    int         hour;
    byte        timerOverflow;
    byte        brkStat;
    unsigned    resetFlag;
    long        hardDiskStat;
    byte        parallelTimeout[4];
    byte        serialTimeout[4];
    unsigned    kbdBuffOfs;
    unsigned    kbdBuffEnd;
} BIOSDATA;
```

- -

Chapter 7: TEXTSCRN.H

Extended functions for managing text displays, and constant names for the default colors.

- -

```
/* TEXTSCRN.H: Stretching text screen operations for QC 2.0 */

/* Text color constants */
#define BLACK       0
#define BLUE        1
#define GREEN       2
#define CYAN        3
#define RED         4
#define MAGENTA     5
#define BROWN       6
#define LTGRAY      7
#define DKGRAY      8
#define LTBLUE      9
#define LTGREEN     10
```

```
#define  LTCYAN        11
#define  LTRED         12
#define  LTMAGENTA     13
#define  YELLOW        14
#define  WHITE         15


/* Added control functions */
void  far  _cleareol (void);                        /* clear to end of line */
void  far  _outtextf (char*, ...);                    /* formatted _outtext */
void  far  _outch (char);                            /* single-char output */
void  far  _textbox (int top, int left, int bottom,      /* text box */
                     int right, int style);
void  far  _savescrn (int page);                    /* save screen image */
void  far  _restscrn (int page);                   /* restore saved screen */
void  far  _setbordwindow (int top, int left,      /* bordered window */
                     int bottom, int right,
                     int borderstyle, int fgcolor, int bgcolor);


/* Inquiry functions */
int  far  maxcol (void);                        /* max column on display */
int  far  maxrow (void);                           /* max row on display */
int  far  maxpage (void);                      /* highest avail video page */
int  far  activepage (void);                      /* currently active page */
int  far  visualpage (void);                     /* currently visible page */
int  far  wherex (void);                     /* cursor col in active page */
int  far  wherey (void);                     /* cursor row in active page */
```

Chapter 8: POPUP.H _____

A library for managing pop-up windows and menus, dialog boxes, and menu
bars. Works in conjunction with the TEXTSCRN library.

```
/* POPUP.H: Prototype and typedef for POPUP.C library */

typedef  struct {
  int    top, left, bottom, right,              /* border location */
         style,                                   /* border style */
         normal, hilite,                         /* text attributes */
         normback, hiback;
  char *text;                                 /* fixed text contents */
  int  lastrow, lastcol;                     /* last cursor position */
} POPUP;

typedef  struct {
  int    row,                               /* row where bar appears */
```

```
           interval,                     /* cols between first chars */
           fore, back;                   /* foreground/background colors */
       char *choice;                     /* pointer to text contents */
   } MENUBAR;

   void far popShow (POPUP *pop);        /* display popup window */

   void far popKeep (POPUP *win);        /* save window state */

   void far popUse (POPUP *win);         /* re-enable a window */

   void far popCenter (POPUP *win, int row, char *string);
                                         /* Center string in window */

   void far popRewrite (POPUP *win, int row,
               int fgcolor, int bgcolor);
                                         /* Rewrite pop-up row in new colors */

   void far popHilite (POPUP *win, int row);
                                         /* Hilight text in popup row */

   void far popNormal (POPUP *win, int row);
                                         /* Set text in popup row to normal attribs */

   void far menubar (MENUBAR *spec);
                                         /* Write the menu bar described by spec */
```
- -

Chapter 10: VCOORDS.H _____

This library implements virtual coordinates in graphics modes.

- -
```
   /* VCOORDS.H: Header for implementing 800 x 600 virtual
                    display area in QuickC graphics */

   /* GLOBALS DEFINED IN LIBRARY, EXTERNALLY VISIBLE */
   extern int      maxx, maxy;           /* max x and y coords */
   extern double xf, yf;                 /* x and y translation factors */

   void far setvcoords                   /* set virtual coord space */
         (int vw, int vh);               /* based on width, height */
   int far dx (int vx);                  /* translate virt X to device X */
   int far dy (int vy);                  /* translate virt Y to device Y */
```
- -

Chapter 11: EXGRAPH.H _____

This library stretches Quick C 2.0 graphics by adding a number of new functions.

```
- - - - - - - - - - - - - - - - - - - - - - - - - - - - - - - - - - - - - -
/* EXGRAPH.H: Extended graphics functions for Quick C 2.0 */

int far bestmode (void);   /* get best graphics mode for adapter */

void far wait (double seconds);/* stop execution for timed period */
                               /* also quits on detecting a keypress */

void far _polyline (int nsegs, struct xycoord vert[], int next[]);
         /* draw a polyline of nsegs line segments, where:      */
         /*     vert[] contains vertices for nsegs + 1 vertices  */
         /*      and next[] contains nsegs + 1 indexes for end points */
         /* NOTE: vert[] must contain device coords, not virtual   */

void far _saveimage (int x1, int y1, int x2, int y2);
/* push defined graphics screen area onto a stack in the heap */
                            /* retrieve later with _restimage() */

void far _restimage (void);
             /* pop graphics screen area off top of image stack */
                      /* restore to screen at original location */
- - - - - - - - - - - - - - - - - - - - - - - - - - - - - - - - - - - - - -
```

Chapter 12: CURVE.H _____

The function described by this header file draws a conic spline (a simple curve between two knots and tending toward a control point).

```
- - - - - - - - - - - - - - - - - - - - - - - - - - - - - - - - - - - - - -
/* CURVE.H: Prototype for function to draw conic splines */

void far _curve (int x1, int y1, int x2, int y2, int xc, int yc);
             /* draw conic spline, where knots are at x1, y1 */
                  /* and x2, y2, control pt is at xc, yc */
- - - - - - - - - - - - - - - - - - - - - - - - - - - - - - - - - - - - - -
```

Chapter 13: BEZIER.H _____

A library for drawing complex curves using Bezier splines in two-dimensional space.

```
-------------------------------------------------------------------
/* BEZIER.H: Prototypes for drawing Bezier curves in 2D */


/* Return q factorial */
double fact (int q);

/* Return coordinates for current "u" */
void far bezierFcn (double *x, double *y, double u,
            double  coeff[], int n, struct xycoord p[]);

/* Draw a Bezier curve */
void far drawBezier (struct xycoord p[], int npts, int segments);
-------------------------------------------------------------------
```

Chapter 25: EMS.H

This library enables Quick C 2.0 programs to use the basic functions that
manage Extended Memory.

```
-------------------------------------------------------------------
/* EMS.H: Basic functions for Expanded Memory (3.n) */

#define  PP0  0                    /* frame physical page offsets */
#define  PP1  0x4000
#define  PP2  0x8000
#define  PP3  0xC000

int  isEMS (void);
             /* Returns TRUE if EMS is installed, FALSE if not */

void  EMSerror (int code);
                     /* Print explanation of EMS error code */

int  EMSstatus (void);            /* Returns EMS device status */

int  EMSframe (unsigned *segment);
        /* Gets segment of 64K page frame used by EMS */
                         /* Returns segment in argument */
                         /* Returns success code directly */

int  EMSpages (unsigned *totalPages, unsigned *freePages);
             /* Gets total EMS pages available, number of free  */
             /*   pages (not already allocated), returns them   */
             /*   to the arguments (page is 16K)                */
             /* Returns success code directly.                  */
```

```
int EMSversion (unsigned *major, unsigned *minor);
                /* Returns the EMS version number via arguments */

int EMSopen (unsigned *handle, int npages);
                /* Allocates npages 16K pages to an EMS handle   */
                /* Handle is returned via argument and must be   */
                /*    used for all EMS I/O's                      */

int EMSmap (unsigned handle, int lpage, unsigned ppage);
                /* Ties EMS logical page associated with handle   */
                /*   to physical (frame) page so that the logical */
                /*   page can be accessed by the caller           */

int EMSclose (unsigned handle);
                /* Releases space allocated to handle and frees  */
                /*    the handle for reassignment                */
------------------------------------------------------------
```

APPENDIX B

Suggested References

A programmer's reference shelf can never be too full. Studying programming is like studying the Bible; the more sources and opinions, the better. They might all be wrong, or inadequate, or obtusely worded, but at least they direct you, as well as furnishing the factual background and the point of departure for your own incursions into the infinitely complex, fascinating underworld of software development.

Here are the works I found useful in writing this book, in approximate order of importance. All are cited within the text at some point or another.

C Language:

Quick C 2.0 documentation by Microsoft Corporation, which accompanies the Quick C product. The present book is not a surrogate manual for those who have pirated Quick C, but rather it interacts with the official documentation. If you have obtained a "backup copy" of Quick C from a friend, you are not only in violation of the law, but you have deprived yourself of an invaluable resource.

The C Programming Language, by Brian W. Kernighan and Dennis M. Ritchie (Prentice-Hall, Englewood Cliffs, NJ, 1978). This is the seminal work on C as a language. No C programmer's library is complete without this book. Often referred to in the literature as "K&R," it furnishes the standard by which all C implementations are measured.

The C Programming Tutor, by Leon A. Wortman and Thomas O. Sidebottom (Brady/Prentice-Hall, Bowie, MD, 1984). This book provides many workaday examples of C programming constructs. In effect, it translates the somewhat difficult language of K&R into everyday situations that C programmers need.

Graphics: —————————————————————————————

Programmer's Guide to PC & PS/2 Video Systems, by Richard Wilton (Microsoft Press, Redmond, WA, 1987). This book is an exhaustive treatment of computer graphics for PCs. Many of the things it explains are done by the Quick C graphics library, but it also contains numerous tricks, algorithms, and listings (Assembly Language and C) useful in practical graphics applications.

Principles of Interactive Computer Graphics, by William M. Newman and Robert F. Sproull (McGraw-Hill, New York, 1979). Somewhat more theoretical than the Wilton book, this work is nevertheless highly readable and contains numerous code examples (written in Pascal, but easily translated into C). The book is one of the seminal treatments of computer graphics. Many consider it an indispensible reference for serious graphics work.

DOS and Related Topics: ———————————————————

Advanced MS-DOS, by Ray Duncan (Microsoft Press, Redmond, WA, 1986). Duncan is perhaps the leading writer on DOS and related topics, and his *Advanced MS-DOS* is a distillation of several other books published by Microsoft and his columns in *Dr. Dobb's Journal*, *PC Magazine*, the Microsoft magazine, and other sources. If you can afford only one DOS book, get this one.

Programmer's Problem Solver for the IBM PC, XT, & AT, by Robert Jourdain (Brady/Books, New York, 1986). Jourdain's book furnishes machine-specific, problem-oriented solutions to a number of programming issues that are not found anywhere else. Especially valuable are his insights into hardware features of the IBM-class machines and software mechanisms for accessing them.

The IBM PC-DOS Handbook, by Richard Allen King (Sybex, Inc, Berkeley, CA, 1983, updated 1987). This book fills in some gaps left by Duncan, and provides some further details.

Memory Resident Utilities, Interrupts, and Disk Management with MS & PC DOS, by Michael Hyman (Management Information Source, Inc., Portland, OR, 1987). Hyman offers short, succinct, and highly practical chapters that deal with difficult programming issues.

Technical Reference (DOS and the target machine), published either by IBM, Microsoft, or the machine's vendor. These are terse manuals sold at added cost with a machine or separately by the vendor. They furnish no-frills, machine-specific information about supported DOS commands, options, and (in the machine manual) a listing of the **ROM BIOS**.

Inside the IBM PC, by Peter Norton (Brady Books, New York, 1986). The leading expert on the IBM PC architecture offers a lucid discourse on a variety of topics interesting to programmers in the PC environment. An essential background work for enhancing one's understandings of the machine's inner workings.

INDEX

ABOUT THE AUTHOR

Stretching **Quick C** is Kent Porter's eighteenth book. All but one of these books deal with computers and software. In addition to books, Porter writes the monthly Graphics Programming column for *Dr. Dobb's Journal*, plus feature articles and product reviews for these and other leading computer magazines. He has also lectured and led seminars on software development both in the United States and overseas. In 1988, he was a guest lecturer at the Computer Science Department of a German engineering school.

Porter lives and works in Silicon Valley, where he is the Senior Technical Editor for the renowned *Dr. Dobb's Journal*, the magazine that made C the language of choice for microcomputer systems software.

A Californian, Porter holds a B.S. in Information Systems from the University of San Francisco.

The Computer Industry Almanac 1989

**The only reference that lists and organizes
the people, companies and trends of this
fast-paced industry.**

"If you just can't get enough facts about computers, this is the place to go."
— Stewart Alsop,
Editor and Publisher, *P.C. Letter*

*"Computers are changing the world in which we live. I recommend the Almanac to
everyone whose life is touched by computers—and that is just about everyone."*
— Regis McKenna,
President, Regis McKenna, Inc. and author
of *The Regis Touch*

*"Computers make sense out of masses of information Here is a mass of information that
helps me make sense out of the computer industry."*
— Benjamin M. Rosen,
Partner, Sevin Rosen Management

The Computer Industry Almanac is the ultimate reference guide that everyone affected by
computers needs. It provides an insider's view of this complicated industry and makes sense
out of the storm of facts and figures it generates. Egil and Karen Juliussen categorize and list
people, products, and trends. Regardless of your experience with computers, you will find this
book both helpful and fascinating.

Included:

- profiles of the top industry companies;
- product trends and product award winners;
- forecasts for the PC marketplace;
- rankings of hardware and software;
- the industry's most influential executives;
- salaries of top executives and engineers;
- and much more!

0-13-167537-0
$29.95

Look for this an other Brady titles at
your local book or computer store. To
order directly call 1 (800) 624-0023,
in New Jersey 1 (800) 624-0024
Visa/MC accepted

Peter Norton's Inside OS/2

**Robert Lafore
and
Peter Norton**

OS/2's reputation for being hard to learn is about to be compromised. Whether you're a student of this new operating system, a hacker, or a professional programmer, with this book you'll master OS/2.

Using easily understood examples, it takes you from the simplest functions up through multitasking, virtual memory management, and interprocess communication. It even shows you how to avoid the potential pit-falls of multitasking such as race conditions and deadlock.

The book includes:

- The elements of multitasking
- Interprocess communication
- Reading files, writing to the screen, and
  number crunching all at the same time
- and more.

Team up with Robert Lafore and Peter Norton to learn OS/2 and move into a new era of microcomputer programming.

ISBN: 0-13-467895-8 • $24.95

IIIBradyLine

Insights into tomorrow's technology from the authors and editors of Brady Books.

You rely on Brady's bestselling computer books for up-to-date information about high technology. Now turn to BradyLine for the details behind the titles.

Find out what new trends in technology spark Brady's authors and editors. Read about what they're working on, and predicting, for the future. Get to know the authors through interviews and profiles, and get to know each other through your questions and comments.

BradyLine keeps you ahead of the trends with the stories behind the latest computer developments. Informative previews of forthcoming books and excerpts from new titles keep you apprised of what's going on in the fields that interest you most.

- Peter Norton on operating systems
- Jim Seymour on business productivity
- Jerry Daniels, Mary Jane Mara, Robert Eckhardt, and Cynthia Harriman on Macintosh development, productivity, and connectivity

Get the Spark. Get BradyLine.

Published quarterly, beginning with the Summer 1988 issue. Free exclusively to our customers. Just fill out and mail this card to begin your subscription.

Name _____

Address _____

City _____ State _____ Zip _____

Name of Book Purchased _____

Date of Purchase _____

Where was this book purchased?   *(circle one)*

    Retail Store   Computer Store   Mail Order

F R E E

Mail this card for your free subscription to BradyLine